# THE
# PRICE OF
# AMERICAN
# FOREIGN POLICY

WILLIAM I. BACCHUS

# THE PRICE OF AMERICAN FOREIGN POLICY

*Congress, the Executive, and International Affairs Funding*

The Pennsylvania State University Press
University Park, Pennsylvania

Library of Congress Cataloging-in-Publication Data

Bacchus, William I., 1940–
    The price of American foreign policy : Congress, the executive,
and international affairs funding / William I. Bacchus.
      p.     cm.
    Includes bibliographical references and index.
    ISBN 0-271-01692-2 (cloth : alk. paper)
    ISBN 0-271-01693-0 (pbk. : alk. paper)
    1. United States—Foreign relations administration.   2. United
States. Dept. of State—Appropriations and expenditures.
3. Program budgeting—United States.    I. Title.
JX1706.Z7B33   1997
327.73—dc21                                 96-49106
                                                     CIP

It is the policy of The Pennsylvania State University Press to use acid-free paper for
the first printing of all clothbound books. Publications on uncoated stock satisfy the
minimum requirements of American National Standard for Information Sciences—
Permanence of Paper for Printed Library Materials, ANSI Z39.48-1992.

*For Professor Jay Clare Heinlein*

*It's wonderful to have an uncle in the business,
especially a constitutional scholar!*

# CONTENTS

# FIGURES AND TABLES

# PREFACE

This book is an examination of the nexus where high constitutional concerns meet the low politics of day-in, day-out activities that determine how well the United States is equipped to carry out its international activities and obligations. As such, it draws from several threads of public policy and political science research and investigation, strands which unfortunately are not woven together as often as they should be: budgeting, Congress, foreign policy, and constitutional law. Some reviewers of this study expressed concern that it did not easily fit into established course structures because it crosses several of them. Perhaps that is the point: in the real world, what happens and how it happens bridges several conventional fields of study, and we would be well advised to remember that fact.

A second motivating concern is that there is all too often a wide gulf between those who formulate and carry out public policies and those who analyze them. As an academically oriented political scientist whose primary career, through happenstance, has been in the government, to me the lack of cross-fertilization is a major failing. For all of the perils and potential conflicts of interest involved, the best remedy for this separation is the "participant-observer" approach. As one who through the years has enjoyed the benefits of being both a participant and an observer, I want to acknowledge my debt here to the conceptual approach most prominently advocated by Harold Lasswell and, more recently, reinforced in important ways by Richard Fenno, especially in his presidential address to the American Political Science Association in 1986. Whatever the opportunities that more sophisticated data and other forms of analysis provide us, there is simply no substitute for close-in familiarity with the events and individuals that are the subjects of our studies. Through luck, I have had the advantage of being a minor participant in many of the events discussed in this book. While some readers may perceive a "pro–executive branch" bias resulting from my own role as senior legislative assistant to the under secretary of state for management (1986–91), I have tried conscientiously to provide a balanced view. Readers must judge the result for themselves.

I am obligated also to thank those of my colleagues who, in a variety of roles, knowingly or unknowingly, have contributed in important ways to this book. First of all, I am indebted to those who were jointly involved in arguing the Department of State's case on budget and management issues in the late 1980s and early 1990s, both before the authorizing and appropriating committees of Congress and within the executive branch (in particular, the Office of Management and Budget). Robert Hopper, Ross Starek, and Mark Johnson all played major roles in that effort, and many others helped. Similarly, without the assistance throughout these years of three exceptional legislative counsels, Jamison Selby Borek, Sally Cummins, and Mary Helen Carlson, I would have learned much less. Under Secretaries of State for Management Ronald I. Spiers, Ivan Selin, and John F. W. Rogers all gave me a chance to play the game. Later on, Brian Atwood and Jim Michel provided the same opportunity at AID. In State's budget office (M/COMP, later FMP) special thanks go to Rich Greene, Bruce Brown, Jim Millett, and Chuck Casper, who were always ready to provide information and to discuss concepts and ideas. Their counterparts at USIA and USAID, Stan Silverman and Rick Nygard, were equally helpful. Bob Bauerlein, Craig Johnstone, Bill McGlynn, Ann Richard, Dan Speckhard, and Mike Usnick, members or heads at various times of the Function 150 staff in its several incarnations, were helpful in the same ways. Equally supportive were Jane Becker, Albert Fairchild, Joe Melrose, and Ruth Whiteside, management officials in the Department of State. Jim Barie, Bruce Sasser, and Mike Margeson of OMB became my close friends, in spite of our "full and frank" discussions of budget issues. Hill staffers, too, made direct and indirect contributions, often in the "partner/adversary" mode discussed throughout the text. Susan Andross, Bob Boyer, Steve Berry, Phil Christensen, Mike Finley, Charlie Flickner, Scott Gudes, Lise Hartman, Warren Kane, Eric Lief, Dick McCall, Ken Nakamura, Doug Olin, John Osthaus, Gardner Peckham, Ken Peel, John Shank, Nancy Stetson, and Chris Van Hollen all helped me learn about Congress and its ways. At a later stage, during the Clinton administration, Boyer and McCall became close colleagues as we all moved to AID. And I would be remiss not to cite my colleagues on the "State 2000" task force in 1992, several of whom are noted for their specific contributions throughout the text: Ambassadors Lannon Walker (for his help on resource allocation), Edward Dillary (for general wisdom and a careful review of the manuscript), David Shinn (organizational issues), and Sandy Vogelgesang (for insights on foreign assistance) as well as Alphonse LaPorta (resource allocation and general management), Ed Casey (economics and departmental politics), Herb Yarvin (systems and technology), and Albert Ossman (political climate and general support).

Finally, I am indebted to Fritz Mosher and Jim Fesler, who got me interested in planning and budgeting; to Allen Schick, who knows more about federal budgeting than anyone; and Jim Lindsay, who has paved the way for meaningful studies of Congress and its impact on foreign affairs. Both Schick and Lindsay served as referees for Penn State Press and made many helpful suggestions for modifications and additions to the manuscript. Mary Brock and Jerry Gagne of USAID, Bob Beckham of State, Ken Nakamura of AFSA, and Wayne Struble of the House Budget Committee all helped with tables and figures.

Especially pleasurable has been the opportunity to continue a friendship of more than two decades with Sandy Thatcher, director of Penn State Press and the editor of two of my previous books published elsewhere. His consideration and encouragement will always be appreciated.

It should go without saying that without the support and tolerance of my wife, Mary, this work could not have been completed. I will always be grateful.

William I. Bacchus
Arlington, Virginia
April 1997

# INTRODUCTION

The power of the purse . . . the basic power of government —Robert E. Byrd, May 19, 1988, U.S. Senate, Morning Business

The President . . . shall have Power, by and with the Advice and Consent of the Senate, to make Treaties . . . and . . . shall appoint Ambassadors, other public Ministers and Consuls . . . [Article II, section 2]; he shall receive Ambassadors and the other public Ministers . . . [Article II, section 3]. Done in Convention by the Unanimous Consent of the States present . . . [Article VII]. —Constitution of the United States, September 17, 1787

What the Constitution does, and *all that it does,* is to confer on the President certain powers capable of affecting our foreign relations, and certain other powers of the same general kind on the Senate, and still other such powers on Congress; but which of these organs shall have the decisive and final voice in determining the course of the American Nation is left for events to resolve. All of which amounts to saying that the Constitution, considered only for its affirmative grants of power capable of affecting the issue, is an invitation to struggle for the privilege of directing American foreign policy. —Edward S. Corwin[1]

The President is the constitutional representative of the United States with regard to foreign nations. . . . [He has] the very delicate, plenary and exclusive power of the President as the sole organ of the federal government in the field of international relations. —Mr. Justice Sutherland[2]

1. *The President: Office and Powers, 1787–1957* (New York: NYU Press, 1957), p. 171. Quoted in Daniel Patrick Moynihan, *On the Law of Nations* (Cambridge: Harvard University Press, 1990), p. 44.
2. Majority opinion, *United States* v. *Curtis-Wright,* 299 U.S. 304, 319–20 (1936). The first sentence is quoted by Sutherland from a report of the Senate Foreign Relations Committee on February 15, 1816, while the remainder is a play on John Marshall, taken from an argument in the House of Representatives, March 7, 1800: "The President is the sole organ of the nation in its external relations, and its sole representative with foreign nations."

Presidential powers are not fixed but fluctuate, depending upon their disjunction or conjunction with those of Congress. —Mr. Justice Jackson[3]

These classic examples of what has been said about the complex relationship of the president and the Congress in carrying out American foreign policy reflect both a consuming interest in the subject and a lack of easy answers.

Expending resources—people and money—in pursuit of foreign policy objectives has never been a straightforward matter. Evidently, there is frequently no direct cause and effect. Some profound policy changes and initiatives have minuscule dollar costs (the opening of China), while expenditures of billions may have no significant policy effect (the Aswan Dam). Consequences may be unanticipated (food aid, instead of raising the subsistence levels for inhabitants of a destitute country, may allow the government of that country to divert funds for other purposes, yielding no benefits for the population). And programs may "find" policies, rather than the other way around.

At first, such matters can look less important (or at least less exciting) than other foreign affairs issues; they seem to be "nuts and bolts," distant from high policy, except in the rare case when providing resources to support a specific policy *becomes* the primary focus, as with Contra aid. Allen Schick is surely right when he asserts that "money is not the root of all foreign policy."[4] Other experts are even less equivocal.[5]

But do not be deceived. The tendency to regard management and budgeting in foreign affairs as mere "housekeeping" loses sight of major policy and operational issues that can determine the ultimate success or failure of foreign affairs initiatives.[6] Resource issues, under certain circumstances, can

3. Concurring opinion in *Youngstown Sheet & Tube v. Sawyer,* 343 U.S. 579, 635 (1952).
4. Allen Schick, "Congressional Use of Its Money Power to Control Foreign Policy," in Appendix T: "Budgeting and Foreign Affairs Coordination," in *Report: Commission on the Organization of the Government for the Conduct of Foreign Policy* (Washington, D.C.: GPO, 1975), app. vol. 6, p. 454. This commission was referred to as the Murphy Commission.
5. See, for example, Thomas Schelling, quoted in I. M. Destler, "Executive–Congressional Conflict in Foreign Policy: Explaining It, Coping with It," in Lawrence C. Dodd and Bruce Oppenheimer, eds., *Congress Reconsidered,* 3d ed. (Washington, D.C.: Congressional Quarterly Press, 1985), p. 348; and John W. Ellwood, "Budget Authority vs. Outlays as Measures of Budget Policy," a paper prepared for the annual meeting of the American Political Science Association, Washington, D.C., September 1986, p. 6.
6. This unfortunate tendency in the Department of State to equate management with "housekeeping" was noted in 1987 by Ronald I. Spiers, then under secretary for management, who spoke at one of the informal "Face-to-Face" discussions sponsored by the Carnegie Foundation for International Peace and the American Foreign Service Association. Reprinted as

bring into the sharpest possible focus the post-Vietnam constitutional confrontation over the proper roles of the executive and legislative branches in making foreign policy. One such episode was the 1995 struggle between the Clinton administration and the newly elected Republican Congress over a triad of related issues: funding for foreign affairs; forced consolidation of the executive branch's organization for conducting international relations; and congressional forays into areas that presidents have regarded as their own, almost exclusive foreign policy terrain. Since this set of interrelated issues is in some senses the culmination of many themes highlighted throughout this book, they are treated in a separate chapter near the end.

Former Senate Majority leader Robert E. Byrd got it right. In one of his well-known "Morning Business" soliloquies (quoted above), Byrd, after tracing the history of England from Edward I to Charles I, concluded that the early English kings learned they "could not veto the absence of money." Specifically, "the Parliament learned early on, early on, that the power of the purse was the basic power of government. And we ought to think of that."[7] When the executive needs resources to carry out foreign policy choices, while simultaneously asserting its primacy under Article II, sections 2 and 3 of the Constitution,[8] the constitutional battle between "separate institutions sharing powers"[9] is well and truly joined.

Even when this inherent tension is overcome or finessed, an important issue remains: How well do resource expenditures match policy directions, however set? It is irrefutable that correspondence of these two is routinely imperfect, and cynics might assert that any match at all is serendipitous.

There is a second important aspect of budgetmaking. Beyond the sheer planning of application of resources to policy and program purposes (i.e., the allocation of benefits) one must consider the influence of outside, but interested, parties. Little known outside the foreign assistance community, for example, is the extent to which priorities can be set by nongovernmental

---

Ronald I. Spiers, "Managing the Department of State," *U.S. Department of State: Current Policy*, no. 747 (September 26, 1985): 1.

7. *Congressional Record* 134 (May 19, 1988): S6176. Hereafter the daily edition of the *Congressional Record* will be cited as it is here; citations identified by page numbers *not* preceded by H or S are from the subsequently published permanent edition. The text is identical in both versions.

8. These sections formally reserve for the president treatymaking and the power to send and receive ambassadors, ministers, and consuls, but they have come to be interpreted much more broadly.

9. Richard E. Neustadt, *Presidential Power: The Politics of Leadership*, 2d ed. (John Wiley & Sons, 1976), p. 101.

organizations (NGOs) and others seeking a share of the assistance business. J. Brian Atwood, Clinton administration USAID administrator, vowed early on to change his agency's focus from "supply driven" (what NGOs and contractors wanted) to "demand driven" (activities and projects that fit the administration's development philosophy).[10] Overcoming the natural tendency to use the budget process to further particularistic political goals, however, is likely to be extremely difficult. The old saying, sometimes attributed to President John F. Kennedy, is clearly correct: "To govern is to choose."[11] One purpose of this book is to show that there is an equally valid corollary: "To budget is to choose."

In this book, perhaps impudently, I attempt a vertical approach to the issues of money and foreign policy. This is *not* a history of federal budgeting, *nor* a treatise on constitutional interpretation, both of which have been done exhaustively and well in the many works cited throughout. Rather, it is a somewhat episodic—perhaps idiosyncratic—attempt to look at grand issues of constitutional responsibility, as played out in the rough-and-tumble, day-to-day way in which the public's business is conducted, and to link them with lesser but still important questions regarding *how,* whatever the current balance between the Congress and the president (the assumption here is that, of those quoted at the opening of this chapter, Corwin is in closest touch with today's reality), scarce resources can be matched most effectively with policy priorities. The initial leap of faith is that these two levels are intimately related: what happens with one is heavily influenced by developments in the other. Another important assumption is that it matters how we as a nation commit our resources to foreign affairs.

In this book, I examine devices and strategems used by proponents of constitutional arguments as well as those employed by advocates of rational budgeting. Most observers think that the primary purpose of budgets, on the expenditure side, is to allocate resources according to established program priorities. This might be called "budgetary logic." But there is also "budgetary politics," for budgets can (and often do) just as easily serve as the key element in distributive politics. Budgetmakers can ensure that farmers receive subsidies for surpluses, displacing the goals of Food for Peace; that states or districts obtain and keep military bases for the economic stimulus they provide, independent of military need; that foreign affairs budget

10. Atwood, talk to USAID employees, U.S. Department of State, July 30, 1993.

11. See, for example, Arnold J. Heidenheimer, Hugh Heclo, and Carolyn Teich Adams, *Comparative Public Policy: The Politics of Social Choice in Europe and America,* 2d ed. (New York: St. Martin's Press, 1983), pp. 8–9.

allotments are used to fund essentially domestic undertakings;[12] or that certain U.S. consulates abroad are kept open even when the need for more efficient, less costly operations strongly indicates they should be closed.

Domestic political considerations—also legitimate but different—may determine what actually happens. Thus the long-term pattern of maintaining military assistance to the Greeks and Turks in the ratio of 7:10 had little to do with perceived foreign policy needs and a great deal to do with the strength of the Greek American lobby. Similarly, the efforts of AIPAC (American Israel Public Affairs Committee)[13] have driven much of the foreign assistance agenda for many years.

Budgets can also serve as congressional oversight mechanisms, as evaluation devices, and as general measures of who wins and who loses in the game of politics. The executive–legislative relationship in this area has not remained static. The general trend has been one of more and more direct congressional involvement at every stage, accompanied by less willingness to allow the executive branch to manage programs without constraints and close guidance.[14] This approach is derisively

12. In the FY 1992 CJS Appropriations Act, for example, $5 million in the Salaries and Expenses (S&E) account for State's Bureau of Oceans, International Environmental, and Scientific Affairs (OES) was earmarked for international grants. For FY 1993, this amount was increased to $31.5 million. A very similar program, heretofore funded for NOAA (National Oceanographic and Atmospheric Administration) and thus within the domestic discretionary ceiling, had been reduced in the same year because of a tight budget ceiling for that category, whereas the appropriators considered the Function 150 account to be more flush. Predictably, for FY 1994, with the end of BEA caps (see below), this amount, except for $5 million, was returned to its former NOAA home. Although only a small amount was involved, this is a classic example of creative budgeting, taking advantage of whatever rules are in effect to serve desired purposes.

13. For a discussion of the role of AIPAC, perhaps the most successful of recent foreign affairs lobbies and certainly the most long-lived, see Chuck Alston, "AIPAC Working to Shore Up Its Clout with Congress," *Congressional Quarterly Weekly Report* 47 (February 18, 1989): 297–300. In subsequent notes, this source will be cited as *CQ Weekly Report*; and *Congressional Quarterly Almanac* will be cited as *CQ Almanac*. Note: *CQ Almanac* and *CQ Weekly Report* volume numbers differ. See also Robert I. Friedman, "The Wobbly Israel Lobby" (Outlook), *Washington Post*, November 1, 1992; and a response by Mayer Mitchell and Thomas A. Dine, who were then AIPAC's board chairman and executive director, respectively, in the letters column of the *Washington Post*, November 14, 1992.

14. There is broad general agreement on this point, although commentators differ over whether this is a positive or a negative development. See, for example, Randall B. Ripley and James M. Lindsay, eds., *Congress Resurgent: Foreign and Defense Policy on Capitol Hill* (Ann Arbor: University of Michigan Press, 1993); and James M. Lindsay, *Congress and the Politics of U.S. Foreign Policy* (Baltimore: Johns Hopkins University Press, 1994). A somewhat contrary view, based on the flawed assumption that purely legislative (i.e., lawmaking) activities present a full picture of congressional activity in the foreign policy arena, is to be found in

called "micromanagement" by the executive, and it receives due attention in this book.[15]

Finally, any study of American budgeting written in the mid-1990s would
be seriously lacking if it did not deal with a growing concern that the system
can no longer cope. In what later could be seen as prescient warnings of
problems to come, several perceptive and thoughtful commentators in 1989
and 1990 simultaneously struck the same note. Tom Mann, picking up on
*Time*'s rhetorical question "Is Government Dead?" devoted an entire chapter in a Brookings "National Priorities" volume to the topic of "Breaking
the Political Impasse";[16] Allen Schick dedicated a whole book to the question of whether we still have a "capacity to budget,"[17] coming up with a
melancholy conclusion; and Joseph White and Aaron Wildavsky lamented
the state of national budgeting in the 1980s by characterizing that period of
their exhaustive study as "the search for responsible budgeting."[18] So it was
obvious that something needed attention. Further evidence was supplied in
ample measure by the grinding budget debates of 1990: the floating,
months-long, and futile summit; a deal at the top initially vetoed by rank-
and-file members of Congress; and then, more from exhaustion than merit,
an agreement struck which no one liked. This episode nearly destroyed the
entire process. It was hard to believe at the time that the Budget Enforcement Act of 1990 could result in five years of budgetary peace.[19] The strug-

---

Barbara Hinckley's *Less Than Meets the Eye: Foreign Policy Making and the Myth of the
Assertive Congress* (Chicago: University of Chicago Press, for the Twentieth Century Fund,
1994). Part of Hinckley's argument rests on the failure of Congress to pass foreign-assistance
authorizing legislation in recent years, but she ignores the passage of State Department authorizing legislation which has always been enacted except for fiscal years 1996–97 (if not always
routinely) and which has become a surrogate for foreign-assistance authorization bills as a
vehicle for indicating congressional policy preferences and demands.

15. This pattern is by no means limited to the area of foreign affairs. It was to become a
major theme of Vice-President Al Gore's "reinventing government" exercise in 1993. For the
flavor of that time, see David S. Broder and Stephen Barr, "Hill's Micromanagement of Cabinet
Blurs Separation of Powers," *Washington Post*, July 25, 1993, which draws on interviews and
testimony from several Clinton and pre-Clinton cabinet secretaries.

16. Thomas E. Mann, "Breaking the Political Impasse," chap. 9 in Henry J. Aaron, ed.,
*Setting National Priorities: Policy for the Nineties* (Washington, D.C.: Brookings Institution,
1990), pp. 293–317.

17. Allen Schick, *The Capacity to Budget* (Washington, D.C.: Urban Institute Press, 1990).

18. Joseph White and Aaron Wildavsky, *The Deficit and the Public Interest: The Search for
Responsible Budgeting in the 1980s* (Berkeley and Los Angeles: University of California Press,
1989).

19. See Chapter 4 below for a consideration of the budget summit of 1990 and the resulting
Budget Enforcement Act (BEA) as it affected foreign affairs. For early commentaries on the
infighting over scorekeeping, see Lawrence J. Haas, "New Rules of the Game," *National Jour-*

gle continued throughout the 1990s. First came the Clinton 1993 budget, passed with *no* Republican votes. Then, even more dramatic, there was the 1995 Republican "Contract with America" budget resolution and the resulting shutdown of much of the government for two extended periods.

Some might be inclined to argue that the works cited just above, all from the period of "gridlock" or divided government,[20] did not accurately reflect conditions in the early part of the Clinton administration, evidenced for example in 1993 by the quickest adoption of budget resolutions in recent U.S. history. But with no Republican help and with widely diverging views among congressional Democrats, the president narrowly averted a disastrous setback on the reconciliation bill. The extraordinary budget happenings of 1995 reinforce the point that, divided government or not, partisan environments work with constitutional roles to produce conflict. It is safe to predict that institutional imperatives will continue to arise and that Congress and the president, whether of the same or different parties, will have important differences over the budget. This book, while it must take account of recent changes in federal budgeting, attempts a longer-term view than either the "gridlock" or the "honeymoon" paradigm suggests.

Chapter 1 is an overview of the post–World War II evolution of foreign affairs funding, including State Department operations and foreign assistance, in the context of an evolving budgetary process. The recurring theme of the interplay of Congress and the executive in ways not always adhering to strict constitutional niceties is also introduced.

In Chapter 2, we turn to obstacles within both branches that make it difficult to find a better budget logic. Among other things, it is argued that

---

*nal* 22 (November 17, 1990): 2793–97; and George Hager, "The Budget: Parties Wrangle over Power to Figure Cost Overruns," *CQ Weekly Report* 49 (December 8, 1990): 4072–73. The battle continued into 1991, in the first instance during debate on adoption of the House rules on January 3. See *Congressional Record* 137 (January 3, 1991): H5–H28. Two useful early evaluations of the BEA appear in *Public Budgeting & Finance* 12 (Spring 1992): Richard Doyle and Jerry McCaffery, "The Budget Enforcement Act in 1991: Isometric Budgeting," pp. 3–15; and Philip G. Joyce, "The Budget Enforcement Act and Its Survival: Congress Hears from Experts," pp. 16–22.

20. The many confrontations of 1993, of course—from the budget agreement to Somalia and Bosnia policy to NAFTA—showed that many of the differences that count are institutional, not partisan. The 1994 Democratic election debacle showed that ignoring partisanship is equally misguided. Worth referring to, albeit in a different context than the authors were analyzing, are James L. Sundquist, ed., *Beyond Gridlock? Prospects for Governance in the Clinton Years—and After* (Washington, D.C.: Brookings Institution, 1993); and David R. Mayhew, *Divided We Govern: Party Control, Lawmaking, and Investigation, 1946–1990* (New Haven: Yale University Press, 1991).

the Budget Enforcement Act of 1990 provided an unexploited opportunity, even if unplanned, for developing a more coherent approach to foreign affairs budgeting. Chapter 2 also explores some of the problems and pathologies that afflict the process today, while Chapter 3 provides some telling examples about how they played out in individual cases.

Chapters 4, 5, and 6 focus on congressional budgeting activities, albeit with heavy executive involvement. In these chapters, I attempt to show how, as the legislative branch is called on to exercise the power of the purse, budget logic often gives way to budget politics. The division of congressional activities posited in this book—between purely budgetary actions, on the one hand, and those which consciously attempt to use the power of the purse to influence foreign policy outcomes, on the other—is frequently ambiguous. Nevertheless, for presentation purposes, Chapters 4 and 5 deal primarily with the former, and Chapter 6 with the latter.

Among the themes to be explored on the budget side is the degree to which State Department and USIA funding and operations have been impacted by being grouped with the Commerce and Justice departments for appropriations purposes and thus subjected to direct resource competition with popular domestic programs. More on the policy side, another set of potentially confrontational situations emerges in cases when Congress takes exception to the ways in which the executive proposes to expend (or withhold) appropriated funds: e.g., some elements of aid to the Contras, certification of the U.N. Food and Agricultural Organization (FAO) as being in compliance with congressionally mandated requirements for budgetary reform[21] or, even worse, programs held to be outside the law, as in the Iran-Contra episode.

As noted, Congress is a player in resource allocation in ways that go beyond just providing funds, and among the trends noticeable during the 1980s and early 1990s were increased "earmarking" for specific purposes and a greater tendency to include very explicit statutory or report language

21. In 1990–91, there was a minor contretemps between State and the House CJS Appropriations Subcommittee (and its chairman, Neal Smith) when the department proposed to withhold funds from FAO on grounds that the organization had not complied with congressionally mandated budget reforms (a policy choice perhaps made easier because of the eccentric leadership of FAO and because appropriations were not sufficient to pay U.S. assessments to all international organizations in which the United States was a member). Smith, from Iowa, was lobbied hard by major American agricultural corporations, and he eventually convinced State that it was not prudent to withhold the FAO funding. Such cases of withholding often cause more problems than the reverse situation (when the executive wants to spend funds for purposes not approved in advance by Congress); it all depends on the issue. The 1974 Congressional Budget Act, of course, was in part a response to the impoundment of appropriated funds by the Nixon administration.

instructions about operations in authorization and appropriations bills ("micromanagement"). What difference this all makes, and how it is done, constitutes the last part of Chapter 6.

Chapter 7 reviews some additional and more contextual (rather than structural or political) features of the process, continuing the earlier emphasis on executive–legislative interaction by examining some of the norms and myths about the budget process. At times, I conclude, "what everybody knows" is not supported by the evidence, and there are some little-noted rules of the game which can provide illumination and guidance.

In Chapter 8, I tie many of the preceding themes together, using the foreign affairs funding, policy, and organizational debates of 1995 as a detailed illustration. While some saw 1995 as a significant departure from bipartisanship in foreign affairs, the contention here is that the extraordinary contentiousness of that year can best be understood as a continuation of past trends.

The obvious remaining question is whether anything can be done to make things better. Chapter 9 therefore suggests different ways of doing business, both in the executive branch and in the Congress, that would likely bring greater coherence to the process, though not guaranteeing any quick fixes.

Chapter 10 is a summary and conclusion. The end result, with luck, will be a better understanding of the importance of the budget process and its impact on our ability to carry out an effective and sensible foreign policy. At a time when the world is moving inexorably toward greater integration in many fields, and greater interdependence in virtually every aspect of life, such an understanding is of prime importance. Our apparent inward turn as a nation, as manifested at least for the moment by an important part of our political leadership, is therefore troubling. Missed opportunities, in large measure attributable to a "bottom line," sometimes neo-isolationist mind-set, are the result of constant battles over financial support for the conduct of foreign policy. The issue becomes one of whether we are willing to commit the resources necessary to remain a superpower—an increasingly difficult proposition at a time when the American people feel shortchanged at home, when the United States trails all other major donors in the percentage of GNP dedicated to sustainable development, and when the State Department is clearly underfunded.[22] Thus, the issues addressed in this book are arguably more important now than they might be in calmer, less confusing times. First, to some history.

22. This sentence is a paraphrase of remarks by Senator Paul Sarbanes, one of Congress's most thoughtful internationalists, to a group of exchange students participating in the University of Maryland Foreign Policy Seminar. The remarks were made at a reception in the Capitol on February 9, 1995.

CHAPTER ONE

# FOREIGN AFFAIRS FUNDING TRENDS AND THE EVOLVING BUDGETARY PROCESS

Today's contentiousness over the price of the nation's foreign policy and over the appropriate relationship between executive and legislative powers in supporting that policy did not begin overnight. At base, these contests began with the U.S. Constitution, itself derivative from the English experience. In a more modern sense, they began in the immediate post–World War II period, as America began to adjust to superpower realities in what rapidly became a Cold War environment. Events such as the Vietnam War and the Iran-Contra affair heightened suspicion between the two branches. Ultimately, the end of the Cold War together with at least a temporary rejection of "big government" in the 1994 elections brought us face to face with a new and unsettling international affairs budgetary regime.

Some review of past developments, evolutionary as well as radical, is relevant to a current understanding. This chapter provides that critical context. First the history of funding for the conduct of U.S. foreign affairs is presented, showing how little of our national wealth has been spent for that purpose. Next is an introductory discussion of the significant changes in the federal budgetary process since passage of the 1974 Congressional Budget Act, including an evaluation of how those changes have affected foreign affairs. This chapter concludes with overviews of the current budget process, in the executive branch and in Congress, as a prelude to more-detailed discussions.

# Numbers: A Flat Curve

In light of both the importance of foreign policy and the attention it receives, it is striking (though easily explainable—here versus there) how little of the federal budget is spent to support it. This is true even in the mid-1990s, which arguably have seen more change in the old order than any other decade since the 1870s, in terms of the global structure, ideologies, and norms that define the international system. At no time since World War II, with the exception of the aberrational Marshall Plan years of 1947–51, has Function 150, the International Affairs category of the budget,[1] accounted for more than 5.28 percent (in 1962) of overall budget expenditures. Since 1981, the level has always been below 2 percent, sometimes far below; by fiscal year 1996, it was less than 1 percent. Similarly, the percentage of total gross domestic product (GDP) devoted to this fundamentally important purpose has been *less than half of 1 percent,* except in the late 1940s and early 1950s, and in recent years it has been much less and on a downward spiral, with only a temporary upward reversal in the early 1990s (see Figure 1). In constant 1996 dollars, the amount spent for International Affairs has been halved since 1984, from $37.5 billion to $18.5 billion, causing major reductions in our overseas presence and activities.[2] In a remark from an unexpected source, but not far from the truth, a Republican SFRC staffer noted in early 1995 that the total amount in the budget for the International Affairs category that year, about $20 billion, was less than the statistical error in the president's total budget of more than $1.6 trillion![3]

The American public, generally held to be antagonistic to foreign expenditures, particularly foreign assistance, apparently believes that much more is spent internationally than is the case. In a 1995 study by a unit of the University of Maryland, the median public estimate was that 15 percent of the federal budget was spent on foreign assistance, whereas the actual amount was around 1 percent. Furthermore, the same sample believed that

---

1. The federal budget, for convenience, is divided into some seventeen "superfunctions," confusingly referred to normally as "functions." Thus, in addition to 150, National Defense is 050; Science, Space, and Technology is 250.

2. Thomas W. Lippman, "U.S. Diplomacy's Presence Shrinking," *Washington Post,* June 3, 1996. This article is an excellent overview of all aspects of Function 150.

3. Related by Frederick W. Weiss, a congressional representative for the American Foreign Service Association, the professional association/union for members of the Foreign Service, at a public meeting held at the Department of State, January 13, 1995.

Fig. 1.   Outlays for International Affairs (Function 150), 1940–1997 (As Percentage of Budget and of GDP)

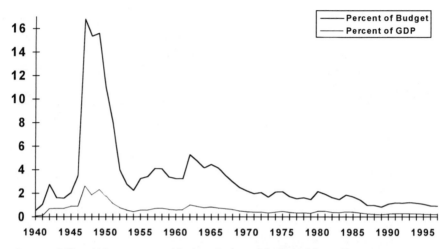

SOURCE: Office of Management and Budget, *Budget of the United States Government Historical Tables, Fiscal Year 1997* (Washington, D.C.: GPO, 1996), table 3.1, pp. 42–49. NOTE: For the data, see Appendix Table 1.

5 percent—five times the actual amount—was an appropriate level for such assistance.[4] Clearly, the public has little idea of what the government does overseas, or how much it costs. Yet, as Madeleine Albright argued during her January 1997 hearings for confirmation as secretary of state,

> Consider the stakes. We are talking here about one percent of the federal budget, but that one percent may well determine 50 percent of the history that is written about our era. Let me repeat that. The one percent that we are talking about may well determine 50 percent of the history that is written about our era.[5]

4. Steven Kull, principal investigator, *Americans and Foreign Aid: A Study of American Public Attitudes. Summary of Findings.* Monograph. (College Park: University of Maryland, Center for the Study of Policy Attitudes and Center for International and Security Studies at Maryland, School of Public Affairs, January 23, 1995), pp. 1–2. For a press summary, see Barbara Crossette, "Foreign Aid Budget: Quick, How Much? Wrong," *New York Times*, February 27, 1995.

5. Senate Foreign Relations Committee, "Hearing to Consider the Nomination of Madeleine Albright for Secretary of State," transcript, typescript, Washington, D.C., January 8, 1997, p. 16.

Admittedly, a focus only on Function 150 understates the total amount spent on foreign affairs, because the intelligence budget, among other items, is included in Function 050 (National Defense) and significant international programs are to be found in other functions such as Agriculture. Many direct defense expenditures—e.g., peacekeeping in Bosnia—also clearly qualify. Nevertheless, even with these added in, the total amounts expended are no more than on the order of double the figures for Function 150, still a minuscule proportion of the total budget if we consider the importance of this category in a world in which domestic versus international distinctions are increasingly archaic. Thus, focusing on Function 150, as this section does, does not significantly distort the basic argument. Figure 1 gives a more detailed view of Function 150 levels, year by year.

Equally surprising is how small a proportion of Function 150 funding is devoted to the operations of the key foreign affairs agencies, as opposed to the amounts allocated to foreign assistance. Function 150 is divided into subfunctions, and it is worth examining this breakdown in more detail (see Table 1).

Subfunctions 151 (International Development and Humanitarian Assistance), 152 (International Security Assistance), and 155 (International Financial Programs, largely of an assistance nature) traditionally have accounted for at least 75 percent of the total for Function 150, with 153 (Conduct of Foreign Affairs, including State Department Operations and Contributions to International Organizations) and 154 (Foreign Information and Exchange Activities) together making up in the neighborhood of 25 percent, sometimes less. (Figures 2a and 2b present this information graphically.) Subfunction 155 includes credit and other financial programs for which the new budget authority varies radically from year to year—depending on whether a large replenishment is made and on the size of repayments—and can even be a negative amount. Figure 2a can therefore be deceptive. Figure 2b, which excludes Subfunction 155 while presenting the same data as shown in Figure 2a for the other subfunctions, is a better visualization of funding trends for most purposes.

Table 2 shows the portions of the total Function 150 appropriation dedicated for the Conduct of Foreign Affairs (Subfunction 153) and for Foreign Information and Exchange (Subfunction 154) in recent years. Yet even these figures overestimate the amounts available for actual diplomatic operations. First of all, Subfunction 153 includes contributions to the United Nations as well as international organization contributions (both for regular assessment and for peacekeeping) which have expanded from $702 million in FY

Table 1. Function 150 and Its Subfunctions

| | |
|---|---|
| Function 150 | International Affairs |
| | Maintaining peaceful relations, commerce, and travel between the United States and the rest of the world and promoting international security and economic development abroad. Excluded are outlays from domestic programs that may tangentially affect foreign relations or the citizens of other nations. |

| | |
|---|---|
| Subfunctions | |
| 151 | International Development and Humanitarian Assistance [USAID, USDA] |
| | Humanitarian assistance, development assistance, security support assistance, grants to and investments in international financial and development institutions, and budgetary costs associated with concessionary agricultural exports |
| 152 | International Security Assistance [Department of State] |
| | The transfer of defense articles and services to foreign governments, including grants, credit sales, and training. Excluded is the military sales trust fund, which is classified under Subfunction 155 |
| 153 | Conduct of Foreign Affairs [Department of State] |
| | Diplomatic and consular operations of the Department of State, assessed contributions to international organizations, and closely related activities in other agencies (such as ACDA) |
| 154 | Foreign Information and Exchange Activities [USIA] |
| | Student and cultural exchange programs and foreign library, radio, or other media information activities designed to promote mutual understanding between the people of the United States and other nations |
| 155 | International Financial Programs [Department of the Treasury] |
| | Export credit, the military sales trust fund, international commodity agreements, international monetary programs and other programs designed to improve the functioning of the international financial system |

SOURCE: U.S. General Accounting Office, *A Glossary of Terms Used in the Federal Budget Process,* exposure draft, January 1993, app. 2: "Budget Functional Classification," pp. 104–5.

Fig. 2a.    FY 1976–FY 1997 Budget Authority, Mandatory and Discretionary, for Function 150: All Subfunctions

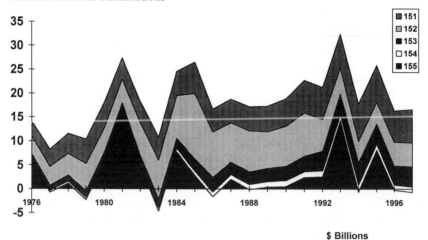

SOURCE: Office of Management and Budget, *Budget of the United States Government Historical Tables, Fiscal Year 1997* (Washington, D.C.: GPO, 1996), table 5.1, pp. 75–77
NOTE: For the data, see Appendix Table 2.

Fig. 2b.    FY 1976–FY 1997 Budget Authority, Mandatory and Discretionary, for Function 150: Less Subfunction 155

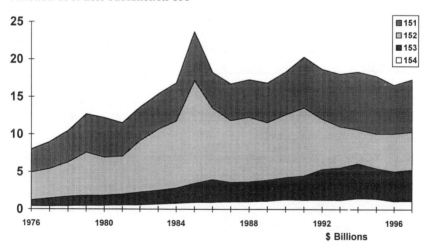

SOURCE: See Figure 2a.
NOTE: For the data, see Appendix Table 2.

Table 2. Portion of Total Function 150 Appropriation Available for Conduct of
Foreign Affairs (Subfunction 153) and for Foreign Information and Exchange
Programs (Subfunction 154)

| Fiscal<br>Year | Subfunction 153 | | Subfunction 154 | | 153 + 154<br>(% of 150) |
|---|---|---|---|---|---|
| | Amount<br>($Millions) | % of 150 | Amount<br>($Millions) | % of 150 | |
| 1990 | 2,933 | 15.60 | 1,317 | 7.00 | 22.59 |
| 1991 | 3,238 | 14.27 | 1,243 | 5.48 | 19.75 |
| 1992 | 4,063 | 19.14 | 1,303 | 6.14 | 25.28 |
| 1993 | 4,327 | 21.35* | 1,248 | 6.16* | 27.50* |
| 1994 | 4,630 | 26.14 | 1,496 | 8.45 | 34.59 |
| 1995 est | 4,063 | 22.48† | 1,421 | 6.76† | 29.24† |
| 1996 est | 3,954 | 24.21 | 1,115 | 6.82 | 31.03 |
| 1997 req | 4,167 | 25.07 | 1,162 | 6.99 | 32.07 |

Subfunction 153 = State Department operations, international organizations
Subfunction 154 = International cultural, educational, and information activities
              (includes broadcasting)

Source: Office of Management and Budget, *Budget of the United States Government Historical Tables, Fiscal Year 1997* (Washington, D.C.: GPO, 1996), table 5.1, pp. 77–78.

Note: est = estimate; req. = request.

*Total used omits International Monetary Fund replenishment which distorts analysis.

†FY 1995 amounts are from FY 1995 data in the FY 1996 historical tables (anomaly in FY
1995 data in the FY 1997 historical tables).

1990 to $1.379 billion in FY 1993, though declining thereafter (e.g., to
$1.254 billion for FY 1996). Second, the percentages for Subfunctions 153
and 154 have increased over six fiscal years 1992–1997 from historical levels of generally less than 20 percent of the Function 150 total, primarily
because the *base* has decreased (with major reductions in Subfunctions 151
and 152) for foreign assistance.

It is also important to note that these categories are not broadly fungible.
Because Subfunctions 153 and 154 are considered by one set of appropriations subcommittees, while 151, 152, and 155 are taken up by others, it is
only with great difficulty that funds can be moved from one category to
another once the president's budget has been sent to Congress and the allocations provided for by the Budget Enforcement Act of 1990 (BEA), discussed in detail below, have been made to subcommittees by the full
appropriations committees in each house.[6] As a result, there is usually insuf-

6. Under the 1974 Congressional Budget Act, the budget committees determine the amounts
allowed for each function, under the terms of subsection 302(a) of that act; and, through the

ficient flexibility to delay programs, as Defense can sometimes do, in order to preserve the institutional base in times of budgetary stringency. Also important to note is that International Affairs did not benefit to the same degree as other areas from massive funding increases of the 1960s and much of the 1970s. Largely because of the unpopularity of foreign assistance programs, suspicion of the United Nations, and higher priorities for defense and domestic programs, the line was held more tightly for Function 150 than elsewhere. There is every reason to believe this pattern will continue, given the increased determination to reduce the federal budget deficit while preserving whatever domestic spending is most visible to worried constituents. This trend has made foreign affairs spending extremely vulnerable, especially given the deep antipathy and skepticism the new Republican majorities, in both the House and the Senate, have shown since 1995 with respect to international activism. Even without overall budget-balancing pressures, International Affairs, especially foreign aid, would have faced major cuts.

From 1960 to 1970, total federal budget outlays more than doubled—from \$92.191 billion to \$195.649 billion (112% growth)—while Function 150 outlays grew from \$2.988 billion to only \$4.330 billion (44% growth) and, as a percentage of total expenditures, declined from 3.24 percent to 2.21 percent. When one considers International Affairs outlays in constant 1982 dollars, the amounts for the late 1980s are virtually the same as for the early 1970s, and both these periods saw significantly lower outlays than the first postwar decade, the 1960s, or the first half of the 1980s. Even the "high" periods such as the Marshall Plan years, the Kennedy buildup, or the CORDS ("pacification") program[7] in Vietnam during the late 1960s are

---

budget resolution, transmit the results to the appropriations committees in each house. In turn, the appropriations committees make allocations to the thirteen appropriations subcommittees under the authority of subsection 302(b). For fiscal years 1991 and later, however, there are special provisions which accomplish the same purpose, under subsections 602(a) and 602(b) of the act, as added by the 1990 BEA. These steps are referred to in the "insider" literature as "302(b)'s" or "602(a)'s." For the best short explanation of this complicated process, see Allen Schick, Robert Keith, and Edward Davis, *Manual on the Federal Budget Process* (Washington, D.C.: Congressional Research Service, Library of Congress, December 24, 1991), pp. 69–71. For an updated and more easily accessible formulation, see Allen Schick, *The Federal Budget: Politics, Policy, Process* (Washington, D.C.: Brookings Institution, 1995), pp. 88–91.

7. CORDS, or Civil Operation and Revolutionary Development Support (the latter part was subsequently changed to the less provocative "Rural Development Support"), was a major development project involving U.S. advisors, largely from AID. The last in a series of similar programs during the latter 1960s, CORDS was controversial within the foreign assistance community for its intrusiveness, for its direct ties to the U.S. military (to whom it reported), and for its expense—then as now.

anomalies. There has been no real growth in dollar amounts since the mid-1950s (see Figure 1 and the data in Appendix Table 1). Yearly variations suggest caution in interpreting such data, but the larger point is unmistakable: foreign affairs funding has not grown at a rate commensurate with expanding responsibilities, or with the rest of the federal budget.

In practice, the situation was even more drastic than these data suggest. One State budget official estimates that the real decline in International Affairs–related purchasing power since the mid-1980s has been on the order of 5 percent a year. That is because, even when inflation has been included in budget submissions in order to approximate a "current services budget" (not always the case), OMB has used a domestic inflation rate. Typically, though, inflation overseas, where much Function 150 money is spent, is higher. Over this same period, this official believes, the difference between the two inflation rates has been on the order of 3–4 percent annually (3% vs. 5–7%).[8] There is still another cause of funding difficulties: the decline of the dollar. In 1995 alone, State's overseas operating costs seemed likely by the end of the year to be some $20 million higher than planned.[9] To add one specific example covering a longer period, the 1985 dollar was worth 255 yen; at a low point ten years later, the dollar's value was 83 yen.[10]

Against these financial problems, operational requirements actually increased. Some thirty new posts had to be opened after the collapse of the Soviet Union. Passport and visa issuance demands greatly increased. Information management, the lifeblood of State, had significantly higher operating costs owing to new demands, better technology, and antiquated systems which had to be replaced. Moreover, administrative costs beyond State's control, such as rents and health insurance, outpaced funding increases.

The increasingly troubled funding situation for International Affairs is not attributable to a lack of congressional attention. Far from it. Ever since the early postwar period, Congress has become progressively more involved in the details of funding for, and the operations of, foreign affairs agencies. Prior to 1951, at a time when the United States made its largest assistance contributions to the rest of the world (both as a portion of the total U.S. budget and as a percentage of total assistance provided by all donors), Con-

8. Conversation with a senior M/FMP official, June 12, 1995.

9. See Steven Greenhouse, "Sinking Dollar Raises the Costs of U.S. Operations Overseas," *New York Times*, April 24, 1995.

10. State Department talking points for congressional use, M/FMP, April 28, 1995 (also the source of the next paragraph). By early 1997, the dollar had risen in value above 110 yen, but the general trend through this period was downward.

gress was content to appropriate general, unspecified amounts. Until much later, there was no requirement even for a foreign assistance authorization act. In the 1950s, Congress started to assert itself, and in the happy days after the Korean War this could perhaps be attributed to growing questions about whether such programs were still necessary to protect American interests.

There was also a growth industry in reorganization, finally resulting in the passage of the Foreign Assistance Act of 1961, which created the Agency for International Development (USAID) and which remains the central legislation to the present, despite periodic, largely unsuccessful reform efforts, most notably in the late 1970s and in 1989, 1992, and 1993–95.[11] Attempts to reorganize the organizational structure and programs for foreign aid did not occur in isolation. State and USIA, as well as Defense and the intelligence agencies, also received considerable attention.[12]

Given this high level of interest, low levels of funding must be ascribed to ambivalence or antipathy, rather than to a lack of attention.[13] In general, there has been a disinclination for individual members of Congress to put scarce resources into programs with little or no political payoff, and few "pork" possibilities, however important in "high policy" terms.[14]

This reality has sometimes led supporters of international programs, especially foreign assistance, to think of creative ways to package budget re-

11. See Stephen Hellinger, Douglas Hellinger, and Fred M. O'Regen, *Aid for Just Development: The Development Gap* (Boulder: Lynne Rienner, 1988), pp. 13–31, for a brief history of the evolution of foreign assistance organization and programs. In 1979, IDCA (International Development Cooperation Agency) was created as a holding company to knit together foreign assistance activities, but it never amounted to much. In 1989, the House Foreign Affairs Committee produced a thoughtful reform package under the sponsorship of Representatives Lee Hamilton and Benjamin Gilman, but it was thwarted, as will be seen. Still later, in 1992, a congressionally mandated commission produced two reports calling for integration of AID into State, while other groups called for reform, but not for integration.

12. The one comprehensive effort to catalog all these studies was John Elting Treat's "Some Lessons from Reports of Previous Commissions: Survey of Previous Reports on Organizational Reform in the Foreign Affairs Community, written for the Commission on the Organization of the Government for the Conduct of Foreign Policy (Murphy commission), June 1974.

13. See Joshua Muravchik, "Affording Foreign Policy: The Problem Is Not Wallet, but Will," *Foreign Affairs* 75 (March–April 1996): 8–13.

14. Sometimes, of course, there *was* "pork." It is interesting to note that at a time of extreme budgetary stringency, the CJS Senate appropriators found a way to preserve FY 1990 funding for DOSTN, the State Department's proposal for a new and very expensive global communications system, owing in some measure to the intervention of one of New Jersey's senators (Frank Lautenberg), who had been approached by a New Jersey company which was a bidder for the prime contract and would have lost a significant financial opportunity had the project been canceled.

quests in ways that would make them either less visible or less significant in appearance. In the early 1980s, for example, one of State's lawyers who was responsible for foreign-assistance funding proposals advocated (together with his OMB budget examiner counterpart) that security assistance be moved to the Defense portion of the budget—from Function 150 to Function 050—on the grounds that an $8 billion request, let us say, might be 40 percent of the total 150 request, but would be only 2 percent of a $400 billion Defense request. It thus would be below the threshold of attention in a Defense Appropriations Subcommittee, but if left in 150, it would be the primary account for Foreign Operations.[15] This proposal never received serious attention, and in any event its merits seemed less compelling by the late 1980s, as the Gramm-Rudman-Hollings Act (GRH) of 1987, the subsequent BEA of 1990 and the end of the Cold War began to place serious pressures on Function 050.

A variation on this theme was proposed by the Bush administration in 1992. With the dramatic increase in U.N. peacekeeping activities—in Cambodia and Somalia, among other places—the argument was made that peacekeeping was a low-cost surrogate for direct U.S. military engagement, and that it should appropriately be funded out of the Defense budget. The Clinton administration also adopted this view and included it as the "shared responsibility" proposal in PDD-25.[16] At first, it seemed possible that these ideas might be accepted, but they died when Senator Sam Nunn, chairman of the Senate Armed Services Committee, said he would go along only if Armed Services rather than the Foreign Relations Committee assumed responsibility for authorizing peacekeeping activities. The SFRC and its chairman, Claiborne Pell, were unwilling to cede this authority, and equally unwilling to take Nunn on frontally. In the end, additional peacekeeping funding was made possible within the 1990 Budget Enforcement Act ceilings for Function 150, but only because the House Foreign Operations Appropriations Subcommittee insisted, for unrelated reasons, on a significant cut in foreign assistance, thus providing the necessary "headroom."[17]

---

15. Discussions with several of the participants.

16. PDD stands for Presidential Decision Document. I am indebted to Ann Richard of State's S/RPP office for this point.

17. Under the BEA, within the overall spending allowed for FY 1991–FY 1993, special "caps" on the Defense, Domestic Discretionary, and International Affairs categories could not be exceeded unless emergency provisions were invoked. They were not in this case. The only way that the added peacekeeping expenses could be funded from Function 150 was if something else in 150 were cut. David Obey, chairman of the House Foreign Operations Appropriations Subcommittee, made this funding possible when he cut security assistance funding.

The importance of congressional schizophrenia vis-à-vis international activities cannot be overemphasized. For it explains much of what happens that is otherwise opaque.

# The Evolving Budget Process

A fact sometimes forgotten in the executive-branch foreign affairs community is that Function 150 activities do not occur in isolation. Major changes in the overall budget process inevitably influence foreign affairs, often negatively. International activities, as suggested above, are not only beset by ambivalence but are also an extremely small part of a very large whole. To understand what happens in foreign affairs, one must consider the full budgeting situation.

Today's federal budget process is quite different from that of two decades ago. These changes, the reasons for them, and their impact on foreign affairs are taken up in much greater detail in Chapter 4. Here, an overview is needed for context.

Congressional assertiveness was at the heart of a drive for change beginning in the 1970s. Passage of the Legislative Reorganization Act of 1970 can be viewed in part as an effort better to equip Congress for its responsibilities, since the legislative branch was widely held to be at a significant disadvantage compared to the executive. That act also attempted to reclaim foreign relations authority that had earlier been allowed to devolve to the president, for example through the War Powers Resolution in 1974. Most saliently, in order to regain control over the budget and emphasize its power of the purse, Congress enacted the Congressional Budget and Impoundment Control Act of 1974. Leroy Rieselbach has provided a succinct summary:

> The law centralized budgetary decision making in Congress and endeavored to produce a coherent, comprehensive budget that compared revenues and expenditures, thus offering a clear picture of the deficit. The act also created new procedures that permitted Congress to curb the president's ability to impound—refuse to spend—duly authorized and appropriated funds. The act did not stem the flow of red ink—members found creative ways to evade its strictures. Congress continued to modify the budget process in 1985 with the Balanced Budget and Emergency Deficit Control Act (the Gramm-

Rudman-Hollings bill) and again in 1990 with the Budget Enforcement Act. The former exacted automatic spending cuts if the deficit exceeded prescribed levels; the latter, renewed in 1993, abandoned a focus on the deficit and sought instead to impose spending limits (caps) on domestic, military, and international outlays.[18]

The 1974 act created today's budget process, still largely intact despite some significant changes. Of special import was its emphasis on expenditures (outlays) as opposed to budget authority and, because of the need to measure the deficit, on "scorekeeping" (how to count). It shifted some power in Congress away from the traditional money committees (Appropriations for expenditures and Ways and Means (House) and Finance (Senate) for revenues) and the authorizers, to the new budget committees and, more unevenly, to the leadership. And it forced the executive to adapt how it prepared, presented, and executed the budget.

At times, normal ways of doing business broke down, leading to the need for the so-called budget summits of 1987 and 1990, and for a functionally similar pair of high-level negotiations in early 1993 and late 1995. These events represented abrasive confrontations between (and to some extent within) the branches generated in large measure by the statutory requirements of the new process. Such episodes revealed the limitations of attempting to resolve complex public policy problems—in this case, deficit reduction—by legislative rather than political means. In the following sections, the basics of the process are outlined, first of all in the executive, where the budget still begins, and then in Congress, where the new approaches are most visible.

# Today's Budgeting: Fragmentation and Complexity

## The Executive Proposes

The president's budget, a complex compilation of requested funding submitted by law to Congress on or before the first Monday in February, is

18. Leory N. Rieselbach, "Congressional Change: Historical Perspectives," chap. 2 in James A. Thurber and Roger H. Davidson, eds., *Remaking Congress: Changes and Stability in the 1990s* (Washington, D.C.: Congressional Quarterly Press, 1995), p. 17. Rieselbach is also the source for the comments immediately preceding the quote. This is a helpful chapter for students of change in Congress.

the aggregation of millions of incremental decisions. Despite efforts to limit presidential budget power, the "single most important component of the president's spending authority . . . [is] the power to propose a cohesive budget embodying an economic program and spending priorities."[19]

Although the budget cycle is usually viewed as being an annual one, in fact at any point in time four different cycles are under way in the executive branch: final audits and accounting for the fiscal year just completed; expenditure of the current year appropriations; defending before Congress the president's request for the coming year; and preparation (often called "formulation") of the president's budget proposal for the following year.[20] Thus, in September 1996, the Department of State, like all other parts of the government, was completing its final accounting for FY 1995, which had ended on September 30, 1995. Simultaneously it was carrying out current operations in the final weeks of FY 1996, using funds appropriated in early 1996.[21] Meanwhile, Congress was attempting to complete action on the thirteen FY 1997 appropriations acts, including Foreign Operations and Commerce-Justice-State, that were of most importance for Function 150, with presidential action to follow.[22] Lastly, in each of the foreign affairs

19. Stanley E. Collender, *The Guide to the Federal Budget: Fiscal 1988* (Washington, D.C.: Urban Institute Press, 1987), p. 25.

20. For useful general descriptions of the executive branch budget process, see (in addition to the GAO *Glossary*, note 25 below) Allen Schick, "Mapping the Federal Budget Process," chap. 3 in Schick, *The Federal Budget*. A helpful textbook treatment is Don A. Cozzetto, Mary Grisez Kweit, and Robert W. Kweit, *Public Budgeting: Politics, Institutions, and Processes* (White Plains, N.Y.: Longman, 1995), pp. 49–63.

21. In a normal year, appropriations would have been completed by September 30, 1995. Since 1975, the federal government's fiscal year has been from October 1 through September 30; prior to 1975, it ran from July 1 to June 30. The change was made in the hope (largely unfulfilled) that Congress, given three extra months, would be able to complete action on annual appropriations bills before the new fiscal year started, thus obviating the need for continuing resolutions to provide interim funding while legislative action was completed. This change necessitated a "transitional quarter" for data purposes, from July 1 to September 30, 1976, which technically was a bridge between FY 1976 and FY 1977. Because of the budget disputes in 1995, FY 1996 appropriations were not completed until April 1996. A series of continuing resolutions (CRs) bridging the period after October was necessary to provide temporary funding for those departments and agencies for which appropriations bills could not be passed. Along the way, two shutdowns of the federal government occurred, one for six days in November and one for twenty days in December and January. Ultimately, eight of the thirteen appropriations bills were passed, including Foreign Operations in late January (see Chapter 8 below), but the remaining five, including CJS, after months of stalemate were combined into a CR for the rest of FY 1996 and were signed into law on April 26, 1996.

22. Congress was again unsuccessful in completing all the FY 1997 appropriations acts on time, so six were combined into an omnibus conference report attached to the Defense

agencies, final decisions and preparations were being made for the submission of requests to OMB for inclusion in the FY 1998 president's budget, scheduled to be sent to Congress in February 1997. Figure 3 illustrates those parallel activities which occur at the same time, at least in "normal" years. By starting at a given month on the edge of the diagram and moving to the center, it is possible to see what should then happen in each successive fiscal year. Of course, there is often slippage, usually causing additional difficulties and lowering the quality of the "product."

The formulation phase of presidential budget presentation deserves some attention, because it is at that stage that many of the problems which impede preparation of an integrated Function 150 budget have their source. To take one year as an example, the process of producing the president's FY 1997 budget began early in calendar year 1995, shortly after submission of the FY 1996 budget request to Congress. First came the development of budget policies at the OMB and presidential level, including economic assumptions which had a strong influence on projections of revenues and the deficit. In due course, OMB produced initial budget-preparation guidelines which were transmitted to departments and agencies; follow-up discussions were conducted with those departments and agencies concerning major programmatic issues. Later in the spring, the central agency budget offices (the Bureau of Finance and Management Policy [M/FMP] in State's case) developed policy guidance, including target figures, for bureaus and posts. Since the process is essentially incremental in nature, the previous year's enacted amounts (in this example, the amounts in the FY 1996 appropriations acts) are almost always the starting point.[23] Even before internal compilations of estimated needs were completed, initial projections were sent to OMB.

Estimates were progressively aggregated at the unit (office or mission), then the bureau, and finally the department/agency level. More often than not, the amounts estimated to be needed exceeded the target allocations provided by OMB and M/FMP, so a way had to be found to prioritize and compress the overall request. As will be seen, State has employed a variety of means to develop an overall departmental request—in earlier years, through a Priorities Policy Group (PPG). More recently, integrative effort have extended in some degree to the other foreign affairs agencies in a pro-

---

Appropriations Act (H.R. 3610). It was passed in late September 1996 by both houses and signed by the president on September 30, 1996.

23. This was true even for FY 1996, in the face of the "Republican revolution" of 1995, regarding both the president's budget submission and the final budget outcomes for Function 150; the changes were mostly similar increments from the FY 1995 base.

Fig. 3   The Budget Cycle

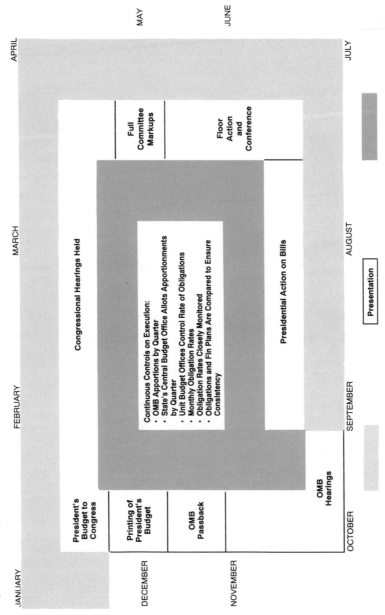

SOURCE: Bureau of Finance and Management Policy, U.S. Department of State.

cess directed by the deputy secretary or, currently, through the Office of Resources, Plans, and Policy (S/RPP), which reports to the secretary.[24] Beginning in the early 1990s, efforts have also been made to inform budget preparation with information from the program planning process, discussed in the context of executive reforms in Chapter 9. Ideally, though not yet the case, budget preparation and program planning would be a single process.

In mid- to late summer 1995, OMB provided technical instructions for budget preparations and submissions, as well as updates on budget policy arising from the midsession review, required to be submitted to Congress by July 15.[25] Using this information as well as bureau requests, the secretary of state made final decisions on priorities and, somewhere around September 15, submitted the department's detailed budget request to OMB, as did the heads of all other departments and agencies. In making these decisions, he was advised by the head of S/RPP, the director of M/FMP (the CFO), and the under secretary of state for management. At this point, owing to the extraordinary budget events taking place in late 1995, the FY 1997 cycle diverged from the norm and was delayed. Ordinarily, between mid-September and late November or early December, OMB would have prepared its recommendations for the president on what to accept and what to reject from the agency presentations, normally operating through a series of hearings focused on individual accounts and programs. These recommendations would have been conveyed to the agencies through a November "passback" (traditionally timed for the day before Thanksgiving!) and subject to "reclamas," or appeals. Sometimes appeals were resolved between OMB and the agency or department, and sometimes the president himself would make the final decision.

---

24. Both the PPG and the S/RPP are discussed at length later in this chapter. The point here is that there must be some mechanism to aggregate all of the individual requests into one complete Function 150 presentation, incorporating those from the Department of State and those from each of the other involved agencies.

25. "A supplemental summary to the budget the President submits to the Congress in January or February. . . . As required by 31 U.S.C. 1106, the midsession review contains revised estimates of budget receipts, outlays, and budget authority and other supplementary information." Accounting and Financial Management Division, General Accounting Office, *A Glossary of Terms Used in the Federal Budget Process*, exposure draft (Washington, D.C.: GAO, February 1993), p. 57. This last source is a helpful primer on the overall process and has been drawn on throughout this section. Appendix I, "Overview of the Federal Budget Process," pp. 87–101, is especially useful. Annually, requirements for specific executive branch actions such as the midsection review are contained in that year's version of OMB Circular A-11, which lists budget presentation requirements.

Once all these decisions were made, the final president's budget would usually have been printed and submitted to the Congress by early February; in this case, it was delayed until March 18, 1996. Then came the congressional budget process (see next section).

After Congress completed action on the thirteen appropriations bills (or on a continuing resolution) and the president signed them, ideally by the beginning of the next fiscal year—in this example, October 1, 1996—OMB apportioned the amounts appropriated to the receiving departments and agencies, and the central budget office (M/FMP for State) issued allotments to the subunits. These allotments are based on financial plans which break down the various accounts into more specific activities. After approval of the allotments, the execution and final accounting phases of the budget process occurred. Meanwhile, work had already begun for the following two years! This timing can be thrown off by presidential elections or by unanticipated political happenings. The only sure thing is that there will be a new twist each cycle, causing some to say there is no such thing as a "normal" budget year.

## Congress Disposes

The complicated and oftentimes mind-numbing procedure by which Congress translates the president's annual budget requests into the final appropriations needed to carry out the nation's foreign affairs consists of three distinct but intimately interrelated processes: budget, appropriations, and authorization. They must function in concert if the results are to be coherent and timely. It is unusual when that happens.

The *budget process* is the means by which, since 1974, the Congress has attempted to establish overall funding priorities—in effect, a congressional counterproposal to the president's budget, albeit one with much less detail. Once the president's budget is transmitted to the Hill, the House and Senate budget committees develop the concurrent budget resolution, scheduled for completion by April 15 (although this statutory deadline has seldom been met).[26] The budget resolution does not have the force of law, but it does provide the framework for all future budget actions; it is developed through hearings and submissions from the various authorizing committees respon-

---

26. This and the following paragraphs owe a large debt to Allen Schick, Robert Keith, and Edward Davis and to their excellent *Manual on the Federal Budget Process*.

sible for legitimizing agency budgets and programs. The budget resolution sets overall levels for the twenty or so major budget functions, such as 150 for International Affairs, and includes nonbinding assumptions detailing how the summary amounts were calculated. If the House and Senate cannot agree on a common resolution, then each house uses its own version during the rest of the process.[27]

Once the budget resolution passes, or after April 15 if it does not, allocations for each of the major budget-function categories (e.g., 150) are sent to the full appropriations committees, together with the allocation assumptions on which they are based, and the *appropriations process* begins. The appropriations committees, in turn, allocate ceiling amounts to their thirteen subcommittees (components of Function 150 go to four different pairs of subcommittees). The subcommittees are free to reallocate within a function, notwithstanding budget resolution assumptions; and, unless there are overall caps in place (such as those included in the 1990 BEA), they are also free to shift funds among functions.[28] Normally, at the end of the process, when all thirteen appropriations bills have been developed, reconciliation bills are intended to bring closure by ensuring that existing laws are changed as needed to conform revenues and expenditures to the levels set in the budget resolution (but see below for exceptions).[29] Otherwise, either appropriations must be cut or additional revenues must be found.

The final element, logically the second temporally, is the general requirement for *authorization* of programs and operating expenses before appropriations can be spent. The traditional theory is that authorizers should be advocates and overseers of the activities in their areas (e.g., the Senate Foreign Relations and House Foreign Affairs/International Relations committees in the case of State, USIA, USAID, and related programs or organizations), while appropriators are conservers of the public purse and, among other things, serve to restrain the enthusiasms of the authorizers. Thus there is a continuing (and intended) tension between the two: the authorizers holding that their program decisions should be implemented without

27. When this happens, final agreement is left until later, generally through reconciliation.

28. Within the domestic category especially, it is still possible for appropriators to shift funding from one function to another so long as they do not exceed that year's overall budget resolution ceiling. Similarly, within International Affairs, it is possible to shift funds from one subfunction to another. For example, as noted above, it was possible in FY 1993 to increase peacekeeping funding (in Subfunction 153)—some $300 million in the end—because the "Foreign Ops" appropriations subcommittees had slashed security assistance substantially.

29. Schick, *The Federal Budget*, p. 214.

Fig. 4.   The Congressional Budget Process

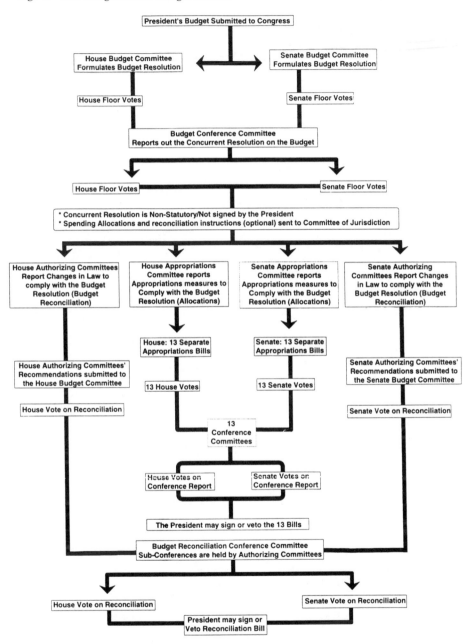

SOURCE: House Budget Committee.

change by appropriators and the latter adamant in their belief that what *they* do is what counts.

Figure 4 presents these intertwined budget, authorization, and appropriations activities as they would normally play out. The possibilities for conflict within the Congress arising from them are almost limitless.

# CHAPTER TWO

# IMPEDIMENTS TO COHERENT FOREIGN AFFAIRS BUDGETING

The outline of congressional and executive branch budget processes just presented, while revealing the complexities involved, does little more than hint at how those processes are translated into ongoing operations or at what problems can arise. Many anomalies in fact exist, which can be categorized as structural inconsistencies, process disconnects, and disincentives to the development of a more coherent process. These anomalies are the subject of the present chapter, along with some first thoughts about possible improvements. In Chapter 3, this analysis is fleshed out as we see how such problems have manifested themselves recently.

## A Fractured Structure

### Executive Branch

*No Central Authority.*

Although it may seem counterintuitive, the executive has generally been no better equipped than Congress for developing a unified approach to funding the nation's foreign policies.[1] Yet a prime motivation for the Congressional Budget Act of 1974 was the Hill's perception that it was at a

---

1. It will be argued subsequently that the inclusion of protective "fences" around Function 150 in the 1990 BEA provided an opportunity, not really exploited, to develop a more integrated presidential budget for International Affairs.

disadvantage because the president presented a consolidated budget and Congress had no counterpart!

A root cause of executive failure is fragmentation. There is no central point formally empowered either to exert control or to link policies and budgets. A strong secretary of state may dominate policy decisions and yet face contrary funding choices—which one might think would naturally conform to policy—that have been made at the working level of OMB. Nobody is in overall charge: not the secretary of state, not the NSC advisor, not even the OMB director. During the endgame of budget preparation, although the secretary may prevail with respect to those programs which are of highest priority to him, budget time is a free-for-all. In Chapter 9 below, a new and integrated approach to linking policy priorities with budget requests is suggested, but, as we shall see, making this work will be a difficult enterprise.

One obvious reason for this lack of focus is that, for many practical policy and budget purposes, the several foreign affairs agencies are essentially independent, even though in theory the secretary of state is clearly *primus inter pares*. Organizational fragmentation in the executive branch began half a century ago. Rather than maintain a unified foreign affairs structure, as for example the British largely did, the American choice after World War II was to establish separate intelligence, foreign assistance, and eventually information agencies, leaving the State Department with "policy" and with traditional diplomatic functions. State's comfortable assumption that policy control ensured program coherence was naive. The existence of numerous organizations, each with a separate budget (and, perhaps more important, with different sets of authorizers and appropriators in Congress), independent grants of statutory authority, separate institutional and bureaucratic goals, and discrete interest-group support invites uncoordinated responses to international developments.

Today, one result of this independence is that special interests surround programs, even within agencies, and their influence is profound. A related problem is that in foreign assistance and other programs, a change in allocations sends political signals, intended or not. Allocations thus come to be seen as entitlements, adding extra complexity to the already difficult problem of shifting resources to higher priorities. This dilemma is especially acute when resources are declining.

A note of caution is in order. Precisely because of this organizational independence, some well-respected experts believe that since departments and agencies remain the fundamental budgetary building blocks, attempts to produce integrated budgets in the absence of integrated organizations will fail. But it is also possible that if the president and secretary of state truly want overall prioritizing and budget integration, considerably greater coherence can result.

Some even question whether a unified foreign affairs budget, comparable to the defense budget, is desirable, given the "difficulties of making clear distinctions between foreign affairs and non–foreign affairs programs, the absence of a unified Department with a single responsible official, and traditional jurisdictional divisions in the Congress."[2] One expert, Allen Schick, has argued that however such a budget might be constructed, many programs with "significant international impacts" would of necessity be classified under domestic functions and carried in the budgets of domestic departments. Thus, "the idea of a foreign affairs budget has questionable operational value. . . . Whatever analytic gain inheres in a foreign affairs budget can be attained by a compilation of international-related programs in the Special Analysis volume of the President's budget."[3] Schick would still attempt to construct a foreign affairs budget, but would limit it to purely foreign programs.[4]

Yet such an executive branch effort seems worth making, even with the inherent limitations. It should be made clear that what is meant by an integrated budget is not simply a combined presentation when the budget is sent to Congress, but a budget in which trade-offs are made throughout— from initial assumptions, through construction of the individual unit and agency proposals during the OMB process.[5]

There are two schools of thought on the possibility of remedying this chronically chaotic condition. One group, the "realists" (some might say "pessimists") includes Charles E. Lindblom, the late Aaron Wildavsky, Allen Schick, and their disciples, who see budgeting as preeminently politi-

2. Arnold Nachmanoff, "Budgeting, Programming and Foreign Policy," in Appendix T, "Budgeting and Foreign Affairs Coordination," in *Report: Commission on the Organization of the Government for the Conduct of Foreign Policy*, app. vol. 6, p. 439.

3. Schick, "Congressional Use of Its Money Power," p. 458.

4. Ibid.

5. It seems necessary to make this point since one Department of State reader of an early draft of the present study took exception to an assertion that there was "nothing like an integrated Function 150 budget." He continued, noting that "while the 'process' may have been inadequate and not well integrated, in the end there was an integrated budget," with a single Congressional Presentation Overview that "pulled all the programs together in one place." Fair enough, but this is a far cry from what most analysts mean by an "integrated foreign affairs budget."

cal in nature.[6] Rational attempts to set priorities may be instruments in decisionmaking, but politics, power, interests, and turf determine outcomes. For this school, unless the secretary of state or some other official controls the budget submissions of all the foreign affairs agencies, it will never be possible to have a unified foreign affairs budget. The extreme wing of this school would go so far as to say that no solution short of reversing the organizational fragmentation of the 1940s and 1950s is likely to work; for them, it would be necessary to create a "Department of Foreign Affairs" along the lines of the Department of Defense, incorporating, along with State, currently independent agencies such as USAID and USIA, and perhaps even some of the foreign affairs components of other departments.

The "rationalists" (or "optimists"), in contrast, believe more in the possible triumph of logic in the budgetary process. The spiritual godfather of this camp probably is Robert McNamara, who, together with his Defense Department "whiz kids" of the Kennedy and early Johnson administrations, set the whole government, for a while, in pursuit of Planning-Programming-Budgeting (PPBS).[7] Shortly thereafter, largely because of a 1965 Johnsonian decree extending PPBS to the entire government, the foreign affairs agencies began experimenting with comparable procedures, usually focused on individual countries. USAID and USIA, with more discrete functions, led the way. However, they were quickly joined, as will be discussed in detail later, by State's more extensive Comprehensive Country Programming System (CCPS). After repeated attempts through the early 1970s, all these mechanisms were discarded.

There are several reasons for failure. These supposedly scientific ap-

6. The literature is voluminous, but the following are of particular importance: Charles E. Lindblom, *The Policy-Making Process* (Englewood Cliffs, N.J.: Prentice-Hall, 1968) and especially "The Science of Muddling Through," *Public Administration Review* 19 (Spring 1958); Aaron Wildavsky, *The New Politics of the Budgetary Process* (Glenview, Ill.: Scott, Foresman, 1988), an updated version of his seminal *Politics of the Budgetary Process* (Boston: Little, Brown, 1964); and Allen Schick, *Congress and Money: Budgeting, Spending and Taxing* (Washington, D.C.: Urban Institute, 1980). Harold E. Lasswell's *Politics: Who Gets What, When, How* (New York: McGraw-Hill, 1936) is in a sense the precursor of them all.

7. The starting point for this effort is usually considered to be Charles J. Hitch and Roland N. McKean, *The Economics of Defense in a Nuclear Age* (Cambridge: Harvard University Press, 1960), based on an earlier study done by the authors for the RAND Corporation. Hitch subsequently became the comptroller of DOD and put the system in place. A particularly useful collection of articles and documents from this period is Fremont J. Lyden and Ernest C. Miller, eds., *Planning Programming Budgeting: A Systems Approach to Management* (Chicago: Markham, 1967).

proaches were often too broadly applied; it was extremely difficult to relate resource use to particular policy objectives. The programming cycles and the annual congressional budget cycles were out of sync. There were great difficulties in relating country-based plans to the agency-based annual budget submissions, except in the broadest sense. Yet the failure of these procedures has not prevented the rationalists from insisting that such efforts must be continued and that the need for synthesis is more intense in times of budgetary stringency. There have in fact been some residual pluses from attempts to think through the resource implications of policy choices.[8]

### Cross-Agency Integrative Experiments in the 1980s.

Better coordination of Function 150 budget preparation in the executive has been repeatedly addressed, largely in vain, over many years. In 1979, OMB with the help of the NSC staff developed a rank-order list of various "decision packages," a response to FY 1981 requests that exceeded the planning ceiling by more than $3.2 billion. State had declined to do the rank-ordering, on grounds that its budget needs could not be compared with those of other agencies. The department also saw no advantage in setting priorities that it could not make stick, since OMB insisted on making the final decisions. Another factor was that this 1979 exercise was almost an afterthought, starting too late to have much impact. Because of the late start, there was no alternative except to force trade-offs solely on budgetary, not policy, grounds.

In 1980 Carter administration OMB Director James McIntyre asked Secretary of State Edmund Muskie to render State's judgment on the relative priorities of various international affairs programs proposed by the several agencies for the FY 1982 budget, and to do so within realistic budget limits. This attempt applied lessons from the 1979 experience. McIntyre's FY 1982 effort began much earlier in the cycle. This time, with a stronger White House mandate, State agreed to participate and a small staff was organized for that purpose. After the predictable interagency battles, it was one participant's conclusion that the process had largely succeeded in paring down submissions to achievable levels, although in some instances OMB did not initially follow State's rankings. State insisted, thus saving the exercise from

---

8. James Barie, a former OMB official in the National Security and International Affairs Division, is the source for this paragraph's summary of problems with previous programming efforts.

irrelevance. It was not perfect, but it was held by one admittedly engaged participant to have promise.[9]

Not all agreed. Some at State thought that a secretary of state could not play the role of honest broker and credibly set priorities for the entire Function 150 account if he were also to protect effectively State's single-agency interests. Others were concerned by the changes in power and authority that such a process portended, however improved it might be. Without a unified department of foreign affairs, this problem may be insurmountable. The realists could be right. In light of such concerns and because there was no central force determined to put them to rest, the scheme did not survive into the Reagan administration.

This did not mean, however, that there were not additional attempts to secure State's judgment on the relative priorities of various activities and expenditures. Two successive under secretaries of state for security assistance, science, and technology (T), James Buckley (1981–82) and William Schneider, Jr. (1982–86), were given broader mandates by State and OMB to look at the programs of other agencies (though not State's) besides attending to their responsibilities for bilateral foreign assistance. These arrangements were largely idiosyncratic. Both Buckley and Schneider had extensive congressional ties, Buckley being a former senator and Schneider a former senior official at OMB. Previously, foreign assistance had been completely uncoordinated, with several bureaus in State, Treasury, and DOD each advancing parts of the program. Buckley put together a partially integrated foreign assistance budget in 1981–82, aided no doubt by the willing involvement of Peter McPherson, USAID's administrator—in clear distinction to Charles Wick, McPherson's counterpart at USIA. Wick fought every effort at integration of Function 150 and relied on his close friendship with President Reagan to circumvent the normal budget-decisionmaking process.

Building on Buckley's first step, Schneider added personality, expertise, Hill contacts, a close relationship with David Stockman at OMB, and prior knowledge of Function 150. While Schneider produced a combined foreign assistance budget, Subfunctions 151 and 152 were still divorced from the rest.[10]

9. Harry J. Shaw, "A Better Budget Recipe," *Foreign Service Journal* 63 (July–August 1986): 38–43, is the source for this summary. A former OMB official, Shaw had headed the State Department staff attempting to produce this early prioritizing.

10. Interview with Ralph Boyce, a member of the Deputy Secretary's Policy and Resources staff (D/P&R), July 19, 1988.

The next episode was initiated by the State Department's comptroller, Roger B. Feldman (M/COMP), and by Under Secretary for Management Ronald I. Spiers (M) in early 1985.[11] At a special meeting with the department's Management Council (composed of assistant-secretary-level officials) on March 15, 1985, Secretary George Shultz approved the idea of a single, independent Function 150 staff reporting to the deputy secretary; the under secretary for management was tasked to work out whatever actions might be necessary within the executive branch to bring the new entity into being.[12] Schneider argued that such an additional layer was not needed, since he could perform the integrative function impartially. Spiers agreed, but expressed concern that institutionally this approach would work well only with Schneider personally in charge. It is also possible that Schneider and his ally McPherson were opposed to any plan that would inevitably share their influence with M and run the risk of being overruled by a higher-level official (or, even worse, by the M staff) on assistance matters.[13] Whatever the facts, John C. Whitehead, former head of Goldman Sachs, newly installed as deputy secretary and designated by Shultz to deal with budgetary issues, ultimately declined to endorse the major reorganization/reform proposed by M. He asked Schneider to take on the assignment for the moment, while agreeing that the issue should be revisited one year hence, when he was more familiar with the intricacies of the problem. He also accepted some modest suggestions from AID and T—directing, for example, that budget submissions for all subfunctions be prepared in a common format, to be developed.[14] When the time came for the review, Schneider had departed, and no move was made to adopt the M plan. It was business as usual; but outside factors acted to revise the 150 budget process in unexpected ways. To begin with, later in 1985 the Gramm-Rudman-Hollings legislation passed, including a 4.3 percent cut in all appropriations.[15] The president's FY 1987 budget, however, sent to the Hill in February 1986,

11. Internal State Department memorandum, July 3, 1985 (in author's files, as are other documents cited in this paragraph).

12. Meeting summary prepared by State's Office of the Comptroller (M/COMP), April 25, 1985.

13. Schneider's and McPherson's views were summarized in a joint memorandum to Deputy Secretary John C. Whitehead on October 2, 1985.

14. Memorandum from Whitehead to McPherson, Spiers, and Schneider, October 30, 1985.

15. The purpose, of course, was to start controlling the federal deficit, sent into orbit in large measure because of the prevalence of "trickle down," supply-side (some even said "voodoo") economics as the governing theory of the first half of the 1980s. See the discussion of GRH in Chapter 4 below.

showed increases both for Defense and International Affairs. This was the famous dead-on-arrival ("DOA") budget, and when the Senate passed the budget resolution it was a disaster for Function 150, and for foreign assistance in particular. Secretary Shultz requested that separate analyses of the impact be prepared by M and T; finding the M analysis "incoherent," he directed that the entire Function 150 analysis be put together in the "T format."[16] Eventually, the secretary erupted, decided to launch a press and public relations campaign against Congress, and decreed (after the dust had settled) that a small staff attached to the Deputy Secretary (known as D/P& R) should assume a central role in managing the 150 budget. At the same time, Shultz decided that State must do a better job in telling its story, in order to force Congress to provide more funding.[17]

Despite some improvements instituted by the two- to three-person D/P&R staff, neither at the end of the Reagan administration nor for that matter four years later when President Bush left office could it fairly be said that there was anything like an integrated Function 150 budget process. At best, as noted above, there was a mechanism during the final stages of budget preparation whereby requests prepared by the separate agencies were added together to produce a Function 150 total and the deputy secretary and budget director made the final trade-offs.

One vignette helps show why all this was so difficult. Ronald Spiers, who had originally proposed the combined Function 150 approach in 1985, later showed exasperation with even these limited efforts to bring one to pass. More than once he complained when members of his staff sought clearances on budget documents from the D/P&R staff, on grounds that Subfunction 153 appropriations, for State operations, were exclusively an M concern![18] But it is inescapable that if Function 150 is to be considered as a whole, then *all* subfunctions must be included.

## Congress: Partner and Adversary

We have already seen indications of what is to be a major theme of this book: the attempt of Congress, over at least the past quarter-century, to

16. Several participants in the events described in D/P&R and M/COMP, confirm this decision by Secretary Shultz.

17. Interview with Boyce, July 19, 1988.

18. The author was one of these staffers. Subsequent under secretaries for management, and the departmental comptrollers/chief financial officers who worked for them, were hardly more sympathetic (at least through 1996) to sharing control of Subfunction 153.

become a coequal partner in the conduct of the nation's foreign affairs, raising constitutional, institutional, and role questions along the way. As will be seen, however, this drive has hardly been coherent or well orchestrated.

### Divided Committees and Subcommittees.

Congress does little to mitigate the fragmentation begun in the executive branch, and its failure to do so has a negative impact on executive reforms. Once the president submits his budget to Congress, a complicated two-house, tripartite committee process begins. First, the two budget committees begin their examination. In their reports, they can include assumptions about the subfunctions to accompany their allocations by function, but they have generally been hard-pressed, especially when the BEA fences/ceilings were in effect, to make major changes; in any event, the appropriations committees are not obliged to follow budget committee assumptions.[19] The appropriators set some priorities among the subfunctions, but even this action is at a high level of abstraction. And once the allocations are made to the subcommittees, it is rare indeed that there are changes. Reallocations can happen, but only if chairpersons agree to "move" an allocation from, say, foreign assistance to international peacekeeping (the former being handled by one pair of subcommittees, peacekeeping by another). Usually, though, each subcommittee can decide priorities for its own piece of the pie.

It is a historical and political accident that foreign assistance is considered by one set of subcommittees, while much of the rest of Function 150 is taken up by another, with small fragments being funded by two additional sets of subcommittees. How this state of affairs came to be is worth a small detour, because it underscores the problems in developing logical processes when political realities intervene. When European recovery efforts began in the late 1940s, they were handled by new procedures rather than by adding onto the existing CJS subcommittee portfolios. In the House, the recovery effort was first assigned to the Subcommittee on Deficiencies, which was chaired by the full Appropriations Committee chairman and which dealt with all "extraordinary" requests. This subcommittee was well known for its skepticism, which extended to foreign assistance: "The Subcommittee on Deficiencies as well as the full committee . . . regarded the foreign aid demands of these years as extraordinary and unusual, not something tradi-

---

19. Even with the more radical 1995 realignment of the budget by the new Republican Congress, the budget committees had surprisingly little latitude; outcomes were dictated by larger forces, such as the "Contract with America" in the House.

tional and regular and therefore meriting consideration by a specialized subcommittee."[20]

In 1949, however, Chairman Clarence Cannon created a Special Subcommittee on Foreign Aid Appropriations, which evolved into today's Subcommittee on Foreign Operations. It had jurisdiction after 1951 over all foreign assistance activities, including military aid which formerly had been part of defense funding. This change mirrored a tendency at the time to pass omnibus foreign affairs authorization bills, and Cannon followed suit.[21]

The Senate appropriators, in contrast, handled foreign assistance at the full committee level until 1969, despite the committee's normal practice of following House jurisdictional patterns in order to facilitate conference consideration of appropriations bills. For example, when the House created a separate Commerce Subcommittee in 1955, the Senate followed suit; when the House returned Commerce to CJS in 1961, the Senate again followed.[22]

Foreign assistance was handled differently in the two houses (though in a way that did not complicate conferences) for very specific reasons, as Stephen Horn describes:

> [I]n order to avoid the "economy" mentality so prevalent in House Appropriations consideration of foreign aid bills, Senator Hayden [the committee chairman] simply never established a foreign aid subcommittee since it would probably have been dominated by the more conservative senior members; instead, until 1969 foreign aid appropriations were considered by the full committee, which had a sympathetic majority for the program. (After Hayden's retirement, a Subcommittee on Foreign Operations was established with five Democratic and three Republican members.)[23]

Yet this division between the handling of appropriations for foreign assistance and for the rest of Function 150, premised on the former's being temporary, endures today and, de facto, drives the entire process. So long as

20. Holbert N. Carroll, *The House of Representatives and Foreign Affairs* (Pittsburgh: University of Pittsburgh Press, 1958), p. 147.

21. Ibid., pp. 147–48.

22. See Senate Committee on Appropriations, *100th Anniversary*, Doc. no. 21, 83d Cong., 1st sess. (Washington, D.C.: GPO, 1967), p. 18; and Stephen Horn, *Unused Power: The Work of the Senate Committee on Appropriations* (Washington, D.C.: Brookings Institution, 1970), pp. 41–42.

23. Horn, *Unused Power*, p. 35.

this pattern endures, executive branch reforms intended to unify resource allocation in that function will face an uphill struggle.

*Budgeteers vs. Authorizers vs. Appropriators.*

Split consideration of appropriations is only the beginning of congressional fragmentation with respect to foreign affairs. The authorizing committees also reveal divisions—internal, between the houses, and between authorizers and others—which likewise impede coherence.

A significant step in executive-congressional interactions and in intra-Congress dynamics was the addition, in 1973, of a statutory requirement for an annual foreign-assistance authorization act. Added at the same time was the condition that, unless there was a specific waiver in statute, there could be no expenditure (obligation) of appropriations without such an authorization. Similar requirements were added for State and USIA operations in 1983.[24] Before then, it was not uncommon for years to pass between authorizations for foreign assistance. In the 1980s it became impossible to pass such bills because of policy controversies, and the authorization requirement then had to be waived. This situation was one of major concern to the authorizing committees, SFRC and HFAC, for it made them mere bystanders to decisionmaking by the appropriators. When it also became difficult to pass State Department authorization bills, their problem of reduced relevance became even more severe.

This requirement for authorization inserted new committees, with a more direct interest in the *content* of policy and not only in its *costs,* firmly into the process, and it placed the opportunity for mandating specific program requirements in the hands of members determined to be players. It also set the stage for protracted conflicts between authorizers and appropriators. In earlier days, the House appropriations subcommittees under the strong and sometimes irascible leadership of Otto Passman (for foreign assistance) and

24. This requirement is found in sec. 15 (a) of the State Department Basic Authorities Act of 1956, as amended (P.L. 84-885); for USIA, in sec. 701 of the United States Information and Educational Exchange Act of 1948, as amended (P.L. 80-402). Updated provisions of these two acts, as well as all other basic legislation relating to foreign affairs, are published annually by the Senate Foreign Relations and the House International Relations (formerly Foreign Affairs) committees in the series *Legislation on Foreign Relations Through [Year]* (Washington, D.C.: GPO), normally in five volumes. Foreign assistance legislation is found in volume 1 each year; legislation relating to State and USIA is in volume 2. See the discussion of the FY 1990–91 authorization and the FY 1990 appropriations acts, where this requirement became directly relevant, in Chapter 5 below. See also James M. McCormick, "Decision Making in the Foreign Affairs and Foreign Relations Committees," in Ripley and Lindsay, eds., *Congress Resurgent*, pp. 145–47.

John Rooney (for State operations) dominated the process. To say the least, Passman and Rooney were skeptics about international activities, while the authorizing committees were generally more favorably disposed. Because the authorizers were weak, it made little difference; but as they came to play a more direct role, if not usually to win, divisiveness escalated. In 1989, the authorizer/appropriator conflict became direct, as Senator Ernest "Fritz" Hollings, chairman of the Senate CJS Appropriations Subcommittee, held the State Department authorization bill hostage and ultimately prevented its passage. His price was the repeal of section 15(a) of the State Department Basic Authorities Act of 1956 and its USIA analogue, those sections containing the authorization requirement (see Chapter 5).

The Congressional Budget and Impoundment Control Act of 1974 added yet another set of interested committees, the budget committees, which were given responsibilities for producing budget resolutions that would set overall funding allocations to guide appropriators. These committees were also responsible for reconciliation legislation, needed to ensure that deficit-reduction targets were met. One result, of course, was additional complexity.[25]

It would be incorrect, however, to attribute the funding shortfalls and impasses in foreign affairs solely to the Congress; all postwar administrations must share responsibility. As has become a cliché, though largely true, there is no natural domestic constituency for international affairs programs. It would therefore seem to be obvious that administrations charged with the effective conduct of foreign policy must expend greater effort—which until now has been only intermittent—advocating these programs. Otherwise, they are likely to get short shrift.

## The Budget Itself

*International Affairs: A Divided Function.*

Another major difficulty in integrating the Function 150 budget, assuming this is desirable, rests within the structure of the budget presentation itself. As just described, throughout the process, both in the executive and in the Congress, the foreign-assistance-related elements (Subfunctions 151, 152, and 155) are considered apart from State Department operations and from the information programs conducted by USIA (Subfunctions 153 and 154, respectively).

---

25. This and related subsequent laws are discussed at length in Chapter 4 below.

There are three possible exceptions—points when an overall "look" is in theory taken and might provide such integration. Each has serious limits. First, there is the possibility, centered within State, of using the S/RPP mechanism which replaced D/P&R,[26] although as will be seen there is a long way to go before this mechanism can be deemed truly effective. Second, there is the senior-level review at OMB, first by the associate director for international affairs and then by the director, when the president's budget is being put together *after* all the executive branch agencies have made their requests and the various branches of OMB have made their decisions. But this review takes place so late in the budget preparation process that only incremental changes are possible. Third, once the budget reaches Congress, the two budget committees make their decisions about what allocation levels to recommend for the several functions, *before* each appropriations committee makes allocations to its thirteen subcommittees.[27] These allocations are at a very high level of generality, and the appropriators are not bound by the assumptions underpinning them. So the possibilities of integration are largely ineffectual.

While each agency is instructed at the beginning of the budget preparation process to submit its requests in accordance with OMB guidelines, the latter are often couched in incremental terms ("no more than a 3.6% increase over the current year," for example) and thus do not really lead to prioritizing, even if the agencies follow them. They do not, of course, necessarily do so; time and again in recent years, State has gone to OMB with a significantly higher request than the guidelines would allow, on the grounds that international circumstances so dictate. This practice has been either unknown or ignored by congressional supporters of the department such as the former HFAC chairman Dante Fascell, who assumed State had been too passive in seeking needed resources. In any event, it is hard to argue that a serious examination of priorities takes place in the executive branch as the International Affairs presentation is developed, except very late and at the most "macro" of levels.[28]

The process followed for the FY 1993 budget is instructive. In the fall of 1991, Deputy Secretary of State Larry Eagleburger had been designated by

26. See Chapter 9 for details about the latter.

27. As noted, the Budget Committee allocations for FY 1991 and later are designated "602(a) allocations," after the provision of the BEA that provides for them, while the further allocations by the appropriations committees to their subcommittees are "602(b) allocations."

28. As will be discussed in Chapter 9, in 1994 State began an effort through S/RPP to change this traditional pattern.

the president and by Secretary of State James Baker as the final decision-maker concerning the overall composition of the Function 150 submission. Several subordinate budgeteers alleged that State had abdicated the strong decisionmaking position it had been given, because its FY 1993 submission to OMB was more than a billion dollars above the ceiling set by the BEA. Some argued that Eagleburger's other duties precluded his giving due attention to the budget proposals, and that he had sent them forward without expressing his funding choices. This action, it was asserted, ceded decision-making authority to OMB. In fact, the actual composition of the foreign affairs budget was resolved in a series of telephone calls between Eagleburger and senior OMB staff, including Director Richard Darman. Knowledgeable cynics in State and in other agencies believe that this move allowed Eagleburger and Baker to go on record as being in favor of increases, while expressing their preferences for reductions in private. They could then argue that while State Department leadership had sought an increase for international affairs programs, OMB had decided to reduce funding for certain of them. In fact, State and OMB participants all agree that OMB followed Eagleburger's choices very closely. While the secretary's priorities apparently prevailed, this "endgame" hardly encouraged rational choices.[29]

*Budget Presentation Makes a Difference.*
    Evolution of federal budgetary concepts has been slow. Until 1951, the budget was organized by object classes having little to do with programs per se. Instead, the budget was calculated in terms of things—furniture, space, people. Starting with the 1952 budget, an attempt was made to identify activities or programs, moving to a "performance budget." There was, however, no explicit attempt to link these activities directly to broader policy goals. It was this linkage that McNamara attempted to forge at Defense in the 1960s. The foreign affairs community, therefore, was not notably behind the rest of the government (see next section).
    Attempts to develop program and performance budgets, however, often meet resistance, and not only within the executive branch. In one recent example, the staff of the Senate CJS Appropriations Subcommittee became exercised at attempts by State's budget shop to move toward functional, crosscutting categories (executive management, economics, etc.) and away from the more traditional categories of function, object class, and organiza-

29. This description of the FY 1993 budget development process is derived from discussions with some of those directly involved, at OMB, at State (D/P&R), and in the Congress.

tional unit. The CJS chief clerk wanted a presentation set up overseas post by overseas post, so that he could easily compare how much was being spent at each embassy. After a protracted dispute, he wrote into the FY 1990 State appropriations bill the requirement that "for fiscal year 1992, the Department of State shall submit a budget justification document to the Committees on Appropriations which provides function, subfunction, and object class information for each activity, subactivity, and bureau within the Department."[30]

The concern, of course, was that in rearranging the budget and presenting it in new ways, it would become more difficult to track what was being spent by whom. Richard Darman's new budget-presentation format for the entire federal budget for FY 1991 (though it did not change the account structure) was subjected to the same criticisms. He was accused by congressional staff of deliberately trying to make the budget more difficult to understand. Darman referred to his approach as one of "thematic crosscuts" which grouped policy initiatives and themes, regardless of where the money was to be spent.[31] This, of course, is precisely what performance budgeting is intended to do: find a way to judge how well an activity is being performed, rather than just what is spent on what.

It is an unresolved question whether one form of budget presentation favors or inhibits funding for particular items. Technically it is possible, especially with the use of computers, to present the same budget in a variety of ways, depending on the purpose to be served, but multiple presentations add confusion for all except the most intrepid budget fanatics.

Intuitively, the executive seeking to maximize funding would choose a budget format that highlights those elements—whether agencies, purposes, or themes—which are likely to be popular with the legislative branch, while downplaying those which are unpopular. The problem, of course, is that it is difficult to pick and choose. At times in the past, nonetheless, OMB has attempted something of this sort, presenting the overall budget in traditional object and agency terms while also presenting special analyses that highlighted themes and priorities.

One related point is worth considering. Although a simple distinction, it

---

30. *Conference Report to Accompany H.R. 2991, State Department Appropriations Act, Fiscal Year 1990* (November 21, 1989), Amendment 110, pp. 51–52. See also sec. 302 of the act as passed (P.L. 101-162, November 21, 1989).

31. See Eric Pianim, "Whether or Not Budget Shrinks, OMB Plans to Condense the Book," *Washington Post*, February 2, 1993, for a brief review of the Darman effort and for speculation about how the new Clinton administration would present its budget.

is useful for some purposes to recognize some differences of kind within Function 150 activities. *Infrastructural and operational costs* include embassies and what is required to build, maintain, protect, and communicate with them as well as people-related costs (the latter by itself is at least 65 percent of State's operating budget).[32] These costs differ markedly from *program expenditures*. Again, to pick up on a consistent theme of this book, programs should be closely related to policy priorities; otherwise, there is little reason for their existence. Diplomatic infrastructure and operations, on the other hand, especially for a great power, must be in place worldwide and must be sustained coherently over time, even if some posts or some activities are far removed from the high priorities of the moment. Logically, this distinction would lead to the conclusion that, optimally, operational and infrastructural expenses would be maintained in a stable fashion following long-term plans, even if program funds were subject to variation according to evolving objectives.[33]

Such an approach has not been followed for State Department funding since World War II. Along with programs, some very important ongoing operational activities have fallen victim to fads, with funding fluctuating wildly at much harm and expense.

## Policy Priorities and Resources: A Difficult Link

### Failed State Attempts to Relate Resources to Policy Purposes

The organizational culture of the Department of State is most attuned to "high policy" and does not consider "low" concerns about money to be of great importance.[34] Hence the indifferent success, over more than three

32. Estimate from the Department of State's Bureau of Financial Management and Planning, November 1993. Depending on the definitions used, some would place this figure even higher.

33. One problem with this idea, of course, is that certain programs (e.g., large-scale development infrastructure activities) take long periods of time to complete, and may be obsolete from a current-policy perspective well before they are completed. This is a chronic dilemma in the realm of foreign assistance, and no satisfactory solution has been found.

34. I draw heavily in this section on "Resource Allocation," annex B to Office of the Under Secretary of State for Management, *State 2000: A New Model for Managing Foreign Affairs*, Publication no. 10029 (Washington, D.C.: U.S. Department of State, December 1992), pp. 145–58. The significant contributions of Ambassador Lannon Walker to that annex (which I drafted) and thus to the following analysis are gratefully acknowledged.

decades, of the department's efforts to set priorities for its *own* part of the budget, never mind the rest of Function 150.

In the Kennedy and Johnson administrations, there were several related efforts to introduce programming to foreign affairs. The first of these, given impetus by the Herter Committee Report in 1962[35] and initially called the Comprehensive Country Programming System (CCPS), evolved into the Foreign Affairs Programming System (FAPS), reflecting a turn away from the country base used initially. This system, never fully accepted within State, was eventually terminated in 1967, in the face of a conflicting government-wide effort to introduce Planning-Programming-Budgeting Systems (PPBS) after the apparent success of PPBS under Robert McNamara in the Department of Defense. The Bureau of the Budget (as it was then called) wanted to use existing agency programming systems, rather than the State-based FAPS system. Some elements of the latter, however, survived into the 1970s: in the Latin American Bureau, as Country Analysis and Strategy Papers (CASP); elsewhere as Policy Analysis and Resource Allocation Papers (PARA). These efforts remained country-based, but were less quantitative and structured than CCPS.[36]

A few years later, the NSC under Henry Kissinger attempted to develop a comprehensive analytical framework for U.S. policy toward countries and regions, including country program budgets, but the results were put primarily to short-term purposes and were not tied into budget preparation.[37] Later, Kissinger's policy planning staff at State assumed some responsibility over USAID's budget, but there was no comprehensive attempt at integration.

During the Carter administration, two major attempts were made to link goals and objectives to resource allocation: Zero-Based Budgeting (ZBB) and Goals, Objectives, and Resource Management (GORM). Although ZBB never met its logical goal of justifying and reprioritizing each program, it did result in a better process. State's bureaus were forced to rank their program priorities under three possible funding levels. Some argue that this "banding" approach was effective for security assistance.

35. The Herter committee report was published as *Personnel for the New Diplomacy*, Report of the Committee on Foreign Affairs Personnel (Washington, D.C.: Carnegie Endowment for International Peace, 1962).

36. For a more extensive discussion of these episodes, see Frederick C. Mosher and John E. Harr, *Programming Systems and Foreign Affairs Leadership: An Attempted Innovation* (New York: Oxford University Press, 1970); and Nachmanoff, "Budgeting, Programming and Foreign Policy," pp. 438–52.

37. Nachmanoff, "Budgeting, Programming and Foreign Policy," pp. 444–45.

In an attempt to carry the ZBB exercise beyond State's salaries and expenses (S&E) and State Department–controlled security assistance accounts, GORM was launched in 1978 as a means of integrating the program budgeting of USAID, USIA, and State. It was received with much grumbling since it came on top of ZBB. The effort foundered, according to some, when President Carter ordered each ambassador to prepare a personal goals-and-objectives statement to be used by the White House to evaluate the overall management-by-objectives program. Coming as it did toward the end of the administration, this duplicative effort to install program- and performance-based budgeting led to the abandonment of all such interagency efforts. It was not until 1985, when State's inspector general insisted on reinstituting a goals-and-objectives program for each overseas mission and bureau, that such a process was restarted, laying the groundwork for the more formal MPP (Mission Program Plan) process begun early in the Bush/Baker period.[38]

A somewhat parallel approach was the Priorities Policy Group (PPG) in State, also attempted during the Carter administration. The notion was that representative assistant secretaries drawn both from geographic and from functional bureaus, should become decisionmakers for the overall departmental budget, providing advice to the under secretary for management (M).[39] This mechanism simply failed to work, and the assistant secretaries sent their deputies, or even their special assistants, to PPG meetings because they felt other, policy-related matters were more deserving of their own time. As early as 1980, the general conclusion was that a better way must be found.[40] Finally, in 1986, Ronald Spiers (M) decided that PPG was worthless and sought resource allocation advice in less formal ways.[41] Although attempts were made in 1988 to revive the mechanism (owing to a budgetary crisis which, it was hoped, would command more attention), the

38. The text of the previous two paragraphs follows closely a draft by Lannon Walker, prepared for the "Management Task Force–State 2000" in 1992. Walker, as a deputy inspector general during the mid-1980s, was an active participant in the events described. See Chapter 9 below for later developments relating to programming and integrated Function 150 budgets.

39. The early history and problems of the PPG are described in Edward Joseph Perkins, "The Priorities Policy Group: A Case Study of the Institutionalization of a Policy Linkage and Resource Allocation Mechanism in the Department of State" (Ph.D. diss., University of Southern California, 1978).

40. See William I. Bacchus, *Staffing for Foreign Affairs: Personnel Systems for the 1980's and 1990's* (Princeton: Princeton University Press, 1983), p. 187.

41. Several interviews with M and with State Department budget officers intimately involved with process, 1988–94.

PPG proved no more useful than earlier and again failed to garner the participation of Department of State bureaus.

In the Bush administration, Ivan Selin as M considered reviving the PPG, but after reviewing its sad history opted not to do so and eliminated it altogether. His successor, John F. W. Rogers, reached the same conclusion after still another review.

Under Secretary Richard Moose in the Clinton administration attempted at first (in 1993) to have more input in budget decisions in informal ways, but in 1994 decided to make a more formal attempt, this time with the key players being under secretaries rather than assistant secretaries. By the end of that year, he concluded that the assistant secretaries were critical to the process, because they were closer to the action, and he began developing still another approach, in the context of formulating the overall Function 150 budget.[42]

A related effort to link policy and budget priorities during the Carter administration also failed. The proposal was advanced that the policy planning staff, the secretary's think tank, should prepare an annual policy priority paper which would be used by the PPG to help relate budgets to policies. The first effort, in 1979, was widely criticized as being too vague and ethereal, providing little help in relating the two. After a second attempt the next year, the idea was scrapped.[43] The lesson of these experiences is an unsettling question: If State itself cannot decide how resources should be related to policy, how can it be remotely possible for the executive as a whole to devise a coherent, integrated, policy-relevant foreign affairs budget?

## Fads and Fluctuations in State Department Funding

Admittedly, it is no easy task for the executive to formulate its priorities. At the micro level, consider the problem of State's chief financial officer, who, supported by staff analyses and on the strength of budget justifications received from the department's offices and bureaus, must make initial decisions on programs to put forward. Pressures of time and staff predilections clearly encourage the rejection of poorly justified submissions, rather than having them redone so that there is a sounder informational base for higher-level decisionmakers. Thus it is inevitable that some lower-priority, better-

---

42. See Chapter 9 for subsequent developments. This paragraph and the preceding one are based on 1994 and 1995 interviews with several M-area staffers close to the process.

43. I was a very minor participant in this exercise.

justified submissions will survive, while some of higher priority will fail. At the other end of the spectrum, high-visibility programs—aid for Eastern Europe and the former Soviet Union, peacekeeping in Haiti or Bosnia—result in a cursory consideration of other major but less prominent requirements.

Obstacles to rationality abound. Budgetmakers think in annual cycles, while major initiatives require many years to complete. It is difficult to base outyear funding on results achieved, allowing some activities that by any sensible measure should be terminated to continue long after their time has passed. The incrementalist bias in the budget process is a severe obstacle to taking fresh looks at priorities and current needs; the wise bureaucrat knows that getting his program or pet project "in the base" is the key, since that makes it likely that the program not only will survive but will receive increased future funding based on yearly incremental adjustments.

Another difficulty is that many times there is insufficient information on which to base a coherent prioritizing decision: we do not know what works and what does not, or even the causal relationships involved. This is a particularly acute problem in certain foreign assistance areas, where it is often a leap of faith to assume that a particular program to promote democracy, for example, actually achieves its intended purposes. Even if a recipient country becomes more democratic, how can one prove that U.S.-sponsored assistance was the cause? The drive for better programming and reporting, integrated into budget preparation, responds in part to such difficulties.

Another group of problems stems from the inability to time and sequence funding in a logical way. Even if $X$ obviously should occur before $Y$, there is no guarantee in today's fragmented funding processes that $X$ will be funded before $Y$. The federal budget process is a classic, unhappy example of what Lindblom years ago described as "disjointed incrementalism."[44]

The demonstrated mismatches between program importance and the attention devoted to particular programs or purposes have resulted in funding for certain ongoing activities being subject to extreme fluctuations, often little related to "budget logic." Consider, first, the long history of the State Department's Foreign Buildings Office (FBO), responsible for designing, constructing, and maintaining State's worldwide network of chanceries and

---

44. David Braybrooke and Charles E. Lindblom, *A Strategy of Decision: Policy Evaluation as a Social Process* (New York: Free Press, 1963), p. 166. See also Charles E. Lindblom's *The Intelligence of Democracy: Decision Making Through Mutual Adjustment* (New York: Free Press, 1965) for his development of this important concept.

consulates, as well as housing, at some 254 posts (as of mid-1996) through-out the world. Given that the current average time from the decision to build a new chancery to moving into it is at least five years,[45] the planning of funding is essential. There has always been a big dilemma here. The department could seek full project funding—everything from site acquisition to design to construction to outfitting—all at once. In such a case, major assets can be tied up for long periods of time, especially if there are delays at any step, as has often occurred. Alternatively, it could seek project funding in stages, allowing resources to be used quickly once appropriated, but running the risk of disconnects if there are breaks in the funding stream or problems with the construction schedule. According to some, for example, one new chancery building remained partially completed for more than five years, adding significant repair costs once the project was resumed.[46] Because of this dilemma, the State Department in the 1970s and 1980s vacillated between full-project and staged funding, switching from one to the other in response to the obvious flaws of the approach then being used. Only in the early 1990s was it possible to put into effect an advanced planning approach that allowed appropriations for construction to be put to use more immediately while minimizing the possibility that funding would not be available for later stages of a project. In 1995, the department completed the final year of the initial five-year construction plan and there had been no funding lapses. The project was extended year by year with OMB and congressional approval, so coherent plans existed through the year 2000. For a department given to ad hoc solutions, this is an important advance.[47]

A counterexample, demonstrating the tendency for funding to get out of control, can be found in State's experience during the mid-1980s to the early 1990s in the diplomatic security area. After the bombings of the U.S. embassy and Marine compounds in Beirut in 1983, considerable attention was devoted to the issue of diplomatic security by the State Department, Congress, and a blue-ribbon commission chaired by Admiral Bobby Inman, culminating in the passage of the Omnibus Diplomatic Security and Antiter-

45. Until recently, the time involved was closer to seven years. Jerome F. Tolson, deputy assistant secretary for foreign buildings, November 5, 1993.

46. This assertion has not been verified with respect to a specific post, although a number of those with whom I discussed this issue believe it to be true. In any event, there is a risk with partial funding, unless there is a consistent plan and the appropriations remain regular.

47. The five-year plan was first sent to Congress as part of the department's Congressional Budget Presentation for FY 1992. Details on the extension come from Jerome F. Tolson, January 24, 1995.

rorism Act of 1986.[48] Shortly thereafter, the tangled story of the Moscow embassy security compromise and of the possible laxity in security practices there intensified the demands by Hill critics for enhanced attention and resources devoted to security, for greater accountability of ambassadors and other senior officials having security responsibilities, and more generally for the development of a more security-conscious State Department and Foreign Service culture. While highly critical of past State efforts in the realm of security, the Congress was initially very forthcoming in authorizing exceptional amounts of money for security programs and especially for construction of new chanceries under enhanced security standards. More than $4 billion was authorized for fiscal years 1986–90, and later amendments allowed this authorization to remain in effect until all funds were expended.[49] However, only about $1.2 billion was appropriated for these purposes, an amount that was by no means adequate to build all of the new secure buildings envisioned in the initial plan.[50] The original version of the plan was unrealistic and extremely costly because it contemplated building *all* new buildings to the highest security standards, regardless of whether they were in high- or low-threat posts, or whether the threat was of a physical or an intelligence nature. The plan required a totally American work force and twenty-four-hour American security over a period of several years once construction started. Costs for new buildings quickly rose to as much as six times that of an equivalent building in the Washington, D.C., area. At a time when foreign affairs resources were extremely tight, the security requirements of what Senator Claiborne Pell on several occasions called the "Diplomatic Fortress Act" seemed to submerge the substance of what U.S. embassies and representatives were abroad to do.[51]

This prominence for security funding had other costs. As is often the case with popular new activities, the Bureau of Diplomatic Security (DS), which

48. P.L. 99-399 (August 27, 1986), 22 USC 4801 et seq. The commission was the Secretary of State's Advisory Panel on Overseas Security, which produced both classified and unclassified versions of its report in June 1985.

49. Section 401 of the act, as amended in 1987 (subsection 3).

50. This history provides one small example of the eternal difference in viewpoint between authorizers and appropriators. In 1991, a very senior minority member of HFAC was incredulous when a department representative testified to the lack of funds as a reason for the slow pace of making security enhancements—refusing to be convinced that the Congress had not provided the full amount authorized in 1986, and that it seemed extremely unlikely that the funds would ever be provided. Authorizers tend to forget that it is the *appropriators* that provide the spendable money!

51. During the 1986–91 period, as a legislative affairs officer for the under secretary of state for management, I was present for several hearings at which Pell used this term.

had been enshrined in statute by the 1986 act, grew very rapidly, as if the high levels of funding would continue indefinitely. Much was wasted, and only two years later, in the late summer of 1988, there was a financial crisis owing to the bureau's inability to cover commitments as well as possible violations of the Anti-Deficiency Act, averted only by a massive, last-minute restructuring of the program which again resulted in waste.[52] By the early 1990s, reality had begun to set in, and the security program was scaled back. New standards of threat were established, so that the circumstances prevailing at a given post guided the security precautions taken there. While State was left with a security apparat that by most standards was excessive for the threats faced, at least the financial crunch of the times began to force some sober reconsiderations. The "DS" example nevertheless provides a spectacular case of how fads can drive funding actions, both in the executive branch and by the Congress.

There are other, less prominent but still pertinent, examples of short-term considerations driving out prudent management approaches. When funding becomes tight, the natural instinct is to defer those expenditures which apparently do not need to be made immediately. But if this practice continues for too long, the institutional and organizational costs can be debilitating. Five current examples help make this point with respect to State: recruitment, hiring, training, intelligence, and facilities maintenance. Observing the department in various capacities since the late 1960s, I have seen the periodic repetition of the same patterns in each of these areas.

In personnel, State's relatively small Foreign Service component depends on regular entry, if the right number of officers at each level is to be maintained; it is better to hire two hundred new officers each year rather than none one year and four hundred the next. Yet from time to time, hiring has been deferred owing to funding constraints.[53] The system pays, as do the officers, for as long as the disproportionately sized cadres remain in the service.

The same is true with respect to recruitment to fill whatever positions are

52. I was a participant, in August and September 1988, in many of the discussions during which this painful adjustment was made.

53. Most recently, such a deferral occurred in the mid-1990s. In 1993, for example, State brought 230 junior officers on board, close to the average historical number. In 1994, budget and employment ceiling limitations forced this number to be reduced to 130, with a further 1995 reduction to 110. The initial intake number for 1996 was 90, possibly to be increased to around 100. All this will cause significant later distortions in a bottom-entry career system where most officers move upward in distinct cohorts, as in the military. Data from State Department Bureau of Personnel officials, January 25, 1995, and May 3, 1996.

available. State, generally smug about the large numbers who take the Foreign Service exam relative to the small numbers hired, spends very little on recruitment, even though this means that the service is not as diverse as it needs to be and that some of the most suitable candidates never apply.[54]

Also, in an age when rapid evolution of the issue agenda means that the tasks which the Foreign Service and the department face will evolve considerably from those of the Cold War days, State's training budget has actually declined in real-dollar terms since 1980. This is truly shortsighted, and the amounts of money involved are minuscule compared either with the department's overall budget or with the total amount spent on Function 150.[55]

Similarly, at several points during this period, State's Bureau of Intelligence and Research (INR) had been subject either to reductions in force (RIFs) or to hiring freezes, thus crippling its ability to collate and organize the overwhelming amount of information made available from Foreign Service reporting and from the intelligence community. This state of affairs reinforces the department's natural tendency to act on the basis of today's news, rather than looking for trends and patterns. State's performance here has, among other things, led to litigation by employees who felt themselves to be disadvantaged.

Finally, the Department of State has made the same mistake as many homeowners with respect to not maintaining its (conservatively) estimated $10 *billion* inventory of buildings and facilities abroad.[56] Year after year, especially in the feeding frenzy of new security-based construction, fixing the roof or the plumbing has been put off for another year at embassies all over the world. In the late 1980s, the FBO chief argued that he could spend $1 billion a year for a ten-year period and only then begin to catch up with

54. The situation has not changed materially from the early 1980s, when I noted that "aggressive recruitment has not appeared to be necessary when upward of 20,000 individuals have been competing for some 200 places. But getting the *right* 200 officers is a more complicated problem." Bacchus, *Staffing for Foreign Affairs*, p. 121.

55. My assertion concerning flat funding comes from conversation with senior managers of the Foreign Service Institute (now the National Foreign Affairs Training Center), January 1994. FY 1996 estimates were that $52 million would be spent for all aspects of training, mostly staff salaries. This figure is 1 percent of a total State Department budget request of around $5 billion, and only 2.5 percent of its core S&E and diplomatic programs budget. These data were supplied by an official in State's Bureau of Financial Management and Planning, February 3, 1995, and are reflected in the FY 1996 *Budget in Brief* issued by the Department of State at the same time. Given cuts from this already low request level, the pattern will continue.

56. Estimate of total value from the Foreign Buildings Office chief Jerome Tolson, November 5, 1993.

needed maintenance.[57] As with your house or mine, deferring repairs only adds to the cost.

In sum, the executive branch has not taken farsighted view about the best long-term application of funds, especially for infrastructure. Nor have congressional surges and cuts in funding been helpful. The FBO example of a coherent five-year plan points to a better future, as will be discussed in Chapter 9.

# Disincentives for a Coherent Process

## State's Resource Timidity

Through the years, State has been legitimately criticized by supporters in Congress for "resource timidity." At times failing to press its case with sufficient intensity and effectiveness with the OMB and the president—and strong advocacy is necessary if adequate funding requests are to be submitted to the Congress—State frequently has started out behind. Even when a secretary of state is seized with the issue, as was George Shultz after the fall 1987 budget summit, larger political considerations can become overriding. The secretary of state is, after all, a very senior political member of an administration and not only the head of a department. Some secretaries may have felt that they must subordinate departmental and Function 150 interests to the overall strategy or, like Secretary of State Alexander Haig, risk being accused of not being a team player.[58]

Dante Fascell, the longtime chairman of State's primary House authorizing subcommittee, and chairman of the full House Foreign Affairs Committee from 1983 until 1992, found the low Function 150 budgets proposed to him by successive administrations to be unsatisfactory and in hearings repeatedly expressed his exasperation to several secretaries of state and under secretaries for management. Fascell's point was simple: "I can't help you if you won't help yourselves," by which he meant that unless State

57. Discussions with Richard Dertadian, DAS for Foreign Buildings, Department of State's Bureau of Administration, in 1988–89.

58. The view around State during the Bush administration was that Secretary James A. Baker found himself in precisely this situation. Warren Christopher, in the Clinton administration, seemed less reluctant to push for additional resources and, as will be discussed in Chapter 4, was somewhat more successful.

fought hard during preparation of the president's budget for adequate funding levels, Fascell and the few strong supporters of the department had little to work with. Especially with less popular programs and during times of budgetary restraint, all of the natural instincts of Congress are to cut, not increase, funding for foreign affairs. Programs that are favored within the foreign affairs total normally do not attract new funding; instead, the present-day tendency is to "earmark," or protect, funds within the lower levels provided in order to guarantee that these preferences are honored. The trick then, is to provide levels to Congress that are high enough to sustain some cuts and earmarks while leaving sufficient funds for necessary, if not favored, operations and programs.

State's top leaders, consumed with the foreign affairs policy issues of the moment, have normally only intermittently become engaged in budgetary matters. Even then they usually do so only in the final hours of congressional sessions, when it is just too late for meaningful change, given the procedural and political constraints. Secretaries Christopher and Albright, however, became more active than their predecessors in the search for resources, as funding for diplomacy, foreign assistance, and other international activities became more and more limited in the mid-1990s.

As is already apparent, an obvious systemic weakness has been the general inattention to resource issues. One good example is the previously noted indifferent success, over many years, of the State Department's efforts to prioritize even its *own operating budget*. Unless senior policy officials are willing to play an active role in resource allocation, it will always be disconnected from policy concerns. An overly cumbersome process, however, practically guarantees they will find other ways to use their time.

Another problem has been the deep reluctance by many at State to delve too deeply into programmatic activities, especially when carried out elsewhere. As early as the mid-1950s, for example, the then under secretary Herbert Hoover, Jr. (the second-ranking official of the department at that time), made it clear that State should have as little to do with foreign assistance as possible, because it was unpopular and a potential source of trouble with Congress.[59] Although there are recent indications that at least some senior State officials do not share this traditional view, the culture still is not program-oriented. Unless the climate changes, program budgeting does not have much of a chance. Programs count. State must ensure they contribute to policy objectives when resources are scarce.

59. William I. Bacchus, *Foreign Policy and the Bureaucratic Process: The Department of State's Country Director System* (Princeton: Princeton University Press, 1974), p. 60.

## Public Unwillingness to Spend on Foreign Affairs, Especially on Foreign Assistance

In no area of international activity has there been so much controversy, year in and year out, as with foreign assistance. Although we think of ourselves as a very generous people, Americans appear to have an innate antipathy to transferring resources to foreigners, except in cases of clear humanitarian need or where there is a perceived requirement for foreign assistance to avert something even worse (generally the threat of communist takeovers that might eventually present a direct challenge to us). In fact, in 1995, the United States ranked *last* among the top twenty-one industrialized countries in the percentage of its GNP devoted to foreign assistance: 0.15 percent compared with a UNICEF target for donor states of 0.70 percent and an average of 0.30 percent for the other top twenty donors.[60] When there have been clear purposes to be served and when there has been relatively united leadership (e.g., during the Marshall Plan for Europe and, more fleetingly, the Alliance for Progress), significant resources have been transferred, as Figures 1 and 2a-b and the supporting Appendix Tables 1 and 2 clearly demonstrate.

Even so, as Figure 2b and Table 2 show in somewhat different ways, foreign assistance generally forms at least two-thirds of the appropriations for the International Affairs function of the federal budget. Given the uproar, it is perhaps surprising that this much has been transferred. The explanation may be that State has at times been even less popular with Congress than foreign assistance!

In contrast to the "popular" assistance circumstances just noted, conflicts have arisen over what kinds of aid to give to whom when the national leadership has been divided and the purposes more ambiguous. Recall the Vietnam era or Central America in the 1980s.

Domestic considerations have not infrequently captured the aid program, most visibly with respect to assistance to Israel and the required ratio of funding for Greece in relation to Turkey.[61] Nixon was certainly correct in arguing that a Middle East peace must be pursued, among other reasons because "the Arab-Israeli conflict totally distorts our foreign aid budget. In

---

60. Robin Wright, "Foreign Aid Hits Lowest Level in Two Decades: Other Rich Nations Follow U.S. in Cutting Back While Poverty Spreads, World Surveys Show," *Los Angeles Times*, June 13, 1995.

61. See Chapter 7 for these two examples of "linked" aid driven largely by domestic politics.

1991, the 60 million people of Israel and Egypt received more than 40 percent of the almost $15 billion the United States allocated to foreign aid, while the over 4 billion people in the rest of the underdeveloped world competed for the leftovers."[62] Add to this the ideological overtones of assistance in such areas as Central America, as well as AID's obvious management difficulties and confusion about its appropriate mission, and by the late 1980s almost everyone with an interest, benign or otherwise, in foreign aid began to clamor for major change.[63]

## Funding Constraints

More generally, the difficulties caused by the still-unresolved general pattern of executive branch fragmentation will be especially debilitating over the next few years. There will be strong pressures to reduce funding in order to attack the budget deficit and, with Republicans in control of Congress, to enhance defense expenditures and reduce taxes at the expense of international programs as well as many domestic activities (with the latter maintaining priority over the former). Under the FY 1997 budget resolution, for example, budget authority and outlay levels for Function 150 would decrease from $15.01 billion (BA) and $15.90 billion (OT) in FY 1996 to $11.86 billion (BA) and $10.90 billion (OT) for FY 2002, or 21.96 percent and 31.45 percent, respectively.[64]

62. Richard Nixon, *Seize the Moment* (New York: Simon & Schuster, 1992), p. 219. He continues by summarizing the total amounts of aid given to these two countries since the mid-1970s and draws the obvious but true conclusion that "we lack sufficient money to help the emerging democracies of Eastern Europe, the struggling economies in Latin America, and the destitute peoples of Africa and South Asia" (p. 220).

63. See Chapter 3. Two articles that appeared toward the end of the Reagan administration summarize the problems neatly, argue the need for much better prioritization as foreign aid resources decline, and advocate a reorientation away from security affairs and toward the kinds of activities that later, in the Clinton administration, came to be called "sustainable development": namely, those related to the environment, population, debt reduction, trade, and small-scale enterprises. See David R. Obey and Carol Lancaster, "Funding Foreign Aid," *Foreign Policy* 71 (Summer 1988): 141–55; and John W. Sewell and Christine E. Contee, "Foreign Aid and Gramm-Rudman," *Foreign Affairs* 65 (Summer 1987): 1015–36. The status of the authors gave these ideas particular import. Obey was chairman of the House Foreign Operations Appropriations Subcommittee, and he continued to serve in that capacity until the Republicans took control of the House in the 1994 elections; Lancaster, an academic in 1988, became the deputy administrator of USAID in the Clinton administration; and Sewell continued his influential role as president of the Overseas Development Council, one of the most engaged foreign assistance organizations in the private sector.

64. Data from sec. 101 of *Conference Agreement, Recommended Levels and Amounts*, H. Con. Res. 178 (June 12, 1996). BA means budget authority while OT means outlays, or the

In addition to very low funding levels there will be continued pressures to categorize some domestic programs as international, thus funding them from Function 150 and creating more "headroom" for appropriations carried in domestic functions (see Chapter 5). Similar attempts have been made to recategorize defense funds and, occasionally, international programs as domestic. All of this underscores the fundamental reality that limited resources will be available for international activities, and that they must be used wisely.

# New Ways Needed for Managing Resources

Yet another disincentive for coherent resource allocation has to do with the existing ways of doing business. To reiterate, at the end of the Bush administration, integration of the foreign affairs budgetary process across agency lines, even within Function 150, occurred only at the macro level and in the final stages of budget formulation. Cross-agency/cross-subfunction prioritizing took place only during the endgame, when the secretary of state and the budget director made final choices and recommended them to the president. To some extent, appropriations subcommittees performed a similar function once the president's budget reached Congress. In each case, little if any attempt was made to consider international activities funded outside Function 150 as a part of the total international resource package. As a result, no resource management process extended effectively across the full range of U.S. government international activities.

While some innovations were made by the Clinton administration (see Chapter 9), there were still significant lacunae. Despite the new challenges the United States faces, including radically different assumptions about world politics, very tight budgets, and newly important activities (from democracy programs to multilateral peacekeeping) that almost *had* to be supported, the prioritizing process remained ineffectual. Some particulars of

---

amounts actually expended. Because of offsetting repayments, the projected amounts for discretionary authority are somewhat higher than those shown: FY 1996, $18.496 billion (BA) and $19.846 billion (OT); FY 2002, $14.175 billion (BA) and $14.469 billion (OT). Either way, the decline in available funding at a time of greater challenges and higher costs of doing business is significant; reductions would have been even greater had the FY 1996 budget resolution remained in place.

what was lacking, identified by the "State 2000" task force, provide a start-ing point.[65]

To begin with, the resource allocation processes have been structured to focus on appropriations accounts (types of money such as P.L. 480 food assistance, development assistance, and S&E), on organizational units, and on countries or programs. They have tended to direct most resources to those countries which are most important to the United States, but the end results do not inspire confidence that resources have been allocated in ways that meet top-priority foreign policy goals in any direct way. That is to say, the resource management process has never begun at the top; and because it has not, there can be no confidence that the real priorities among, say, export enhancement, collective security, Middle East peace, and Third World sustainable development have really been considered and balanced against one another. What should be the other part of the equation—an effective bottom-up program process to help set such priorities and feed them into budget preparation—is embryonic and incomplete.

Just as significant, current budget and resource-management practices are closely attuned to the pending fiscal year and encourage duplication among agencies and bickering over budget allocations within the executive branch, between the executive and the Congress, and among several appropriations subcommittees in each house. More attention to strategic planning would force greater budgetary attention to the outyears, especially important for long-term projects.

In a more coherent process, the executive would justify as directly as pos-sible to the Congress its rationale for given levels of funding—defining U.S. current and multiyear foreign policy goals and showing how foreign affairs budgets should be allocated to attain those goals. Then the executive should further explain how these overall goals and allocations play out in regional or country objectives and budget requests.

Many would argue that a reformed resource-management process should begin in Washington but be built up from the field in order to consider trade-offs *at the country level*. With this approach, after Washington had established foreign policy goals and provided budget-planning guidance, the regional bureaus, overseas missions, and managers of major programs would be required to present an integrated foreign affairs budget showing how the proposed programs and expenditures would accomplish country-level or worldwide policy objectives.

65. The following paragraphs draw heavily from Annex B, "Resource Allocation," of the *State 2000* report (see note 34 above).

Reflecting a difference of opinion going back at least to the 1960s, the critics of this country-based approach argue that it cannot pick up crosscutting priorities or react quickly to new needs, especially regional or global ones. A secondary critique is that ambassadors and their deputy chiefs of mission (DCMs) are not normally equipped to run such an operation; as a consequence, the kind of field-driven determination of outputs that would be required is simply unrealistic. All agree, however, that the policy and resource-management processes must be better linked so that new, unanticipated policy priorities—not addressed in initial planning—are met by needed resource shifts. Planning and continuous coordination, rather than ad hoc solutions, must prevail.

Within State, despite some improvements, the internal resource-management process is still viewed by many who are responsible for programs and operations as too centralized, inefficient, limited with respect to setting priorities (especially across bureau lines), and insufficiently linked to policy. Data to support effective prioritizing are often unavailable. And it is still largely true that once an activity or program is incorporated into the budget base, it assumes a life of its own and is seldom reexamined. The incremental nature of the federal budget process provides no incentives and in fact imposes some disincentives for doing so.[66]

In such a climate, when cost savings must be found, there is a grinding internal process of negotiations, approximations, and snap judgments, usually at the margins. The 1987 cost-reduction exercise ordered by Secretary Shultz and the 1992 "Strategy 1993" review are cases in point.[67] Typically, when additional resources are "obtained" in this way, few if any of the recommended cuts or reforms are implemented, because they are not tied to program goals and are viewed solely as the product of temporary budget constraints. Better ways of prioritizing must be found when these con-

66. There is perhaps no better example of the pervasiveness of budgetary incrementalism than the fact that the process of developing appropriations language each year begins with the exact text of the previous year's legislation. Any change raises questions both in OMB and among appropriators. With such a procedure, incrementalism almost invariably triumphs—even in the "radical" 104th Congress.

67. The Shultz-mandated exercise, a result of the 1987 funding problem, is discussed in a case study of the authorization and appropriations process during that year in Chapter 5. "Strategy 1993" was a somewhat similar exercise commissioned by Under Secretary for Management John F. W. Rogers in 1992. Both were very precise in their recommendations, and neither resulted in much significant action. Some of the National Performance Review's follow-on activities (e.g., the "Streamlining" exercise in late 1993) fell victim to the same problems, as did State's Strategic Management Initiative II (SMI II) in 1995–96.

straints are more long-lasting, as will almost certainly be the case in coming years.

This chapter has examined a number of the problems and anomalies that plague both executive and congressional budgeting for foreign affairs, not the least of which revolve about the relationships between the two. Before turning to a more detailed examination of some of these themes, using recent authorization and appropriations bills as examples, it will be helpful first to explore some additional elements of congressional-executive interplay in foreign affairs—this time by way of episodes that reveal considerations beyond budgets and funding.

# CHAPTER THREE

# HOW THINGS WORK TODAY

## *Beyond the Budget*

Up to this point, our concern has been almost entirely with budgeting and funding issues in the traditional sense: how requests for appropriations are developed and how they work their way through Congress. But a key premise of this book is that the influence of money, and therefore of the Congress which ultimately provides it, reaches far beyond mere funding into the structure of government, the programs that are conducted, the mistakes that are made, and the innovations that should be tried.

Recent history illustrates some of the almost endless variations of the executive-legislative relationship. By considering four such vignettes, our examination of specific bills in Chapter 5 can be more sharply focused.

## Foreign Aid After the Cold War: The Search for a New Mission

As is already apparent, a very large proportion of the combined congressional and executive attention to international affairs during the postwar period has been directed at foreign assistance. Two recent episodes provide useful insights into the problems involved. The first of these cases deals primarily with how assistance programs are managed; the second is concerned with more fundamental questions of the purposes of such assistance activities and, ultimately, whether they are in our national interest.

## The Failed Hamilton-Gilman Reforms of 1989

In retrospect, a major opportunity for needed reform, just in time to "catch the wave" provided by the breakup of the Soviet Union and its empire, was missed in 1989. This opportunity was the Hamilton-Gilman report,[1] the result of a request by HFAC chairman Dante Fascell and ranking minority member William Broomfield. Lee Hamilton, perhaps the most respected member of the committee, and Ben Gilman, his well-thought-of minority counterpart, managed to produce a report that, if enacted, almost certainly would have provided a sounder basis for U.S. foreign assistance. Among other things, it suggested that the Congress should consider scrapping the Foreign Assistance Act of 1961 (FAA)—the basic enabling legislation (often amended) which had guided the "program," if that is an appropriate term, for more than thirty years—and replacing it with a new International Economic Cooperation Act which would clarify the objectives of the foreign aid program and distinguish clearly between development assistance and economic support funds (ESF), the economic portion of security assistance. It was argued that "a fresh start is unlikely if Congress simply revises and adds yet more amendments to an already cluttered act. The current 500 pages of foreign assistance legislation, developed over the past 28 years, are strewn with obsolete, ambiguous and contradictory policies, restrictions and conditions."[2]

In particular, the study argued for an end to "earmarks" (see Chapter 6) or funding set-asides. Hamilton-Gilman almost certainly would have provided better coordination among U.S. government agencies, with other donors, and with recipient governments. Measures were also proposed that would have improved program flexibility.[3]

Hamilton-Gilman could not overcome entrenched ways of thinking. The Bush administration refused to support it, advocating instead its own version of reform. Perhaps even more telling, however, was Fascell's inability to control his own committee. When foreign assistance legislation was taken up by the various HFAC subcommittees, the seductiveness of maintaining earmarks for "client" states (states that often hired former committee mem-

---

1. More formally, the *Report of the Task Force on Foreign Assistance to the Committee on Foreign Affairs, U.S. House of Representatives,* February 1, 1989, H. Doc. 101-32 (Washington, D.C.: GPO, 1989).

2. Hamilton-Gilman report, p. 29. See also John Felton, " 'Earmark' Tradition Shows Staying Power on Hill: Panel Members Willing to Discard Obsolete Restrictions, but Not Their Voice in Setting U.S. Policies," *CQ Weekly Report* 47 (April 22, 1989): 903–4.

3. See the Hamilton-Gilman report, pp. vii–viii, for a summary of recommendations, and pp. 29–42 for the full texts.

bers or staffers as lobbyists, or that similarly used representatives of contractor organizations having a financial stake in a specific program) proved
overwhelming. It was business as usual. Even Gilman, in a section of the
report entitled "Reservations," argued for the maintenance of "a limited
number of exceptions" to the general principle of "no earmarks." Not surprisingly, these were for Egypt and Israel, Turkey and Greece, and consti-
tuted the lion's share of the funding—and the problem.[4] The final outcome
was typical: there was no foreign aid authorization bill in 1989. Foreign aid
reform would be deferred.

## Whither USAID? 1990–1996

By 1992, preparing reform plans for foreign assistance had become a
growth industry, one that continued into the Clinton administration. Many
proposals emerged, but no consensus.

The first attempt resulted from the increasing displeasure with AID's performance, notwithstanding internal reform efforts, voiced by appropriators
on the Foreign Operations subcommittees.[5] Partially in response to a bar-
rage of criticisms by GAO and the AID inspector general over several years,
in late 1990 the FY 1991 Foreign Operations Appropriations Act[6] established a Commission on Management of the Agency for International Development Programs (usually called the "Ferris commission," after its
chairman, George M. Ferris, Jr.), consisting of five members to be appointed
by the president. Owing to Bush administration reluctance to have a congressionally sponsored "outsider" report prepared on this increasingly volatile subject, the commission was not chartered until the following
September, and then only after Senator Patrick Leahy threatened to hold up
appropriations for the remainder of FY 1992 if the commission had not
delivered its report by April 1992.[7] When completed, the report contained

4. Ibid., p. 43.
5. See, for example, Directorate for Policy, U.S. Agency for International Development, *US
AID Policy: Democracy and Governance* (Washington, D.C.: USAID, November 1991). Another interesting effort, keyed to improving the quality of agency performance, was U.S.
Agency for International Development, *Report of the AID Incentives Project: Reforming the
Incentives System* (Washington, D.C.: USAID, January 1992).
6. P.L. 101-513, November 13, 1990, sec. 557. Note that this kind of commission typically
is mandated in authorization legislation; because of the usual problems, however, there was no
authorization bill that year.
7. On September 20, 1991. USAID was funded through March 1, 1992, on a continuing
resolution. After that date, either a new CR or an appropriations act would be needed.

some reasonable, if limited, suggestions for improved management. It called for much greater focus and agreement on a more limited agenda, for a new Foreign Assistance Act, for AID programs organized by type rather than by recipient country and, more controversially, for integration of AID into State.[8]

Early in 1992, concerned about possible reactions to the impending Ferris report, and recognizing both the unpopularity of foreign assistance and the need for President Bush to emphasize domestic issues in the 1992 campaign, the White House launched a preemptive strike. It created a joint OMB-AID "SWAT team"[9] to make its own recommendations on improving AID's organization, management, personnel systems and, especially, accountability for actions taken.[10] The administration hoped to make it plain that it was dealing with foreign assistance problems on its own. In April 1992 the SWAT team report was completed, its recommendations having been largely dictated by OMB over AID objections.[11] But by the spring of 1992, it turned out that no one cared. Neither the Ferris report nor that of the SWAT team drew much attention. AID's problems remained.

By mid-1992, others were beginning to address the problem of future assistance programs, increasingly with an eye toward a presidential transition. Senator Leahy, the instigator of the requirement for the Ferris report, wrote both to President Bush and to then-Governor Clinton, proposing a congressional-executive foreign assistance summit shortly after the election, with the purpose of designing a new program and drafting new foreign assistance legislation.[12]

The Carnegie Endowment for International Peace sponsored two studies,

8. The Ferris commission's report was published outside normal GPO channels as *The President's Commission on the Management of AID Programs: Report to the President—An Action Plan* (Washington, D.C.: President's Commission, April 16, 1992). See Chapter 8 below for the next integration/merger effort.

9. Predictably, USAID management was reluctant to participate, but really had no choice. Asked by OMB to take part, I served on one of the subordinate task forces.

10. Details of the creation of the SWAT team are from an OMB press release, "Administration Acts to Ensure Accountability over A.I.D. Programs," January 22, 1992 (in my files). One press treatment derived from this statement was Don Oberdorfer and Bill McAllister's "Short Takes: SWAT Team Formed to Study AID 'Management Problem,' " *Washington Post*, January 28, 1992.

11. Thus, in April 1992, OMB leadership rejected the initial SWAT team draft report as not being tough enough and required major changes in some areas (e.g., in procurement). This information comes from several USAID and OMB participants in the SWAT team exercise.

12. These letters were sent on August 12, 1992. The proposed summit did not take place, although there were extensive consultations between the Clinton transition team and all the key foreign assistance players in Congress.

the first addressing the future international operating environment for the United States[13] and the second more explicitly drawing the implications of this environment, including those for foreign assistance and other U.S. government operations.[14] Unlike Ferris, the Carnegie studies did not advocate moving AID into the State Department. The State Department's internal study, *State 2000: A New Model for Managing Foreign Affairs,* conducted simultaneously, reached the same conclusion.[15]

Still other reviews were carried out by John Mullen, an AID attorney commissioned by Acting Secretary of State Lawrence Eagleburger,[16] and by an ad hoc group sponsored by the Overseas Development Council with Rockefeller Foundation support.[17] The latter group would have preferred a new Development Cooperation Agency to replace AID and recommended moving all responsibilities for economic support funding to State. Articles by individual experts also appeared: for example, one by former Secretary of State James Baker, who argued for the elimination of AID and the creation of a Freedom Fund for Eastern Europe and the former Soviet states.[18] Finally, the Clinton transition team carried out its own review.

By the time the new administration took office on January 20, 1993, however, nothing had been settled, and on February 5, Secretary of State Christopher announced that his deputy, Clifton Wharton, had been asked to undertake a sixty-day (later changed to ninety-day) review of the future of foreign assistance.[19] By the accounts of those participating, after an initial

13. Carnegie Endowment for International Peace, *Changing Our Ways: America and the New World* (Washington, D.C.: Carnegie Endowment, 1992). Winston Lord, a former policy planner for Henry Kissinger and U.S. ambassador to China, and who would soon be assistant secretary of state for East Asia and Pacific Affairs in the Clinton administration, chaired this review.

14. Carnegie Endowment for International Peace and the Institute for International Economics, *Memorandum to the President-Elect: Subject—Harnessing Process to Purpose* (Washington, D.C.: Carnegie Endowment/IIE, 1992). Richard Holbrooke, also a former State Department official and subsequently ambassador to Germany and assistant secretary of state for European and Canadian Affairs in the Clinton administration, chaired this study.

15. I was executive secretary and co–study director of the "State 2000" task force.

16. John E. Mullen, "United States Economic Foreign Aid: A Program for the Post Cold War into the 21st Century Based on Broad-based International Economic Growth and the US National Interest," internal State Department memorandum, October 1992.

17. The Independent Group on the Future of U.S. Development Cooperation, *Reinventing Foreign Aid: White Paper on U.S. Development Cooperation in a New Democratic Era* (Washington, D.C.: Overseas Development Council, December 1992).

18. James B. Baker III, "Special Report: The Stakes for Them—and Us," *Newsweek* (April 5, 1993): 24–25.

19. Warren R. Christopher, "Message to State Department Employees" and "Implementa-

period of inactivity caused by transition priorities, Wharton and a team assembled by him began what amounted to a new review, trying to integrate the work of all of that had gone before. Somewhat confusingly, a parallel and not always consistent White House/NSC review of all international affairs programs, including assistance, was carried out simultaneously. Both exercises encountered difficulty, going through numerous drafts and changes in drafters in an attempt to bring coherence. Neither the final Wharton report nor PRD-20 (the NSC product) proved to be definitive, and they are perhaps best seen as necessary steps toward redefining the goals of foreign assistance and the missions and roles of the many involved components of the U.S. government.

What emerged was a broad set of strategies addressing global issues—specifically, environmental problems, population and health, broad-based economic growth, humanitarian assistance, and the promotion of democracy—all under the rubric of "sustainable development." There was to be greater focus on crosscutting concerns, with less priority for individual countries and for political and strategic considerations, a change argued to be possible with the end of the Cold War.[20]

In addition to big changes in the activities proposed for the agency, there were ongoing efforts from 1993 to 1996 to improve the way USAID carried out its business, in response to the critiques cited above. Atwood and his key staff quickly concluded that without rapid and radical change, the existence of USAID as an independent agency was at risk. Their efforts were given impetus by the vice-president's National Performance Review (NPR), which gave considerable attention to USAID,[21] and by appropriations language mandating the submission of changes in statutory provisions needed

---

tion Directive for Reorganization," February 5, 1993. Printed in *Dispatch* 4, no. 6 (February 1993): 69–73 (published by the Bureau of Public Affairs, U.S. Department of State).

20. Summarized from a USAID general notice of November 8, 1993, entitled "Excerpts from Remarks of the Hon. J. Brian Atwood, Administrator, U.S. Agency for International Development, to Interaction, Washington, D.C., November 4, 1993." Interaction was one of many development-oriented private groups before whom Atwood spoke after being sworn in in May. In addition, there were frequent congressional consultations, meetings with employees, and press briefings and interviews, yielding many similar formulations of his plans. For a good press example, see John M. Goshko and Thomas W. Lippman, "Foreign Aid Shift Sought by Clinton: Proposal Would Drop Friendly Nation Focus for Broad U.S. Goals," *Washington Post*, November 27, 1993. A somewhat earlier formulation is a column by Atwood, "Taking Exception: Don't Write Off AID Yet," *Washington Post*, June 17, 1993.

21. Vice-President Al Gore, *Creating a Government that Works Better & Costs Less: Report of the National Performance Review* (Washington, D.C.: GPO, 1993). For a fuller discussion, see Chapter 9 below.

to carry out NPR recommendations.[22] The result was a major reorganization plan and a frenetic set of reform efforts, which in the end seemed likely to produce significant results.

Two benchmarks in all this were, first, a "foreign aid reform summit" convened by Lee Hamilton on September 21, 1993, and attended by almost all the key players: Secretary Christopher, Deputy Secretary Wharton, Brian Atwood, National Security Advisor Anthony Lake, as well as David Obey, Speaker Thomas Foley, and Senator Paul Sarbanes (Leahy was unavailable). According to participants, the summit led to a substantial meeting of the minds, but also to some potentially serious problems.[23] Second, later in the fall, a discussion version of the proposed FAA rewrite was circulated on the Hill and, based on extensive comment, was revised. It was resubmitted early in 1994 as the Peace, Prosperity, and Democracy Act (PPDA) of 1994, and was introduced by request on February 2, 1994.[24]

By April, Carroll J. Doherty offered a commentary entitled "Foreign Aid: Stalemate Stalls President's Overhaul of Foreign Aid";[25] by June, it was clear that it would be extremely difficult to produce a new act in 1994, given the primacy of domestic issues (health care, welfare reform) and the disinclination of such normal supporters as Sarbanes and Hamilton to become the "white knights of foreign aid" in the face of a tough election. These factors, together with the absence of Cold War pressure and with a climate of budget stringency, doomed the positive prospect of truly "fixing AID."[26] Con-

---

22. FY 1994 Foreign Operations Appropriations Act, P.L. 103-87, September 30, 1993, under the heading "OPERATING EXPENSES OF THE AGENCY FOR INTERNATIONAL DEVELOPMENT." Included in the requirement were a redraft of the 1961 Foreign Assistance Act, personnel system reforms, improvements in agency project and program management, and a reduction in the number of USAID missions abroad. Though subsequently relaxed, the original language provided that no funds under this heading could be obligated after March 31, 1994, unless these requirements were met.

23. For details, see Dick Kirschten, "Rescuing AID," *National Journal* 25 (October 2, 1993): 2369–72.

24. As H.R. 3765. AID produced an executive summary and textual analysis, which was circulated extensively on the Hill, using this title. For a positive evaluation of the new bill, see "A Face Lift for Foreign Aid" (editorial), *Washington Post*, February 18, 1994. The point was made, however, that the continued set-asides (earmarks) for the former Soviet Union and the Middle East left very little in a tight budget for the global purposes being promoted.

25. *CQ Weekly Report* 51 (April 2, 1994): 807–8.

26. See, for example, Steven A. Holmes, "The Thin Purse: A Foreign Aid of Words, Not Cash," *New York Times*, December 5, 1993. In an editorial at about the same time, "Foreign Aid: Better, but Threatened," November 28, 1993, the *New York Times* applauded the AID reforms, but warned that "all this good work could be undone. Overly mechanical White House budget-cutting formulas would reduce funding for Mr. Atwood's new programs by as

troversy over some parts of the new bill, ironically those for which State and not USAID was responsible (promoting peace, promoting democracy) led to its demise.

By early 1995, faced with a new Republican Congress much less amenable to the new foreign assistance strategy outlined by Atwood and his colleagues, the administration decided not even to resubmit the PPDA for congressional consideration.[27] With the larger issues that surfaced in 1995, the independent survival of USAID and intense budgetary pressures, it became obvious that the early Clinton years would have been a more propitious time to reform the process. Delay was fatal.


# The Dramatic Growth of Congressional Involvement

For all their prominence, foreign aid issues tell only part of the story. The increase in congressional involvement in international activities can be further illustrated by two additional cases. The first was widely seen as an embarrassing debacle for all involved in both branches, and the second was a quiet example of the positive results that are sometimes possible.


## The Red Scare and the Moscow Chancery

The decade-long attempt to come to terms with how to construct a new chancery in Moscow, once it was discovered that the building under construction was seriously compromised by Soviet bugging, illustrates several points: congressional suspicion of the State Department; legitimate and fanciful concerns with security vis-à-vis what was then seen as a genuine threat from the Soviet Union; and attempts by some individual members of Congress to find political advantage.

It is striking that money was never the defining component of the Moscow issue (though not totally absent), despite persistent financial problems from 1986, when construction was stopped on the bugged building and the

---

much as 50 percent. . . . A.I.D.'s leaner management and more focused approach deserve reward, not punishment. Administration budget slashers ought to take a second look."

27. Details in this and the preceding paragraph come from a discussion with a senior USAID legislative official, February 8, 1995.

Soviet contractors were banished from the new embassy compound, until 1992 when Congress (after several false starts) finally provided a means for getting on with construction of a replacement. Rather, the debate focused (1) on the desirability of alternative approaches to the construction of a secure new chancery, owing to different assessments of the threat of penetration through electronic means; (2) on making the Soviets pay for the damage; and (3) on preventing them from gaining any advantage, most especially by not allowing them to move into *their* new chancery in Washington. Domestic political considerations played a significant role, for Congress wanted to ensure that any political price associated with this "fiasco" would be paid by the State Department, rather than by members of Congress who might have approved one or another course of action during the long dispute. There were also attempts by executive branch agencies, notably State and the CIA, to scapegoat each other, both with respect to the compromised building and with respect to the site provided in Washington for the new Soviet chancery. Each attempted with some success to enlist its congressional authorizing and appropriating committees in these efforts. Neal Smith of House Appropriations and Claiborne Pell of the SFRC, for example, were steadfast in arguing that the threat was overdramatized, and that less secure (and less expensive) options would do. Senator Fritz Hollings— under constant pressure from the intelligence community, to which he was intimately connected by staffers serving him in his Intelligence Committee capacity—and Olympia Snowe were the hard-liners for maximum (and expensive) solutions and, incidentally, for blaming State for all that had gone wrong.[28] A way out was found only with the dissolution of the Soviet Union and the resulting assessment that there was nothing to be gained politically by continuing the highly public contretemps over what all saw as an embarrassment to the United States, to State, to the CIA, and (of no small importance) to the Congress. Almost miraculously, in the FY 1993 appropriations bill, funding was provided to complete a new chancery, agreement was gained on allowing the Russians to use the new Washington embassy they

28. From the extensive press coverage of this episode, see the following CQ *Weekly Report* articles: "A Hill–State Department Impasse," 45 (December 26, 1987): 3199; Elizabeth A. Palmer, "House Passes Embassy Decision into Hands of White House," 49 (May 18, 1991): 1302–3; Elizabeth A. Palmer, "An Olympian Effort," 49 (May 18, 1991): 1303; Joan Biskupic, "Spending Bill Includes Money for New Moscow Embassy, 49 (July 13, 1991): 1903; Carroll J. Doherty, "Senate Juggles Arms Issue in State Department Bill: Measure Seeks to Limit Weapons but Help Producers, Sidesteps Moscow Embassy Controversy," 49 (August 3, 1991): 2185–86; and John R. Cranford and Pamela Fessler, "Trading Up," 50 (June 20, 1992): 1818.

had inherited, and U.S. claims were vitiated in return for favorable property agreements and terms of construction in Moscow.[29]

But nothing had ever been easy regarding the Moscow chancery. Hardly had this positive end to the congressional struggle been achieved when executive branch disagreements over what construction option to pursue, always a factor in congressional considerations, resurfaced. Moscow city officials, seeing hard-currency possibilities, pushed for using the funding to purchase and rehabilitate two apartment buildings adjacent to the compound, in light of new circumstances—the reduced threat since the demise of the Soviet Union—that they argued would permit the United States simply to finish work on the existing, bugged building. State headquarters pushed for either constructing a smaller but secure building on the compound or taking off the top of the bugged building and replacing it with a smaller amount of secure space. Those at post, driven largely by "creature comfort" considerations (nobody likes a massive construction project literally in one's front yard, especially in a difficult environment), argued for refurbishing the original office building, located some distance from the compound where the housing was located, for secure use. The post thus ignored the security inadequacies of that building, which had prompted the plans for a replacement office building in the first place!

So it was that the new Clinton administration carried out yet another review, concluding in 1994 that removing the top floors of the existing building, putting secure floors in their place, and finishing the lower floors for unclassified use made the most sense. Either constructing a new totally secure building, while retaining the existing one for unclassified use, or dismantling and rebuilding the bugged office building would have cost too much, and would have required a return to Congress for additional funding. This choice was no doubt aided by warnings from the exasperated appropriations subcommittee chairmen Neal Smith and Fritz Hollings: if State did not proceed quickly, it ran the risk, in a tight budget situation, of a rescission taking away the funds appropriated for the project. With this clarifying focus, State decided after congressional consultations to proceed with what

29. The language in the Appropriations Act (P.L. 102-395, October 6, 1992) was deceptively simple, given the long controversy: "ACQUISITION AND MAINTENANCE AND BUILDINGS ABROAD. For necessary expenses for carrying out the Foreign Service Buildings Act of 1926 . . . and the Omnibus Diplomatic Security and Antiterrorism Act of 1986 . . . $570,500,000, of which not to exceed $140,000,000 is available for construction of chancery facilities in Moscow, Russian Federation, to remain available until expended as authorized by 22 U.S.C. 2696(c)."

(after a temporary renaming as "Hard Hat") had come to be called "Top Hat"—taking off the top floors, replacing them with secure space, and finishing the lower floors for unclassified use. The department authorized the contractor to begin design work in late 1994. Although there were the inevitable complications, work proceeded on schedule, with the construction contract being let on May 2, 1996, and work beginning soon thereafter.[30] With luck, the chancery would be completed in 1999, twenty years after work began![31] Congress, for its part, seemed by this time willing to accept *anything,* so long as it did not have to embarrass itself by taking up the issue once again.

## Innovation in Refugee Programs

Another, more positive example, occurring at about the same time and even in part in the same venues, shows that major new problems can be dealt with effectively if Congress and the executive work together and if the latter will try something unusual. This case has to do with new procedures developed in 1989 and 1990 for processing refugees seeking to leave the Soviet Union (primarily but not exclusively Russian Jews).[32]

Between 1986 and 1989, emigration from the Soviet Union increased from 4,000 to all destinations to more than 60,000 annually to the United States alone, with another anticipated jump on the horizon.[33] Not surprisingly, by early 1990 U.S. mechanisms for handling these refugees were outstripped by the phenomenal exodus. The process was complicated and extremely expensive. To begin with, the Soviets did not allow immigration directly to the United States, so even those wishing to go there had to apply for a visa to Israel. An added complexity was that because there were no Israel–USSR diplomatic relations, there were no direct flights to Israel and

30. Details for the two preceding paragraphs are from discussions with the State Department legislative affairs officer (1993–97) and with State's official responsible for the design and construction of the Moscow building (January 25, 1995, and May 7, 1996).
31. See "Construction of Embassy in Moscow to Resume," *Washington Times*, November 1, 1995. See also Lee Hockstader, " 'Top Hat' to Cap Off Moscow Embassy Saga: $240 Million Rescue Operation Expected to Start This Fall," *Washington Post*, February 22, 1996.
32. This case study is derived from William I. Bacchus, "U.S. Refugee and Diplomatic Programs in a Rapidly Evolving Foreign Policy Climate: Measuring Program Success," a paper prepared for the annual meeting of the American Political Science Association, San Francisco, September 1990.
33. Princeton Lyman, "Testimony as Director, Department of State Bureau of Refugee Programs Before the Commission on the Conference for Security and Cooperation In Europe," typescript, Washington, D.C., March 7, 1990.

emigrants had to use either Vienna or Rome as intermediate transit points. Thus all applied for Israel and, if allowed to leave, then proceeded to Rome or Vienna, where they might have to stay for months while applying for entry to the United States or some other destination. In the meantime, emigrants were supported by private relief organizations, through expensive contracts paid for by the United States under agreements with the Austrian and Italian governments. Nevertheless, under this cumbersome approach some 47,000 Soviet refugees came to the United States in FY 1989, and 46,000 arrived during the first six months of FY 1990.[34] There were increasing delays, not only because of larger numbers but because of a 1988 change in Immigration and Naturalization Service (INS) policy. In response to legitimate questions about whether all Soviet Jews should automatically be eligible for refugee status, the INS decided to return to case-by-case adjudication rather than grant virtually automatic entry. Interviews in Rome and Vienna were carried out to determine whether the individuals had been subject to persecution or had a well-founded fear of it.[35]

Thus, by late 1988 it was clear to Bush administration transition officials as well as to career officers charged with refugee affairs that alternatives for managing the flow of refugees from the Soviet Union had to be found in order to respond to many more potential refugees, more time-consuming processing requirements, and growing political demands to go back to admitting qualified Soviet refugees automatically. Understandably, Secretary Shultz felt that the Reagan team should not make radical changes as they left office, and he passed the problem along to the new secretary, James A. Baker III.[36]

Transition papers reflected major divisions on the issue of automatic entrance by categories. In early 1989, a senior member of the policy planning staff (S/P) was asked to prepare a summary package on the contentious issues involved. Working with Ivan Selin, the new under secretary for management who also was responsible for refugee matters, she developed a radical approach. In April, the study they prepared argued for closing down the Rome-Vienna processing facilities and shifting the base to Moscow, with as

34. Ibid., supplemented by information from the Bureau of Refugee Programs, 1990.

35. These are the standards that by law must be applied in determining eligibility for refugee status. See the Immigration and Naturalization Act, 8 USC 1101(a)(42), for this definition. For an effort to refine the categories of eligible individuals, see sec. 599(D) of the Foreign Operations Appropriations Act, FY 1990, P.L. 101-167, November 21, 1989.

36. Information on the decisionmaking process leading to establishing the new procedures comes from interviews with several participants and close observers during the spring and summer of 1990.

much of the work as possible being done elsewhere (or, in the jargon developed, "offshore"). After initial thoughts about doing this "offshore" processing in Helsinki or Bonn, Selin decided that it should be in Washington. Of great importance was an early decision that, given the extraordinary efforts that would be required, management feasibility would drive policy, rather than, as is so often the case in State, the other way around. At first there was opposition within the executive branch and a certain amount of derisive commentary from Congress. Soon, however, virtually everyone who counted was lined up in support for one simple reason: there was no viable alternative. Rome-Vienna could not continue.

By September 1989, the decision was made to move as quickly as possible to the new process, on the grounds that it would be cleaner and easier to administer a speedy transition than a more protracted one. Almost the only objections came from the private relief organizations working with the refugees in Rome and Vienna. Those organizations stood to lose their contracts because, under the new system, refugees would remain in Moscow until interviewed and adjudicated, and would then leave directly for their new homes.

This process was all made possible by the work of what came to be called the Washington Processing Center (WPC), the "offshore" facility administered jointly by State and INS. The key was that WPC scheduled all interviews and maintained most records, drastically cutting down the work load in Moscow. Eventually it became possible to transmit needed records electronically rather than by diplomatic pouch, eliminating one cumbersome element of the offshore approach.[37] Because a category approach was being used, and was eventually accepted by Congress, only those applications which were in eligible categories had to be processed. Later on, a way was found to enter index information on all applicants in a computer database, largely so that cases of special interest to Congress could be quickly tracked and their status reported.[38]

Of equal importance to the WPC concept was the active help of Congress in funding both the new operation and the expanded number of refugees.[39] All in all, the new process worked very well. By early 1993, WPC was being

---

37. Interview with a refugee programs official, April 9, 1993.

38. Subsequent interviews in November 1993 confirmed that this tracking system was in place and operating effectively.

39. An extra $75 million for refugee programs was made available through the Dire Emergency Supplemental Appropriations Act for FY 1990, H.R. 4404 (P.L. 101-302, May 25, 1990).

evaluated to determine whether it was still needed, once the backlog had been cleared, expected at that time to occur within eighteen months.[40] Ultimately, WPC was kept, in fair measure because of a new development: the 1994 extension of legislation to facilitate exodus from the former Soviet Union, a measure that added new cases at roughly the same rate the older cases were being resolved. As of 1996, the WPC was expected to operate indefinitely and was continuing to function well.[41]

So, sometimes, when the logic is right and the need is apparent, change is possible, even when some are opposed because it reduces or eliminates their role.

Notwithstanding recent successes such as the Washington Processing Center, neither the Congress nor the executive has showed any general adeptness or inclination for developing a coherent approach to funding foreign affairs, guided by an overview of total needs and by the relationships of the various components. This is not new. Current congressional-executive relations with respect to the financing of our foreign activities are more a continuation of the past than a new departure.

40. Refugee programs official cited above, April 9, 1993.
41. Telephone interviews with an official in State's Bureau of Population, Refugee, and Migration Affairs, February 3, 1995, and June 10, 1996.

# CHAPTER FOUR

# CONGRESSIONAL FOREIGN AFFAIRS FUNDING

## *Plus Ça Change . . .*

As we analyze the congressional role in managing America's international presence, it is useful to begin at the macro level, with the changes in the overall budget and funding processes that have occurred over the past quarter-century. The watershed was in 1974, with the passage of the Congressional Budget and Impoundment Control Act, which purported to provide Congress with the tools for unifying its approach to resource allocation, thus leveling the playing field with the executive which had enjoyed this ability, at least in theory, ever since the president began to submit an overall budget to Congress in 1921.

We begin with the changes made by the 1974 act, followed by the impact of several recent budget summits. Next, an overarching theme—the irrelevance of foreign affairs in overall budget politics—is introduced. Finally, a seemingly second-order but nevertheless important element—score-keeping—is presented, since it can distort decisions about how our limited resources for international affairs should be marshaled.

## The Congressional Budget Act of 1974 and Its Consequences

In Chapter 2 above, the three distinct but interrelated congressional processes involved in funding federal activities were introduced: budget, appropriations, and authorization. A brief reprise will set the stage for a discussion of how these processes have evolved since the 1970s and how they affect foreign affairs.

The *budget process* is the relative newcomer, having existed only since 1974. Its output, when it works, is a budget resolution to guide further congressional action. Budget allocations by major budget functions are transmitted to the full appropriations committees, which further subdivide resources by making allocations to the thirteen pairs of subcommittees.

With these allocations in hand, the *appropriations process* begins. A subcommittee need not use the full amount of its allocation, and it can shift funds from one budget function to another so long as the subcommittee has jurisdiction over the sending and receiving of accounts.

Along the way, the *authorization process* occurs in parallel with appropriations. We shall see that the existence or absence of authorization for specific activities adds an element of potential tension between authorizing and appropriations committees, the latter being tempted to act on their own if authorization legislation is delayed. The conflict between these committees has if anything been exacerbated by the new budget process, and changing rules add complexity and potential for more strife.

## The Budget Act

Any discussion of the role of Congress in the financial aspects of the conduct of foreign policy, these days, must give due attention to the Congressional Budget and Impoundment Control Act of 1974 and its successors (the Gramm-Rudman-Hollings Act of 1985, a modification thereto in 1987, the contentious Budget Enforcement Act of 1990 and, for some purposes, the Clinton budget of 1993 and the budget stalemate of 1995.)[1] The 1974 act

---

1. These key acts are as follows:

- Congressional Budget and Impoundment Control Act of 1974 (CBO), P.L. 93-344, July 12, 1974. Titles I–IX are referred to as the Congressional Budget Act.
- Gramm-Rudman-Hollings (GRH): Balanced Budget and Emergency Deficit Control Act of 1985, Title II of P.L. 99-177, December 12, 1985.
- Gramm-Rudman-Hollings II (GRH II): Balanced Budget and Emergency Deficit Control Reaffirmation Act of 1987, Title I of P.L. 100-119, September 29, 1987.
- Budget Enforcement Act of 1990 (BEA), Title XIII of P.L. 101-508 (Omnibus Budget Reconciliation Act of 1990), November 5, 1990.
- Omnibus Budget Reconciliation Act of 1993, P.L. 103-66, August 10, 1993.

In 1995, there was no reconciliation or other budget act, illustrating the chaotic outcome that year.

See other sources cited (especially Schick, Keith, and Davis, *Manual on the Federal Budget*

is perhaps the prime example of the "law of unintended consequences" in recent governmental history. For structural and political reasons, this seems particularly true for Function 150. The act made funding for foreign affairs captive to the larger conflicts between the president and Congress, especially conflicts over funding domestic programs and defense.

Analyzing the Congressional Budget Act has become a popular sport, and it is impossible to review the extensive literature here.[2] I should, however, make several points relevant to this study. First of all, the budget process and the two budget committees established by this act have been hamstrung throughout their existence by the well-founded suspicions of preexisting authorizing and appropriating committees, although it is not much of an overstatement to say that there was no significant effect until 1981. Also, while the first budget resolution did not set targets for each function,[3] and therefore in theory limited the discretion of the appropriations committees, in practice there was little penalty for exceeding the set limits; they were little more than goals. Moreover, after the appropriations bills had been consid-

*Process*, and Schick, *The Federal Budget*) for fuller discussions, especially of how the overall budget process was affected by each of these acts. A particularly useful summary can be found in James A. Thurber, "If the Game Is Too Hard, Change the Rules: Congressional Budget Reform in the 1990s," chap. 8 in Thurber and Davidson, eds., *Remaking Congress*, pp. 130–44.

2. For those interested, however, the following are recommended: Wildavsky, *The New Politics of the Budgetary Process*; White and Wildavsky, *The Deficit and the Public Interest*; Ellwood, "Budget Authority vs. Outlays as Measures of Budget Policy"; Schick, *The Federal Budget*; Schick, Keith, and Davis, *Manual on the Federal Budget Process*; and Irene S. Rubin, *The Politics of Public Budgeting: Getting and Spending, Borrowing and Balancing*, 2d ed. (Chatham, N.J.: Chatham House, 1993). Perhaps the most succinct and coherent, though unfortunately not widely available, is Allen Schick, *Five Reforms in Search of Budget Control: Congress Versus the Federal Budget*, a CRS Report for Congress (Washington, D.C.: Congressional Research Service, January 1992). Other works that deserve attention are Rudolph G. Penner and Alan J. Abramson, *Broken Purse Strings: Congressional Budgeting, 1974–1989* (Ann Arbor and Washington, D.C.: Gerald R. Ford Foundation and the Urban Institute, 1988); Donald F. Kettl, "Myths, Trends, and Traditions in the Budgetary Process," a paper prepared for presentation at the annual meeting of the American Political Science Association, Washington, D.C., August 31–September 4, 1988; and Donald F. Kettl, *Sharing Power: Public Governance and Private Markets* (Washington, D.C.: Brookings Institution, 1993). For the early period after the passage of the 1974 Congressional Budget Act, see Rudolph G. Penner, ed., *The Congressional Budget Process After Five Years* (Washington, D.C.: American Enterprise Institute, 1981); and W. Thomas Wander, F. Ted Herbert, and Gary W. Copeland, eds., *Congressional Budgeting: Politics, Process, and Power* (Baltimore: Johns Hopkins University Press, 1984).

3. The 1974 act originally called for two budget resolutions each year, although at first there were in fact one, two, or three, depending on the year. Since 1983, no more than one has ever been completed in a given year.

ered, reconciliation could correct whatever differences existed and provide additional resources whenever the political exigencies of the moment required them.

In 1981, of course, the Reagan administration effectively turned this process to its own purposes, putting a totally different "spin" on reconciliation. Following a "reconciliation first" strategy, the Reagan team, led by the OMB director and former member of Congress David Stockman, forced an early reconciliation vote, trying to lock in programmatic cuts in an "all or nothing" vote that precluded powerful appropriations subcommittee chairmen from protecting their favorite programs later on.

The purpose was to demonstrate significant cuts in expenditures, making it possible to justify the major tax reductions that the administration, following its supply-side economic predilections, would later propose and guide to enactment. Interestingly, some initial Stockman allies, notably Chairman Pete Domenici of the Senate Budget Committee, agreed to go along for the opposite reasons. Having been seized with the size of the deficit, they thought the reconciliation debate would prove that a tax cut was both ill-advised and politically indefensible.[4]

Even during 1981 this innovation was undercut by still other parliamentary maneuvers. The new budget process still had little fundamental impact on how the power of the purse influenced government operations, at least in international affairs.

## Gramm-Rudman-Hollings and Its Origins

The budget process changed substantially in 1985, with the Balanced Budget and Emergency Deficit Control Act of 1985 (Gramm-Rudman-Hollings, P.L. 99–177), enacted in response to the failure to meet Congressional Budget Act deadlines, annual deficits exceeding $200 billion and, arguably, a total lack of executive or legislative branch discipline.

GRH made the 1974 budget process "real" for the first time because it tied the results of the budget resolution, the actions of the appropriations committees, and reconciliation to *specific targets for deficit reduction.* Ultimately it did not work, for it focused on estimated rather than actual deficits and utterly failed to meet deficit targets during the five years it was in effect. It succeeded, however, in directing renewed attention to the budget process.

4. See David Stockman, *Triumph of Politics* (New York: Harper/Avon, 1987), pp. 173–84, for this episode.

Its failings were noted only after the fact, while its sanctions were real until 1990 and, in fact, forced a reversal of the process.

Under GRH, if estimated spending would result in a failure to meet the deficit reduction targets established by legislation, then each affected account (largely but not exclusively the discretionary spending accounts) would have to be reduced, or "sequestered," by a percentage sufficient to bring estimates back in line with the deficit reduction targets.[5] A limited sequester actually occurred for a time in 1987, before the budget summit agreement discussed in the next section was put in place. It was quickly learned that GRH made it virtually impossible to maintain a rational funding process. Changes in the economic climate and in critical economic forecasts could cause significant increases in the size of the projected deficit, triggering funding aberrations through sequesters.

Because of this critical logical inconsistency, the "constant deficit reduction targets through variable spending level approach" was turned topsy-turvy in 1990, when the BEA reversed the process and set *expenditure* limits rather than deficit limits. Although this approach made budget planning much easier to manage, the deficit could not be controlled solely by spending ceilings. Then, after including "revenue enhancements," President Bush set off his 1992 campaign difficulties with "Read my lips: no new taxes," and all concerned accepted at least implicitly that the deficit would not be reduced as quickly as originally required in GRH.

The operational impact of GRH was that the limits for the various major categories ("superfunctions") established by the spring budget resolution, and then "crosswalked," as provided for in section 302(b) of the Congressional Budget Act, to the appropriations subcommittees, had to be taken seriously. For the first time the thirteen subcommittees in each house had to adhere to set limits. Parenthetically, this gives great power to the CBO and budget committee staffs, who largely determine which "crosswalks" go where.

A second feature of GRH was also important. Since GRH required that specific deficit targets be met for each of the following five years, the operational question became how much was actually expended as opposed to how much was appropriated. Thus "outlays" became more important, for GRH purposes, than budget authority, the traditional budget measure.

---

5. Sequestration is a procedure, under GRH and subsequent legislation, by which expenditures are reduced—owing to estimates of lower economic growth, lower than estimated revenues, or greater than allowed expenditures—to meet legislated targets.

Almost immediately, it became obvious that GRH targets could not be met without draconian spending reductions which Congress and the executive, whatever the rhetoric, were unwilling to endure. It was this growing realization, together with a lack of confidence in the economy (as demonstrated by the October 1987 stock market crash), that set the stage for the first in a series of budget summits. Mechanical, statutory devices were sought to control the deficit without having to suffer more pain than the traffic could bear. The search for such mechanisms was, in a way, the failure of politics.

## Budget Summits: Short-Term Relief, Longer-Term Problems

### Black Monday and the 1987 Summit

In retrospect, the budget summit of October and November 1987 proved to have been a political and budgeting watershed, although its immediate impact on the budget deficit was slight. The forces and approaches it set in motion continue to define the overall process. First, when the president and Congress approached the brink of sequestration as required by GRH and in fact as actually ordered by the president,[6] they backed away, in part because of uncertainty and uneasiness resulting from the stock market's fall on Black Monday. The summit agreement, since it covered FY 1989 as well as FY 1988, deferred larger issues of economic policy until the next administration and Congress. Second, and important for this study, the summit underscored the likelihood that, as an unintended consequence of the changes in budgeting over the past twenty years, international affairs will be handled like the rest of the budget, probably with lower outcomes. Finally, it appeared at the time, although it became less clear later, that the way the summit agreement was constructed might add impetus to the eventual formulation of an integrated foreign affairs (Function 150) budget in both the executive and the Congress.

Without repeating the ins and outs of the summit, in essence it was a

---

6. Providing an example of the reason for fearing GRH sequesters, the fall 1987 budget agreement restored about $17.6 billion over sequester levels for FY 1988. See Lawrence J. Haas, "Assessing the Budget Ballet," *Government Executive* 20 (February 1988): 16–18.

complicated trade-off of budget cuts and revenue increases, a way to avoid the even worse impact of sequestration. The summit was born of politicians' fears of a loss of faith in the government's ability to deal with the nation's economic problems: cooperative action was required to end the several-years-long impasse between the president and Congress.

After nearly a month of meetings between senior administration officials and appropriations, budget, and tax committee chairmen as well as with ranking members and some members of the leadership, including a great amount of contention and kibitzing, an agreement in principle was reached on November 20, 1987. Then the problem was to convince the whole Congress (and incidentally parts of the executive) to accept the deal and to incorporate it in implementing legislation. A CR, or continuing resolution (P.L. 100-202), provided funding for the entire government for FY 1988 and together with the Budget Reconciliation Act of 1987 (P.L. 100-203), cut the anticipated deficit by $33.4 billion in FY 1988 and $42.7 billion in FY 1989, accomplished by reducing spending in the CR and increasing revenues in the reconciliation act. An additional element of the agreement was that the president's budget for FY 1989 would be submitted with requested funding that would show no more than a 2 percent growth over 1988 amounts, and the FY 1989 budget resolution would make this same amount available. This is what in fact occurred, albeit with a fair amount of trouble along the way.

Unlike its GRH parent, this summit agreement explicitly carried international affairs as a separate component, along with defense and domestic discretionary spending, a pattern to be followed in the 1990 BEA. In the end, most observers believed this approach to be beneficial, although it created some risks. Under the final agreement, Function 150 accounts were allocated some $800 million more ($60 million for State operations, $150 million for international organization contributions, and $590 million for foreign assistance) than had been allocated earlier in the year in the initial budget resolution. Presumably, congressional leaders gradually came to the opinion that the earlier cuts in 150 had been excessive, a change in thinking for which Secretary of State Shultz and Deputy Secretary John Whitehead took and generally deserved substantial credit.[7]

Nevertheless, an apparent increase of funding for foreign affairs at the same time that there were significant cuts in domestic programs presented a

7. Whitehead to Shultz, "after action" memorandum on lessons from the process, December 29, 1987 (in my files).

delicate political problem, most especially for Fritz Hollings and Warren Rudman, the chairman and the ranking member of the Senate CJS Appropriations Subcommittee, co-authors of GRH and, more to the point here, the appropriators for Commerce and Justice, departments that were taking cuts.[8] Rudman in particular threatened to work against the agreement on the floor; in State's estimation, public opposition from Hollings would have killed it. Luck and prior work paid off. The "Gramm-Rudman-Hollings baseline" from which the summit negotiators were working was actually higher for Function 150 than the agreed presummit amount by some $600 million, owing to its having been keyed to the higher 1987 actual-funding levels; not those in the earlier FY 1988 budget resolution. The ambiguities caused confusion even for those closely involved. One difference in explanations to Congress by State versus OMB led congressional participants to suspect trickery. The explanation was that the former was talking in terms of budget authority, while the latter had been discussing outlays.[9] In any event, all this meant that the deal could be sold as a cut, rather than as the increase it in fact was over what would have been available to Function 150 without the summit. As one participant noted, "Throughout the negotiations, attempts have been made to keep these 'optics' so that 150 will not be shown as increasing while domestic discretionary spending is decreasing."[10]

## Congress to Shultz: "Tell Your Boss to Raise Taxes!"

Beginning in the summer of 1987, in the period leading up to the first budget summit, Secretary of State Shultz endorsed a major effort undertaken at State, under the direction of Deputy Secretary Whitehead, to try to find ways to reduce expenses. Closing posts abroad, freezing hiring, longer tours of duty overseas to reduce travel and relocation costs, deferral of any expenditures possible, and even reductions in force (RIFs) were all considered. The effect on morale was noticeable, and complaints from within State soon reached Congress. Throughout the annual cycle of hearings before the budget, appropriations, and authorizing committees, Shultz was repeatedly

8. Reports of Hollings's and Rudman's concerns were passed from Senate Budget Committee staff to their State counterparts. The Budget Committee was supporting the summit, of course, while Hollings and Rudman had stood aloof from the process, in part because members of the Appropriations Committee were largely excluded from it. Internal D/P&R memorandums, November 12, November 19, and December 9, 1987 (in my files).

9. Letter from Howard Baker to Shultz, November 16, 1987 (in my files).

10. Memorandum from Robert Bauerlein (D/P&R) to Shultz, November 12, 1987 (in my files).

asked whether conditions were in fact so dire that the proposed steps were really warranted. In each case, he responded that they were, and members saw him as blaming Congress. This perception raised the level of heat, of course. At one point, before the budget summit changed everything, Dan Mica, chair of the HFAC subcommittee that dealt with the department, said: "Pell [Sen. Claiborne Pell, chairman of the SFRC] and I are going to have to ride white horses and help save the State Department from its own ineptness in dealing with Congress."[11] In the end, their grudging help proved to be unnecessary.

Congress, faced with lower than desired budget limits for favored domestic programs and with real constraints on defense, had little sympathy for the "orphan" international programs with their minuscule constituencies. The larger context, of course, was that the same constraints faced in international funding were felt throughout the government. These pressures finally loosened the screws at the budget summit, at the cost of impairing deficit reductions.

Eventually, members seized familiar answers to the funding crunch: a tax increase, of course, anathema to the president and his closest advisors. Time and time again, Shultz, Whitehead, and Under Secretary for Management Ronald Spiers found their pleas for funding dismissed with a derisive "Tell your boss to raise taxes!"[12] While privately they might have agreed with this solution, they were in no position to say so. This battle continued intermittently until the fall 1990 BEA and, in altered form, through the 1992 presidential election and into the Clinton administration. But for FY 1988, the crisis was averted.

Since Function 150 benefited unexpectedly from additional funding via the budget summit, Shultz's doomsday predictions were never put to the test. Although it was asserted that the reform and cost-cutting efforts would continue, there was great disbelief. In the end, the skeptics were proved right: they would have to wait until the next crunch.[13]

11. John M. Goshko, "Democratic Chairmen Devise Plan to Avert Layoffs, Closings at State Dept.," *Washington Post*, November 5, 1987. This turn of events was just one more element in the complicated congressional scenario of late 1987, discussed below.
12. I was present at more than one such hearing, notably when Secretary Shultz appeared before the Senate Budget Committee early in 1988 and when Under Secretary for Management Spiers appeared before HFAC later that spring.
13. For a discussion of the end results, see Elaine Sciolino, "State Department Given a Budget Reprieve: Congress Forestalls Crisis for About a Year by Providing Funds to Prevent Cuts," *New York Times*, January 19, 1988. She was referring to the $60 million added to State Department operations funds at the summit.

## Later Budget Summits

The prime mover of the successful fall 1987 budget summit—that there would be a failure of confidence in the ability of the government to deal with the nation's problems if budget bickering continued too long—had by 1990 obviously been forgotten by a new administration (most particularly Budget Director Darman and White House Chief of Staff Sununu) and by a recast congressional leadership (Tom Foley as speaker, not Jim Wright; Richard Gephardt as majority leader, not Foley; Leon Panetta as budget chairman, not Bill Gray; George Mitchell as Senate majority leader, not Robert Byrd; Byrd as Senate appropriations chairman, not John Stennis; James Sasser as Senate budget chairman, not Lawton Chiles). Only the Republican House leader Robert Michel and the Senate minority leader Robert Dole held the same positions as they had in 1987.

Because it arguably became the biggest political drama of the decade—overshadowing even Iran-Contra and the Reagan revolution of 1981—the initially failed budget summit of 1990 and its fallout assumed greater importance than its predecessor. The summit presented the ultimate illustration of the confrontation of old and new ways of conducting the nation's business with respect to budgets: namely, the interplay of revenues and expenditures.

For the whole idea of a budget summit, with the final deal cut between the president and the congressional leadership of both parties, undercuts the normal role that the Appropriations, Ways and Means, and Finance committees traditionally play. This time, the pygmies revolted, sending down the plan crafted on high to the acute embarrassment of the president and the leadership. Perhaps the savviest participant was Bob Dole. Commenting in early September 1990, possibly with a sense of foreboding, he noted that "the bottom line around here is you've got to have the votes . . . so you've got to be fairly careful what goes into the package or it'll all blow up on the floor."[14]

The outlines of the story are well known: Republican insistence on cuts in domestic discretionary spending and entitlements and, above all, until

14. Quoted in *CQ Weekly Report* 48 (September 8, 1990): 2822. The decline of committees in favor of majorities under the 1974 Congressional Budget Act and especially under GRH is brilliantly detailed in John B. Gilmour, *Reconcilable Differences? Congress, the Budget Process, and the Deficit* (Berkeley and Los Angeles: University of California Press, 1990). Ironically, the failed summit and its aftermath shows perhaps that this is not always a one-way game: the committees can become the instrument of a backbench majority, against the leadership. This was not a case of the floor majorities taking power away from committees, as the Gilmour thesis posits; rather, the majority handed power back to the committees in a revolt against the leaders and the president. Power gravitates where it can be used; in Congress, this can well be the committees.

late in the game, on "no new taxes"; Democratic demands for reduced defense spending in the post–Cold War era and for fairness in generating revenue. As the enormity of the problem began to sink in, both sides began to move. The Democrats began to look at the heretofore sacrosanct notion of cutting entitlements, although they had quite different views from those of their Republican colleagues about what and how much to cut. And the president, much to the consternation of conservative Republicans, especially in the House, indicated that the famous "no new taxes" pledge had loopholes in it.[15] Throwing both taxes and entitlements into the mix was heavily responsible for bringing down the budget resolution that codified the first agreement, as members began to hear from outraged constituents whose Medicare premiums and taxes would go up.

Above all, there was the gigantic game of chicken, with each side trying to exploit the situation to the very end. Both lost. By the time either considered crying uncle, it was too late.

For context, it is worth listing the principal steps in this extraordinary sequence. Because the appropriations bills intended to codify the summit agreement were still uncompleted by the end of the fiscal year, the president reluctantly agreed to a short continuing resolution, providing funding and thus avoiding a 32.4 percent sequester, that was to last until midnight on Friday, October 5.[16] During this breathing period, furious efforts were un-

15. More specifically, in order to try to move the stalled negotiations, Bush issued a written statement on June 26, 1990. "It is clear to me," said Bush, "that both the size of the deficit problem and the need for a package that can be enacted require all of the following: entitlement and mandatory program reform; tax revenue increases; growth incentives; discretionary spending reductions; orderly reductions in defense expenditures; and budget process reform—to assure that any bipartisan agreement is enforceable and that the deficit problem is brought under responsible control. The bipartisan leadership agree with me on these points." See George Bush, "Statement on Federal Budget Negotiations," in *The Public Papers of the Presidents of the United States*, 1990, bk. 1 (Washington, D.C.: GPO, 1991), p. 868. Pamela Fessler, "Cover Story: Bush's Sudden Shift on Taxes Gets Budget Talks Moving," *CQ Weekly Report* 48 (June 30, 1990): 2029–32, deals with initial reactions and predictions of the difficulty of the coming negotiations, which of course were amply borne out. From the later perspective of the 1992 campaign, Bob Woodward's four-part series, "Making Choices: Bush's Economic Record," *Washington Post*, October 4–7, 1992, details the statement's impact and addresses Bush's primary-campaign renunciation of the 1990 deal as a mistake. Parts 1 and 3 of the series are especially relevant.

16. Press coverage of the ensuing events discussed in this paragraph was voluminous. The most comprehensive summary is contained in a series of articles in *CQ Weekly Report* 48 (September 29 and in particular October 6, 1990). A portent of what was to come can be seen in Susan F. Rasky's "Accord to Reduce Spending and Raise Taxes Is Reached; Many in Congress Critical," *New York Times*, October 1, 1990 (several related articles were also published by the *Times* that day). As noted, when the agreement was voted down by the House in the

dertaken first to revive the original deal (including a prime-time Bush TV address that, if anything, solidified opposition) and then to negotiate a different one. By the end of the week, when the first CR ran out, another short-term CR was vetoed by the president, shutting down the government over the weekend of October 6–8. Finally, a second legislative package emerged, this one bare bones, with the details to be worked out by the appropriate committees in each house. Once this legislation was passed, by the House on Sunday the 7th and the Senate on Monday the 8th, the president signed a second CR, this time extending the deadline until midnight on October 19. During the next two weeks, most of the focus was on the revenue side, with many taxation plans emerging and with appropriations subcommittees struggling to complete their work on expenditures, the macro levels of which had finally been set by the second budget resolution of October 8. By the time one version had been voted down by the rank and file in the House, and a second, not liked by anyone, had passed narrowly, it was October 26, with the elections only ten days away. Congress slipped out of town, fearing the reaction. Although few incumbents paid the electoral price, the victory margins of many were reduced.[17]

Foreign affairs was not a major issue. As will be seen in the next section, the only significant decision was to treat Function 150 as a separate item, as in the 1987 summit, and to "fence" or "cap" International Affairs expenditures for FY 1991–93. Domestic discretionary expenditures and defense spending were dealt with similarly.[18]

---

early hours of October 5 and the president vetoed the continuing resolution, resulting in a weekend shutdown of the government, there was a press explosion. See both the *New York Times* and the *Washington Post*, especially October 6–8, for details.

17. "In the Senate, 31 of 32 incumbents seeking re-election won. . . . In the House, the anti-incumbent sentiment was translated into marginal victories rather than outright defeats. Of the 407 House incumbents who sought re-election in 1990, 392 won—a 96 percent re-election rate. . . . Still, there was ample cause for concern: About 85 incumbents won with less than 60 percent of the vote, roughly double the number of 1988. Fifty-three House members were re-elected with their lowest winning percentage ever, while 57 won with their lowest vote share since they were first elected." *CQ Almanac* 46 (1990): 902. The advantages of incumbency, of course, are well known. Even during the Democratic debacle of the next congressional election, in 1994, 91.4 percent of all incumbents won (85.1 percent of Democratic incumbents and 100 percent of Republican incumbents). See data in *National Journal* 26 (November 12, 1994): 2852.

18. For a perceptive account of the budget summits from 1987 through 1990, from the quite different perspective of a relatively junior Democratic member (and political scientist), see David E. Price, *The Congressional Experience: A View from the Hill* (Boulder: Westview Press, 1992), esp. chap. 7, "Budget Politics." Price concludes that a big part of the problem is that "the easiest vote on the budget is almost always no" (p. 91), and he continues with a

# The Minimal Role of Foreign Affairs in Overall Budget Decisions

What is instructive is the minuscule role that Function 150 played in all of this. Within the Bush administration, there had all along been a small controversy between State and OMB over whether that function should be "fenced," as it had been previously, and thus treated as a separate category. OMB Director Darman argued that a fence (or "fire wall") would be counterproductive in the outyears (he was seeking a five-year agreement), since it would lock in International Affairs expenditures to a set funding ceiling. He thought expenditures should grow disproportionately, responding to new challenges and opportunities in the international environment. While agreeing with this assessment, the State Department was most concerned with the first year or so and feared that, without a "fence," cuts would be necessary in order to provide additional, unexpected but necessary funding for the Iraqi crisis and for Operation Desert Shield.[19] For if there were no fence, Function 150 would be lumped together with the domestic category as "Other," from which the necessary reductions in a zero-sum game would have to be made. Instead of seeking increases over the Senate Budget Committee's allocation, using a baseline that included the repeal of section 614 of the CJS Appropriations Act and the results of the Dire Emergency Supplemental,[20] State felt that the main effort would be to protect current levels. The department argued, and Darman eventually agreed, to seek the fence.[21] The failed summit agreement did in fact contain such a fence (now called a "cap") and the separate category was maintained, though at a lower level than State would have liked. The budget resolution that passed after the

---

thoughtful analysis of why this is so. To underscore a general point, nowhere in this chapter does Price make a specific reference to the impact of the budgetary debates on foreign affairs.

19. At this time, of course, October 1990, "Desert Shield" had not yet become "Desert Storm."

20. As will be seen in detail in Chapter 5 below, sec. 614 of the State Appropriations Bill held funding at a low, sequester level in the absence of an authorization bill, so its repeal would increase the current-year baseline (i.e., funding level) available. Similarly, it was hoped that State would receive additional funds in the Dire Emergency Supplemental. If both events happened, the baseline for subsequent budgets would be higher. However, if Function 150 were fenced, or capped, as State argued for and Darman was initially against, then taking advantage of this situation would not be possible. Protecting the bird in the hand won out, and Function 150 was fenced.

21. Details here come from State and OMB staffers privy to the discussions.

events described above maintained virtually the same level of expenditures as the summit agreement for FY 1991.

A second element is also illuminating. Darman argued, and this time State agreed, that Function 150 should be deferred until the outlines of the larger agreement were in place—on the assumption that, if raised earlier, International Affairs would become a target for poaching. Once again, the lack of a constituency for foreign affairs was seen as a given, not even debatable, by its supporters.

This low importance accorded foreign affairs in high budget politics should not have been surprising, for in a way it was a logical extension from past decades. At the beginning of the Reagan administration, it will be recalled, there was a major effort led by David Stockman to cut domestic spending dramatically in order to reduce the size of the government and to provide resources for repairing perceived weaknesses in defense spending. The first Reagan budget envisaged increases in the range of 10 percent real growth for defense, on top of the significant increase seen in the last Carter budget, while almost all of the rest of the discretionary accounts (including State, USAID, and USIA) were expected to take cuts or at best maintain their current levels.[22] In effect, the foreign affairs agencies were to be treated as "domestic" for budgetary purposes, notwithstanding their intimate relationship to national defense.

Although Secretary of State Alexander Haig used a variety of bureaucratic tactics to reverse the initial decisions and had some success, State and its sister agencies were objectively worse off than had been proposed under the Carter "lame duck" budget.[23] This change set off a concerted long-term campaign by upper-level State Department managers to have the department designated "a National Security agency," as a way of getting otherwise unobtainable budget increases. Ultimately, in late 1983, this campaign led to a halfhearted acquiescence by OMB Director Stockman and NSC Executive Secretary William P. Clark that "it has been agreed that the State Department will be exempt from future across-the-board personnel cuts required of domestic agencies and will be treated on a par with DOD and CIA in such matters."[24]

It was never clear, however, whether the president concurred with or even

22. See Stockman, *Triumph of Politics*, pp. 109–72, for the story of the first Reagan budget's preparation. As Stockman himself admits, it was extremely difficult to develop accurate figures for the increases/decreases proposed.

23. Ibid., pp. 126–31, 151–53, describes Stockman's early budget battles with Haig.

24. Memorandum from Clark to Secretary Shultz, August 29, 1983.

knew about this memorandum, or whether this step had any impact. Years afterward, those seeking greater funding for the department, such as the American Foreign Service Association, continued to press management to renew this campaign, obviously not realizing that the wheel had turned, that defense spending had become a target in the final years of the Reagan administration, and that a formal National Security designation could hurt foreign affairs funding. Mechanical solutions to political problems seldom work. In fact, as we shall see, once Gramm-Rudman-Hollings was enacted in 1985, State's problem was not the size of the administration's budget request but, rather, congressional decisions, given an overall budget ceiling, to allocate scarce resources in a different pattern than had been proposed by the president. Just when State convinced the White House that it needed more funding, Congress found higher priorities.

This history is troubling for foreign affairs advocates. Even when a powerful secretary of state presses his case directly with the president, there is no guarantee of success. Shortly after the budget summit of November 1987, Secretary Shultz pleaded with President Reagan for a larger than 2 percent increase for the State Department's operations. (Each of the three discrete categories in the agreement was separately limited to a 2 percent real growth.) Thus, what Shultz was asking was difficult, but could have been accomplished either by reducing other parts of Function 150 or by approaching Congress with a request to divert some additional funding from defense or domestic programs. Instead, the secretary was told that he had to accept his share of the pain.[25]

One modestly successful exception to this pattern—whereby executive branch advocates of additional funding for international affairs got short shrift at the White House—is interesting because of the tactics used by Secretary of State Warren Christopher and his allies, including USAID Administrator Brian Atwood. Christopher became convinced in late September 1993 that the contemplated FY 1995 budget being prepared by OMB would not provide enough resources to carry out the president's publicly stated foreign policy goals, announced to the U.N. General Assembly in a September 27, 1993, speech. An interagency team was put to work on what was named the "Big Pie" exercise, whose purpose was to demonstrate to the president with some specificity which of his new policy goals—foreign and domestic—could not be met unless funds were added to the budget request. The theme of the presentation was that modest investments in international

---

25. Several State Department sources confirm the details of this episode.

affairs would save billions in crisis response and defense funding that would be needed if the United States had to react to wars and other catastrophes. One had to look at the overall "big pie," and not consider international affairs in isolation. Initially, Christopher reportedly was seeking some $4 billion above an OMB mark of $19.6 billion (a cut of some 10 percent from FY 1994), but later reports cited a figure of something less than $3 billion.[26]

Besides personally engaging the president's prestige, an opportunity made possible in part because Clinton took part directly in the reclama process, rather than leaving it to his budget director as in the earlier rejections of State pleas just discussed,[27] Christopher and Atwood used a second ploy. To counter the indifference or outright opposition to foreign assistance, they attempted to show that there was a constituency for these programs, orchestrating a lobbying campaign by private-sector organizations and charitable groups that resulted in a letter to the president signed by almost two hundred organizations.[28]

The flavor of this effort was captured succinctly and brilliantly by the *National Journal,* in a short item on its "Inside Washington" page, under the caption "Wow, Catch Warren's End Run," which is worth quoting in its entirety:

> The State Department calls it the "big pie" plan. What it amounts to is a $4 billion interagency food fight. Facing a proposed budget cut of nearly 10 per cent, Secretary of State Warren M. Christopher has asked for a 8 per cent raise. He wants to reorder national security spending to free up more money to develop overseas markets and avert environmental and humanitarian crises. In a Nov. 24 memo to the President, he argued that Clinton's "legacy" as a forger of post–Cold War foreign policy is at stake. State is backed by Treasury, but

26. Details here come from discussions with participants, and from Thomas W. Lippman, "Christopher Lobbying for $3 Billion More in Foreign Aid," *Washington Post,* December 17, 1993.

27. Function 150 was not the only budget category with advocates in this process, of course. For a description of this important yet little understood aspect of budgeting, see Clay Chandler and Stephen Barr, "As Budget Specter Looms, Clinton Hears Wishes," *Washington Post,* December 17, 1993.

28. Steven A. Holmes, "State Department Seeking Funds of Other Agencies," *New York Times,* November 11, 1983. This article was to my knowledge the first public mention of the "Big Pie" effort; it is unclear whether the information in it was leaked by advocates of greater funding for Function 150, or by opponents!

opposed by Defense and the CIA. The Office of Management and Budget reserved comment.[29]

When the budget was submitted to Congress, on February 7, 1994, the general view among those involved was that Christopher had managed to obtain considerably more than $1 billion in additional budget authority, although the nature of the process makes it impossible to know definitively what OMB would have done without "Big Pie." Through some budget legerdemain that should be familiar by now, the size of the increase was disguised by making the FY 1994 appropriated amount appear higher than it actually was, by creatively adjusting how supplemental appropriations were counted. Nonetheless, given the tight circumstances, those who felt opportunities were being missed by a failure to fund international activities at the levels needed to support important U.S. initiatives took some heart at the outcome.[30]

In some respects the next budget, in late 1994, was a reprise of 1993. This episode provides some additional insights into executive branch budget politics. Once again, OMB's allocation for Function 150 was deemed to be too low by Secretary Christopher and Craig Johnstone, who headed the S/RPP office that developed the interagency submission. After a difficult battle, once again resolved personally by President Clinton, the secretary succeeded in adding several hundred million dollars in budget authority and some $150 million in outlays (actual, spendable current-year money). Close observers agreed that this represented a bigger success than the more visible "Big Pie" which, while producing more BA, included almost no new outlays.

There were several reasons for this outcome. Christopher was more knowledgeable the second time, both about International Affairs programs in the budget and about technical budget matters. The intensive process of internal seminars and hearings, which refined and helped justify the request and which increased Christopher's knowledge of the details, led to a submission some $1 billion higher than OMB's initial target figure.

According to some old OMB hands, Director Alice Rivlin and her staff then chose to ignore a traditional OMB maxim: Try to avoid going head to

29. *National Journal*, 25 (December 4, 1993): 2871.

30. Details come from discussions with participants. The final Function 150 request in the president's budget for FY 1995 was $20.881 billion, compared with an estimated amount of less than $20 billion without "Big Pie" (internal summary prepared by the Department of State's Office of Resources, Plans, and Policy, April 25, 1994).

head with the secretary of state (any secretary) because of his presence and stature. Admittedly, this had not worked well, as we have seen, for Secretary Shultz with President Reagan in 1987. Possibly with this history in mind, OMB declined State Department offers to try to "cut a deal" so that an agreed position could be presented to the president. OMB did not feel, given the major cuts necessary in the domestic area, that International Affairs should be exempted from the pain. This was a miscalculation, for in the seminal meeting, according to all consulted, Christopher overpowered Rivlin, successfully arguing that while International Affairs funds made up only 1 percent of the federal budget, the Clinton administration would long be remembered for its success or failure in foreign policy. Both the president and the vice-president were very high on Christopher's performance. When someone mentioned this, the president is reported to have said: "That's why he is secretary of state."[31]

At least *inside* the Clinton administration, the foreign affairs community had learned how to use an asset—an engaged and knowledgeable secretary of state—that had been virtually ignored earlier. Outside, during the budget crisis of 1995 when deficit reduction was the primary goal, it was another story. Still, international funding declines then could hardly be blamed on a lack of attention by the secretary of state.

More evidence of a renewed determination to reverse the decline in funding for foreign affairs became evident in late 1996 and early 1997, through an orchestrated campaign to force public (not to mention presidential and congressional) attention to the dangerous consequences of a reduced U.S. diplomatic and programmatic capability. Warren Christopher (in his departure statements), Madeleine Albright (in her confirmation hearings and first public statements as secretary of state), Senator Richard Lugar (a well-respected senior Republican member of the SFRC), and an independent task force of former officials and other luminaries all weighed in, raising the alarm.[32] The initial result was a FY 1998 budget submission to Congress

31. This and the preceding paragraph are based on interviews between February and May 1995 with OMB, State, USAID, and USIA officials who participated in the reclama process, including several who were present at the final meeting.

32. See Warren Christopher, "Investing in US Leadership: Budget Cuts are Threatening America's Ability to Make a Difference in the World," opinion, *Christian Science Monitor*, January 21, 1997. Madeleine Albright's views were expressed, in her confirmation hearing statement quoted previously (Chapter 1, note 5), where she also mentioned Senator Lugar's strong opinions; and in her first press conference as secretary. In the latter, after describing her goals in that position, she said,

Fundamental to all of this is our ability to work with Congress to obtain the resources required to protect our interest and advance our leadership. As you know, funding for

that was more than $1 billion higher than the FY 1997 appropriations level, and about that much more than OMB's original proposed amount. Another billion, mostly for later years, was to be added to pay U.N. arrearages.[33] Whether the budget and appropriations committees, still in pursuit of a balanced budget by the year 2002, would go along seemed problematic.[34] But there was a general belief among internationalists in the executive branch that a corner was being turned, although the future would remain difficult.

# The Unreal World of Budget Scorekeeping

Of all the new features of the Congressional Budget Act of 1974, as amended by GRH I and II (the 1987 budget summit) and by the BEA of 1990, perhaps the most mystical, least understood, yet fundamentally important is "scorekeeping." With set limits on expenditures, a way must be found to determine how much can be spent in each account. This is a complicated business because the rate of expenditure can vary significantly from one account to another. For example, money provided for foreign buildings generally is spent at the rate of about 18 percent of the appropriated amount per year, since new buildings abroad take years to complete. In contrast, contributions to international organizations, essentially executed by sending

---

international affairs has declined sharply in recent years, despite the vast political changes that have increased the number of foreign countries and created both new threats to our security and new opportunities for building a more stable and democratic world. (Transcript, Bureau of Public Affairs, U.S. Department of State, Washington, D.C., January 24, 1997)

The Task Force on Resources for International Affairs was co-sponsored by the Brookings Institution and the Council on Foreign Relations, and its co-chairmen were former congressmen Mickey Edwards and Stephen J. Solarz. Its press release, "Blue Ribbon Panel Finds U.S. Foreign Policy Objectives Imperiled by Budget Cuts," was issued on January 13, 1997.

33. Thomas W. Lippman, "Clinton to Seek U.N. Dues Fund, Higher Foreign Affairs Budget, *Washington Post*, January 14, 1997; and Jonathan S. Landay, "Clinton May Boost Diplomatic Funds: But he faces Congress intent on Budget Cuts," *Christian Science Monitor*, January 16, 1997.

34. For the reaction of Representative Sonny Callahan, chairman of the House Foreign Operations appropriations subcommittee, see Ben Barber, "House Republican Calls Chances Slim for More Foreign Aid," *Washington Times*, January 15, 1997. A more positive prognosis is Tyler Marshall, "Latest U.S. Bout of Isolationism May Be Ending," *Los Angeles Times*, January 13, 1977.

a check, may "outlay" at close to 100 percent. Thus, if funds are shifted from the first account to the second, even though the budget authority may remain the same, the outlays (i.e., the rate of spending) may differ significantly, and one runs the risk of exceeding the allowable cap for some accounts and thus triggering a sequester. Another problem can occur when funds appropriated for one purpose are later designated for another use; this may lead to a scoring of the expenditure de novo, even though no outlay took place originally. Thus, "double-scoring" is possible when scorekeeping "case law" is developed issue by issue by CBO and OMB staffers.[35]

Three examples of scoring conventions and determinations will help show the range of possibilities as well as the otherworldly quality of the process: (1) a rather routine new international agreement, which is a pure case of double-scoring; (2) a recent case of a "mistake" in appropriations, which led to exceeding the cap allowed under the BEA for international affairs and thus to a sequester; and (3) one creative attempt, of which many examples could be cited, to circumvent the rules. Whether such a system can or should long survive must be an open question.

## The International Rubber Agreement, 1988

In a cursory and noncontroversial debate, the U.S. Senate on September 7, 1988, ratified the International Natural Rubber Agreement of 1987 (INRA II), 97–0. However, the seeming ease of this action belied the difficulties that State, OMB, and the Senate Budget Committee encountered in reconciling the terms of the treaty with funding practices required by the new budget procedures, thus emphasizing how the latter affect the conduct of foreign policy, often in unintended ways.[36]

This agreement was a successor to the International Natural Rubber Agreement of 1979 (INRA I), which had expired in October 1987. The

35. For Budget Act junkies, it should be noted that double-scoring is a distinct issue from the more politicized question of "static" vs. "dynamic" scoring which arose after the 1994 congressional elections. The latter question refers to how to treat tax cuts for scoring purposes—only on their literal impact at the time or, alternatively, on the basis of growth they might be expected to generate. For a sample of this controversy, see the *Washington Post* editorial, "A Rubber Stamp CBO?" November 16, 1994. Since double-scoring as used here is on the expenditure side, it can occur just as readily regardless of whether static or dynamic treatments of revenue changes (e.g., tax cuts or increases) are employed.

36. Details for this section are drawn from statements by Senators Chiles and Pell, *Congressional Record* 134 (September 7, 1988): S11778–79 and S11790, and from discussions with State Department participants.

purpose of both treaties, as with similar commodity trade agreements, was to moderate price fluctuations by buying (in this case) rubber when prices were low and selling when prices rose. To fund U.S. participation, P.L. 96-271 (FY 1981) authorized and P.L. 96-536 appropriated $88 million which was to remain available until expended. By the time INRA I expired, some $53 million had been used in the purchase of "buffer stock." The remaining $35 million was subsequently returned to the Treasury.

Under the second treaty, the $53 million contribution (by mid-1988 estimated to be worth $59 million in potential receipts from sales and remaining buffer stock, owing to an increase in rubber prices) was to be transferred to the International Natural Rubber Organization (INRO), the slightly revised mechanism for administering the agreement. This outcome had been specifically contemplated by the first treaty and was a key element in what followed.

Since INRA I was a commodity agreement that worked in favor of the United States, there was virtually no opposition to U.S. participation in INRA II. Yet, for Budget Act reasons, it came close to foundering when State broached the new treaty with Congress. The initial reaction of OMB was that new enabling legislation, such as that passed for INRA I, would be required. OMB apparently sold this interpretation to CBO and the Senate Budget Committee. Since this would be a new authorization and appropriation, it would involve new budget authority in the amount of approximately $65 million, the full estimated U.S. commitment for INRA II. More important, given GRH conditions, the new legislation would also involve outlays of virtually the same amount (which, it will be remembered, count directly in the scorekeeping). This requirement would have been a major problem and might well have meant that U.S. participation, even if the treaty were ratified, would have to be deferred until there was "headroom" to accommodate that amount of outlay.

Frantic work by State's lawyers, who relied on the INRA I provision that initial contributions could be rolled over to a successor agreement, and who noted that the provision had been ratified by the Senate, led to an acceptable outcome. In a colloquy on the Senate floor at the time the treaty was ratified, Senator Lawton Chiles, of the Budget Committee, said that he saw "no problem" with transferring the buffer stock, and that the Budget Committee would "not score such a transfer against any implementing legislation." Chiles continued by arguing that, nonetheless, new legislation would still be needed, since without it there would be no authorization for the United States to meet its full commitment. Senator Claiborne Pell, speaking for

Foreign Relations, placed in the record a carefully crafted statement which had been prepared by State. The statement made the administration's point that the previous contributions "remain available without further legislation to meet the United States' INRA II obligations to the buffer stock account." Since rubber prices in the interim had increased so that payments were unnecessary, Pell was correct in terms of current conditions, and Chiles's information was wrong.

Thus a problem had been avoided. But this near miss involving a well-supported treaty was entirely a result of scorekeeping conventions, nowhere enacted into law, that had been developed by CBO and endorsed by a deficit-conscious OMB. This is the power of the purse raised to a constitutionally questionable impact on the president's (not to mention the Senate's) treaty power.

## Foreign Military Financing, FY 1991 (1990)

In the immediate aftermath of the bruising October 1990 budget battle, which resulted in the BEA with its ceilings on the three primary budget categories, there was a rush to complete work on the remaining appropriations bills. A combination of haste and exhaustion highlighted the scorekeeping and sequester provisions of the new law. During final staff drafting of the "Foreign Military Financing" (FMF) portion of the Foreign Operations Appropriation Bill (P.L. 101-513), the loan guarantee portion of about $403.5 million was inadvertently double-counted, appearing both as a separate item and as part of the total figure for the grants portion of the program.[37] As a result, the "Foreign Ops" bill brought the total outlay (expenditure) total for Function 150 to some $395 million above the allowed ceiling. This error was discovered at the time the bill was being enrolled, but the House parliamentarian ruled that it could not be corrected as a technical matter and that a statutory fix was therefore required. By then, however, Congress had adjourned.

The automatic result was an across-the-board 1.9 percent sequester (or reduction) in each discretionary account and subcategory (or "PPA")[38] throughout Function 150, thus reducing the overall 150 amount by about

37. Details here from discussions with executive branch and congressional participants in the FMF episode. See also Carroll J. Doherty, "Slip of the Pen Triggers Cut in Discretionary Programs," *CQ Weekly Report* 48 (November 17, 1990): 3888.

38. PPA (program, project, or activity) is an element in a budget account. Sequestration cuts must be taken equally from each of the PPAs, which are defined by appropriations acts and

$389 million. Ultimately, this amount was restored in the spring of 1991, but in the meantime there was financial uncertainty, not to mention a few permanent losses in cases where restored funding came too late to allow expenditures to catch up before the end of the fiscal year. Some at OMB argued that since this was so obviously a mistake, OMB could make first-quarter and, if necessary, second-quarter FY 1991 apportionments at the pre-sequester level, relying on the strong likelihood of a statutory correction before final apportionments were necessary. Richard Darman, however, re-fused to approve this approach, according to some because he did not want to be the first to appear to be finding a way around the painfully negotiated provisions of the BEA.[39] Once again, scorekeeping was a driving force in decisionmaking.

## Funding Unemployment Insurance Extensions, FY 1992 (1991)

A third example of the impact of scorekeeping was seen throughout the summer and fall of 1991, with respect to repeated efforts to extend unem-ployment insurance funding in the face of a troublesome economic situa-tion. President Bush had twice vetoed Democratic plans to accomplish this extension, on the grounds that the need did not exist and, in one case, be-cause he did not wish to invoke the "emergency" provision of the BEA,[40] which would have allowed domestic discretionary expenditures to rise above the level stipulated in that act, without sequester.

In late October, Senate Majority Leader Mitchell proposed that the presi-dent "put Americans first" by freezing the foreign assistance budget for FY 1992 at 1991 levels, and both the State Department and the foreign assis-tance budgets for later years at those same levels, in order to pay for the

accompanying documentation. See Schick, Keith, and Davis, *Manual on the Federal Budget Process*, p. 215, for a more technical definition; a similar treatment appears in Schick, *The Federal Budget*, p. 213.

39. OMB and executive branch sources. OMB normally apportions, or provides, appro-priated funds for obligations/expenditures in equal, quarterly amounts spread across the fiscal year. Even if there were no statutory correction, the argument went, the reduced apportion-ment necessary to fit totals under the sequester amounts could be taken in the third and fourth quarters.

40. Technically, sec. 251(b)(2)(D) of Gramm-Rudman-Hollings, as amended by sec. 13101 of the 1990 Budget Enforcement Act. See note 1 above for fuller citations of the relevant legislation.

unemployment benefits.[41] This proposal was both a result of frustration and a shrewd political effort to embarrass the president, already under attack for having no domestic agenda and for being overly interested in foreign affairs. Officials at State and OMB, recalling the recent demise of the foreign assistance authorization bill, which failed almost entirely because of the same feeling that domestic needs should be served first, were very concerned during the first two weeks of November that if the Mitchell proposal were to come to the floor it would pass overwhelmingly, devastating the State Department and USIA budgets.[42] For one thing, Mitchell had been circulating charts purporting to show massive International Affairs funding increases during the 1980s. State believed these charts to be extremely misleading because most of the growth had come from new activities mandated by Congress, such as enhanced diplomatic security, immigration law changes, and additional help to refugees. At any rate, Mitchell's data made those who were inclined to support State, such as Chairman Hollings of the CJS appropriators and his key staffer, very wary of a floor fight.[43]

Ultimately, minor adjustments in the tax structure were made in the compromise bill, and the Mitchell threat to Function 150 ended; but this episode suggests the difficulties that will confront international funding in tight times. The initial fear in the foreign affairs agencies was that this problem would arise in FY 1994, when the three separate caps under the BEA expired and there was to be only one overall cap for government-wide domestic spending. In the end, the Clinton budget for FY 1994 and the budget resolution adopted by Congress in March 1993 were tight for all, but they did not disproportionately cut Function 150. Nonetheless, foreign affairs funding, unless the climate improves, will be at risk to pay for domestic programs.

41. For two discussions of Mitchell's proposals, see his statements in *Congressional Record* 137: the first on November 1, 1991, pp. S15785–88; the second on November 7, 1991, pp. S16311–12, with the text of his amendment on p. S16322.
42. I rely here on discussions with relevant OMB and State officials at the time. See "Foreign Aid Bill Fails; Domestic Need Cited," *CQ Almanac* 47 (1991): 470–78, for a legislative summary of what happened with respect to the foreign assistance authorization bill in 1991; details of the fall 1991 House defeat of the conference report are at pp. 477–78. I recall being told of the following exchange by a Hill staff acquaintance who was on the floor during the debate and vote on the conference report: STAFFER (*to member with a long history of support for foreign aid*): "Joe, how come you're not going with us this time?" MEMBER: "Jim, I can't vote for foreign aid when seniors in my district are eating cat food."
43. Informal memorandum prepared by the Department of State's Management Legislative Affairs staff, November 13, 1991 (in my files).

Thus far, our attention has been focused primarily on budget procedures and politics that engage the entire Congress, and only secondarily on the activities of the authorizing and appropriating committees, where the issues and controversies are so often played out—sometimes in cooperation, but often in conflict. It is to these latter relationships that we now turn.

# CHAPTER FIVE

# AUTHORIZERS AND APPROPRIATORS

*High Priests, Cardinals, and the Rituals of Congress*

Those who routinely work in and with the Congress learn quickly that very different norms and mores guide the work of the authorizing and appropriating committees. The motivations and operating styles of each are distinct and often conflicting. Perhaps the main characteristic they share is that they regard the budget committees and the new congressional budget process as Johnny-come-latelies and interlopers interfering with the "real" work of Congress. In this chapter, the very different optics through which authorizers and appropriators see the world (and what that difference means for the conduct of foreign affairs) are vividly demonstrated by a series of interrelated foreign affairs authorization and appropriations bills considered between 1987 and 1991. Lesser attention will be given to some subsequent ones. In Chapter 8 I shall show how easily these differences survived a change in party control of Congress in 1995. Before turning to these cases, however, it will be useful to look at the committees themselves, beginning with the appropriators.

## Appropriators: The CJS Subcommittees as a Microcosm

The jurisdictions of the thirteen House and Senate appropriations subcommittees do not match the functions in which the president's budget is presented to the Congress or the budget resolution is considered (some twenty primary functions are used). Thus, a single pair of subcommittees will routinely have jurisdiction for parts of more than one function; and a single function, such as 150, may be divided among multiple subcommittees (four in this case). Appropriations subcommittees are therefore forced to consider trade-offs, unintended by any conscious decision in either the executive or the Congress, between completely unrelated functions and activities. In a time of zero-sum budgeting, which is quite different from the "You scratch my back and I'll scratch yours" approach by which funds have been provided since the beginning of the Republic, this necessity is especially true for the Commerce-Justice-State appropriators.

The work of these subcommittees is a microcosm of recent executive–congressional battles, because their deliberations and choices show the same pressures and tensions that affect the appropriations process as a whole. During the Reagan administration, for example, the president inevitably submitted budget requests with lower amounts for domestic discretionary spending than the Congress would approve as well as higher requests for defense (and, by 1985, for international affairs) than could be accommodated within GRH ceilings. Once Congress made its inevitable increases in domestic programs, something had to give. Tables 3a, b, and c and 4a, b, and c illustrate how this occurred, using FYs 1988, 1993, and 1994 as examples for appropriations.

For FY 1988, the budget resolution allocations for FY 1988 ("Section 302[b] Crosswalks")[1] for these subcommittees amounted to approximately $14.440 billion, so the amounts appropriated in late 1987, $14.024 billion, represented a cut of 2.0 percent ($416 million) from what was theoretically available under the budget resolution passed in June 1987.[2] The budget resolution figures in turn were about $376 million below the administration's requested amounts (2.6%). For most years, these would be useful comparisons, indicating the extent to which the budget resolution reflected congressional intent to fund a block of agencies/programs at higher or lower levels than the president desired, on the one hand, and the extent to which the appropriations committees had their funding predilections constrained by the overall congressional spending target, on the other. However, for FY 1988 this figure is quite misleading, because the enacted figures in Table 3a represent the *final*, continuing resolution amounts, which incorporate the

1. See above (chapter 1, note 6) for details of the allocation process.
2. Budget allocation estimates (sec. 302[b]) are from S. Rept. 100-182 to accompany H.R. 2763 (CJS Appropriations Bill, FY 1988), September 25, 1987. Figures from the Senate Budget Committee vary slightly, owing to rounding.

Table 3a. Appropriations Under the CJS Appropriations Act, FY 1988

| Agency | Final Budget Request | Final Appropriation* | Difference | Percent Difference |
|---|---|---|---|---|
| Commerce | $2,093,254,000 | $2,408,948,000 | $315,694,000 | +15.1 |
| Justice | 5,321,180,000 | 5,018,504,000 | (302,676,000) | −5.7 |
| Justice related | 552,785,000 | 511,161,000 | (41,624,000) | −7.5 |
| State | 3,888,807,000 | 2,688,175,000 | (700,632,000) | −20.7 |
| USIA | 941,857,000 | 820,021,000 | (121,836,000) | −12.9 |
| Other State related | 237,623,000 | 250,300,000 | 12,627,000 | +5.3 |
| Judiciary | 1,460,678,000 | 1,329,934,000 | (130,774,000) | −9.0 |
| Related agencies | 819,669,000 | 1,003,092,000 | 183,443,000 | +22.3 |
| TOTAL | $14,815,903,000 | $14,024,395,000 | ($791,508,000) | −5.3 |

Budget Resolution 302(b) allocation = $14,440,000,000

SOURCES: S. Rept. 100-182 to accompany H.R. 2763 (CJS Appropriations Bill, FY 1988), September 25, 1987, pp. 126–28, for request levels; S. Rep. 100-388 to accompany H.R. 4782 (CJS Appropriations Bill, FY 1989), June 20, 1988, pp. 7–9, for final FY 1988 appropriations levels.

NOTE: Some line entries have been omitted; therefore, totals are greater than the sum of entries shown.

*Post budget summit.

Table 3b. Appropriations Under the CJS Appropriations Act, FY 1993

| Agency | Final Budget Request | Final Appropriation | Difference | Percent Difference |
|---|---|---|---|---|
| Commerce | $2,887,918,000* | $3,287,187,000 | $399,269,000 | +13.8 |
| Justice | 10,018,488,000* | 9,663,372,000 | (355,116,000) | −3.5 |
| Justice related | 775,006,000* | 586,811,000 | (188,185,000) | −24.3 |
| State | 4,601,498,000 | 4,377,417,000 | (224,081,000) | −4.9 |
| USIA | 1,144,039,000 | 1,164,105,000 | 20,066,000 | +1.6 |
| Other state related | 314,187,000 | 312,802,000‡ | (1,385,000) | −0.4 |
| Judiciary | 2,838,134,000† | 2,534,837,000 | (303,297,000) | 10.7 |
| Related agencies | 1,429,134,000 | 1,869,711,000 | 440,557,000 | +30.8 |
| TOTAL | $23,779,002,000 | $23,616,242,000§ | ($162,760,000) | −0.6 |

SOURCES: S. Rept. 102-331 to accompany S. 3026 (CJS Appropriations Bill, FY 1993), July 23, 1992, pp. 124–46; H. Rept. 102-709 to accompany H.R. 5678 (CJS Appropriations Bill, FY 1993), July 23, 1992, pp. 6–7, 110–33.

NOTE: Some line entries have been omitted; therefore totals are greater than the sum of entries shown.

*House report shows the request as $2,884,918,000 for Commerce, $9,965,478,000 for Justice, $677,507,000 for Justice related. Differences result from the House using projected offsetting receipts to slightly reduce the apparent request.

†Senate figure, reflecting a subsequent budget amendment; House figure is $2,809,334,000.

‡Because of the $180 million Israeli transmitter recission (see text), new budget authority for this category was only $132,802,000; the figure here gives better comparisons of requests vs. appropriated amounts.

§Senate figure; the House figure, because of adjustments in scoring, is $23,571,683,000.

Table 3c. Appropriations Under the CJS Appropriations Act, FY 1994

| Agency | Final Budget Request | Final Appropriation | Difference | Percent Difference |
|---|---|---|---|---|
| Commerce | $3,575,936,000 | $3,635,714,000 | $59,778,000 | +1.7 |
| Justice | 9,839,212,000 | 9,578,395,000 | (260,817,000) | −2.7 |
| Justice related | 541,703,000 | 496,402,000 | (45,301,000) | −8.4 |
| State | 4,624,199,000 | 4,034,463,000 | (589,736,000) | −12.8 |
| USIA | 1,228,766,000 | 1,142,570,000 | (86,196,000) | −7.0 |
| Other State related | 329,366,000 | 308,450,000 | (20,921,000) | −6.4 |
| Judiciary | 3,164,560,000 | 2,743,368,000 | (421,192,000) | −13.3 |
| Related agencies | 1,624,343,000 | 1,457,419,000 | (166,924,000) | −10.3 |
| TOTAL | $24,928,085,000 | $23,396,781,000 | ($1,531,304,000) | −6.1 |

SOURCES: S. Rept. 103-105 to accompany H.R. 2519 (CJS Appropriations Bill, FY 1994), July 22, 1993, pp. 128–42; H. Rept. 103-157 to accompany H.R. 2519, June 24, 1993, pp. 6–7, 112–31; additional data on final appropriations amounts provided by Senate CJS Subcommittee staff, January 1994.

NOTE: Some line entries have been omitted; therefore, totals are greater than the sum of entries shown.

Table 4a. Budget Requests vs. Final Appropriations Under the CJS Appropriations Act, FY 1988

| Agency | 1987 Appropriation | 1988 Request | House Committee | Senate Committee | Final 1988 Appropriation* |
|---|---|---|---|---|---|
| Commerce | $2,122,817,000 | $2,093,254,000 | $2,489,970,000 (+19.0%) | $2,536,333,933 (+21.0%) | $2,408,948,000 (+15.1%) |
| Justice | 4,949,943,000 | 5,321,180,000 | 5,248,750,000 (−2.4%) | 5,303,943,000 (−3.3%) | 5,018,504,000 (−5.7%) |
| State | 2,683,103,831 | 3,388,807,000 | 2,580,579,000 (−23.8%) | 2,519,126,000 (−25.8%) | 2,688,175,000 (−20.7%) |
| USIA | 826,991,176 | 941,857,000 | 816,352,000 (−13.3%) | 819,705,000 (−13.0%) | 820,021,000 (−12.9%) |
| Judiciary | 1,259,708,000 | 1,460,678,000 | 1,371,210,000 (−6.1%) | 1,405,108,000 (−3.8%) | 1,329,934,000 (−9.0%) |
| Related agencies | 917,043,000 | 819,669,000 | 929,579,000 (+13.4%) | 923,757,000 (+12.7%) | 1,003,092,000 (+22.4%) |
| TOTAL | $13,459,625,007 | $14,815,903,000 | $14,164,560,000 (−4.4%) | $14,275,122,933 (−3.6%) | $14,024,395,000 (−5.3%) |

SOURCES: S. Rept. 100-182 to accompany H.R. 2763 (CJS Appropriations Bill, FY 1988), September 25, 1987, pp. 126–28, for FY 1987 appropriation, budget request, and Senate committee entries; S. Rept. 100-388 to accompany H.R. 4782 (CJS Appropriations Bill, FY 1989), June 20, 1988, pp. 7–9, for final FY 1988 appropriation levels.

NOTE: Some line entries have been omitted; therefore, totals are greater than the sum of entries shown. Data within parentheses reflect percentage differences from request levels.

*Post budget summit.

Table 4b. Budget Requests vs. Final Appropriations Under the CJS Appropriations Act, FY 1993

| Agency | 1992 Appropriation | 1993 Request | House Committee | Senate Committee | Final 1993 Appropriation |
|---|---|---|---|---|---|
| Commerce | $2,988,756,000 | $2,887,918,000* | $2,873,159,000 (−0.5%) | $3,331,812,000 (+15.4%) | $3,287,187,000 (+13.8%) |
| Justice | 9,319,233,000 | 10,018,488,000* | 8,945,371,000 (−2.4%) | 9,766,207,000 (−3.3%) | 9,663,372,000 (−5.7%) |
| State | 3,748,123,000 | 4,601,498,000 | 4,326,257,000 (−6.0%) | 4,326,195,000 (−6.0%) | 4,377,417,000 (−4.9%) |
| USIA | 1,087,094,000 | 1,144,039,000 | 1,141,902,000 (−0.1%) | 1,198,879,000 (+4.8%) | 1,164,105,000 (+1.6%) |
| Judiciary | 2,341,540,000 | 2,838,134,000† | 2,458,523,000 (−14.4%) | 2,449,504,000 (−13.7%) | 2,534,837,000 (−10.7%) |
| Related agencies | 1,904,789,000 | 1,429,154,000 | 1,675,007,000 (+17.2%) | 1,663,569,000 (+16.4%) | 1,869,711,000 (+30.8%) |
| TOTAL | $22,287,011,001 | $23,779,002,000‡ | $22,260,535,000 (−6.4%) | $23,595,854,000 (−0.8%) | $23,616,242,000 (−0.7%) |

SOURCES: S. Rept. 102-331 to accompany S. 3026 (CJS Appropriations Bill, FY 1993), July 23, 1992, pp. 134–46; H. Rept. 102-709 to accompany H.R. 5678 (CJS Appropriations Bill, FY 1993), July 23, 1992, pp. 6–7, 110–33. Final FY 1993 appropriations figures from S. Rept. 103-105 to accompany H.R. 2519 (CJS Bill, FY 1994), July 22, 1993, pp. 128–44.

NOTE: Some line entries have been omitted; therefore, totals are greater than the sum of entries shown. Data within parentheses reflect percentage differences from request levels.

*House report shows the request as $2,884,918,000 for Commerce, $9,965,478,000 for Justice. Differences result from the House using projected offsetting receipts to slightly reduce the apparent request.
†Senate figure, reflecting a budget amendment; House figure is $2,809,334,000.
‡Senate figure; the House figure, because of adjustments in scoring, is $23,571,683,000.

Table 4c. Budget Requests vs. Final Appropriations Under the CJS Appropriations Act, FY 1994

| Agency | 1993 Appropriation | 1994 Request | House Committee | Senate Committee | Final 1993 Appropriation |
|---|---|---|---|---|---|
| Commerce | $3,287,187,000 | $3,575,936,000 | $3,247,962,000 (−9.2%) | $3,658,906,000 (+2.3%) | $3,635,714,000 (+1.7%) |
| Justice | 9,663,372,000 | 9,839,212,000 | 9,389,351,000 (−4.6%) | 9,664,002,000 (−1.8%) | 9,578,395,000 (−2.7%) |
| State | 4,377,417,000 | 4,624,199,000 | 4,047,916,000 (−12.5%) | 4,135,442,000 (−10.6%) | 4,034,463,000 (−12.8%) |
| USIA | 1,164,105,000 | 1,228,766,000 | 1,084,770,000 (−11.8%) | 1,144,072,000 (−6.9%) | 1,142,570,000 (−7.0%) |
| Judiciary | 2,534,837,000 | 3,164,560,000 | 2,791,385,000 (−11.8%) | 2,656,478,000 (−16.0%) | 2,743,368,000 (−13.3%) |
| Related agencies | 1,869,711,000 | 1,624,343,000 | 1,554,364,000 (−4.3%) | 1,509,251,000 (−7.1%) | 1,457,419,000 (−10.3%) |
| TOTAL | $23,616,242,000 | $24,928,085,000 | $22,770,994,000 (−8.7%) | $23,604,764,000 (−5.3%) | $23,396,781,000 (−6.1%) |

SOURCES: S. Rept. 103-105 to accompany H.R. 2519 (CJS Appropriations Bill, FY 1994), July 22, 1993, pp. 128–42; H. Rept. 103-157 to accompany H.R. 2519, June 24, 1993, pp. 6–7, 112–31; additional data on final appropriations amounts provided by Senate CJS Subcommittee staff, January 1994.

NOTE: Some line entries have been omitted; therefore, totals are greater than the sum of entries shown. Data within parentheses reflect percentage differences from request levels.

*increases* from the budget summit for State. A better comparison is the request amounts against the amounts originally voted by the two appropriations committees, as shown in Table 4a.

Table 4a is a variation of Table 3a, cut down to exclude the related agencies for Justice and State, while expanded to include actual amounts appropriated in 1987 *and* the amounts originally proposed by the two committees. The disparity between the large increases for Commerce and small decreases for Justice, compared with the major decreases for State and USIA, is even more striking than in Table 3a, because it shows the levels to which the two foreign affairs agencies would have been cut but for the "bailout" they received in the budget summit. It also shows amounts that would have been appropriated in other titles of the appropriations bill had not the budget summit reductions (averaging 3.7%) been needed to avoid sequester.[3]

Table 4a shows clearly how State benefited for FY 1988 from the budget summit, as discussed above. Under the original subcommittee versions of the appropriation, State would have been below its requested amount by 23.8 percent (House) or 25.7 percent (Senate), compared with "only" a 20.7 percent reduction from the request in the final CR.[4] Similarly, Commerce did not receive the 19 percent or 21 percent increase indicated by the committees, but only 15.1 percent; while Justice went from a 2.4 percent or 3.3 percent decrease, to one of 5.7 percent.

The point of Tables 3a and 4a, of course, is to demonstrate the major cuts in requests for State and USIA which the subcommittees felt necessary in order to fund, according to their own priorities, other programs within their jurisdiction. Without budget resolution and GRH requirements—limiting appropriations and forcing spending reductions, respectively—it would have been possible to have it both ways: fund State and USIA at requested

---

3. Under GRH rules at the time, sequestration had to occur if the estimated deficit would be more than $10 billion above the target figure. Sequestration procedures originally enacted were declared unconstitutional by the Supreme Court on the grounds that they violated the constitutional separation of powers (because the comptroller general would have acted jointly with OMB in preparing the estimates). New procedures were subsequently adopted. In September 1988, concern about the possibility of exceeding the sequester ceilings in FY 1989 led to cuts in funding levels for all appropriations bills not yet enacted; this reduced State's S&E account by about $10.5 million. In the 1990 BEA, the sequester rules were changed, but many of the same principles, especially across-the-board cuts for defined categories, persisted.

4. As explained above, however, there was some legerdemain here: the appropriated amount was substantially higher than the spring 1987 budget resolution figure, though lower than the GRH baseline used in the summit.

(and probably needed) levels *and* appropriate for "their" domestic programs at desired levels.

It should be remembered that for fiscal years 1991–93, as a result of the BEA, Function 150 was "fenced" and protected as a separate category, so it could not be raided to the benefit of either domestic or defense funding. For FY 1994, although this protection disappeared, with minor exceptions all categories were treated initially the same way in the budget resolution. Still, this fact did not provide complete safety for international agencies, either under the BEA fences in FY 1993 or under the convention adopted for FY 1994 (see Tables 3b–c and 4b–c, constructed on the same bases for FY 1993 and FY 1994 as Tables 3a and 4a were for FY 1988). For FY 1993, State received the largest percentage reduction of the major agencies (4.9%), comparing budget requests with final appropriations, while Commerce received a significant increase at the expense of other domestic categories. However, the amount received by State that year, with the BEA fences in place, was much less a reduction than occurred in FY 1988 (20.78%), before the fences came into existence, or in FY 1994 (12.8%), after they had disappeared. USIA, in each of the three years cited, did relatively better than State, though never as well as Commerce. The picture is mixed: in all three years, the Judiciary also received major cuts compared to requests.

Obviously, a defensible argument can be made that for fiscal years 1988, 1993, and 1994, the budget and appropriations processes worked. Congress was forced to prioritize spending, as intended; and State and (at least for 1988) USIA were found wanting in comparison to the Economic Development Administration, Legal Services Corporation, and several smaller programs, all of which were "zeroed out" or proposed at very low levels by the administration but funded in much higher amounts by congressional action. It can be argued equally well, however, that this result was an unintended consequence of the *structural* arrangements by which the International Affairs budget was considered, rather than a conscious and considered trade-off between contending programs. It certainly cannot be said that it represented a comparison of all programs, or even an especially rational one. One can make a strong case, for example, that logic would call for trade-offs among all Function 150 programs and operations once a budget resolution had set the targets for that broad category. Yet because the Function 150 allocations are "crosswalked" (in the jargon of GRH and the BEA) to multiple appropriations subcommittees, such comparisons among related activities across the whole foreign affairs universe cannot be made by Congress under the current procedures.

A final, longer-in-time view of these realities can be seen in Table 5, which compares the percentage differences between administration requests and the final amounts appropriated in CJS acts from FY 1982 through FY 1996. It compares, first, Function 150 differences with those of all other categories in these acts, then does the same for the two primary domestic agencies, Commerce and Justice, and for State and USIA. Although there are some problems of data comparability with Tables 3a–c and 4a–c, the pattern is clear: the non-150 portions of these acts are invariably cut less than the international ones, with or without caps or fences, and this has been true for an extended time period.

There is a second important structural issue that is an artifact of the current budget process, though of little practical operational concern in most years before 1985. With the advent of GRH, "outlays" became highly relevant not only in political arguments over the size of the deficit, but with

Table 5. Percentage Changes in CJS Appropriations, Administration Requests vs. Final Appropriations, FY 1982–FY 1996

| Fiscal Year | CJS (less 150) | CJS (150 only) | Commerce | Justice | State | USIA |
|---|---|---|---|---|---|---|
| 1982 | + 16.44 | − 9.01 | + 17.71 | + 7.50 | + 8.68 | − 11.64 |
| 1983 | + 22.99 | − 6.29 | + 39.35 | + 6.15 | − 1.65 | − 17.88 |
| 1984 | + 15.65 | − 3.07 | − 39.59 | + 5.07 | − 2.34 | − 8.33 |
| 1985 | + 11.41 | − 1.61 | + 26.82 | + 0.79 | − 0.16 | − 8.08 |
| 1986 | + 5.63 | − 8.83 | + 20.90 | − 2.22 | − 5.78 | − 16.27 |
| 1987 | + 21.66 | + 14.87 | + 23.50 | + 20.50 | + 21.72 | − 12.84 |
| 1988 | + 2.27 | − 17.51 | + 14.02 | − 4.04 | − 21.27 | − 12.82 |
| 1989 | − 1.80 | − 0.19 | + 12.87 | − 4.46 | − 0.32 | + 0.21 |
| 1990 | + 9.99 | − 5.18 | + 11.08 | + 4.54 | − 3.80 | − 1.40 |
| 1991 | − 2.11 | − 18.40 | + 8.24 | − 5.28 | − 25.31 | + 0.50 |
| 1992 | + 2.56 | − 1.28 | + 13.77 | + 2.26 | − 7.04 | + 2.65 |
| 1993 | − 0.88 | − 2.28 | + 13.83 | − 3.54 | − 4.87 | + 1.75 |
| 1994 | − 3.71 | − 8.83 | + 1.67 | − 2.65 | − 12.75 | − 7.01 |
| 1995 | − 3.30 | − 2.89 | + 0.25 | − 2.24 | − 2.44 | − 3.84 |
| 1996 | − 11.90 | − 8.64 | − 22.65 | − 4.04 | − 5.47 | − 16.53 |

SOURCES: OMB Central Budget Management System for FY 1982–89; Senate and House Appropriations Committees for FY 1990–96.

NOTE: Assumptions change from year to year in some cases, but data are consistent within a given year. For 1982–89, either April request levels or midsession requests (i.e., final requests after budget amendments) are the base, while for FY 1990 and later, the initial presidential request is used. For FY 1994, Department of State figures do not include a $670,000,000 peacekeeping supplemental; with it, the State figure would be − 2.12%. Percentages throughout may not equate to those in other tables if a different base is used.

respect to real-world losses of flexibility in budget making. For outlays (amounts spent) compared to revenues define the deficit. Thus, budget resolution estimates of outlays associated with specific grants of budget authority, the traditional budgetary measure, had to be calculated to ensure that amounts appropriated would not exceed available limits. Compounding the analytic and budgeting problem was the fact that outlays projected to result from appropriations of previous years but expected to be expended in the current year also had to be estimated.

As seen above in the International Natural Rubber Organization, FMF, and unemployment insurance extension cases, one consequence of these procedures is that "scorekeeping," the calculation of outlays by the Congressional Budget Office, becomes critical. Those staffers who develop the sometimes arcane rules and then apply them, needless to say, have considerable power.[5] Appropriators have to worry about fitting their programs not only within BA ceilings but within those for outlays as well. The result, when expected outlays are very close to the limits that would trigger sequestration, is to limit severely the reallocation of funds from one program or account to another. This, incidentally, is a reason to accept the absolute amounts and percentages of cuts portrayed in Tables 3a–c and 4a–c with a degree of caution; sometimes the budget authority amounts, as shown in those tables, must be reduced for outlay reasons, even if the appropriations committees would not otherwise call for cuts. In the State Department accounts, for example, this has sometimes been the case for contributions to international organizations, since amounts appropriated there are fully expended in the initial year.

To drive home the critical point: *different types of programs "outlay" at different rates.* The practical effect of such differences was demonstrated at the height of State's 1987 budget crisis, during Senate floor consideration of the department's FY 1988–89 authorization bill.[6] With security funds "fenced off," and thus politically and legally untouchable, there was a frantic search by congressional and departmental staffers for other sources of

---

5. This, in my opinion, is a more general problem. Staff sometimes come to exercise greater power, in the modern Congress, when they control critical pressure points in the process or when they serve members who have no ability to analyze issues independently because of time pressures. By all reports, the CBO staffers, some of whom have become widely known, exert yeoman efforts to be consistent and to follow the intent of the law, but at times the results seem capricious to those in the executive who are charged with carrying out the programs Congress has approved.

6. The Foreign Relations Authorization Act, Fiscal Years 1988 and 1989, P.L. 100-204, December 22, 1987. I was a participant in the episode described.

funding. Attention momentarily focused on State's FBO account, which had some $900 million committed to building projects but not yet obligated (and therefore theoretically available). However, diverting all of these funds to operating expenses, which would have devastated construction much needed for security purposes, was highly undesirable on programmatic grounds and would have produced less than $200 million in outlays during FY 1988. Giving up $900 million in BA for $200 million in spendable funds was simply too much. While this particular outcome was sensible, outlay problems often limit the ability of legislative and executive budgeteers to make prioritizing choices. Such a limitation was particularly evident in FY 1991, in the wake of the BEA summit of October 1990, when many theoretically possible transfers from lower-priority accounts (e.g., payments for services at embassies abroad or embassy construction) to the starved S&E operating account for State could not be made because of differing outlay rates.

To restate the point of this discussion: budget innovations since 1974 have radically changed the processes by which funds are supplied for the entire government—and have exactly the same impact on foreign-policy-related activities as elsewhere. The result of attempts to rationalize and prioritize, paradoxically, can be to circumscribe the range of choices that would result in true prioritizing under conditions of resource constraints.

## Authorizers: The SFRC and HFAC (HIRC) in Search of Modern Roles

The biennial Foreign Relations Authorization Act, commonly called the "State bill" (although it also includes USIA, the "radios," refugee programs, international organizations and, in recent years, USAID's operating expenses),[7] is in theory a relatively routine way of meeting the statutory requirement that no appropriated funds can be "obligated" (i.e., committed

7. The primary radios are the Voice of America, Radio Free Europe, and Radio Liberty. Also included more recently have been Radio Martí, broadcasting to Cuba, and a new radio intended for China. See also the case on funding for the radios in Chapter 7. ACDA authorizations are normally handled in a separate bill, and USAID has of course been a part of the Foreign Assistance Authorization, if there is one. However, the FY 1994–95 Foreign Relations Act for the first time included operating expenses (OE) but not program authorizations for USAID.

for expenditure) without having been previously authorized. Its purposes are to authorize appropriations for agency operating expenses, to create programs, and to provide needed statutory authorities for administration and operation of the nation's foreign affairs agencies. In the 1980s and 1990s, however, these bills became attractive vehicles for congressional assertiveness in attempting to share foreign policy powers with the president. Few alternatives have the same potential for actually being enacted; for, unless the requirement for authorization is waived in statute, the president must have this bill. This is especially important when, as since 1985, it has been impossible to pass a Foreign Aid Authorization Act. Most on the Hill see foreign assistance authorizations as more appropriate expressions of foreign policy but will turn to the State bill if it is the only alternative.

Thus, the SFRC and HIRC have come to have a strong and persistent interest in passing the State bill. It is usually the *only* important piece of legislation they can produce, and legislation enacted is one important measure in Congress of the relevance of committees. In turn, this makes the committee members extremely reluctant to go along with waivers of the requirement for authorization, even though they routinely are forced to do so for foreign assistance. Among other things, threats by appropriators to insert such waivers in the CJS appropriations bill gives them leverage and heightens tensions between authorizers and appropriators. So while on the one hand there is a growing disposition by the authorizers to take on presidents on foreign policy issues, they also feel they must simultaneously guard their flanks against incursions by the appropriators. Increasingly, in a development paralleled elsewhere in Congress, the authorizers feel themselves under attack and in danger of losing their significance.

# A Time of Troubles: 1987–1991

The way this authorization process has evolved recently is worth an extended look because it provides a story-line survey of the range of possible interactions between the executive and Congress and within the latter. For the full flavor, a look at some of the parallel appropriations developments is helpful. In fair measure, these fractious encounters form a larger story that might be called "When Things Go Wrong."

## Authorization and Appropriations, 1987

Calendar year 1987 can fairly be called a disaster in terms of executive–congressional cooperation in the conduct of an effective foreign policy. Probably what will be most remembered is the Iran-Contra affair and the highly publicized, contentious, but ultimately inconclusive joint congressional hearings that resulted. But things were little better in terms of recurring legislative requirements, in particular the FY 1988–89 Foreign Relations Authorization Act, the (failed) FY 1988 foreign assistance authorization bill, and the two parallel appropriations bills. The first of these finally became law after a full year of intra- and interbranch contention; the second was never passed, under threat of a veto of two different versions; and the two appropriations bills were included in a massive CR (the results of which are in part detailed in Tables 3a and 4a), blurring the authorization/appropriations distinction and producing additional strains along the way. Hanging over everything was the continuing impasse between the Reagan administration and the Democratic-controlled Congress over what was arguably the fundamental political issue of the 1980s: the appropriate size of the government (and the resulting amount of government spending) and whether defense and international programs should receive increased support at the expense of domestic discretionary funding and even entitlement programs. Only the politicians' fear of the unknown after Black Monday, October 19, allowed a temporary escape, deferring the basic issues to the next administration.

The State bill was trouble from the very beginning. Early in the year, hearings on it before the International Operations Subcommittee of HFAC became highly charged, with tough exchanges between Secretary Shultz and other administration witnesses and Chairman Dan Mica, ranking minority member Olympia Snowe, and many of their colleagues. Issues ranged from the problems at the Moscow embassy,[8] sharp disagreements over funding levels, and policy differences that eventually became the subject of amendments in the bill. Shultz argued that the Congress would be irresponsible if it did not authorize funding at requested levels, while (as detailed in Chapter 4) members of Congress, especially Democrats, contended that the only way to do this was to "Tell your boss to raise taxes," since domestic programs could not and would not be subject to further cuts.

---

8. Mica and Snowe made a quick, flamboyant, and publicity-oriented trip to Moscow during the spring recess to explore the bugging of the new office building and the circumstances of the Lonetree/Bracey Marine security cases.

The House bill as reported by the committee on March 27, 1987, contained several elements disturbing to the administration, but the dialogue continued. On March 30, OMB informed Republican members of the Rules Committee (including the ranking member, Trent Lott, who was opposing the bill—but not Snowe, who was generally supporting it!) that the president would veto the bill if passed in its current form, because of low funding levels. This was an unwise breach of normal etiquette. Mica angrily pulled the bill from the House calendar, feeling that his efforts to have it considered in the House before the April 15 budget resolution deadline, thereby possibly avoiding even lower funding levels,[9] had not been appreciated and that State was ungrateful. Although this had been OMB's tactical choice and was in fact opposed by State management, Mica and Snowe blamed State, specifically Under Secretary Spiers.[10]

By the time the bill finally reached the House floor in mid-June, the atmosphere had worsened and the budget situation was no better. As a result, one usual check against floor mischief did not work. In earlier times, State and committee staffs collaborated closely to head off unwanted and unwarranted amendments. This time, however, the House managers were determined to pass an authorization bill at any cost, to avoid losing any more power to the budget and appropriations committees. Thus they "took" even what they considered to be objectionable amendments in order to gain the support of their sponsors for the overall bill. The staffs even collaborated in drafting compromise amendments, especially in the security and Soviet-bashing area, that arguably were worse than those they were alleged to be forestalling.[11]

Much the same thing happened on the Senate side, and the bill reported by the Foreign Relations Committee on June 23 was not appreciably better

9. For a more detailed discussion of this initial confrontation on the bill, see John Felton, "Administration Wants More Money: Funding Impasse Imperils State Department Bill," *CQ Weekly Report* 45 (April 4, 1987): 621–22. Mica's theory, seen also in 1989, was that passing an authorization bill before the first budget resolution somehow avoided constraints the latter might bring. Others believed this notion to be erroneous; for even if higher amounts than those contained in the budget resolution were authorized, they would not be appropriated.

10. For the Hill version, see Dan Mica and Olympia Snowe, "Taking Exception: The State Department Created the Fix It's In" (op-ed article), *Washington Post*, October 29, 1987. The author, working this bill for the department under the direction of Spiers, is convinced that OMB senior staff made the call to Lott; I was in fact arguing against it with OMB working-level staff even as it was being announced.

11. To some, this willingness to accept virtually any amendment became known as the "General Assembly syndrome," since that U.N. body was known at times to engage in the same practice.

overall than the House version, although it did include a quite different constellation of amendments opposed by the administration. An added Senate element was the well-known hostility of Senator Jesse Helms, ranking minority member of the SFRC, both to State and to Shultz personally. The bill also contained an example of a most egregious kind of prohibition on spending: section 107 (which became section 122 of the final act), prohibited the use of any funds for expenses associated with closing posts, reserving $500 *million* of the amounts proposed for the Administration of Foreign Affairs account for operating seven specified posts (which State intended to close but some in Congress wanted to keep open), with the rest available for the original purposes only if those posts remained open. This was modified to a $50 million penalty on the Senate floor in October, but remained in the final authorization act, leading to some interesting maneuvers during the final hours of the session.[12]

By mid-summer, many in State were arguing that no bill at all was better than the one likely to emerge from Congress. But that would have been possible only if the statutory requirement for authorization were waived. This was to be a major issue.

After much uncertainty about whether the bill would be taken to the Senate floor at all, four wild days of debate finally occurred, with final passage on October 8. Eighty-six amendments were added, sponsored by some forty members of the Senate. Many were policy-related, while others were clear examples of either "micromanagement" or vindictiveness against State or even against specific officials. Indeed, some members of the Senate pronounced themselves embarrassed by the circuslike atmosphere.[13]

Meanwhile, executive–legislative contention over the budget continued, although foreign affairs was only a minor part of it. Appropriations bills were moving to completion, and the budget summit was imminent (although no one knew it in mid-October.)

At the same time, State Department officials and Mica and Snowe amused themselves by exchanging charges and countercharges in the op-ed pages of

12. The $500 million penalty was voted by the SFRC and described in S. Rept. 100-75, accompanying that committee's bill reported to the Senate floor. There, an attempt to strike the provision failed, with the final result being a reduction of the penalty to $50 million. The final provision (sec. 122 of P.L. 100-204, December 22, 1987) was similar to this final Senate provision.
13. See Don Oberdorfer and Helen Dewar, "Senate's State Dept. Bill 'Cacophony of Confusion,' " *Washington Post*, October 11, 1987; Nathaniel C. Nash, "Telling the State Department How to Run Foreign Policy," *New York Times*, October 12, 1987; and John Felton, "Senators Load Up State Department Measure," *CQ Weekly Report* 45 (October 17, 1987): 2535–38.

the *Washington Post* about who was at fault (rather than, as one might expect anywhere but Washington, in more private communications). On October 19, Elliott Abrams, assistant secretary of state for inter-American affairs, wrote a piece entitled "Wrecking State: What in the World Does Congress Think It's Doing?" Predictably, this article elicited the Mica and Snowe response of October 29: "The State Department Created the Fix It's In," which presented a bill of particulars about how inept the department was in its congressional relations. Mica and Snow argued that State must recognize not only the government-wide budgetary constraints, but also "that its seeming distaste and disdain for Congress' traditional and legitimate role have taken their toll and [that State] must begin to repair the damage . . . and make a sincere effort to work with Congress at solving the problems that concern us all." Not to be outdone, Shultz's staff produced a rebuttal under the secretary's signature, entitled "Will Congress Not Listen to Reason: The Curtailment at State Is a Part of a Larger Disaster Looming in Our Overall International Affairs Budget."[14]

The conferences on authorization and appropriations will long be remembered by the participants, if not fondly. By early December substantial progress had been made in eliminating many odious provisions contained in one or both versions of the authorization bill. In the end, though, it was not enough. After starting with some 170 differences between the House and Senate bills (State had prepared no fewer then 175 position papers on items of difference, those to which the department objected), all but about 30 were "solved" at the staff level; the rest were taken to several sessions of the conference. There, many major items of concern to the administration were dropped or deferred, but in the end the result was not acceptable to Shultz and State. Even though the budget summit allowed the conferees to set higher authorization levels than were contained in either the House or the Senate bill, as discussed above—viz., $4.1 billion for FY 1988 and $4.2 billion for FY 1989, compared with $3.6 billion in the Senate bill and $3.9 billion in the House version for FY 1988—a veto seemed to be in the offing because of the accompanying provisions. Nevertheless, the House adopted the conference report on December 15, 1987, as did the Senate the next day.

Within the administration, an active debate was renewed as to whether the bill should be vetoed because of several offensive provisions: (1) the penalty of $50 million if any foreign service posts abroad were closed; (2) a

---

14. Secretary Shultz's piece appeared on November 8. Although some at State counseled against continuing this debate, they were overruled.

requirement to withdraw from the agreements allowing the Soviets to construct and occupy a new chancery site at Mt. Alto in Washington, D.C., in exchange for the new U.S. embassy in Moscow; and (3) earmarks on contributions to international organizations. Secretary Shultz decided to recommend a veto, hoping initially that a replacement bill without the offending provisions could be passed before the end of the session.[15]

Realistically, though, it would have been difficult to pass a new version before Congress adjourned. A veto would have meant *either* that State and USIA would have no authorization, legally forcing them to shut down, obviously an untenable result; *or else* that the requirement for authorization would have to be waived in the CR that was still being worked. If the requirement for authorization were waived, the authorization bill (and the work of the SFRC and HFAC) would become irrelevant.

Fascell and his staff therefore concocted a shrewd approach, closely held and not immediately understood at State. Under normal circumstances, the authorization bill conference report would have been enrolled by the clerk of the House shortly after its adoption on December 16 and sent expeditiously to the White House for presidential consideration. Each day State's inquiries were met with the bland assertion that the conference report was being processed, but that the end-of-session passage of a large number of bills was delaying its enrollment and transmission to the president.[16] Obviously, until the White House received the bill officially, it could not be vetoed. So Fascell arranged with the House leadership to have the passed conference report held at the clerk's desk, rather than being processed immediately. This meant that the uncertainty was prolonged and the administration could bring less pressure on the appropriations committees to waive the requirement for authorization; for, in principle, if Hill pressure were great enough, the authorization bill could still become law. Fascell's thinking was that if the bill were to be sent quickly to the White House and were

15. For more details on the bill as it emerged from conference, before the waivers added in the appropriations bill (see below), see Steven Pressman, "Administration Unhappy with Congressional Strings: Congress Clears State Department Measure," *CQ Weekly Report* 45 (December 19, 1987): 3123–25.

16. To quote the preeminent source on congressional procedures: "Once both houses approve the conference report, the papers are delivered to the house that originated the measure. A copy of the bill as finally agreed to by Congress is prepared by an enrolling clerk. The 'enrolled bill' is signed by the Speaker and presiding officer of the Senate, or by other authorized officers, and sent to the president." Walter J. Oleszek, *Congressional Procedures and the Policy Process*, 4th ed. (Washington, D.C.: CQ Press, 1996), p. 294. Fascell was able to engineer the tactics described simply by ensuring that the enrolling clerk acted with "all deliberate speed."

then vetoed, the votes probably did not exist for an override. Moreover, the nearness of Christmas made time very short. After a veto in these circumstances, Congress would have had little choice but to waive the requirement for authorization, and the authorizing committees would have been left out in the cold. But if the bill were held until the CR was completed, a good argument could be made that there was no need to waive the authorization requirement since an authorization bill was still alive. If there were no waiver, then according to Fascell's logic the president would have to sign the authorization bill.

The eventual outcome, however, was unacceptable to nearly everyone—except, ironically, Dante Fascell and his staff. CJS appropriator Neal Smith at first argued for waiving the authorization requirement, but in a small private meeting with Smith, Fascell, and key staffers, Speaker Jim Wright decided that the authorization bill should be passed if at all possible, given all the work Fascell and the authorizers had done. Thus, during intense discussions over the weekend before Christmas, with Congress almost frantic to pass the CR and adjourn, Smith and the CJS appropriators, with Fascell's active participation, developed an expedient approach: instead of waiving the authorization requirement, three of the authorization provisions most offensive to the administration would be waived for a two-year period, while the rest would become effective when the bill was signed, as it was believed the president would have no choice but to do. The waived provisions were those requiring that the embassy construction agreements with the Soviets be voided, setting earmarks on contributions to international organizations and imposing financial penalties if any overseas posts were closed. Key SFRC staff, not part of the deal, were adamant about keeping the post-closing provision, so they were not told about the deal until afterward! Thus Fascell, master of the art of the possible, *got a bill,* something that was more important to him than the survival of any specific provisions. Mica was loyal to his chairman, and Snowe's objections were simply ignored. Resigned to the impossibility of obtaining the authorization waiver and thus to the inevitability of this alternative approach, State argued unsuccessfully for waiving two additional provisions: one mandating the forced closure of the PLO office in New York (felt to be contrary to international law); and one requiring the polygraphing of State's Diplomatic Security officers (intensely opposed by Shultz personally). Fritz Hollings refused to go along with a waiver of the polygraph provision and, of course, was successful because, as chairman of the Senate CJS Subcommittee, he had to be on board for such an unusual approach to work. Subsequently, the president's signing statement interpreted these two provisions in a way that State and the White House hoped would make them tolerable.

The appropriators (somewhat smugly, others thought) conveyed their decision to the White House, to State, and to the SFRC and HFAC. Faced with this dictum, the administration decided that it must accept the remainder of what it considered to be a marginal authorization bill, albeit with the reservations expressed in the president's signing statement. Similarly, the authorizers were forced to acquiesce in this outcome, some feeling that they had been thwarted by State with the cooperation of the appropriators. The authorization bill was sent to the White House and was not vetoed.[17] While State had escaped, for two years, what it saw as the worst provisions,[18] it was forced to accept others it had strenuously opposed. The authorizing committees (except for the small group that had engineered this outcome) were left smarting from a clear demonstration that in the final crunch the appropriators held the power. The appropriations subcommittees were quietly satisfied. Not surprisingly, this outcome would be remembered during work on the next set of appropriations and authorization bills.

While all this authorization activity was occurring, of course, consideration of the parallel appropriations bills (Commerce-Justice-State and Foreign Operations) was also under way. CJS was relatively uneventful, compared to earlier years, though subject to the funding limitations and differing priorities previously discussed, thus leading to an administration veto threat. The bill passed the House on July 1, and the Senate on October 15, with the results detailed in Tables 3a and 4a. However, partly because of the veto possibility and partly because of the budget summit, the bill was not taken to conference; eventually it became a part of the CR and thus a vehicle for the unusual two-year waiver of authorization provisions just discussed.

The conference report on the CR, which contained the CJS bill as well as

17. Details about Fascell's approach come from postmortems with members of his staff, supplemented by information from the same sources in May 1994.

18. Section 305 of the CJS Appropriations Act, 1988 (sec. 101[a] of the Continuing Appropriations Act, 1988; H.J. Res. 395, 101 Stat. 1329, approved December 22, 1987), stated simply: "SEC. 305: The following sections of H.R. 1777 (the Foreign Relations Authorization Act, Fiscal Years 1988 and 1989) are waived during Fiscal Years 1988 and 1989 in the event that H.R. 1777 is enacted into law: Sec. 122, Sec. 151 and Sec. 204." This language put an end to the $50 million penalty if posts were closed, since the authorization to which it applied was effective only during these two fiscal years; but, as the lawyers ultimately concluded, the Moscow chancery–Mt. Alto and PLO office prohibitions once again became effective in FY 1990.

the other twelve appropriations measures, finally passed both houses at about 2 A.M. on December 22, ending almost a week of nearly around-the-clock negotiations, and was signed into law by the president later that same day. It must be remembered that while overall funding levels were set by the budget summit, they were at a very high level of generality, so there was room for a fair amount of dickering over funding for specific programs. In addition, because of the inclusion of many legislative provisions in the CR (routine but theoretically subject to points of order since substantive legislation on an appropriations bill is not permitted under the rules of either house), there was a full range of nonmonetary issues. As usual, the CR, especially in the Senate, had been the successful target of a great number of parochial "Christmas tree" amendments.

## Foreign Assistance, 1987

In a parallel and simultaneous drama, the situation for foreign assistance was if anything worse. Having passed an authorization bill in 1985 (for FY 1986–87) for the first time since 1981, the HFAC and SFRC hoped very much to reaffirm a pattern of authorization committee involvement by repeating this success for FY 1988–89. It was not to be. HFAC's first attempt, H.R. 1630, was dead for practical purposes as soon as it was voted out of committee on April 9, 1987. This quick death largely reflected the ongoing unpopularity of foreign aid, now heightened in some quarters because of the restrictions imposed on domestic spending. The White House and congressional Republicans opposed the bill on different but by now familiar grounds: the $11.07 billion proposed was below the president's request of about $12 billion; and the bill contained too many earmarks and restrictions with respect to where assistance should be allocated.

In the face of these objections, seemingly endless consultations and attempts at compromise continued over the following months. Finally, the House passed an alternative, H.R. 3100, on December 10, which maintained the freeze on funding but allowed greater flexibility in assistance allocation.

The SFRC, meanwhile, had reported its own version, S. 1274, on May 22, again with a funding level that was unacceptably low to the administration. Several attempts by SFRC Chairman Pell to take the bill to the floor failed, owing to opposition from Senate Republicans and the administration and to Majority Leader Byrd's disinclination to engage in a foreign aid floor fight.[19]

To jump ahead briefly in time, the futility of attempts to pass foreign assistance authorizing legislation is probably best shown by the desperate efforts of HFAC, continuing throughout the following year (1988), to move *any* kind of bill. In an effort to force the Senate to deal with foreign aid, HFAC used a complicated maneuver, attaching the bill, H.R. 3100, to the rule under which a routine but necessary reauthorization bill for the Overseas Private Investment Corporation (OPIC) was to be brought to the House floor. With adoption of the rule, H.R. 3100 became part of the OPIC bill. The notion was that, in conference, the Senate could recede to the House and thus adopt H.R. 3100 without ever having a vote on it on the Senate floor. The House did its part, but the SFRC refused to play this game. HFAC eventually adopted a clean version of the OPIC bill, intending to send it routinely to the Senate. Through yet another twist, however, a version of the OPIC bill was instead added by Pell on the Senate floor to the FY 1989 Foreign Operations Appropriations Bill conference report (September 30, 1988) and accepted by the House. Once again, H.R. 3100 was left by the wayside.

Back to 1987. The FY 1988 "Foreign Ops" (foreign aid) appropriations bill, in contrast to the related State authorization and CJS appropriations bills, was completed in reasonably good order, though subject to some of the same old problems of foreign aid's unpopularity as well as the larger dynamic of the budget conflict between the president and Congress. The House bill, reported by Appropriations on August 6, reduced administration requests by $690 million below the 1987 appropriation, citing BEA limits. In a development that would prove important later, the bill earmarked $532 million for the Guaranty Reserve Fund (GRF), a loan guarantee program employed when recipient countries cannot pay for weapons purchases from the United States. Fearing that this earmark would reduce appropriations for other assistance programs—the result in the House bill—the administration argued that the GRF did not require funding for FY 1989. The Senate did not deal with the bill in the full Appropriations Committee until late November. By waiting until after the budget summit, the Senate was able to "plus up" foreign assistance by some $600 million in BA

---

19. Several Senate and State Department staffers believed that a further consideration late in the year may have been to avoid another SFRC floor show such as the spectacle that had greeted the State bill earlier that same year, lasting four long days in October.

and $200 million in outlays over what had tentatively been decided earlier.[20] Eventually, the CR allowed $13.6 billion for foreign operations—much below the administration's initial request of $15.8 billion, but about the same amount as was provided for FY 1987. It is also worth noting that the Reagan administration had increased foreign aid funding throughout its tenure, relating it to defense increases, so that the FY 1988 amount was substantially higher than the 1981 foreign aid budget. These increases were all in security assistance, rather than for development or humanitarian purposes. A summary of Function 150 funding from 1976 on can be found in Appendix Table 2.

## Authorizers vs. Appropriators Once Again, 1989

Since the purpose of the case studies in this chapter is not to provide a complete legislative history but rather to demonstrate salient issues and tactics, the events of 1988 will be largely omitted. It is worth noting, however, that while one tends to think in terms of discrete battles and pieces of legislation, the congressional process is continuous and what goes before affects what comes after. Scarcely two months after the December 1987 imbroglio just described, with the salted wounds of all concerned still providing pain, the relentless cycle began anew. The administration submitted its FY 1990 appropriations requests for CJS and for Foreign Operations and its proposals for a foreign assistance authorization. Because the budget summit deal of 1987 covered two fiscal years, for the first time in many years, all thirteen appropriations bills were enacted before the beginning of FY 1989 (i.e., by October 1, 1988). Although there were the usual problems of fitting budget authority to outlays, as well as the expected complement of late-night surprise amendments, calendar year 1988 was placid when compared with recent years.[21]

20. As noted, this outcome had resulted because the budget summit used a different, and higher, baseline than the budget resolution earlier that year which had been the basis of allocations to the appropriations committees/subcommittees and, therefore, the benchmark for the initial appropriations marks. The net result, of course, was to sell as a cut what was in fact a considerably higher figure than originally included! It was a cut only from the higher baseline; from the earlier one, it was an increase.

21. The CJS bill became P.L. 100-459, approved October 1, 1988. Key statutory provisions included a long, clearly substantive provision with respect to the Afghan Resistance, calling for among other things a special envoy to the resistance with the rank of ambassador (sec. 306). Similarly incorporated, in section 305, was the latest version of the congressional balancing act vis-à-vis construction of a new chancery in Israel. In the late-night amendments category, though not on the CJS bill, was the creation of an "ambassador-at-large for burdensharing,"

In 1989, by contrast, the realities of power relationships between authorizers and appropriators again presented themselves, with some new twists.

With respect to the State authorization bill, there was an unstated but shared determination among department and HFAC staffers to avoid the problems of 1987. A new Bush administration, with a new secretary of state and eventually a new under secretary for management, no doubt helped, for they were able to disavow the actions of their predecessors that had so infuriated the Congress (and did, to a degree not altogether seemly, given they were of the same party). With HFAC, there was a new chairman of the International Operations Subcommittee, with Mervin Dymally of California replacing Dan Mica (who had relinquished his seat for what proved to be an unsuccessful try for Lawton Chiles's Florida Senate seat). Thus, the heat that had so roiled consideration of the FY 1988–89 authorization bill was largely absent in 1989.

House subcommittee and full committee hearings and markups were almost a love feast, and the House passed the bill (with the usual number of floor amendments) on April 12, before the scheduled date of the first budget resolution. This time there was no repeat of the acrimony that had caused so many problems two years before. What was most clear during this process was Fascell's determination (as in 1987) to have a bill and remain a player. Thus, the committee staff, early on, divided the administration's proposals into "A" and "B" packages, with the latter containing items on which other committees might assert jurisdiction. Package "B" was severed from the main bill, with promises to help reattach these provisions at a later stage (which, by and large, did not happen). The point, of course, was to avoid the delays that would inevitably result from referral to other committees. Sometimes, getting a bill is more important than its contents.

On the Senate side, things were not so tranquil. Early on, during committee markup of the bill in May and June, some of the problems that would dog the end of the year began to appear. Important constitutional issues arose, the most troublesome being Senator Moynihan's proposal for an amendment requiring that the administration "obey the law" (a proposal prompted by the Iran-Contra episode; see Chapter 6).

Nevertheless, a Senate bill was reported, after the usual problems with the SFRC's gaining a quorum and with tactical infighting between Pell and Helms (and, even more so, between their staffs). It was taken to the Senate

---

engineered by DOD and the Defense committees. State did not learn about the latter provision until some two weeks later, when a lawyer was reading through all the bills!

floor in mid-July, with the usual "secretary of state for a day" syndrome leading to many amendments and five full days of floor action, but culminating with passage of a bill late on July 20 that the administration, while objecting to certain sections, could live with (except for the Moynihan provision just mentioned).[22] The bill contained more than eighty amendments, most of which HFAC argued were "nongermane" under House rules and would have to be stricken in conference.[23]

Then the fun began. It took the better part of three months to bring the bill to conference, owing to the widely different agendas of the two committees. As seen, the House had been struggling with an attempted major reform in foreign assistance, which had been vitiated within HFAC by the desires of the geographic-area subcommittees to protect or punish recipient countries in accord with member views of those countries' performance relative to U.S. interests. They had nevertheless passed a foreign assistance authorization bill, H.R. 2655, on June 29.[24] While the SFRC had managed to report out a contentious foreign aid authorization bill (S. 1347) on July 12,[25] it was widely viewed as dead and unlikely ever to be brought to the floor, given leadership views that the result would be a debacle.

Predictably, the SFRC and HFAC could not initially agree on the parameters for conference on both these authorization bills: the former wanted to ignore foreign aid, but to allow consideration of its multitude of (nongermane by House rules) amendments to the State bill; while HFAC, as with H.R. 3100 the previous year, concocted an approach that would meld the House-passed foreign assistance authorization to its own version of the foreign relations (State) bill in a single conference report, thus bypassing the need for Senate floor action on a stand-alone foreign assistance bill. Given the profound differences in foreign aid, however, it is not surprising that the Senate was unwilling to accept this parliamentary ploy. The two sides

22. For a detailed account, see Pamela Fessler and John Felton, "The State Department: Senators Use Bill as a Forum for Foreign Policy Views—Raft of Amendments Puts the Chamber on Record on Questions Ranging from Cambodia Arms Aid to the PLO Talks," *CQ Weekly Report* 47 (July 22, 1989): 1879–82. Sanctions on China were another big issue, together with PLO-directed items.

23. The *Washington Post*, in its July 20, 1989, coverage of the Senate floor debate, made sport of "the sweeping statements on foreign policy made by the Senate in its annual diplomacy rite of authorizing the State Department's bill for Fiscal 1990."

24. For an extensive commentary on what happened on the House side, see *CQ Almanac* 45 (1989): 609–23.

25. Helms, for example, made it very clear in committee that he found the bill most unacceptable and would be offering a substantial number of "corrective" amendments on the Senate floor. See *CQ Almanac* 45 (1989): 623–25 for SFRC action.

remained at an impasse—first being unable to conference quickly before the August recess, as Fascell and his staff wanted; then missing early and mid-September targets. There was no formal action at all between late July and early October, when at last the staffs began meeting individually and collectively to see if progress could be made in preparing for a conference. Many doubted, however, that it would occur; or, if it did, that it could produce an agreed bill. This apparent failure of the authorization process had notable implications for what was to come next: a revealing confrontation between authorizers and appropriators, with State and USIA caught squarely in the middle.

As the authorizing committees jockeyed for an advantage neither ever found, the appropriations subcommittees moved steadily toward completing their tasks. The Foreign Operations subcommittees (headed by Obey and Leahy), assuming early on that there would be no new Foreign Assistance Authorization Act and essentially ignoring the painful attempts just described to produce one, passed bills through the House (July 21) and the Senate (September 26). They would complete conference and, on November 9, file a report which was eventually accepted by both bodies (after trips back and forth between the houses) on November 16. This first attempt, however, was vetoed on November 19. A revised bill passed both houses and was signed by President Bush just before the end of the session, on November 21.[26] Although section 10 of P.L. 91-672, the Foreign Military Sales Act Amendments, 1971, required that there be an authorization before there could be a foreign assistance appropriation, this requirement was waived (as happened almost every year) in the appropriations act.[27]

## Endgame: The Authorization Waiver Problem

What happened in the end with the Commerce-Justice-State Appropriations Act, however, was *not at all* routine. Although the battle over the bill was hard-fought, with the usual funding issues over specific programs, the process was predictable until conference. This outcome was facilitated, if not

26. The bill had been vetoed primarily because of a Moynihan-sponsored "leveraging" provision (similar to that on the State Department bill, presented in some detail in Chapter 6). The second bill, H.R. 3743, was passed on November 20, 1989, and became law (P.L. 101-167) on November 21. The vetoed bill was H.R. 2939.

27. In the present case, the waiver appears in sec. 553 of P.L. 101-167. The chronology of the 1990 Foreign Operations Appropriations Act presented in this paragraph is taken from *CQ Almanac* 45 (1989): 780, 785, 792, 797, 800.

to executive branch liking, by the passage of the budget resolution early in the year, providing clarity about spending levels. The bill passed the House on August 1 and the Senate on September 29, and an initial conference report was filed on October 20.[28]

The appropriators, especially Neal Smith, placed great stock on "getting their work done on time." Smith always attempted to have his bill come to the House floor first among the thirteen appropriations bills if at all possible, and this work ethic was pervasive in his overall approach. But in the fall of 1989 he faced a dilemma: What to do about the absence of a State authorization bill, given the now familiar statutory requirement that there could be no expenditure of appropriations without prior authorization? Unlike the pattern for foreign assistance, this requirement was seldom waived for the State bill, and then only when no opportunity arose to authorize a favored program.

Smith had two choices: either delay completion of the CJS appropriations bill, to allow for the possibility that there might be an authorization act, or find a way to pass the appropriation as soon as possible, either by waiving outright the authorization requirement or by another approach that dealt with the various possible outcomes. He tried the latter.

The October 20 conference report on the appropriations bill (H.R. 2991) included section 614, which provided that since no authorization act had become law for either USIA or State, the authorization requirement was waived until November 30, 1989. Meanwhile, the two agencies would be held either to 1989 funding levels or to the 1990 level as passed by the Senate, whichever was lower. If an authorization bill were passed prior to November 30, then the CJS 1990 funding levels would apply immediately; and if there were no authorization bill by then, the requirement for an authorization would be waived, and funding would revert to the appropriations bill's same 1990 levels.[29] Fascell apparently had agreed to this approach but had argued for a later date, February 15, 1990, to allow for more time to pass an authorization. Smith, however, wanted finality by the end of the first session of the 101st Congress. He calculated that November

28. The legislative history of the FY 1990 CJS bill (H.R. 2991) is summarized in the printed version of the act (P.L. 101-162, November 21, 1989). The conference report was accepted by the House, with the exception of one amendment, on October 26. The Senate accepted the conference report on October 31, receding from that amendment, but added other amendments in the process. After two more excursions back and forth, the House agreed to the report on November 7; the Senate concurred on November 8, 1989.

29. See the text of the conference report in *Congressional Record* 135 (October 20, 1989); the text of sec. 614 is on p. H7322.

30 would come after Congress adjourned, and was therefore a reasonable limit.[30]

Had there been no movement on an authorization conference, it seems likely the Smith approach would have been accepted, albeit with grumbling, by the authorizers. It was in fact formally agreed to by the full House when the CJS conference report was approved on October 26. That same day, however, driven by Fascell's and Pell's need for relevance, the authorization conference met, a step many thought was futile. This assumption was proved wrong.

Thus, when the full Senate took up the CJS appropriations conference report on October 31, the authorization conference was continuing (albeit with little initial indication of progress). Pell, with the backing of Helms and the full SFRC, decided to take on the appropriators, offering a floor amendment that struck the waiver of the authorization requirement on the grounds that a waiver was "not in accord with the legislative process and [was] unjustified under current circumstances." Revealingly, Pell further noted that "the authorization waiver would undermine the prospects for enactment of the State Department Authorization Act."[31] For the authorizers, their survival as players of influence was at stake. A bitter debate ensued between Pell and the Senate CJS subcommittee chairman Hollings. State was accused by each side of siding with the other, with threats and attempts to gain a statement of support taking place during the days just before the vote. In fact, the department tried to stay neutral. Senators Helms and Rudman, the ranking minority members of the SFRC and CJS, respectively, each played an active role in support of his chairman; this was an institutional issue, not a partisan one.[32] The result, which many saw as in part reflecting the unpopularity of Hollings and as a payback for previous wrongs, was a recorded vote accepting the Pell amendment by 53–45.[33]

Technically, the Senate had amended a House amendment (the original section 614) to the appropriations bill, so the conference report had to be taken up again by the House. On November 7, after intense consultations

30. Congressional staff sources involved in the Fascell–Smith negotiations.

31. The quotations come from *Congressional Record* 135 (October 31, 1989): S14405; debate on the Pell amendment is on pp. S14405–11.

32. See in particular Rudman's remarks about the Pell–Hollings fight and State's frantic attempts to stay neutral. Rudman was scathing in his contempt for State's lack of backbone. *Congressional Record* 135 (November 1, 1989): S14479.

33. See *Congressional Record* 135 (October 31, 1989): S14411. Hollings lost several members of the Senate Commerce Committee, which he chaired, and even a few appropriators, while Pell, for the first time in memory, had the unanimous support of the SFRC.

between the two CJS subcommittees, a new conference report was taken to the House floor. It in effect accepted the Pell section 614 language, stating that State and USIA would remain on continuing resolution levels (the lower of the 1989 levels or the Senate-passed 1990 ones) indefinitely, without the November 30 end date. If an authorization were passed, "the conferees are agreed that . . . steps will be taken to restore appropriations for the Department and the Agency using the levels originally recommended in the conference agreement on H.R. 2991 as a guide." The revised conference report passed the House on November 7 and the Senate on November 8 with little discussion, and it was signed into law as P.L. 101-162 on November 21, 1989.[34]

Unfortunately, since this language did not provide for an automatic return to the FY 1990 CJS bill levels if there were an authorization, but only for "steps" to fund the two agencies at a higher level, there were to be further difficulties.

The authorization drama continued. A key meeting of the conference was held on October 31, the same day as the Pell-Hollings confrontation over the need for such a bill. Perhaps it was not accidental that both events occurred on Halloween. In any event, the conferees began edging toward the obvious compromise: no consideration of the House-passed foreign assistance authorization in this bill, with the Senate in turn dropping its insistence on its "nongermane" amendments. Once this threshold was crossed, the shared interests of the two committees in producing a final bill began to weigh heavily. Finally, agreement was reached and a conference report on H.R. 1487 was filed on November 9. Interestingly, it was not signed by Helms, although Richard Lugar and Nancy Kassebaum, the other Senate minority conferees, did so. The bill passed both houses routinely, in the House on November 15 and in the Senate on November 16.

But there was at least one remaining trouble spot.[35] In spite of discussions throughout the fall, no agreement had been reached about the Moynihan amendment on "leveraging"; that is to say, the use of third-party or third-country funds for purposes for which U.S. assistance was prohibited. The

---

34. For the text of the revised language and final passage, see *Congressional Record* 135 (November 7, 1989): H8036; for the Senate repassage, see *Congressional Record* 135 (November 8, 1989): S15255–57. The theory was that if an authorization bill were passed, a legislative vehicle could be found to repeal sec. 614.

35. Debates on the conference report may be found, for the House, in *Congressional Record* 135 (November 15, 1989): H8698–H8703 and, for the Senate, in the November 16 *Congressional Record*, pp. S15811–26.

conference had adopted a substitute to the Senate version (sec. 109) intended to meet administration constitutional concerns, but it was not enough. On November 21, President Bush vetoed H.R. 1487. The House promptly repassed the bill minus the offending section, as H.R. 3792, with Fascell noting that it was no longer needed, since it was included (in different form) in the Foreign Operations appropriations bill.[36]

Late that same evening, Majority Leader George Mitchell attempted to bring H.R. 3792 up under unanimous consent. Without such an agreement, the Senate could not complete its work on adjournment night. There was no time for a filibuster. Hollings placed a hold on the bill. Mitchell tried again, and Hollings again objected. He made his terms for allowing consideration to take place very clear: the authorizers must agree to a repeal of the requirement for authorization before appropriations could be expended! In other words, they could have their authorization bill only if they gave up the requirement that there *had* to be an authorization bill. Negotiations continued to no avail until the Senate adjourned sine die some hours later. There would be no authorization passed in 1989, and State and USIA would operate on low "section 614" funding levels until this was fixed.[37]

During the long congressional recess until late January 1990, State worked hard to find a way out of the dilemma, which would first require passage of the authorization bill and then restoration of full funding by repeal of section 614 of the appropriations bill. Both eventually occurred. The cost, however, was delay and uncertainty that disrupted operating programs, caused confusion for the 1990 budget summit, and complicated passage of the following year's (FY 1991) CJS appropriations.

The authorization "fix" came first, and was much simpler. Pell and Hollings, having looked over the brink, backed away. Hollings withdrew his opposition to the bill, and Pell agreed to remove section 301, which ironically would have legislated a new requirement for authorization prior to appropriation for the Board for International Broadcasting (also authorized in this bill and appropriated for in the CJS bill). The final vote was 98–0, after desultory debate. Moynihan promised to revisit the "leveraging" issue

---

36. Fascell's comments are in the *Congressional Record* 135 (November 21, 1989): H9294.

37. For the Senate dialogue between Mitchell and Hollings, and Hollings's explanation of why he objected, see *Congressional Record* 135 (November 21, 1989): S16559–66. It was unclear whether Moynihan, whose amendment had been "stripped" in order to make H.R. 3792 acceptable to the president, would have objected if Hollings had not. For a short but accurate summary of the final days of consideration of the State bill, see "State Department Bill Fails," *CQ Weekly Report* 47 (November 25, 1989): 3261.

and raised another point, concerning a provision to make permanent a modification to the McCarran-Walter Act (see Chapter 6).[38] President Bush signed this troubled bill into law on February 16, 1990, but not without putting Congress on notice that he regarded at least nine provisions as constitutionally dubious, in that they interfered with his right to conduct foreign policy, and interestingly reserving the right to interpret or ignore those provisions as he saw fit.[39]

Fixing section 614 was another matter. The first problem arose when the Senate Budget Committee questioned whether there was room under the budget resolution to "restore" some $163 million (the difference between the CR level and the amount originally appropriated) to State's operating budget.[40] The appropriators, disturbed at the possible damage, argued that section 614's restrictions were on expenditures rather than appropriations, and that room had deliberately been left under the total expenditure (outlay) ceiling for removing those restrictions if an authorization were passed. The budget committees asserted that while this might have been true at the time of passage, subsequent congressional action to provide emergency relief for victims of Hurricane Hugo (e.g., in South Carolina, Hollings's state) and other purposes had used up all available "headroom."

Thus, when Representative Neal Smith made the first attempt to repeal 614 on March 22, Representative Bill Frenzel, the ranking minority member of the House Budget Committee, objected to his bringing up H.J. Res. 471, the vehicle for repeal, on the consent calendar. His reasoning was that the appropriators collectively had already breached the allocation level in the FY 1990 budget resolution, owing to the disaster relief legislation passed at the end of the previous session. Frenzel's objection was sustained and Smith's motion failed, since it required unanimous consent.[41]

Five days later, on March 27, 1990, Smith tried again, this time under

38. See *Congressional Record* 136 (January 29 and January 30, 1990): S467–74 and S543–47 for the final Senate debate, as well as *CQ Weekly Report* 48 (February 3, 1990): 346.

39. See John Felton, "Bush Throws Down the Gauntlet on Provisions He Opposes: Reserving the Right to Ignore Parts of Routine Measure, President Ups Ante in Battle over Prerogatives," *CQ Weekly Report* 48 (February 24, 1990): 603–4, for the specific causes of complaint.

40. The exact amount was a matter of some contention, owing to different opinions of how to interpret sec. 614. Several legal opinions were written in the executive branch, and there were several exchanges of correspondence between the CJS appropriators and State. One of State's legislative counsels eventually prepared an opinion that raised the available levels above what others, including the appropriators and the Treasury, initially felt they should be; although the issue was not resolved until February 1990, her views guided the process.

41. The House floor debate may be founded in *Congressional Record* 136 (March 22, 1990): H1020–22.

suspension of the rules, requiring a two-thirds vote for passage. The arguments were the same, and so was the outcome, which featured some vote switching, apparently by those who did not want to be on record as assisting the State Department. The vote was 276–149, six votes short of the needed majority.[42]

After two House defeats, those still interested in fixing section 614, in particular Neal Smith, decided that the next move must be made in the Senate. Ultimately it was concluded that the vehicle should be the Dire Emergency Supplemental for FY 1990 (H.R. 4404), rather than a freestanding bill.[43] On April 26, 1990, Hollings offered the required amendment, and it was adopted without controversy. In the end, the conference report was accepted in both chambers without further problems.[44]

Unfortunately, half a year had been lost, and there were complications for State throughout the rest of FY 1990. Disaster had been avoided, but once again there was a clear demonstration of the difficulties of providing rational foreign affairs budgeting, with the usual executive–legislative problems being compounded by a three-way congressional battle among the budget, authorization, and appropriations committees. In particular, the relevance of the authorizing committees had to be questioned,[45] a theme that was to receive major attention during the 1993 deliberations of the Joint Committee on the Organization of Congress, considered in Chapter 9 below.

42. For the House debate, see *Congressional Record* 136 (March 27, 1990): H1133–37; recorded vote at H1140. The point about not "assisting the State Department" is derived from conversations with House staffers at the time.

43. This maneuver provided cover for the State and USIA provisions, since other items in the supplemental were popular.

44. Senate debate on the correction is to be found in *Congressional Record* 136 (April 26, 1990): 55107–15. The report was adopted in both houses on May 24 and was signed the next day.

45. See, for example, John Felton, "Authorizer Sees Relevance Slip," *CQ Weekly Report* 48 (June 2, 1990): 1737, for the comments of HFAC Chairman Dante B. Fascell on his determination to pass a foreign assistance authorization bill in 1990 even though the requirement for one had been waived in the Foreign Operations Appropriations Act. Fascell said that the need for authorization panel action "has been less and less and less. It [the tendency to waive authorization requirements] has made our work almost irrelevant." As Felton noted, "The principal purpose of even considering the authorization bill is to assert the jurisdictional authority of the two committees that write such legislation: House Foreign Affairs and Senate Foreign Relations." A later example underscores the point: "Mitch McConnell, the new chairman of the powerful Senate subcommittee responsible for foreign aid, abandoned the Foreign Relations Committee for the Appropriations Committee two years ago. 'The difference between us and them is that we're shooting with real bullets,' he explained. 'We spend the real money.' " Elaine Sciolino, "Global Concerns? Not in Congress," *New York Times*, January 15, 1995.

## Authorization and Appropriations, 1991 and Later

With these events fresh in mind, neither the State legislative team nor their Hill counterparts were eager to repeat earlier miscues. In the spring of 1991, less than a year after the section 614 fix was finally accomplished, State submitted a draft authorization bill for FY 1992–93 containing many revisions and extensions of administrative authorities, including some that were targeted at repealing past congressional attempts to "micromanage" (from an executive branch point of view) administrative operations.[46] Changes on the Hill boded some new possibilities. On the House side, Representative Howard Berman replaced Mervin Dymally as chairman of the House International Operations Subcommittee (of HFAC), when Dymally moved on to chair the Africa subcommittee. Berman, a mainline liberal Democrat, clearly would have more latitude to develop a bill than his predecessor, while Olympia Snowe of Maine, the ranking member, continued her active involvement and skepticism regarding specific issues, most notably those relating to the Moscow embassy. In the Senate, a revolt of staff and some members led to greater emphasis on subcommittees, accepted by Chairman Pell but resisted by the ranking minority member Helms.[47] In the end, the Terrorism, Narcotics, and International Operations Subcommittee was revived, chaired by John Kerry (D–Mass.) with Hank Brown (R–Colo.), just from the House, as ranking member. For the first time in years, the Foreign Relations Authorization Bill was considered initially at the subcommittee not the full committee level. Kerry and Brown took this opportunity seriously. There was more interaction than usual between the administration and members and staff in crafting the bill.

The primary issue during 1991 was what should be done about the increasingly embarrassing Moscow embassy project. State at first abandoned its advocacy for tearing down the bugged building, promoting instead the construction of secure space on top of the existing building; the intransigence of Snowe and Hollings, however, doomed this alternative plan to failure, for the moment. The authorization bill contained a provision leaving the decision to the president, albeit with a requirement for reports intended to keep Congress as an active player. The appropriators were initially in a

46. See H.R. 1435 and S. 579, introduced by request as a courtesy by the respective committee chairmen (Fascell and Pell), for the text of the administration's proposal (prepared by State and USIA, as cleared by OMB).

47. See Carroll J. Doherty, "Foreign Relations: Subcommittee Plan Created to Revive Senate Panel," *CQ Weekly Report* 49 (February 2, 1991): 306.

deadlock, since Neal Smith was as adamantly opposed to tearing down a "perfectly good building" as Hollings was insistent on it. But the arrival of a new under secretary for management at State, John F. W. Rogers, and a highly political new ambassador to the USSR, Robert Strauss, led to yet another review, culminating in yet another plan: build a new, secure building next to the bugged one and leave until later the decision about what should be done with the latter. Given the clear view by most in Congress that it was time to dispose of this issue, Hollings and Smith, after heavy lobbying, agreed to this plan, and the CJS conference report funded it. Only Snowe remained opposed. She managed, in House floor action on the CJS conference report, to strike language designating this specific option as the only one that could be funded, but at the same time she was unable to prohibit its inclusion. Thus, while the issue had not been fully resolved, it had at least been finessed with respect to these two bills.

Several foreign policy issues remained on the authorization bill, especially once it became clear that the foreign assistance bill, as always, was in serious trouble. Conference negotiations on many of them resulted in provisions that were at least minimally acceptable to the administration.

A few issues still threatened the success of the two bills. One, showing how appropriations and authorizations can interrelate, had to do with a proposal by Senator Frank Lautenberg (D–N.J.), attached in slightly different form to both bills, which (1) prohibited the issuance of "Israel only" second passports and (2) prohibited multiple passports for U.S. officials if the purpose were to acquiesce in or comply with the Arab League policy of banning admittance to travelers whose travel documents showed that they had been or were going to Israel. Since neither bill could, realistically, be vetoed, the signing statements for both indicated that the secretary of state would be directed not to implement them if they interfered with the president's constitutional responsibilities for the conduct of diplomatic relations.[48] Other provisions drew similar comments. Nevertheless, there was no serious consideration given to vetoing either bill, and both were signed on October 28, 1991.

Along the way, there were continuing efforts by the authorization committees to increase their relevance. Berman and Snowe decided early on— even though the BEA ceilings applied to appropriated amounts and not to

---

48. Presidential signing statements for P.L. 102-138 and P.L. 102-140, contained in George Bush, *The Public Papers of the Presidents of the United States*, 1991, bk. 2 (Washington, D.C.: GPO, 1992), pp. 144–46 and 348–49, respectively.

those authorized—to have their bill scored by the CEO as if it were an appropriations bill and to ensure that the totals authorized in the bill (or in the existing permanent authorization that would be used) could not exceed the president's request levels, which were within the BEA ceilings. The administration could hardly have complained about this procedure, given Darman's earlier insistence on following the letter of the BEA. However, as always, a number of congressional initiatives were included in the House bill, and this meant that proposed amounts for S&E and foreign buildings, already at minimal levels, were in part diverted to these new purposes, leaving major shortfalls.

For similar reasons, the leadership of HFAC (for USIA) and of the SFRC (for both State and USIA) initially thought seriously about not authorizing any amounts for the second year of the two-year bills, in order to allow themselves to revisit funding for those agencies the next year and thus remain players in the game. Although they finally decided to authorize appropriations for FY 1993 as well as for FY 1992, they did so at low levels, leading to problems of insufficient authorization in some categories. In earlier years this problem had not arisen, because the authorizers could simply authorize either "such amounts as may be necessary" or, if they included figures, make them high enough to ensure coverage of any amounts likely to be appropriated. But under the BEA their felt need to be players did not permit such latitude.

## Conflict Resolution Is Essential

Taken together, the three State authorization bills enacted between December 1987 and October 1991, and the six CJS appropriations bills accompanying them (along with more selective examples from the foreign assistance side), show a pattern of ultimately finding ways to dampen potential conflict between the branches, notwithstanding harsh feelings at many points, whenever a failure of the legislative process became a real possibility. In 1987 only the most offensive portions of the authorization bill were waived, not only to avoid a veto but also to preserve some role for the authorizers. In 1989, in fact, there was a veto over the Moynihan "leveraging" provision that could not be accommodated by a waiver, given the battle between Hollings and Pell, but accommodation nonetheless eventually occurred. In 1991, with none of the parties even considering a waiver of the requirement for authorization, the administration resorted to a comprehensive presidential signing statement, enumerating objectionable provisions that would be taken as advisory or not implemented.[49] Whether this approach—which in some respect amounts to the unilateral assertion of a line-item veto, albeit on legislative provisions rather than on funding ones, the usual context— can succeed depends on whether Congress chooses to challenge this action and whether the courts accept jurisdiction or instead invoke the "political issue" doctrine and decline to rule. Nevertheless, the increasing use of signing statements to signal that the president will not implement a statute he believes to be unconstitutional raises major constitutional issues itself.[50]

In 1993, the legislative history of the FY 1994–95 Foreign Relations Authorization Act demonstrated many of the same trends discussed above, even though divided government no longer prevailed. Once again, an impasse over peripheral foreign policy issues stalled final passage as in 1989, this time primarily because of a dispute over the future of international broadcasting (see Chapter 7)—and the act passed only in April 1994. And as in earlier bills, there were several examples of attempts to use the requirement for authorization to influence foreign policy, some of which are evident in the discussion of post-Chadha congressional "control devices" in the next chapter.

As Chapter 8 will amply illustrate, the struggle in 1995 and early 1996 over the FY 1996–97 authorization bill was strongly demonstrative of increasing interbranch confrontation, abetted by the return of divided government and an intensely partisan atmosphere. Congress searched for even more creative means to exercise its influence, especially in the area of withholding funding in order to force desired actions. In the end, Congress overreached, producing no authorization at all.

Perhaps the larger point is that, divided government or not, the institutional imperatives of the two branches, especially in a time of change and uncertainty, will lead to confrontation (if not impasse) whichever party is in control. For Congress to remain relevant, it must be dampened.

## Incentives for Congressional Fragmentation

The events described in this chapter illustrate one effect of fragmentation in foreign affairs funding, both fragmentation between kinds of committees

49. See the signing statement for P.L. 102-138 (note 48 above).
50. See Michael Glennon, *Constitutional Diplomacy* (Princeton: Princeton University Press, 1990), for a strong constitutional argument that the president must faithfully execute the laws once enacted, even if he disagrees with them.

(budget, appropriations, authorizing) and fragmentation within the appropriations arena. One issue, then, is whether congressional interests would be best served by a serious attempt to consolidate activities in a way that would allow Congress to develop a coherent, across-the-board Function 150 international affairs budget. There is a persuasive argument, perhaps counterintuitive, that those interests would not be well served, at least by traditional measures. Simply put, the more fragmentation there is, then the larger the number of committees and subcommittees and the more chairmanships will be available. This is nothing new. One commentator writing in 1958 argued that

> no one committee of the House of Representatives can coordinate more than a fraction of the international business coming before the lower chamber. Because of the critical importance of money, the Committee on Appropriations has the opportunity to survey the broadest range of policy. . . . [T]he money committee has not exploited this opportunity.[51]

Ranging more broadly, John Gilmour reached essentially the same conclusion concerning contemporary realities:

> Broad legislation that overlaps several committees' jurisdictions or policies whose success depends on simultaneous, coordinated actions by multiple committees do not move well through the fragmented structures of Congress.[52]

Gilmour's argument, in fact, is that the new budget process was necessary precisely because of a need for overarching devices to subdue the parochialism of the existing congressional structures. If so, the results have hardly been spectacular to date. Fragmentation persists.

One must ask whether it is in the interest of the Congress to consider a structure that enforces discipline and a joint look at Function 150. In candor, it is not. For such a structure would undermine independent action. The only place where Congress now considers 150 as a whole is in the budget resolution/summit process, and then largely as an afterthought. One must conclude that Congress is likely to change its approach only if the executive makes changes that force it to do so.

---

51. Carroll, *The House of Representatives and Foreign Affairs*, p. 211.
52. Gilmour, *Reconcilable Differences?* p. 100.

In this and the previous chapter, we have seen a complicated and fragmented interaction between the executive and legislative branches on budgeting for international affairs. Examples have already been provided to show what happens when the Congress moves actively to use the power of the purse to influence or even to determine policy outcomes, instead of those outcomes being consequences of choices made for budget reasons. Now it is time to address more directly what a creative Congress can do when it turns its mind to the task.

CHAPTER SIX

# CONGRESSIONAL ACTIVISM

## Presidential Power vs. the Power of the Purse

As we have seen, the different perspectives of the executive and the Congress on mainstream budget issues, as well as divisions among committees and between the houses, can make for highly political resource-allocation outcomes with little evidence of prioritizing logic. But this is only the beginning of the uneasy relationship between resources and foreign policy.

Of equal importance is the increasing use by Congress of *its* constitutional powers beyond purely budgetary ones to influence executive-branch foreign policy decisions and actions themselves. As James Lindsay has perceptively written, "The Congress . . . uses the appropriations power to give teeth to its other constitutional powers on foreign policy."[1] There have been sporadic periods of congressional assertiveness throughout U.S. history, but there has been a more consistent push in this direction roughly since the time when the Gulf of Tonkin Resolution generated second thoughts in Congress not long after it was passed in 1965.[2] As recently as October 1993, members of

1. Lindsay, *Congress and the Politics of U.S. Foreign Policy*, p. 86.
2. The Johnson administration had asserted that on August 2 and 4, 1964, American ships conducting covert operations in the Gulf of Tonkin were attacked by North Vietnamese torpedo boats. Arguing self-defense, the president ordered the first bombings of the Vietnam War on North Vietnam. He then asked Congress to support his actions, support that was later construed as a congressional agreement to expand the war. Subsequently, critics alleged that the facts were not as presented, in particular that the second attack did not occur. This incident may fairly be said to have initiated the period of congressional assertiveness which is the larger topic of the present book. Among other things, "Tonkin Gulf" was a prime mover for passage, in 1973, of the contentious War Powers Resolution. The Tonkin Gulf Resolution was H.J. Res. 1145, 78 Stat. 384, 88th Cong., 2d sess., August 10, 1964; it was repealed by P.L. 91-672, January 2, 1971. The War Powers Resolution was P.L. 93-148. See Harold Hongju Koh, *The*

President Clinton's own party threatened to strengthen the 1973 War Powers Resolution over the issue of withdrawing U.S. troops from Somalia, and although a major confrontation did not result, when all was said and done the president had to agree to a March 31, 1994, withdrawal date.[3] Predictably, congressional aggressiveness leads to forceful and sometimes intemperate executive branch reactions.[4] Such fractiousness became a virtual certainty after 1995, of course, with the Republican takeover of both the House and the Senate. The unsuccessful attempt led by Representative Henry Hyde (R–Ill.) to repeal the War Powers Resolution that year should not be read as a backing off in any sense from the defense of congressional prerogatives. Rather, it was an admission that War Powers had proved by all accounts ineffectual. Even so, a bipartisan group managed to defeat the effort by a 217–201 vote, declining to accept the Republican leadership's argument that "Congress should allow a president to act as commander-in-chief and use its power to withhold funding to block military missions overseas."[5] Many Republicans, and some Democrats, were not eager to appear to be strengthening the hand of President Clinton.

---

*National Security Constitution: Sharing Power After the Iran-Contra Affair* (New Haven: Yale University Press, 1990), pp. 38–40. In a fascinating reprise thirty-one years later, General Vo Nguyen Giap, the North Vietnamese commander in 1964, affirmed that the August 2 attack had occurred, but not the one on August 4. This information came in reply to a question from former Defense Secretary Robert McNamara at a conference in Hanoi. Tim Larimer, "McNamara and Giap Revisit Gulf of Tonkin," *International Herald Tribune* (New York Times Service), November 10, 1995.

3. See Adam Clymer, "Democrats Study Amending War Powers Act," *New York Times*, October 24, 1993.

4. Conscious efforts have sometimes been made to right the balance when those in the executive branch believe it has tipped too far. For one recent episode, see Chuck Alston, "Separation of Powers: Bush Crusades on Many Fronts to Retake President's Turf," *CQ Weekly Report* 48 (February 3, 1990): 291–95.

5. See Kenneth J. Cooper and Dan Morgan, "House Declines to Repeal War Powers Resolution: Vote on 1973 Act Constraining Presidential Action Marks a Rare Defeat for Gingrich," *Washington Post*, June 8, 1995. Traditionally, Republican presidents had been especially vocal against War Powers (although every president since its passage had argued its unconstitutionality at one point or another), and the Republican minority in Congress had supported its presidents. Democrats, on the other hand, had passed War Powers and continued to support it. Thus the support for the repeal by Speaker Gingrich and the opposition by Representative Lee Hamilton, the ranking minority member and former HFAC chairman, represented a continuation of the past pattern, even though the roles of the two parties were now reversed. Bill Clinton, fearing correctly that the Republicans did not have the votes to succeed, decided at the last minute to withhold a letter of support for the repeal. Another useful commentary, written six months later during the battle over whether or not to commit troops to Bosnia, is Gabriel Kahn, "Even Without Repealing War Powers, House Defines New Role for Hill in Foreign Policy," *Roll Call*, November 2, 1995.

Not every foreign policy action presents the opportunity for Congress to use its power of the purse as policy leverage, and that is one reason why some members of both parties prefer to leave legislation such as the War Powers Resolution on the books—legislation, they argue, that draws on constitutional power other than that of the purse. But when it takes money to carry out a policy, then the seemingly pure and exclusive authority of the president in Article II, sections 2 and 3, of the Constitution can run squarely against the Congress's exclusive rights to raise revenues and appropriate funds, in Article I, sections 7–9. While absolutists on each side of the argument argue for the exclusivity of their position,[6] those less engaged are likely to recognize that there are constitutional limits on each side,[7] and to see the situation as a classic example of Neustadt's famous "separate institutions sharing powers."[8] In this chapter, some recent examples of congressional foreign policy activism are examined, along with a catalog of techniques the Congress uses to exert its influence.

## Resources Provide Leverage: Foreign Aid Conflicts

The largest share of expenditures by the United States on foreign affairs, as noted in Chapter 1, is on foreign assistance. Only here are there programmatic activities that in any way approach those in the domestic or defense

6. White House Counsel Boyden Gray, at least in the early years of the Bush administration, held a "separation of powers" meeting each Thursday morning with his associates and with lawyers from several agencies. The purpose of these meetings was apparently to hold the line against possible congressional incursions into presidential territory and, according to some participants, to find issues on which the Congress could be challenged. Justice Department letters stating the administration position on numerous pieces of pending foreign affairs legislation during this period invariably made lengthy and shrill arguments about the constitutional flaws and dangers such legislation contained. A typical formulation was that "section X is impermissibly intrusive" into the president's powers and would be the cause of a veto or, if passed, would be ignored. As with the boy who cried wolf, after a number of these letters were received, the Hill seemed to ignore them; sometimes they went unread by the members or even by their staff.

7. See, for example, Louis Fisher, "The Power of the Purse," chap. 7 in *Constitutional Conflicts Between Congress and the President*, 3d rev. ed. (Lawrence: University Press of Kansas, 1991), which recognizes the limits on both branches, even from the perspective of an advocate of congressional preeminence. For an updated and powerful treatment of another major constitutional issue, also see Fisher's *Presidential War Power* (Lawrence: University Press of Kansas, 1995).

8. Neustadt, *Presidential Power*, p. 101.

arenas in size. Moreover, foreign aid, especially in the military area, has been highly visible and an instrument either of support for existing regimes or for rebel groups attempting to dislodge them. Thus, much of the congressional activity directed to influencing policy has occurred here. At times, as in 1995, the entire program has come under challenge, threatened either by isolationist-leaning members who want to reduce U.S. involvement abroad or by others who believe scarce resources should be spent on domestic problems. More often, though, the controversy has surfaced in specific situations, when the president and the congressional majority end up on opposite sides. Such episodes can put the respective powers and interests of the two branches in the clearest light. Bosnia is just the latest example. But the case of the Contras in Nicaragua and (in certain respects) the mirror-image situation in El Salvador are perhaps the most revealing, because of the numerous twists and turns, the length of time involved, and the side issues.

## Contra Aid

Perhaps no single recent foreign affairs episode illuminates so many complexities as the nine-year struggle over assistance to the U.S.-supported rightist Contra rebels in Nicaragua, locked in bloody conflict with the leftist Sandinista government of Daniel Ortega. Partisan politics, deeply held ideological concerns (primarily over the degree to which the governing Sandinistas were an extension of Havana/Moscow), executive–legislative and intralegislative divergences, parliamentary maneuvering and, above all, explicit attempts by opposing camps to apply resources directly in support of favored policies, regimes, and opposition groups all played a part. This situation of course was complicated by other developments in Central America, in particular the "reverse" situation in El Salvador, where the rebels were on the left, supported by the Sandinistas, and the government was on the right. A detailed survey would consume volumes, so my goal here is to highlight some of these important themes in the narrower budgetary context of this study.

Nicaragua was the centerpiece of Democratic–Republican disagreements over Central American policy throughout the Reagan administration. The Sandinistas, beginning as rebels, finally displaced the right-wing, oppressive Somoza regime in 1979. From the very beginning the American right believed that the Sandinistas were not an indigenous social-reform government but were instead part of a Cuban design to install communist governments throughout the hemisphere. The liberals, mostly Democrats who had assisted the Sandinistas during the Carter administration, were slower to accept this possibility, and many never did.

By late 1981, the Reagan administration concluded that assistance to the Contras was necessary—if not to bring the Sandinistas down, then at least to apply pressure for democratic reforms. Having concluded that Congress would be reluctant to go along, and thinking perhaps that open assistance to the Contras would be counterproductive, the device chosen was $19 million of covert aid funneled through the CIA. President Reagan approved this plan in November of that year.[9] In 1982, an additional $29 million, still covert but agreed to by Congress, was included in the Intelligence Authorization Act, along with the first of the famous Boland amendments, named for their sponsor, Representative Edward Boland (D–Mass.). This amendment prohibited covert actions to overthrow the Sandinistas and earmarked the funding to be used solely for stopping arms shipments from Nicaragua to leftist guerrillas in El Salvador.[10]

In 1983 (for FY 1984), Congress for the first time approved Contra aid openly, providing up to $24 million for military assistance. This occurred only after several fits and starts, setting what was to become a familiar pattern. First the House passed a bill approving $80 million to be used by friendly Central American nations to interdict arms to the guerrillas, but the Senate Intelligence Committee would not even take up the bill. The House responded by enacting virtually the same $80 million provision in the FY 1984 Intelligence Authorization Bill. The Senate, still determined to provide direct Contra aid, passed an intelligence authorization that contained more than $28 million of the $35 million requested by the president. There was also action on the defense appropriations front (where intelligence appropriations are considered). The House banned further aid, while the Senate allowed $29 million to $50 million. The conference compromise was the capped $24 million cited above.

This bruising battle continued into 1984, beginning with a presidential request in March for a supplemental $21 million. The Senate supported the provision, voting 30–61 against deleting it. The House voted against including it by a substantial margin (177–241). On June 18, the Senate tried

9. See "Chronology of Hill–Reagan Tug of War . . . ," *CQ Weekly Report* 46 (March 26, 1988): 806–7 for a useful short summary of these complicated events. An equally useful 1989 *CQ Almanac* chronology is cited subsequently (note 16 below).

10. A helpful compilation of the unclassified Boland amendments is contained in *Congressional Record* 133 (June 15, 1987): 16075–81. A short summary can be found in *CQ Almanac* 43 (1987): 72.

again, first voting for additional aid, 58–38, but then reversing itself a week later by an 88–1 vote, after key Intelligence Committee Democrats announced they were ending their support. Obviously, this was a calculated reversal by the majority in the Senate that still supported Contra aid, as it became clear that further direct aid could not pass at that time. Of course, the Senate was controlled by the Republicans from 1981 to 1986, while the House was in Democratic hands, so the repeated divergences between the two houses were at least as much partisan as institutional.

Two further attempts later in 1984 were also unsuccessful. First, in August, the Senate approved and the House rejected $28 million in the Intelligence Authorization Act for FY 1985; when the Senate attempted once again to provide aid, in October, on the Continuing Resolution for FY 1985, the House again prevailed and all aid was banned. There was, however, a promise that the president would get another vote on $14 million (split the difference, a traditional way of resolving conflict between the two houses) in early 1985, after the election. As we now know, this failure by the administration to convince Congress to provide direct government support for the Contras led to some creative but ill-conceived, and often illegal, alternatives, both private and governmental. Iran-Contra may date to this extended hiatus in legal Contra assistance.

By the spring of 1985, though, there were new developments. In April, the Senate passed the promised $14 million on its version of a supplemental appropriations bill, but by a narrower margin than usual and only after a Reagan promise that it would be used only for nonmilitary purposes. Later that month, the House rejected this bid. However, after Nicaraguan President Daniel Ortega visited Moscow, the House reversed itself and agreed to $27 million in nonmilitary aid—after defeating both a Boland amendment banning aid indefinitely and an amendment by Richard Gephardt proposing a delay rather than a prohibition. Ortega's ill-timed trip brought the House along, at least for nonmilitary aid. In the end, with the limits of the possible clarified, the Senate accepted the $27 million House package, after first trying for $38 million in the conference on the Supplemental Appropriations Bill (P.L. 99-88).

This was a classic example of "testing the waters" to see the most or least that a majority will accept. Repeated House victories demonstrate another feature of such battles: if one house makes it clear that it would rather have no bill if it cannot prevail, it will often win, so long as the other house is less intransigent and is willing to accept half a loaf. For much of the Contra battle, the House, with its tighter rules and in firm Democratic control, could afford to be less compromising.

In 1986, the conflict became more intense, and the parliamentary maneuvering more complex. Prohibitions, filibusters, cloture votes, discharge petitions, and tabling resolutions all came into play. The upshot, however, reflecting a changing assessment of the Sandinista threat, was that for FY 1987 Congress provided the $100 million (of which $70 million was for direct military purposes) requested by the president in February. The final tactical maneuver was to attach this provision, which had started out in the Senate version of the Military Construction Appropriations Bill, to the Omnibus Appropriations Act (P.L. 99-591) in the closing hours of the session, where it was protected. (The entire package had to be voted "up or down," leaving the House little choice but to accept.) House opponents of military aid for the Contras had been outmaneuvered by the Senate this time. Even in the wake of initial disclosures about Iran-Contra, House efforts to place a six-month moratorium on $40 million of this aid were blocked by the Senate.[11]

Yet by 1987 (for FY 1988), enthusiasm had cooled, and once again opponents of military assistance, largely House Democrats, gained the upper hand. In an era of hopes produced by the Oscar Arias peace plan, distaste occasioned by Iran-Contra, and mounting evidence of Contra ineptness, as well as unanswered questions about the means used to support the Contras, levels of support were sharply reduced. In a series of continuing resolutions, $25.8 million was provided, but under very restrictive conditions linked to peace talks between the two Nicaraguan factions.

The struggle continued. In 1988, this general pattern persisted, ending with limits allowing only "nonlethal" assistance in the amount of $27.14 million (part of a total package of some $48 million), although there were attempts by conservative Republicans to resume military aid. If one is interested in process and tactics, however, much more was involved. This year was especially dramatic and contentious. In particular, the narrow (219–211) February 3, 1988, House defeat of President Reagan's request for $36.25 million in new Contra aid (including $3.6 million of military aid but with hidden costs bringing the total to some $60 million) was seen by some as "one of the most important congressional rebuffs ever to a president's

11. Since both houses had to veto the assistance, problems associated with a one-house veto, declared unconstitutional by the *Chadha* decision (see below), were avoided.

foreign policy."[12] A subsequent House Democratic attempt to pass humanitarian aid for the Contras was killed by a coalition of Democrats and some Republicans (who wanted a vote on their own plan), and the resulting impasse—each side saying the next move was up to the other—suggested no action was likely. *Congressional Quarterly* saw this turn of events as leaving "President Reagan's most cherished foreign policy in confusion and subject to the most bitter partisan rhetoric ever on the contra issue."[13]

This impasse might have been the best outcome, although the results were long in coming. For on March 23, the Nicaraguan Resistance Front (the Contra alliance) and the Nicaraguan government reached agreement for a sixty-day cease-fire. On the 25th, the *Washington Post* lead on this event ("Aid Cutoff Cited as a Key to Accord: Managua and Contras, Achieving Truce, Concur on Role of Congress") asserted that the decision of Congress not to provide additional military aid was a key factor according to both sides. The Contras had concluded there was no political will in the United States to continue the war, so they were willing to try to end the killing and test the good faith of the Sandinistas, while the latter said that the cutoff of funds to their opponents was a sine qua non of the agreement and had allowed them to be more flexible concerning political freedoms.[14] Someone, probably Winston Churchill, once said that 90 percent of the time in diplomacy the right choice was to do nothing; the mark of genius was knowing when the 10 percent was called for. There was no genius here, but perhaps there was some serendipity.

The prediction in one article's title—that "Hill Leaders Expect Prompt Passage of Contra Assistance"[15] for humanitarian purposes, owing to the cease-fire agreement—proved to be too sanguine. Later attempts for a Contra package were thwarted either by a temporary collapse of the peace process, as in July, or by administration balking. Eventually, $27.14 million in nonmilitary aid to the Contras and associated aid to Nicaragua for other purposes was attached to the Defense Appropriations Bill, with a requirement that spending be completed by March 31, 1989. The bill was signed

12. See "Foreign Policy," *CQ Almanac* 44 (1988): 458.

13. John Felton and Janet Hook, "House Defeat Clouds Outlook for Contra Aid," *CQ Weekly Report* 46 (March 5, 1988): 555.

14. Julia Preston in the *Washington Post*, March 25, 1988. A *Washington Post* editorial on the same day applauded the move, while warning of further troubles to come. Charles Krauthammer, however, in an op-ed column, came to a different conclusion: "The Contras Surrender: The Democrats Get Their Way."

15. Bill McAllister and Don Phillips in the *Washington Post*, March 25, 1988.

into law at the end of September.[16] One last attempt to release military aid died when the White House failed to provide support, perhaps to avoid reviving Nicaragua, Contras, Iran-Contra, and all the associated baggage just before the imminent presidential election.

Early in 1989, the new Bush administration largely defused the Nicaragua issue, ending most of the furor over whether military aid or force should be used to overthrow the Sandinistas. Secretary of State Baker negotiated an agreement with the Hill early in the term: to use diplomacy, keep the Contras intact, and continue to provide "nonlethal," humanitarian aid of almost $50 million,[17] with additional amounts for civilian war victims and for USAID support functions and $9 million to support free elections.[18] However, this aid was to continue only until the Nicaraguan elections scheduled for February 25, 1990.

The Contra period ended for all practical purposes with the opposition leader Violeta Chamorro's unexpected victory over Daniel Ortega in those elections. This event was followed by an immediate request from President Bush for $300 million in U.S. assistance for *Nicaragua* (no longer for the Contras), virtually all of it for economic purposes. The funds were provided in the infamous Dire Emergency Supplemental, FY 1990 (P.L. 101-302) on May 25, 1990.[19] An additional $218 million was requested and appropriated for FY 1991, as was $75 million for FY 1992.[20]

Still, the issues that had so long roiled Congress bubbled up from time to time. In June 1992, for example, the Bush administration suspended $104 million in aid to Nicaragua at the behest of Senator Jesse Helms, the most implacable foe of the Sandinistas, on the grounds that Chamorro had turned over the military and police to the Sandinista Front, that there had been serious human rights abuses, and that American property which had been expropriated by the Sandinistas was not being returned. Some $54 million of this amount was released in December 1992 by the administration, citing improvements; and the remaining $50 million was released on April 2, 1993, by the incoming Clinton administration, after a March visit by Cha-

---

16. See *CQ Almanac* 45 (1989): 470–504 for an exhaustive review of the entire history of Contra funding in Congress; details for FY 1989 in this paragraph may be found on p. 498.

17. *CQ Weekly Report* 47 (December 9, 1989): 3341.

18. *CQ Almanac* 46 (1990): 770.

19. This was the same legislation that "fixed" sec. 614 of the FY 1990 CJS Appropriations Act, discussed above.

20. U.S. Agency for International Development, *U.S. Overseas Loans and Grants and Assistance from International Organizations: July 1, 1945–September 30, 1992*, Doc. CONG-R-0105 (Washington, D.C., 1993), p. 105.

morro's son-in-law (a Nicaraguan minister) assured the new U.S. government that progress was continuing. Anti–foreign aid to the end, Senator Helms denounced this action as a "$50 million foreign aid giveaway . . . an outrageous waste of the American people's money and an insult to them." Part of Helms's unhappiness can be attributed to the failure to take similar steps with respect to frozen military aid to El Salvador, whose government was much more in favor with him.[21]

Several facets of this history deserve emphasis. One cannot help noticing, for example, the heat generated over such modest amounts of money,[22] compared with funding for, say, Greece or Turkey. One might argue that these two cases (see Chapter 7) provide another example of the disconnect commonly found between the importance of a policy and the resources applied. On the other hand, the Contra episode may have produced as direct a linkage between policy goals and efforts to support them financially as can be found. It also shows the tendency to "follow the headlines" that has been decried by congressional members in recent times. Sometimes, too, gamesmanship, committee and intralegislative prerogatives, and (above all) matters of perceived principle add great intensity to the commonly noticed struggles between parties and branches. The episode also shows that bipartisanship is hardly the norm, currently, with respect to how major foreign policy issues are contested. Especially, though, it shows the determination of members of Congress, whether of the president's party or not, to be players in foreign policy and to use the tools they have. We are well past the days of congressional acquiescence, and it is time for the executive to realize it. This is not just dry constitutional law; this is high politics.

## Moynihan and "Leveraging"

As the Contra aid case shows, major policy differences can lead to creativity in devising funding procedures. When, as here, such innovative thinking crosses the limits of what is legitimate and lawful, corrective action is inevitable, especially when constitutional issues are present. In the aftermath of Iran-Contra, there were a variety of efforts to devise legislative restrictions

21. Steven A. Holmes, "Nicaragua to Get Blocked U.S. Aid: Administration Cites Progress on Issues of Concern in Releasing $50 million," *New York Times*, April 3, 1993.

22. According to *Congressional Quarterly*, some $311.7 million in direct aid to the Contras, in all categories, was provided over nine years (FY 1982–FY 1990); plus $40.3 million in non-U.S. government funds, including $3.8 million from the Iran arms sales diversion. *CQ Almanac* 45 (1989): 571 (box), extending the chronology previously cited.

that would make such abuses difficult or impossible. Special attention was given to timely notification of Congress concerning covert action and to limitations on arms sales to countries supporting terrorism.[23] One set of examples is directly relevant here. These were the so-called leveraging amendments that initially appeared during 1989 on both the State Authorization Bill for FY 1990–91 and the Foreign Operations Appropriations Act for FY 1990. The term "leveraging" was used because the appropriations versions of these provisions prohibited using offers of foreign assistance as "leverage" to encourage recipient countries to take actions that the U.S. government was prohibited by law from doing. The authorization versions sponsored by Senator Daniel P. Moynihan had a similar intent, but included broader, more ambiguous prohibitions on seeking third-party help for activities that were unlawful for the executive branch to undertake. Hence the characterization by some that these were simply "obey the law" amendments.[24]

Louis Fisher has made perhaps the most pungent commentary on the congressional view of the need for legislation: "Of the revelations emanating from the Iran-Contra affair, the most startling constitutional claim was the assertion that whenever Congress uses its power of the purse to restrict the President in foreign affairs, the President may pursue his goals by soliciting funds from private citizens and foreign countries."[25] It is worth comparing these two parallel provisions, since the differences between them help to demonstrate inevitable ambiguities in constitutional interpretation. It was a given that the administration strongly preferred no legislation and, if it had to accept it, preferred to have the language drawn as narrowly as possible.[26] Thus the issue was whether there was language the administration could

---

23. Among these were Senator William Cohen's "48 hour" bill requiring notification of Congress forty-eight hours before the executive could act, discussed in *CQ Weekly Report* 46 (October 15, 1988): 2981–82; and the bipartisan Hyde-Berman bill in the House, described in *CQ Weekly Report* 46 (April 23, 1988): 1076–77. See also *CQ Almanac* 45 (1989): 541 for a slightly different summary, including discussion of the proposal for an independent inspector general for the CIA, but excluding discussion of the Cohen proposal.

24. E.g., Senate Majority Leader George Mitchell during debate on the Moynihan provision (*Congressional Record* 135 [July 18, 1989]: 15026). The phrase was often used later by Moynihan.

25. Fisher, *Constitutional Conflicts*, p. 210.

26. For a comprehensive, if very pro-Congress view, see Theodore Draper's massive *A Very Thin Line: The Iran-Contra Affairs* (New York: Hill & Wang, 1991). Chapter 26, "Unfinished Business" (which appeared in virtually identical form as "The Constitution Is in Danger," *New York Review of Books* 37 [March 1, 1990]: 41–44), is directly relevant to this discussion of the "leveraging amendments" and contains Draper's somewhat overwrought interpretation.

reluctantly accept while Congress would think it sufficient. In the case of the appropriations bill, there was; in Moynihan's authorization bill, there was not.

The appropriators started with a straightforward prohibition of the use of foreign aid on behalf of any "military or foreign policy activity which is contrary to United States law," and they specifically barred leveraged solicitation of third countries to take actions that the U.S. government could not legally take. Significant changes were made at the insistence of the White House, but in the end President Bush vetoed the foreign assistance bill on the grounds that while the provision might be constitutional, it was sufficiently ambiguous about what activities were legitimate as to "chill the conduct of our nation's foreign affairs."[27] To save the bill, further modifications were agreed to by Congress. For one thing, the prohibition clause was modified to state that no funds appropriated by the act could be provided "in exchange for" carrying out prohibited activities; this new language was intended to connote that what was prohibited was a direct relation between the aid and the action. A catalog of diplomatic activities by U.S. government officials that were not limited was added. Included in this catalog were statements of views "to any party on any subject," the ability "to express the policies of the President," and the ability "to communicate with foreign officials about the kinds of actions prohibited."[28] When this still was not enough to satisfy the president's counsel, C. Boyden Gray, Obey agreed to make a statement on the House floor on November 21, in which he said that the "in exchange for" clause "should be understood to refer to a direct verbal or written agreement."[29] With this final change, the bill was signed by the president the same day.

The parallel Moynihan authorization amendment was more obnoxious to the administration, even after several redrafts, and was the proximate cause of the veto of the first version of the FY 1990–91 State bill (H.R. 1487) discussed at length in Chapter 5.[30] This version was more sweeping

27. George Bush, "Statement on Signing the Foreign Operations, Export Financing and Related Programs Appropriations Act" (November 21, 1989), in *The Public Papers of the Presidents of the United States*, 1989, bk. 2 (Washington, D.C.: GPO, 1990), p. 1574.

28. Clauses are quoted from sec. 582 of P.L. 101-167, the FY 1990 Foreign Operations Appropriations Bill, as passed. Very similar language was incorporated into "Foreign Ops" appropriations legislation for at least the next five years.

29. *Congressional Record* 135 (November 21, 1989): H9231.

30. For conference work on the Moynihan provisions (before the veto), see Robert Pear, "Congress to Limit Bush on Spy Funds: Lawmakers Agree to Restrict President's Power to Seek Aid from Foreigners," *New York Times*, November 9, 1989.

since, unlike the appropriations provision, it contained criminal penalties for violations (up to five years in prison, or fines, or both), broadened the funding prohibition to *any* law that specifically cited the prohibition section, did not have language stating there must be an explicit quid pro quo for a violation to occur (like the appropriations "in exchange for" clause), and required a presidential notification to Congress that was held by the executive to be unconstitutional.[31] These differences, in the opinion of the executive branch, crossed the line: they were "an impermissible intrusion on the President's constitutional prerogatives."[32] After the veto, the House passed a new version of the bill, omitting the Moynihan provision (sec. 109 of H.R. 1487), as H.R. 3792. As we have seen, the quarrel between Pell and Hollings kept it from final passage until early 1990. Later in 1990 and again in 1991, Moynihan threatened to push for his original language, but did not, perhaps because the moment for Iran-Contra had at least temporarily passed and because most other members thought that the appropriations language, repeated in subsequent foreign operations bills, was adequate and that trying for more was not worth a renewed battle with the president.[33]

How serious was this matter? Theodore Draper viewed what the executive had done (and what Moynihan and the appropriators were trying to prevent from recurring) as placing the Constitution in danger:

> The question is not whether the president has some prerogatives in foreign policy by virtue of his unique status as the elected representative of all the people. It is whether he alone can "make," "manage," or "conduct" foreign policy. The idea that the president and his agents can do anything they please in foreign policy brought on the Iran-contra affairs. . . .
>
> Not every dispute of the Constitution endangers it. This one, however, is qualitatively different. An authoritarian, autocratic presidency in "the management of foreign relations" is still a clear and present danger, "most susceptible of abuse of all the trusts committed to a Government." And what ever one may think of the constitu-

---

31. Interviews with State lawyers during this episode in order to determine why the appropriations language was acceptable but the authorization provision was not. Comments based on sec. 582 of the appropriations bill, as passed, and on the vetoed H.R. 1487 version of the appropriations bill; these were the final versions.

32. Letter from Deputy Secretary of State Lawrence Eagleburger to Chairman Pell and others on the Senate version as it then existed, July 17, 1989 (in my files).

33. See Moynihan's Senate floor comments: *Congressional Record* 137 (January 30, 1990): S546 and *Congressional Record* 138 (January 17, 1991): S989.

tional issue, there remains the question: Do we want that kind of presidency?[34]

Contrary to Draper's interpretation of the history of the Moynihan amendment, the executive branch (at least not all of it) was *not* making a claim for total primacy of the presidency, nor for the president's ability to use nonappropriated funds for purposes for which he could not legally use appropriated money: hence the eventual acquiescence in the final appropriations version of the leveraging provision. It is true, however, that there were shades of difference within the administration; it is my understanding that Abraham Sofaer, the State Department's legal adviser, was prepared to accept the Moynihan provision; but the White House general counsel, C. Boyden Gray, was taking a harder line and remained convinced that it went too far.[35] In the end, the reason that Moynihan, notwithstanding his public statements, did not later actively pursue the amendment was simple: the votes were not there.

It must be remembered that this case is about the proposed corrective to the Iran-Contra actions by the executive, not about those actions themselves. Moynihan argues plausibly that impeachable offenses were committed during Iran-Contra, since the president was legally bound to see that the laws were faithfully executed, not to find a way to evade those laws (e.g., the Boland amendments prohibiting military aid to the Contras) which he did not support.[36] The question here is whether the Moynihan amendment went too far the other way, undercutting the president's ability to carry out foreign affairs—thus the executive branch concerns about specifying actions that were not prohibited, which Moynihan and the appropriators both acquiesced to in the final versions of their respective amendments. The overall lesson must be that creative funding as an answer to foreign affairs budget problems must in the end work within the law. In a way, the actions that precipitated the leveraging amendments show the outer limits of the executive primacy doctrine. As Draper argues, if they could do this under the Constitution, it is hard to imagine what they could not do.[37]

34. Draper, "The Constitution Is in Danger," p. 46ff. (*A Very Thin Line*, pp. 595–96). The internal quotations are from sources Draper cites, the last phrase coming from a letter from James Madison to Thomas Jefferson, May 13, 1798.

35. Discussions with State Department lawyers closely involved with working the issue of the Moynihan amendment during 1989.

36. Moynihan, *On the Law of Nations*, p. 143.

37. See Draper, "The Constitution Is In Danger."

## Codicil: The McCarran-Walter Fix

The leveraging amendment case lies close to the heart of congressional–executive struggles, because it pits the strongest powers of each branch—purse and foreign relations—directly against each other. There are, of course, many other examples where the issue is joined less starkly. Direct funding issues may not be involved, but a president can be forced to take a provision he objects to in order to obtain legislation (and funding) he must have. This might be characterized as the "quid pro quo technique" of congressional assertiveness. Take, for example, another series of amendments, also sponsored by Moynihan, which were played out in parallel to leveraging. These were his attempts to repeal or override provisions of the McCarran-Walter Act, which allowed foreign citizens to be denied nonimmigrant (visitor) visas for reasons of political affiliation or belief. Passed in 1952 over the veto of President Truman, at the height of the McCarthy "Red scare," this act had been an embarrassment to the United States, in the eyes of liberals, ever since. Moynihan thus succeeded in having adopted an amendment (which became section 901) to the 1988–89 State Authorization Act whose meaning was clear:

> Notwithstanding any other provision of law, no alien may be denied a visa or excluded from admission into the United States, subject to restrictions or conditions on entry into the United States, or subject to deportation because of any past, current, or expected beliefs, statements, or associations which if engaged in by a United States citizen in the United States, would be protected under the Constitution of the United States.[38]

This provision had a one-year sunset limit, in the hope that it would provide time and impetus for a more complete rewrite of the McCarran-Walter Act then under way in the House Judiciary Committee. Moynihan could not amend or repeal McCarran-Walter directly on the State bill, because that law was under the jurisdiction of the two Judiciary committees, not Foreign Relations.[39] When the rewrite did not occur, in 1988 Moynihan sought and obtained two more years of life for section 901.[40] When by 1989

38. P.L. 100-204 (H.R. 1777), December 22, 1987, sec. 901(a).
39. On this point, see *CQ Weekly Report* 45 (December 19, 1987): 3125 (summary box).
40. In sec. 555 of P.L. 100-461, the Foreign Operations, Export Financing, and Regulated Programs Appropriations Act, 1989. In addition to extending the date by two years, sec. 555 made some substantive changes in the text, the temporary status of which Moynihan reversed when sec. 901 was made permanent in the next State authorization bill.

the rewrite of McCarran-Walter was still pending, Moynihan succeeded in making section 901 permanent legislation, under section 128 of the 1990–91 State bill. In each instance, the Reagan and then the Bush administration opposed the change, but decided that the issue did not rise to the importance of a veto.

How State had implemented section 901 became an issue. Although the department was willing to forgo the old requirements, the Department of Justice and the Immigration and Naturalization Service argued that the operable provision of McCarran-Walter was still law and that all the Moynihan amendment did, therefore, was to provide the possibility of waiving the requirement; it did not eliminate it. Moynihan, exasperated, clearly indicated his concerns some six months after the passage of the 1990–91 State bill, and he signaled where he was going in a letter to Edwin Williamson on the eve of the latter's confirmation hearing as State's legal adviser. In a list of topics Moynihan suggested he might raise was the following:

> (1) McCarran-Walter—I am informed that, notwithstanding the permanent adoption of Section 901 of Title 8 barring the government from considering ideology in granting non-immigration visas, the Administration has taken the legal position that the ideological exclusion provisions of the McCarran-Walter Act (contained in 8 U.S.C. Sec. 1182[a] [27]–[29]) are still operative, that prospective visitors must be queried about their ideological associations and beliefs and that their names must be checked against a "lookout list" containing the names of so-called subversives. The Administration takes the position that it is only required to grant "waivers" to persons on the "lookout list."
>
> I will be interested to know your opinion concerning, among other things: the merits of this legal position, its consistency with the legislative history of Section 901, the legal purpose of requiring a "waiver" when the Administration is forbidden by law to take ideology in to [sic] account, and the Administration's legal basis for maintaining and adding to the "lookout list."[41]

Williamson was duly confirmed, but Moynihan obviously was not satisfied with the responses he received, either then or in a September letter from Acting Secretary Lawrence Eagleburger, responding to the same arguments,

41. Moynihan to Williamson, July 31, 1990.

made to him personally in a July 27 meeting with Moynihan. Eagleburger wrote:

> I can confirm to you that the Department of State is also concerned about the practical and policy difficulties inherent in the present approach to implementing section 901.[42] The Department, however, is not in a position unilaterally to change the Executive's approach and both Department of Justice approval and coordinated changes in INS practice would be required.[43]

The issue was apparently brought to an end later that year, when the Immigration Act of 1990 was unexpectedly passed, resulting in a comprehensive rewriting of the basic immigration statute. It repealed McCarran-Walter, replacing it with a prohibition not substantially different from section 901. The new act stated that

> an alien . . . shall not be excludable or subject to restriction or conditions on entry into the United States . . . because of the alien's past, current, or expected beliefs, statements, or associations, if such beliefs, statements or associations would be lawful within the United States, unless the Secretary of State personally determines that the alien's admission would compromise a compelling United States foreign policy interest.[44]

However, there was one last flurry in this episode, played out in 1991 during congressional consideration of the FY 1992–93 State Authorization Bill. Simply put, the atmosphere between the Democrat-controlled Congress and the Republican executive was so poisonous that key players, especially Moynihan and Howard Berman, did not trust the department to carry out the new provisions of law with respect to exclusions. First, Moynihan and the Senate insisted on, and the House conferees accepted, a provision requiring a report by the secretary of state "on a timely basis" of those excluded either for terrorist reasons or under the foreign policy provision.[45] Second,

42. I.e., continuing to interrogate visa applicants about their beliefs and affiliations, maintaining excludable individuals on a lookout list, and requiring them to apply for a waiver to take advantage of sec. 901.

43. Eagleburger to Moynihan, September 11, 1990.

44. P.L. 101-649, November 29, 1990, subsection 212(a)(3)(C), which was codified as 8 USC 1182(a)(3)(C).

45. P.L. 102-138 (H.R. 1415), sec. 127.

the conferees insisted on a program to purge the Automated Visa Lookout List (AVLOS), or any similar lists, of the names of aliens who were no longer excludable owing to the repeal of McCarran-Walter.[46] This was a complicated business because the lookout list contained various categories of excludables, including suspected terrorists[47] and narcotics traffickers, and records did not always show why a name was on the list, making purging difficult. Ironically, in the spring of 1993 there was some criticism of the department because the suspected ringleader of the World Trade Center bombing had slipped through the lookout system and entered the country, even though he was on the list!

A major difference between this set of issues and those related to "leveraging" is that few constitutional questions were perceived in the McCarran-Walter matter. Congress could enforce its views; the provisions were part and parcel of the immigration law for which Congress had clear responsibility. So Congress used the power of the purse, and the requirement for activities to be authorized before funds could be expended, to bring a reluctant executive to heel. But the issue was much more sensitive and protracted than it had to be. For a lack of trust between the two branches, a contempt within Congress for the practical difficulties involved, and a deeply held belief by some who administered the lookout system that McCarran-Walter was correct national policy all served to exacerbate matters. In this instance, however, the Congress was positioned to have its way.

## Congress Works Its Will (I): Transfers and Reprogrammings

With these examples in mind, it is instructive to examine the techniques Congress uses to exploit the opportunities and responsibilities the constitu-

46. P.L. 102-138, sec. 128.

47. Interestingly, in 1995, after the Oklahoma City and World Trade Center bombings, both versions of the State Authorization Bill for FY 1996-97, as well as some freestanding legislation, proposed a partial revival of McCarran-Walter. These proposals added an exclusion for members of terrorist organizations, as well as for those who actively supported or advocated terrorist activities, to the already existing language (which excluded those who had actually engaged in, or seemed likely to engage in, terrorist activity in the United States if admitted). This of course was counter to Moynihan's basic point that *actions*, not words or beliefs, should be the test. According to legislative affairs officials at State, the (Democratic) administration's decision was not to oppose this provision, because it was so popular in Con-

tion gives it to influence policy. Typically, these techniques are not derived from magisterial constitutional doctrines but, rather, are day-to-day tactical weapons. Since the important *Chadha* decision of 1983, which prohibited one- or two-house "legislative vetoes" of executive branch actions and thereby provided many new considerations for "separation of powers" arguments,[48] the use of other control devices, which of course existed earlier but were revisited and reemphasized after that decision, has in the opinion of most observers increased substantially.[49]

We begin with the most obvious of these devices, those providing direct control of the executive's ability to use funds, especially in ways not originally authorized and appropriated. Reprogrammings and transfers are tech-

gress. Absolute principles turn out to be not so absolute when the political winds of the moment are contrary. For an example of this proposed provision, see sec. 166 of S. 908, as reported from the Senate Foreign Relations Committee on June 9, 1995.

48. *Immigration and Naturalization Service* v. *Chadha*, 103 S. Ct. 2764 (1983). A full account of this important case is Barbara Hinkson Craig's *Chadha: The Story of an Epic Constitutional Struggle* (New York: Oxford University Press, 1988). Chadha, a native of Kenya, entered the United States on a student visa. When he attempted to renew it, the INS ordered him deported. In an appeal hearing, an immigration judge decided that his deportation should be suspended. Such suspensions were provided for in the Immigration and Naturalization Act, but had to be reported to Congress, where they were subject to a resolution of disapproval by either house. After the House of Representatives "vetoed" the suspension of Chadha's deportation in 1975, a new hearing gave him no relief. Chadha's lawyers persuaded the U.S. Court of Appeals to rule the veto provision unconstitutional. The Supreme Court, to which the House appealed, reaffirmed the Court of Appeals decision. In his majority opinion, Chief Justice Warren Burger found that any actions taken by either house containing matter "which is properly to be regarded as legislative in character and effect" must follow the constitutionally defined process of passage by both houses and presentation to the president. It held that vetoing Chadha's deportation suspension was a legislative action, defined as one that has the "purpose and effect of altering the legal rights, duties and relations of persons outside the legislative branch." Further, the one-house veto approach did not meet constitutional requirements. This finding was drawn broadly, leaving little room for congressional acts of this nature, for either one-house or two-house vetoes, and more than two hundred other statutory provisions similarly fell. The preceding analysis is from Craig, *Chadha*; for the quotations, see p. 226.

49. As Craig (ibid., p. 36) points out, "Presidents had taken exception to legislative vetoes ever since their 'invention' in the early 1930s," but until the 1970s they were written into law rather sparingly, averaging fewer than three a year. Between 1970 and 1975, however, no fewer than eighty-nine laws had been passed with legislative veto provisions. Thus the stage was set for a challenge, and one reason *Chadha* happened was that some constitutional lawyers were looking for cases to use in order to challenge the legislative veto. For a partial catalog of these post-Vietnam/post-Watergate efforts—including, among others, the War Powers Act, international agreements under the Atomic Energy Act, federal pay raises under the Federal Pay Comparability Act, fuel allocations under the Emergency Petroleum Allocation Act, and presidential records under the Presidential Recordings and Materials Preservation Act—see ibid., pp. 36–37. All allowed one- or two-house vetoes of administrative actions that were legal under the statutes in question.

niques originally intended to allow the executive branch to shift funds, within prescribed limits, to purposes different from those proposed in the original budget presentations to Congress, on which congressional decisions presumably were made. *Reprogramming,* involving the movement of funding within appropriations accounts (State has about twenty such accounts, so this is a relatively narrow authority to begin with), has gradually become more difficult, perhaps in part reflecting congressional determination to recoup powers lost through *Chadha.* Until 1983, only the appropriations committees had to be notified; since then, the authorizers have had to be notified as well.[50] A 1987 amendment attempted to restrict end-of-year reprogramming, disallowing it within the final fifteen days of the period for which funds had been appropriated.[51] For State and USIA, reprogramming is now required by statute for amounts over $500,000 or 10 percent of the amount in an account, whichever is less, for the creation or elimination of any program regardless of the amount, or for reorganizations of any significant impact. So not a great deal of money is involved—merely an additional limitation (and until 1991 the limit was only $250,000!).[52]

A final consideration is that sometimes new accounts are created in order to "fence off" funds for particular projects, such as for the inspector general function government-wide in 1988[53] and as was considered but ultimately

50. Required by sect. 123 of P.L. 98-164, November 22, 1983, Foreign Relations Authorization Act, Fiscal Years 1984 and 1985, which added sec. 34 to the State Department Basic Authorities Act, the permanent enabling legislation for State. Identical language appears in each annual CJS appropriations bill.

51. Sec. 121, P.L. 100-204, Foreign Relations Authorization Act, Fiscal Years 1988 and 1989, December 22, 1987. It redesignated the previous sec. 34 for the Basic Authorities Act as sec. 34(a) and added the new limitation as sec. 34(b).

52. This was changed in sec. 606(b) of the FY 1991 CJS Appropriations Bill (P.L. 101-515, November 5, 1990) after a major effort by State; the corresponding authorization language, in sec. 34 of the State Department Basic Authorities Act, was changed to conform by sec. 117 of the FY 1992–93 Authorization Act (P.L. 102-138, October 28, 1991). Additional efforts to simplify reprogramming requirements never received much interest. In 1993, for the FY 1994–95 Authorization Bill, the department proposed an easing of reprogramming requirements (e.g., an end to extra notifications about the use of diplomatic security funds) which the authorizers seemed inclined to accept. HFAC also wanted to raise the reprogramming limit to $1 million from $500,000, reportedly in the hope that this would negate the need to do reprogramming notifications on the troublesome issue of closing diplomatic and consular posts (see case following); the Senate followed suit, and the change was incorporated in the final Act (sec. 122[c]). Since the CJS appropriations acts for FY 1994–FY 1996 retained the lower limit, however, this change had no practical effect. These details come from an M legislative staffer, August 6, 1993, and June 14, 1994.

53. Inspector General Act Amendments of 1988, sec. 108; technically, this section amended sec. 1105(a)(25) of Title XXXI, USC. Note that this can backfire, as it did in the sec. 614

not done for State's security programs. A related device is to write prohibitions against transfer or reprogramming into the legislation, as with development assistance funds in the "Foreign Ops" appropriation for FY 1989.[54] The amendments to the Inspector General Act in 1988, however, later caused some problems for State's inspector general, because creating the "fence" kept funds from being transferred *in* as well as protecting from transfers *out*. Whether creating an independent account is a good or bad idea depends on whether the program in question needs to be protected or, conversely, is popular enough that it will be able to "poach" off others when times are tight. If the latter is the case, then fencing the program off so funds cannot be reprogrammed out of (or into) it may be counterproductive.[55]

Reprogramming is a gray area of potential executive–legislative conflict and has not yet been fully tested. The executive branch believes that it is required only to "notify" Congress and then to wait fifteen calendar days to receive objections before proceeding to expend the reprogrammed funds in the new account. To them, it does not matter legally if one or more committees object. Some in Congress, on the other hand, insist that congressional approval is required before proceeding to expend the funds, in effect giving each of the four committees involved a veto, and that the fifteen days in question are legislative days. Obviously, this interpretation if followed would severely constrain reprogramming and could easily be argued to run counter to the *Chadha* decision. To date, State has only sparingly tested its interpretation in the face of opposition to proposed reprogrammings, recognizing that what may be legal may not be politically wise. Instead, the usual State response has been to attempt to repackage the request, or even to drop it, in order to meet congressional concerns.

Technically, *transfers* are movements of funds across accounts and require explicit, advance legislative authority. In effect, a transfer amounts to a new authorization/appropriation, except in relatively rare instances where the need is recognized and authority has been given in advance. A recent exam-

---

situation from November 1989 to May 1990, resulting ironically in (unsuccessful) attempts to transfer State inspector general funds above the sequester limit to another account to avoid lapsing them.

54. P.L. 100-461, October 1, 1988.

55. As a general rule, central agency budgeteers want as small a number of accounts as possible, so that funds can be moved around to meet developing situations. Program managers want protection, at least when funds are tight, so they want to be sure that funds appropriated for their programs cannot be moved at the whim of management. Therefore, they tend to favor separate accounts and, for that matter, tough reprogramming and transfer provisions which also make it more difficult to move funds around.

ple of a major controversy over transfer authority was the attempt, late in the 1988 congressional session, to transfer funds from Defense (Function 050) to Function 150 in order to pay for peacekeeping. While all involved stated that they applauded the goal, they were reluctant to provide the necessary authority on any of the obvious vehicles (appropriations bills for either part of Function 150 or for defense funding), and in the end the transfer did not happen.[56]

As with reprogramming authority, State has attempted to gain additional authority to transfer both authorizations and appropriations from one account to another, in light of the tight budget situation and some close calls. For example, there was a frantic search in the summer of 1990 to fund urgent, unanticipated evacuations of American citizens from certain Middle East countries when the Gulf War was beginning. Such expenses were normally expected to be funded from a small "Emergencies in the Diplomatic and Consular Service" account; but little money was available late in the fiscal year, and Congress was in recess so that a statutory supplemental appropriation was not a viable approach. In this instance, some creative legal work, both at State and on the Hill, concluded that the S&E account could be used as a supplement to the emergencies account. Transfer authority would have negated the need for such legerdemain.[57] Congress gradually came to accept the need, although it was unwilling to allow transfers in anything like the amounts desired by the department (10 percent of the total appropriated to large accounts, 35 percent to smaller ones, no limits on the emergencies accounts). Instead, by 1993, both the authorizing and appropriations committees seemed willing to provide more limited transfer authority: the authorizers would allow appropriations to exceed authorizations by 10 percent (except for the largest account, where the limit would be 5 percent); the appropriators would permit 5 percent of any account to be transferred, with any receiving account being increased by a maximum of 10 percent; and such transfers would be subject to reprogramming notification procedures.[58] Most experts conclude that in a time of tight funding, transfers as well as reprogrammings are essential for efficient resource use.

56. See the case, later in this chapter, having to do with funding U.N. operations (including peacekeeping), where similar issues arose repeatedly.

57. As a member of the M legislative staff, I was an observer and sometime participant in these efforts. The exhausted condition of the emergency account could have been a big problem, since in normal practice the same activity cannot be funded from multiple accounts. However, since both State and the appropriators agreed on the purpose, it was possible to do so.

58. These provisions were to be found in sec. 112 of both the House and the Senate version of the FY 1994–95 Foreign Relations Authorization Bill, in sec. 122 of the final act as passed,

# Congress Works Its Will (II): Other Post-*Chadha* Control Devices

In addition to transfer and reprogramming requirements, there are many other legislative and nonlegislative means available to a Congress determined to become an equal player in the foreign policy game. These techniques, especially effective with respect to programmatic activities that require funds, include earmarks, floors, ceilings, outright prohibitions, and conditional and contingency funding. Less directly related to funding, but carrying the implied or explicit threat of statutory action, are certifications that the required determinations have been made or specific actions have taken place, reports on progress in the use of funds in certain categories, or measures demonstrating other kinds of performance. Overarching is the basic requirement for authorization to establish policy and programs, and for appropriations to allow them to be carried out.[59] Legislation is always possible if congressional concerns are not satisfied.

The employment of these surrogates for the legislative veto is not necessarily more favorable to the president and the executive branch, since they tend to limit administrative flexibility. As Louis Fisher notes, "No one should underestimate the ingenuity of Congress to think up devices that will be more cumbersome for the President than the legislative veto. The temptation will be strong for Congress to grant powers for shorter periods, forcing the President to return to Congress for extensions. Of course either House, by inaction, could deny the President the authority."[60]

Jessica Korn, in her thoughtful study of the landmark *Chadha* case, concludes that "the impact that *Chadha* has had on the balance of power between the branches is not entirely clear." She then places subsequent developments in a broader but consistent context: "The essence of the findings in this paper . . . is that preserving a formalism such as the separation of powers should not be assumed to oppose the capacity of government institutions to fulfill their functional responsibilities. These findings even

---

and in sec. 502 of the FY 1993 CJS Appropriations Act (P.L. 102-395, October 6, 1992). Identical language was used in the FY 1994 and FY 1995 CJS acts, as sec. 502 of both P.L. 103-121, October 27, 1993, and P.L. 103-317, August 26, 1994.

59. See Schick, Keith, and Davis, *Manual on the Federal Budget Process*, chap. 7, "Authorizing Legislation," pp. 113–24, and Schick, *The Federal Budget*, chap. 7, "Authorizing Legislation," pp. 110–28, for useful discussions of these requirements.

60. Fisher, *Constitutional Conflicts*, p. 149.

allow for the possibility that the preservation of such formalisms might, in fact, enhance such functional capacities."[61]

To return to the more prosaic world of Hill operations, each of the techniques and approaches highlighted below requires attention, especially where they have particular wrinkles for foreign affairs.

*Earmarks*[62] have been particularly contentious recently, as funding levels have remained static while program costs and demands have risen. They are a means of guaranteeing, either in authorization or appropriations statutes or in report language, that specific amounts are spent for designated purposes, often pet projects of influential members, regardless of the total funding available. Report language is not legally binding, but is often so politically. Generally, earmarks are of the "X amount shall be expended on for Y" nature, but there are variations. At times, *ceilings* may be set on the maximum that can be spent for a particular purpose, while at other times *floors* are set, requiring that at least a certain amount be spent. As authorizing committees have felt their powers ebbing, they have resorted increasingly to earmarks in an attempt to constrain the actions of the appropriators, forcing them into desired spending allocations. In November 1989, during joint Senate consideration of the CJS Appropriations Bill for FY 1990 and the accompanying FY 1990–92 Authorization Bill, earmarks in the latter for State and USIA became a point of contention between Appropriations Committee Chairman Robert Byrd and the Senate Foreign Relations Committee. Byrd argued that authorizing "floors" were an impermissible intrusion into the business of the appropriators, and he succeeded in having them stricken throughout the authorization bill.[63]

Sometimes excessive earmarking has approached the ridiculous. The House version of the FY 1988–89 Foreign Relations Authorization Bill contained set contribution amounts for each of more than twenty international organizations in which the United States participates, rather than following the usual practice of setting amounts by a few broad categories. The Senate, hearing dire threats of a veto, consolidated the amounts into one single category, specifying earmarks for only five organizations; the conference

61. Jessica Korn, "The Political Effects of Separation of Powers Jurisprudence: The Case of *Chadha* and the Legislative Veto," a paper prepared for the annual meeting of the American Political Science Association, Washington, D.C., August 29–September 1, 1991, p. 36.

62. An earmark is usually equivalent to a floor, because it normally sets the minimum amount expendable, unless the legislation states that "no more than X" may be spent.

63. See *CQ Weekly Report* 47 (September 23, 1989): 2456 for Byrd's views on earmarks, in this instance with reference to the Treasury and Postal Service Appropriation Bill for FY 1990.

report compromised with eleven. The appropriators, not amused, overrode all of this, leaving allocations to the executive, subject to congressional notification.[64] Similarly, proposed earmarks in the Foreign Assistance Act of 1987 (which never became law, in part because of earmarks) at one point contained earmarks that collectively *exceeded* the total amount likely to be available under any foreseeable outcome![65]

The ultimate folly results when different committees are in direct conflict vis-à-vis their earmarks. For FY 1987, the authorization committees directed that at least $6.5 million be used for the office of State's inspector general; the appropriations bill for the same period, viewing this as excessive (and perhaps to emphasize who had the clout), directed that "not to exceed $4,000,000" be available for the Office of the Inspector General.[66] Funds not appropriated cannot be spent, so the appropriators won this joust.

By 1993, there was scattered evidence that earmarking, at least of the most egregious sort, had become somewhat of an embarrassment. In an admittedly limited case—viz., the designation of research funds to home districts—a study of the House Science, Space, and Technology Committee showed earmarks had declined by half. Interestingly for current purposes, the committee concluded that "only one of the four bills—Commerce, Justice and State—had more earmarks, which rose from $60 million two years ago to $82 million for 1984."[67] In 1993 and 1994, for example, USAID succeeded in convincing the "Foreign Ops" appropriators to reduce foreign affairs earmarks substantially, although a substantial return to the older patterns occurred in 1995.[68] However undesirable from the executive's per-

64. The specific texts for the several versions of H.R. 1777, the authorization bill in question, may be found in sec. 102 of the House bill, the Senate bill, and the final act (which, as noted above, became P.L. 100-204, December 22, 1987). The appropriations provision, in sec. 101(a), Title III of the continuing resolution (P.L. 100-202, December 22, 1987, which contained the State Department appropriation), stated under the heading "Contributions to International Organizations" that "notwithstanding section 102(a)(1) through (11) of H.R. 1777 . . . $480,000,000 [is] to remain available until expended." In other words, this language explicitly overrode the earmarks in the authorization bill.

65. Interview with a State Department congressional relations officer who was intimately involved with foreign assistance legislation, September 30, 1988.

66. *Congressional Record* 132 (October 15, 1987): H10616.

67. Described by Mary Jordan, "Congressional Earmarking on the Wane, Review Finds: Designated Research Funds Down by Half in 4 Bills," *Washington Post*, November 11, 1993.

68. This opinion, from a USAID budget official in June 1995, was substantiated by the conference report on H.R. 1868, the Foreign Operations Appropriations Bill for FY 1996, agreed to in the fall. While there continued at least temporarily to be fewer formal earmarks,

spective, this is hardly surprising. What Richard Munson has termed "parochial earmarks" are almost irresistible to congressional seekers of reelection. Moreover, they can give other members a stake in a particular appropriations bill, and they are a way to build up obligations for return favors in the future.[69]

From the executive point of view, the trend is in the wrong direction. Louis Fisher describes how the absence of legislative vetoes has led to tighter controls:

> [F]or about a decade Congress has required the Agency for International Development (AID) to obtain the prior, written approval of the Appropriations Committees before transferring funds from one appropriations account to another. In 1987 OMB Director James Miller III advised Congress that the committee veto violated the constitutional principles of *Chadha*. The House Appropriations Committee basically said, "Fine. We'll repeal the committee veto and also your authority to transfer funds." OMB, realizing that the political dynamics were heading in an undesirable direction, backed down. The regular language, including the committee veto, was enacted into law. Two years later, compromise language was adopted, allowing AID to transfer funds provided it adhered to "regular notification procedures." That phrase means that AID must notify the Appropriations Committees about proposed transfers and wait fifteen days. If the committees object during that period, AID does not proceed or proceeds at great cost to itself.[70]

Similarly, in 1993, both the authorizing and the appropriating committees for State divided the existing S&E account, attempting to separate administrative expenses from operating programs. The two successor accounts were labeled "Diplomatic and Consular Programs" and, for what was left, "Salaries and Expenses." While there was some method in this, given the recent tendency to try to cut administrative accounts by set percentages (this change would make the account at risk much smaller), the negative aspect was less flexibility, owing to tougher rules for transfers between accounts

---

there was a proliferation of "directives" as to how money should be expended. While less binding, the political costs of not following them could be significant.

69. Richard Munson, *The Cardinals of Capitol Hill: The Men and Women Who Control Government* (New York: Grove Press, 1993), pp. 64–68.

70. Fisher, *Constitutional Conflicts*, p. 151.

versus reprogramming within accounts. Ideally, for the executive there would be just one account, subject only to reprogramming rules.

Such fragmentation can be extremely negative, as USAID's experience has shown. With the requirement to separate OE (operating expense) funds from program funds, that agency has been forced to shift to contracting rather than direct administration, because contractors can be paid from program funds while salaries for employees must come from OE. This has resulted not only in a loss of control but in higher expenses, owing to overhead and a misuse of AID's talent pool, now forced in considerable measure to become contract administrators rather than development professionals.[71]

*Prohibitions* state explicitly those purposes for which funds cannot be used, or for which they can be used only if specified conditions are met. For example, a tiff between the Drug Enforcement Agency (DEA) and the ambassador to Egypt over whether a regional DEA officer should be assigned to Cairo (DEA wanted him there; the post thought that its staff was already too large and that DEA's officer should be assigned elsewhere, if at all) led to a statutory requirement that if one DEA agent were assigned to a post (there already was an agent with responsibilities for Egypt in Cairo), then two must be assigned.[72] In another example of how intraexecutive squabbles are translated into law when one side persuades its friends in Congress to act while the other does not, "Foreign Ops" appropriations bills have included language that prohibits cutting staff or changing the locations of USAID's regional inspectors general assigned to posts abroad, which State had wanted to do.[73] And, as we have seen, several times during

71. These details come from AID staff members, summer 1993–January 1994.

72. P.L. 100-204, December 22, 1987, Foreign Relations Authorization Act, Fiscal Years 1988 and 1989, sec. 801 (22 USC 2656 note).

73. This case is particularly illustrative, since the issue persisted: State was generally trying to cut down overseas representation of all agencies, for foreign policy and security reasons, and AID's inspector general was equally adamant in his opposition. For FY 1988 (P.L. 100-102) the language was as follows: "That except as may be required by an emergency evacuation affecting the United States diplomatic missions of which they are a component element, none of the funds in this Act, or any other Act, may be used to relocate the Overseas Regional Offices of the Inspector General to another country." For FY 1989 (P.L. 101-461), the last part became ". . . to relocate the Overseas Regional Offices of the Inspector General to a location within the United States without the express approval of the Inspector General." For good measure, this section (by amending the Diplomatic Security Act) also removed the secretary of state's authority to set overseas staffing levels for the AID Inspector General offices. This could have been challenged by SFRC because that act was within the latter's jurisdiction, but the committee did not choose to contest the change. The FY 1990 act (P.L. 101-167) repeated this language.

the eighties the Congress has placed limitations or prohibitions on the closing of posts abroad.[74]

Three recent Helms amendments further demonstrate the possibilities.
First, section 132 of the State Authorization Bill for FY 1988–89 expressly
prohibited the use of funds to acquire or maintain an official residence for
the secretary of state, the result of a contentious disagreement between
Helms and Secretary of State Shultz.[75]

Second, section 102(g) of the FY 1994–95 State Authorization Bill required the president to certify that the United States was not supporting any
U.N. agency or affiliated agency which granted any official status, accredita-
tion, or recognition to any organization which promoted, condoned, or
sought legalization of pedophilia or which included as a subsidiary or member any such organization.[76]

Third, and most creatively, both the 1986 Diplomatic Security Act (sec.
414) and the FY 1988–89 Authorization Act (sec. 130) contained Helms-
sponsored provisions attempting to change a basic tenet of U.S. Middle East
policy over the past forty years: namely, that Jerusalem could be accepted
by the United States as the capital of Israel only as part of a comprehensive
Middle East settlement.[77] The amendment as introduced stipulated that
money for a new embassy chancery in Israel, needed for reasons of security
enhancement, could be expended only for a site located within five miles of
the Knesset, in Jerusalem; another new building, in Tel Aviv, would thus
become a consulate general, not the embassy. In both 1986 and 1987, Shultz
declined to play this game. Hence, the final provision in both acts stated
that no money could be spent for site acquisition, development, or construction of any new facility in Israel, Jerusalem, or the West Bank, despite the

74. See Chapter 5 on the FY 1988–89 authorization penalty in the event posts were closed
as well as the discussion of post closings later in this chapter.

75. P.L. 100-204, December 22, 1987. For a discussion of the SFRC hearing at which this
provision was added, see David B. Ottaway, "Senators, Diplomats in Housing War: Helms
Proposes Impossible Conditions for Secretary's Residence," *Washington Post*, May 7, 1987.
State did not plan to buy a residence, although it believed that it would be desirable for security
reasons to have a permanent place, rather than having to equip the residence of each new
secretary with security hardware. However, the department had been offered an attractive and
large residence in the District of Columbia, and it was the acceptance of this gift that Helms
was successful in preventing.

76. P.L. 103-236, April 30, 1994. An example of the certification was published in *Washington Monthly* 26 (December 1994): 49 as the "Memo of the Month," a feature poking fun
at bizarre government activities.

77. The relevant statutes were P.L. 99-399, August 27, 1986, and P.L. 100-204, December
22, 1987, respectively.

serious need. Only in 1988, facing even more urgent security requirements, did the secretary accept a compromise, originally proposed by the Helms staff in 1987, allowing construction but deferring the issue of whether the new building in Tel Aviv or the one in Jerusalem would be the embassy. After considerable maneuvering, this compromise was included in the FY 1989 State Appropriation Bill.[78] In effect, Helms tried to use a construction issue to force a major redirection of foreign policy.[79] This is a more dramatic example than most, but it does show how the power to prohibit the expenditure of funds, which clearly belongs to Congress, can be used in creative ways to challenge presidential policies and prerogatives.

Equally direct, if lesser, challenges to the president's powers were put forward during consideration of the FY 1992–93 Foreign Relations Authorization Bill, in the form of amendments by Senator Hank Brown of Colorado. Brown, who at the time was the ranking minority member of the subcommittee that had initial jurisdiction on this primary legislation for State, was intent on developing a reputation as a fiscally responsible conservative and as a consumer advocate. During subcommittee and full SFRC markup, he introduced amendments making his point on both these agendas.

Most interesting was an amendment prohibiting funding for the International Coffee Organization (ICO), which Brown regarded, with convincing evidence, as a cartel whose primary purpose was to keep coffee prices high, to the detriment of U.S. coffee consumers. The United States had become a member owing to an arrangement between the presidents of Colombia and the United States; the quid pro quo for continued Colombian participation in the war against drugs was U.S. membership and support for the ICO,

---

78. Sec. 305 of P.L. 100-459, October 1, 1988.

79. Ironically, State never found a new site in Tel Aviv that both it and the Israeli government would approve. The language of the Helms amendment precluded the start-up of construction in Jerusalem, where a site was easily obtained, until work had begun in Tel Aviv; simultaneous construction and occupancy of the two facilities was required. There was an informal suggestion by the Helms staff that they might modify their own amendment to allow construction in Jerusalem under the same conditions as in the amendment. State was reluctant, since it would thus lose any leverage on the Israelis to expedite site acquisition in Tel Aviv. Even more ironic, by the end of 1993 the search for a new Tel Aviv site had been suspended, and some $20 million had been committed to a major overhaul of the existing building, notwithstanding its problems, because work could not wait any longer (owing to structural and security imperatives). The new facility needed in Jerusalem was still on hold because of the Helms amendment. The amendment, then, was finessed through circumstance rather than intent. Discussions with an FBO senior official in November 1993 and January 1995. For related developments in 1995, see Chapter 8.

one of whose major beneficiaries was Colombia. A sound argument might have been made that this amendment was unconstitutional because it interfered with the president's Article II, section 2 powers, but a possible confrontation was avoided in conference when the House insisted, under strong administration pressure, that the amendment be modified. The final version (sec. 179 of P.L. 102-138) was a "sense of the Congress" provision stating that when a new international coffee agreement was negotiated, the interests of U.S. consumers should be given "highest priority." Of constitutional import is the fact that State's lawyers had concluded that a failure of Congress to authorize or appropriate funding for the U.S. assessment for the ICO would *not* abrogate the obligation of the United States under international law to make its contribution to the shared costs of that organization, nor could the absence of an authorization force the end of U.S. membership.[80] The episode is of interest primarily because of the possibilities for constitutional challenge had the amendment passed in its original form, not because of the actual outcome. Two years later, though, Brown succeeded in adding his original amendment to the SFRC version of the FY 1994–95 authorization; perhaps because in the interim State had decided to withdraw from the ICO, mooting the issue, his amendment survived in the final act.[81] In the end short-circuited, this minor dispute represented a direct clash of the president's powers to negotiate international agreements with the funding powers of the Congress.

*Conditional funding* is a technique that has not yet been fully exploited by Congress, although its use is increasing. Its usual form is to require that certain conditions be met (reform of the U.N. budget, say, or good faith peace talks), usually to be certified by the president, before appropriated funds are released. The most obvious recent examples are assessments to the United Nations and related organizations and assistance to the Contras. *Contingency funding* is a variation, keyed more to possible but unpredictable events than to expected performance. State's "Emergencies in the Diplomatic and Consular Service" account and USAID's "International Disaster Assistance" account are two examples.

*Quid pro Quos* are another technique, generally involving actions (not necessarily statutory) that the executive needs from Congress and for which a price is exacted. Through the years, for example, the Senate has used its

---

80. Conversations with these lawyers at the time of the passage of the Brown amendment.
81. Sec. 428 of P.L. 103-236, April 30, 1994.

confirmation power with respect to presidential appointees, especially ambassadors, to force policy changes, to make political points and, most recently, to persuade the president to accept proposed legislative actions. Thus it was in 1995 that SFRC Chairman Jesse Helms was "taking hostages again," holding up ambassadorial confirmations until the president agreed to accept his legislation reorganizing the foreign affairs community by merging USAID and USIA into State.[82] This is a classic "use what you have" tactic, and whether it works depends entirely on how much the executive wants or needs what the Congress can withhold. (Sometimes, quid pro quos are attempted in reverse. As is discussed below, the Kennedy administration apparently offered significant benefits if a troublesome appropriations chairman would resign his position!)

Any consideration of congressional controls over policy would be incomplete without mention of *reports,* perhaps the most widely used technique of all. In recent years, formal reporting requirements have proliferated. They may be either one-time reports addressed to a particular issue, annual reports on a particular topic (e.g., the well-known human rights reports), or submissions required when the executive takes a specified action (e.g., completing an executive agreement with another country).

The 1988–89 Foreign Relations Authorization Act, for example, included, by actual count, thirty-four required reports for State alone, either one-time or recurring.[83] While some are legitimate oversight devices—e.g., describing implementation of newly authorized programs and activities— many have mostly nuisance value. Some seem destined never to be read, since those who initially commissioned them have turned their attention to new issues by the time they are prepared. The OMB and the departments and agencies mount occasional campaigns, usually of limited success, to eliminate reports that serve no current purpose. There often seems to be a disinclination to let the executive "off the hook." Sometimes, though, the

---

82. Al Kamen, "In the Loop," *Washington Post,* June 26, 1995. The most notable recent example of withholding confirmation was the delay endured by Melissa Wells, a career Foreign Service officer, nominated by President Reagan to be ambassador to Mozambique. She had to wait from October 1986 to September 1987, not because of any problem with her qualifications but because of Helms's disagreement with U.S. policy toward Mozambique's leftist government.

83. Similarly, a compilation prepared in December 1993 by the Department of State's Bureau of Legislative Affairs contained 124 statutorily required recurring reports, many of which had to be submitted each time a particular, specified kind of action was taken. This figure does not include one-time reports that had been required by statute and that had been submitted.

same congressional committees that originated the reporting requirements in their legislation subsequently assist in terminating them.[84]

Admittedly, reports can also serve the political purposes of their sponsors with less administrative disruption than legislative requirements to establish or modify programs. Such reporting requirements can be cited to those pressing Congress for action, without committing the government to undesirable particularistic actions. Should the study or report indicate a need for corrective action, then Congress can always legislate on the next bill—or so the argument goes. The executive branch, moreover, would frequently rather be required to report on a matter of interest, if this is the only alternative to operational legislation, and has been known to suggest such an approach.

Interesting constitutionally has been the requirement, since passage of the Case-Zablocki Act in 1972, that the secretary of state transmit to Congress the text of all written international agreements (other than treaties, which are handled through established constitutionally based procedures) within sixty days. This legislation was born after Congress discovered a number of classified or secret agreements, mostly from the Vietnam era, about which nothing had been known. Over the next fifteen years, Congress continued to be dissatisfied with the information it was receiving, and with such executive stratagems as "arrangements" and simultaneous, parallel policy statements by the United States and another government (stratagems that did not fall under Case-Zablocki, according to the executive). Finally, exasperated after several attempts to refine the requirement, Congress passed an amendment to the FY 1988–89 Foreign Relations Authorization Act, stating that if an executive agreement were not transmitted within sixty days,

> then no funds authorized to be appropriated by this or any other Act shall be available after the end of that 60-day period to implement that agreement until the text of that agreement has been so transmitted.[85]

84. The HFAC, for example, issued two lists of reporting requirements, entitled *Required Reports to Congress on Foreign Policy* and *Foreign Assistance Reporting Requirements* (published by the GPO in 1988 and 1989, respectively). Their intent was to eliminate unnecessary and obsolete reports. I am indebted to James M. Lindsay for calling these publications to my attention.

85. P.L. 100-204, December 22, 1987, sec. 139(a). The original Case-Zablocki Act was P.L. 92-403, August 22, 1972, which added the text quoted here as sec. 112b, Title I, USC. For additional information concerning the periodic spats over whether the executive was meeting these requirements, see Fisher, *Constitutional Conflicts*, pp. 241–43.

While the executive occasionally had legitimate problems with the timely transmission of agreements, its often cavalier attitude led to stronger restrictions that otherwise might have been imposed.

Recently, congressional creativity in ensuring that it receives required reports has increased. The FY 1994 Foreign Operations Appropriation Act stated that

> none of the funds appropriated [for operating expenses by] this Act may be obligated after March 31, 1994 unless the Administration has acted to implement those recommendations of the Report of the National Performance Review which can be accomplished without legislation and has submitted the necessary package of proposed legislation to accomplish . . . the remaining recommendations.[86]

Not surprisingly, these actions were completed on time and so reported. This device drew the attention of several other Hill staffers working on foreign-affairs-related committees, and will therefore surely reappear.

There are, of course, *informal reporting* requirements and requests. All federal departments and agencies receive substantial amounts of mail from members, much of it routine and of a casework nature; but a certain amount is central to ongoing policy issues. One good example is the case of the repeal/continuation of the McCarran-Walter legislation, where some of the key interactions were between Senator Moynihan on one hand and State's legal adviser Edwin Williamson and Deputy Secretary Larry Eagleburger on the other. Much of the business between the branches is conducted in this way; legislation is not the only means.

Sometimes this relationship leads to foolishness. Section 723 of the initial SFRC discussion draft of the State Authorization Bill for FY 1996–97, circulated in the spring of 1995, was entitled "Deadline for Responses to Questions from Congressional Committees." Officials of State and other foreign affairs agencies, if asked a written or oral question by an SFRC or HIRC (formerly HFAC) committee member acting in an official capacity, would have to respond within twenty-one days unless the agency head wrote to each member explaining why a response could not be made in that period. The hooker was that

---

86. P.L. 103-87, September 30, 1993, under the heading "Operating Expenses of the Agency for International Development."

an officer or employee of the United States who knowingly and wilfully violates [this provision] shall be fined in accordance with title 18, imprisoned for not more than 2 years, or both.

While this section survived the subcommittee markup, it was deleted in the full SFRC version reported to the floor.[87]

*Whimsy.* One final category of legislative creativity is worth a brief mention, even though it has little to do with Congress's attempting to exert control over the conduct of foreign policy. These are the nuisance amendments, whose purpose can only be to raise the blood pressure of everyone in the executive branch! A classic example is section 152 of S. 908 (the FY 1996–97 State Authorization Bill), as passed by the Senate: "The National Foreign Affairs Training Center is hereby redesignated as the 'National Center for Humanities, Education, Languages, and Management Studies.' " The first letters of the new name, of course, spell N.C.-HELMS! Not to be outdone, the House threatened to counter with an amendment that spelled out *their* chairman's name, "GILMAN." Not surprisingly, this provision was dropped in conference.[88]

In the same SFRC bill, section 502 added a provision to the Arms Control and Disarmament Act to the effect that nothing in the amended chapter, having to do with nuclear weapons,

shall be construed to authorize any policy or action by any Government agency which would interfere with, restrict, or prohibit the acquisition, possession, or use of firearms by an individual for the lawful purpose of personal defense, sport, recreation, education, or training.[89]

---

87. An almost comedic aside accompanied this provision. In his final commentary during the Sunday, June 25, 1995, edition of ABC's *This Week with David Brinkley*, Brinkley after citing section 723 tweaked SFRC Chairman Jesse Helms, noting that there must be more important things for Helms to do. On the July 2 program, Brinkley announced that he had heard from the senator, who said that this provision was only broached in a staff memo and that he disavowed it. How it got from a staff memo into a draft bill adopted by the SFRC subcommittee on which Helms sat is a mystery.

88. See Al Kamen, "In the Loop," *Washington Post*, May 26, 1995. In the end, the House ("GILMAN") amendment, which apparently was to be introduced on the floor, was not offered. Background on this amendment comes from a State legislative affairs officer and lawyer in the House Legislative Counsel's Office, July 1995.

89. See Al Kamen, "In the Loop," *Washington Post*, May 24, 1995, for a somewhat cynical comment on this provision.

This wording actually survived in the (vetoed) conference report as section 1605.

The real point of such amendments, of course, is to grab the attention of the executive branch or to pander to a particular domestic constituency. Most do not survive to become law, but they do put down markers that the Congress cannot be ignored.

These often innovative restrictions on executive branch flexibility can have a surprisingly fine-tuned congressional impact when adroitly applied. Even when there are no legal restrictions, executive branch agencies are always wary of making expenditures opposed by key committees, knowing that statutory earmarks and prohibitions are likely to follow.

Such devices are much more widely used today than in earlier years. Partly because Congress now has more staff and much more staff expertise than in earlier years (even with the Republican reductions in 1995),[90] and partly because staffers feel they must justify their existence, more and more issues and operations are being scrutinized. Finding an amendment to be sponsored by *their* boss becomes a paramount concern. Whether or not that amendment forces a suspect policy change or an unnecessary report may well be of secondary concern. And the danger that these devices will be used in ways that do not serve the national interest is increased in times of high mutual suspicion between the branches.

90. The sometimes exaggerated growth in congressional staff has leveled off since 1980. See Thomas E. Mann and Norman J. Ornstein, *A Second Report of the Renewing Congress Project* (Washington, D.C.: American Enterprise Institute and Brookings Institution, 1993), pp. 68–69. However, the professional staff of the House Foreign Affairs Committee did grow from 11 in 1971 to 85 in 1991. In 1971, all were assigned to the full committee; in 1991, 40 were on subcommittee staffs. Comparable figures for the Senate Foreign Relations Committee were 13 and 37, and 30 support staffers were added in the latter year. The SFRC continues to have few staffers assigned to subcommittees. See James M. McCormick, "Decision Making in the Foreign Affairs and Foreign Relations Committees," chap. 6 in Ripley and Lindsay, eds., *Congress Resurgent*, pp. 128–29. House Republicans in 1995, in addition to cutting the number of committees, also reduced committee staff size by about 30 percent, from 1,854 positions in 1994 to 1,233 in 1995. Comparable numbers for the Senate were from 1,200 to 950. The reduction for the SFRC was somewhat less than the 13.4 percent for Senate committees as a whole, because its leadership argued successfully that they had taken a large cut previously. This information comes from Stanley I. Bach, Congressional Research Service, Library of Congress, May 1, 1995. See also Janet Hook and Paul Nyhan, "Reorganization: Task Force Recommends Steep Senate Cuts," *CQ Weekly Report* 53 (January 28, 1995): 265; Paul Nyhan, "Organization: Cuts in Committee Spending Approved by House Panel," *CQ Weekly Report* 53 (March 11, 1995): 735; and Jonathan D. Salant, "Appropriations: Panel Approves Bill to Cut Congressional Operations," *CQ Weekly Report* 53 (June 17, 1995): 1707–8.

# The Use of Congressional Controls: Two Examples

## Contributions to International Organizations, 1985–1996

Under the treaties by which the United States is a member of the United Nations and its related organizations, members are required to contribute to the expenses of those organizations following formulas established by the U.N. General Assembly (UNGA) or some other designated governing body. Initially, in 1947, the U.S. share was set at 39.89 percent of the U.N. budget. This share was gradually reduced after 1957, following a standard pushed by the United States and adopted by the General Assembly that no member state's contribution should exceed 30 percent. By 1972, the U.S. assessment for the United Nations was 31.57 percent. In December 1972, UNGA, again at U.S. initiative, adopted a 25 percent limit for any one country, a limit that theoretically remains in effect.[91]

In 1979, the United States for the first time, at the behest of Congress, began withholding small amounts of funding for U.N. organizations carrying out activities that the U.S. government, or at least Congress, opposed. Under the Kemp-Moynihan amendment, the first targets were projects benefiting the PLO. Prohibitions on aid to Cuba were added for FY 1981, and for UNESCO in FY 1982. By FY 1983, the United States was also withholding funds for SWAPO, for preparations for the Law of the Sea Conference, and for a U.N. conference on the Israeli–South African alliance.[92]

New variations on the theme were soon to appear, driven first by a conservative distaste for the United Nations, on grounds that the United States was consistently outvoted by left-wing coalitions; and, second, by a growing, more general concern that the U.N. bureaucracy was out of control and that funds provided by member states were being inefficiently used. Reflecting the first strand was the requirement of the 1983 Kasten amendment for annual reports, showing the coincidence of U.N. votes by other members with those of the United States and comparing this information with the amounts of U.S. foreign aid received by each country. The clear intent was to demonstrate U.S. powerlessness in influencing U.N. actions, and even to

91. Contributions to specialized agencies and to peacekeeping may differ in percentage from those for the United Nations proper and are not always set by the same procedures.

92. This information comes from the Office of Budget, Bureau of International Organization Affairs (IO), U.S. Department of State, and is derived from the relevant authorization and appropriations acts. SWAPO was the South-West Africa People's Organization, one of the contending forces in Namibia which had been recognized by the United Nations, to the displeasure of South Africa and some conservative members of the U.S. Congress.

set up further action with respect to continuing U.S. membership or contributions. In 1984, another Kasten provision required withholding the U.S. share of interest expenses for external U.N. borrowing and for wage increases that the United States opposed.[93]

In 1985, three related developments accelerated the process of tying U.S. contributions to U.N. performance. First, the Sundquist amendment required withholding the U.S. share of salaries of Soviet citizens seconded to the U.N. Secretariat, on the grounds that those funds were routinely "kicked back" to the Soviet government.[94] Other proposals that same year, not adopted, would have added prohibitions on funding additional U.N. activities. To this point, congressional strictures on the United Nations resembled the traditional control techniques (primarily prohibitions and reports) discussed above, and the cumulative amounts withheld were very small, much less than 1 percent of the U.S. assessment and totaling $7,293,263 through the end of 1985.[95]

Second, outside actions affected significantly the amounts withheld, the rationales employed, and the creativity of the means chosen. Budget realities intruded on U.N. funding. GRH sequestration required a cut of approximately 10 percent across the board in allocations to international organizations. This was a disproportionate reduction because the full amount had to be absorbed from this category; other State Department accounts had already received their full appropriation. In addition, there was an regular appropriations shortfall attributable to GRH limits, to an innovative effort at U.N. reform, and to the by-now-routine withholdings from specified activities such as the PLO.

Third and foremost in 1985, however, was the reform effort itself, in the form of the Kassebaum-Solomon amendment,[96] requiring that the United States limit its contributions to 20 percent of the U.N. operating budget (vice the assessed rate of 25 percent) unless the United Nations adopted weighted voting procedures to give a stronger budget voice to the principal

93. The 1983 amendment appears in the first unnumbered paragraph following sec. 101(b)(1) of P.L. 98-51, Further Continuing Appropriations for Fiscal Year 1984 (H.J. Res. 413), November 14, 1983. The 1984 amendment appears under the heading "Contributions to International Organizations" in the FY 1985 State Department Appropriations Act, H.R. 5712 (P.L. 98-411, August 30, 1984); virtually identical language appeared in every subsequent State Department appropriations act through at least FY 1996.
94. Sec. 151, Foreign Relations Authorization Act, Fiscal Years 1986 and 1987, P.L. 99-93, August 16, 1985.
95. Data from IO's Office of Budget.
96. Sec. 143 of P.L. 99-93.

contributor countries. This approach would have required revision of the enabling treaties, and would have opened up such issues as the Security Council veto of the five post–World War II powers. Because of the risks involved, the president chose not to raise the weighted-voting issue at the United Nations, accepting instead the reduced payment levels permitted. That those who guided U.S. policy in the administration were among the harshest critics (from the right) of the United Nations may also have influenced this decision. In fact, for FY 1987, the United States fell even further behind assessed levels, because the president's budget only requested amounts consistent with Kassebaum-Solomon.

This experiment in "contingency funding" is what is most important for current purposes. Instead of authorizing and appropriating set amounts for set purposes, contingency funding requires that certain actions take place and that they be accepted by specified procedures as meeting the stipulated requirements before funds are released. This approach is both superficially attractive and a constitutional alternative to the "legislative veto" disallowed by the *Chadha* decision. However, as later events would show, it is difficult to control and runs the risk that funds originally set aside for a set purpose will lapse and be returned to the Treasury, even as other programs are desperately short of funds. Under GRH and subsequent modifications, lapses are a greater problem now than they were in less difficult times.

Given the president's request, funds withholding continued for FY 1987, but new elements were added. First, the United Nations began a highly visible budgetary reform (although not one involving weighted budgetary voting). Second, it began to feel the financial pinch, thus justifying Kassebaum-Solomon in the eyes of its advocates but also raising the concerns of U.N. supporters as the U.S. arrearages grew to major proportions. The Group of Eighteen (G-18) experts, established in December 1985 to review U.N. administrative and financial practices, was initially disposed to sweeping changes. However, these were diluted by UNGA, and the G-18 final report in December 1986 was much more modest. This turn of events set off battles throughout 1987 over whether what had been done was enough to lighten the Kassebaum-Solomon restrictions.

In the FY 1988–89 Foreign Relations Authorization Bill, that question was answered in the affirmative and a substantial modification to Kassebaum-Solomon was adopted. Under the complex revised provision,[97] 40 percent of the assessed contribution could be paid automatically any time

97. Sec. 702 of P.L. 100-204, amending sec. 143 of P.L. 99-93.

after October 1 of the year in question. An additional 40 percent might be paid on a presidential determination that (1) the revised U.N. budgetary decisionmaking procedure was being implemented; (2) progress was also being made toward a limitation on seconded employees; and (3) progress was being made in reducing the size of the U.N. Secretariat staff. Finally, the last 20 percent could be paid thirty days after the presidential determination, unless in the meantime the Congress had adopted a joint resolution prohibiting such payment.

In late November 1987, *before* the FY 1988 State authorization and appropriation bills had been passed, and therefore while the original Kassebaum-Solomon was still law, Secretary General Javier Pérez de Cuellar was promised by Deputy Secretary of State John C. Whitehead that $90 million of what the United States owed would be paid to enable the United Nations to meet its December payroll, in addition to $10 million previously paid.[98] State argued that, notwithstanding the statute, it had authority to pay this amount. Thus a major contretemps was set off, but eventually the funding envisaged in the budget summit ($144 million) was in fact authorized and appropriated, with the final $44 million being made available later from FY 1988, still well below the assessed contribution level of $209 million for calendar year 1987. Here matters stood until the summer of 1988, when the sudden need for U.N. peacekeepers in the Persian Gulf after the Iran-Iraqi truce made U.N. funding again highly visible.

A small detour is warranted, because the search for greatly increased peacekeeping funds over the next several years is revealing with respect to many of the themes explored in this book. On July 27, 1988, SFRC Chairman Claiborne Pell attempted to modify the CJS appropriation bill on the Senate floor to provide more funding for peacekeeping in the Near East and elsewhere by transferring funds from DOD, on the grounds that the latter's costs would be cut since it no longer needed to provide escort services in the Gulf. Although there was logic on his side, Pell's approach was not one likely to succeed in the controlled world of appropriations, where floor surprises are not welcome. Pell was soundly put down by CJS Chairman Fritz Hollings, who said: "Let us be serious here for a moment."[99]

In mid-September that year, the administration notified Congress that the president had determined that the reform requirements of the revised Kasse-

---

98. Reported by the *New York Times* in a series of stories on November 13, 20, 24, December 1, 3, and 4, 1987.

99. *Congressional Record* 134 (July 27, 1988): 18972–75.

baum-Solomon amendment were being met, and that the administration therefore proposed to release the remaining $44 million available for the U.N. assessment. Almost immediately, Senator Jesse Helms, always an unreconcilable foe of the United Nations, filed the expected resolution of disapproval of the president's certification. All this was accompanied by a full-scale administration effort to gain congressional approval to transfer peace-keeping funds from Defense to State, essentially as originally proposed by Pell. It was not to be, but later years would see several creative approaches to the funding of peacekeeping.[100]

Over the next several authorization bills, the Congress also tried a variety of funding provisions for the main U.N. account, all reflecting the joint pressures to make the United Nations accountable but viable. As always, this issue was a useful reminder that there is not just one Congress, but many. To continue this thread, the FY 1990–91 Foreign Relations Authorization Act, passed in early 1990 after the many difficulties detailed above,[101] contained a provision applauding recent progress in reforms but still applying pressure. It provided that the president

> shall withhold 20 percent of the funds appropriated for the United
> States contribution to the United Nations or any of its specialized

100. Funding for rapidly increasing peacekeeping costs—$29.4 million in FY 1988 (the longtime base level), $115 million by FY 1991, $460 million by FY 1993, and more than $1 billion for FY 1994—came from two basic sources: Function 050 (the Defense function) and Function 150 (International Affairs). GRH and BEA caps and fences complicated the problem of funding these generally well supported activities. For FY 1993, for example, the Senate appropriators wished to shift funds from 050 to 150 for peacekeeping; Senator Sam Nunn, the Armed Forces chairman would agree only if he retained authorizing authority, which the SFRC rejected. However, cuts in military-related foreign assistance funding engineered by Representative David Obey provided some 150 "headroom," which was allocated to CJS to fund peacekeeping. Finally, for FY 1995, an arrangement was worked out in the Clinton administration and with Congress to divide peacekeeping costs into two categories. While State had until then managed all peacekeeping operations, under the new approach Defense would take the lead for peacekeeping operations under Chapter VII of the U.N. Charter (involving the use of force or threat of the use of force, with or without the consent of the states involved), while the State Department would retain the lead for those under Chapter VI (the traditional noncombat operations carried out by neutral forces with the consent of the states affected). That year, the State Department's request for FY 1995 under this split approach was $533 million, including $23 million for remaining arrearages, and $519 million survived in the final CJS Appropriation Act (P.L. 103-317, August 26, 1994). Details of this approach come from the FY 1995 *Budget in Brief*, prepared by State's Bureau of Finance and Management Policy (February 1994), pp. 61–64. In addition, $670 million in supplemental appropriations was provided for peacekeeping for FY 1994.

101. Namely, the problems caused by the Pell-Hollings dispute in November 1987 over the requirement for an authorization bill before appropriations could be expended.

agencies for any calendar year until the President determines and reports to the Congress that the United Nations or any such agency

is continuing implementation of the same reform elements specified in the prior bill. They were (1) taking appropriate account of U.S. views in "consensus based" budgeting; (2) continuing progress in eliminating the abuse of secondment in the U.N. Secretariat; and (3) implementing the 15 percent staff cut recommended by an intergovernmental review group.[102]

The FY 1992–93 bill, passed in the fall of 1991, repealed some of these earlier provisions, made payment of the final 20 percent of assessed contributions contingent only on further progress in consensus-based budget-making, continued to require presidential reports to Congress of such determinations and, for the first time, explicitly provided for payment of arrearages from past years, if in the U.S. interest, notwithstanding the provisions of prior authorizations.[103] In 1993–94, the House and Senate versions of the FY 1994–95 authorization bills repeated almost identical provisions, with the Senate adding two additional requirements: (1) that 10 percent of authorized U.N. funding for FY 1994 and 20 percent for FY 1995 and subsequent years be withheld until the president certified that the United Nations had established an Office of the Inspector General with specified powers; and (2) that U.N. funding for FY 1995 was authorized only if the key management position at the United Nations was held by an American citizen (although a waiver was provided if the secretary of state certified confidence in the non-American incumbent and explained why this was in the U.S. interest). The House proposed eliminating the annual reports to Congress (they were retained in the Senate version) and also endorsed the inspector general concept, albeit as a "sense of the Congress" provision. In the delayed conference compromise, the Senate position generally prevailed, except that the requirement for U.S. participation in U.N. management became a "sense of the Congress" provision, rather than a direct requirement. The House was also unsuccessful in eliminating the annual report.[104]

102. Foreign Relations Authorization Act, Fiscal Years 1990 and 1991, P.L. 101-246, February 16, 1990, sec. 406(c).

103. Foreign Relations Authorization Act, FY 1992–93, P.L. 102-138, October 28, sec. 162.

104. The House provision was sec. 163 of H.R. 2333, passed in June 1993; the parallel Senate provision was sec. 165 of S. 1281, passed and substituted for H.R. 2333 on February 2, 1994, with the inspector general requirement appearing in secs. 166 and 170D and the American-manager provision in sec. 167. The House endorsement of an inspector general was in sec. 194 of H.R. 2333. The conference result, P.L. 103-236, April 30, 1994, contained the

In 1995–96, both the House and the Senate version of the authorization bill continued the same skeptical attitude toward the United Nations. While the full House bill was identical to the prior authorization act with respect to these provisions, the Senate bill as reported from the SFRC eliminated the earlier provision providing for the payment of arrearages from past years. The conference report incorporated the House approach; but, as will be seen, the bill was vetoed by the president.[105] Thus the prior provisions remained in effect. On the appropriations side, some U.N. funding was restored by the CR in late April 1996, but the United States remained by far the biggest debtor.[106]

U.N. funding will remain an issue of contention, especially with a much more skeptical Republican Congress and much greater general concern about peacekeeping. While both the late Bush and the Clinton administration committed themselves to making up all arrearages except those specifically prohibited by law, as of September 30, 1995, the United States was still by far the biggest debtor nation with arrearages of $1.434 billion, divided between regular assessments ($527.2 million) and peacekeeping ($907.2 million). All other nations combined had arrearages of $1.866 billion, the grand total being $3.330 billion.[107]

In 1996, the arrearage issue helped deny Boutros Boutros-Ghali a second term as U.N. Secretary General. In the face of charges by congressional Republicans, in particular SFRC chairman Jesse Helms, that Boutros-Ghali had failed to carry out U.N. reforms with sufficient vigor, President Clinton and permanent representative to the United Nations Madeleine Albright became convinced that there was no hope of congressional agreement to arrearage payments unless he was replaced. Once Kofi Annan of Ghana

---

Kassebaum-Solomon follow-on provision as sec. 409; the inspector general and management provisions were secs. 401 and 402, respectively.

105. Sec. 2521 of H.R. 1561, passed by the House on June 8, 1995; sec. 204 of S. 908, passed by the Senate on December 14, 1995; sec. 2521 of the conference report, filed March 8, 1996.

106. See, for example, Barbara Crossette, "U.N. Agencies Feeling the Pain as the U.S. Lags on Payments," *New York Times*, March 11, 1996; Barbara Crossette, "Four Months into Its Budget Year, the U.N. Says It Is Broke," *New York Times*, April 30, 1996; and John M. Goshko, "Payment from U.S. Will Ease, Not End, U.N.'s Money Woes," *Washington Post*, April 30, 1996.

107. U.N. data, summarized in "United Nations: To bury or to praise," *Economist* 337 (October 21, 1995): 24 (box). Restoration of some current-year funding for peacekeeping in the April 26, 1996, CR did nothing to resolve the arrearage problem, although it did keep the United States from falling even farther behind for that account. U.S. sources argue that the amount owed is less, not counting funds withheld for policy reasons, or in excess of statutory percentage limits.

was elected to replace Boutras-Ghali, the dialogue began anew, although convincing Helms to go along would clearly be no easy task. The president's FY 1998 budget submission, sent to Congress in February 1997, contained a plan to pay off all of the arrearages the administration deemed were owed (a somewhat lesser amount than the United Nations hoped to receive).[108]

Peacekeeping, as a result of the U.N. role in the Iraq-Kuwait crisis, in Cambodia, in Somalia, and in a number of other recent cases—preeminently Bosnia—will continue to be of particular importance, although the future will be complicated by a growing concern that the United Nations is not up to the task.[109] By 1995 this feeling had intensified, so that not only was funding limited but there were increasingly serious efforts in Congress both to constrain the president's ability to commit U.S. forces to peacekeeping and to limit the time and the conditions under which they could serve.[110] Also intriguing is what lessons Congress will learn from this episode and whether contingency budgeting will be used more frequently as a way of imposing its stamp on foreign policy.

## Post Closings and Openings, 1980–1996

Throughout the 1980s and 1990s, State's desire to save money by closing diplomatic and consular posts of low priority became an issue of contention and controversy. Indeed, it generated heat out of proportion to its importance, in my opinion. Still, it is worth detailing some of the byplay involved, for at least three reasons. First, in most of the cases we have seen relating to congressional attempts to impose particular courses of action on the executive, there have been prohibitions or limits on spending, minimum amounts

---

108. See Barbara Crossette, "White House Steps Up Efforts to Deny U.N. Chief a 2d Term," *New York Times*, November 7, 1996; Barbara Crossette, "Boutros-Ghali vs. 'Goliath': His Account," *New York Times*, November 20, 1996; John M. Goshko, "New U.N. Chief Empha-sizes Reform, but Without 'Arbitrary' Personnel Cuts," *Washington Post*, January 10, 1997; and John M. Goshko, "In Shift, U.N. Chief Meets With Helms on Reforms," *Washington Post*, January 24, 1997. Helms's reaction to the administration U.N. funding plan was highly negative, in part because it depended upon a supplemental appropriation which would be considered by appropriations committees and not by *his* SFRC. See "Plan to Fund U.N. Draws Helms Fire," *Washington Post*, January 30, 1997.

109. See Elaine Sciolino, "New U.S. Peacekeeping Policy De-emphasizes Role of the U.N.: A Sharp Shift from Clinton's Campaign Stance," *New York Times*, May 6, 1994.

110. The final FY 1996 CR did restore some $81 million above the level in the CJS confer-ence report to State's appropriations for peacekeeping, for a total of $359 million, but this was still $86 million below the president's request of $445 million and well below the $519 million appropriated for FY 1995.

to be spent for a particular purpose, or conditions that had to be met before funds could be expended. Legislative requirements regarding post closings add some new and rather creative wrinkles (if vindictive in the eyes of many at State) to this catalog, starting with the point that in these instances the executive usually wishes to close a post to reduce costs, while the Congress[111] generally desires that it remain open and that funds be expended to operate it. This case, in a small way, sets the usual image of executive eagerness to spend and congressional restraint on its ear.

The second illuminating aspect is the extent to which the congressional willingness to punish State if certain posts were closed has been staff-driven, with one individual SFRC staff member leading the charge for more than a decade. Far more than is recognized by most beyond the Beltway, many congressional "decisions" reflect the predilections of determined staffers, not the views of busy members. Many points of serious conflict, including post closings, can be traced to executive irritation when serious proposals are dismissed cavalierly.

Post closing is revealing for a third reason: it illustrates the very different perceptions dominating the executive versus the Congress, and clarifies the perspectives of each. At State, the question of where posts are needed is normally seen as a matter of how best to conduct business; as trade patterns change, or as transportation allows easier movement over longer distances, the need for outposts away from the capital declines, especially when there are demands to open new embassies and posts in newly independent states.[112] Congress, reflecting what it takes to be the opinion of the American public, is much more inclined to see the issue symbolically ("lowering the American flag for the last time"; "cut and run"). Congress is also more subject than the executive to lobbying to keep posts open. Important constituents (e.g., businesses with overseas operations there or ethnic groups residing in a member's state or district) may urge that a given post stay open. Moreover, foreign officials often see the loss of a U.S. consulate as a blow to the status of their city or area;[113] and the personal views of congres-

111. Or at least the authorizers. State's appropriations subcommittees, notably on the House side, have often encouraged State to save money by closing some posts, but they have not been willing to take on their authorizing colleagues.

112. One informal Department of State study in the late 1980s found that since 1789, some 750 posts had been opened and more than 500 closed—with many having been opened and closed multiple times, owing to changed conditions.

113. A well-known example is the inevitable visit of the mayor of Salzburg, Austria, to Chairman Dante Fascell of HFAC whenever the Salzburg consulate was proposed for closing. The mayor's concern was that, given the internal tension between cosmopolitan Vienna and

sional members or staff about the importance of a particular post, often based on background or knowledge, may well differ from those of the executive.[114]

Now to some specifics. In section 108 of the FY 1980–81 State Department Authorization Act, passed in late 1979, Congress directed that ten specified consulates not be closed or, if closed by the date of enactment, that they be reopened as soon as possible. This provision was in response to State's decision to go ahead with the closings in spite of congressional concerns.[115]

By the time the next authorization bill passed, however, in 1982, State had not in the opinion of SFRC staff fully complied, thus leading to the inclusion of a provision[116] which earmarked funding for operation of seven of the ten posts and which stated in addition that no other new posts could be opened until all seven had been reopened.[117] A problem of the "unanticipated consequences" variety shortly emerged when the government of Burma, owing to a deterioration of relations with the United States, refused to allow Mandalay to be reopened, thus making any other new openings impossible under the terms of section 103. Therefore, the next authorization act, for FY 1984–85, amended this section by adding a clause ("to the extent such reopening is authorized by the foreign government involved") and by requiring a report on the status of foreign government authorizations to reopen posts and the status of reopenings.[118] Meanwhile, although State reopened or kept open the remaining posts in question, after a hiatus of a

---

the more bucolic west, Salzburg would suffer if it could no longer claim it was important to the United States. One (unverified) story has it that a former senior staff member of HFAC was an ally of the mayor, having spent a pleasant honeymoon there! In 1993, when State finally succeeded in closing Salzburg, the department still had to defer until after the annual summer music festival, so that the consulate would be available to provide services for the many American visitors, thus illustrating an additional congressional concern.

114. The most interesting example was Bratislava, Czechoslovakia, now the capital of Slovakia, which Claiborne Pell, the SFRC chairman, insisted be opened and remain open. He had served there as a Foreign Service officer in the 1940s, had closed the post when the Soviets invaded Czechoslovakia, and maintained a strong belief it should be opened throughout the intervening period. In a way, he was vindicated in 1993, when the consulate became an embassy, after Czechoslovakia dissolved into the Czech Republic and Slovakia.

115. The posts were Salzburg, Bremen, Nice, Turin, Göteborg, Adana (Turkey), Tangier, Mandalay, Brisbane, and Surabaya (Indonesia).

116. Sec. 103 of the Foreign Relations Authorization Act, Fiscal Years 1982–83, P.L. 97-241, August 24, 1982.

117. The three posts omitted from the prior list of ten were Adana, Tangier, and Surabaya, none of which attracted sufficient congressional interest to be kept open.

118. P.L. 98-164, September 22, 1983, sec. 1371.

few years the department renewed its pursuit of post closings in 1986 and 1987, as financial pressures began to build in the wake of GRH. This course of action was given especially strong consideration in 1987, during the cost-cutting review mandated by Secretary of State Shultz. A new aspect was that State was by this time required to notify the authorizing committees as well as the appropriators that it intended to reprogram post-closing savings for other purposes.[119]

In 1986, State closed Nice and Bremen, two of the seven posts that had been at issue earlier, notwithstanding considerable congressional grumbling and the assertion by some staffers that this move was in violation of the requirements of the 1982 statute. In 1987, the department indicated the likely need to close others, closer to the heart—including Göteborg, of interest to an important Pell constituent; Salzberg, of interest to HFAC and Fascell; and Turin, dear to important constituents of several members.

Given the generally confrontational atmosphere surrounding the FY 1988–89 State Authorization Bill (see Chapter 5), it was almost inevitable that post closings would be an item of contention. From personal knowledge, I can attest that the motivation of one senior SFRC staffer, still smarting from his belief that State had ignored the will of the Congress (and thus had thwarted his own judgment), was at least as much to punish the department as it was to redefine which posts should be closed and opened. As already noted, the final provision prohibited spending any funds for post-closing costs, prohibited any spending on State's Bureau of Administration unless all posts that had been open on January 1, 1987, remained open, and earmarked $50 million of S&E funding to "be available only to operate United States consulates in Salzburg, Strasbourg, Göteborg, Lyon, Düsseldorf, Tangier, Genoa, Nice, Pôrto Alegre, and Maracaibo."[120] There was a small escape clause, which allowed a post to be closed only in order to open one of higher priority with congressional notification, but only if the total number of posts remained at least as great as those in existence on January 1, 1987. This was one of three provisions waived for two years in the accompanying appropriations act. In 1988, using the waiver, State closed Göteborg, Tangier, Düsseldorf, and Turin, amid congressional displeasure but no retaliation.

At times, intracongressional politics spill over to issues such as post clos-

119. These new requirements, as cited above, were added to the State Department Basic Authorities Act by the FY 1984–85 State and USIA Authorization Act.

120. Sec. 122—the quoted passage is from subsection 122(b)(1)—of P.L. 100-204, December 22, 1987.

ings. The same 1988–89 legislation just discussed directed in section 123 that the embassy in Antigua and Barbuda be closed unless the president determined and reported to Congress that such action was not in the national security interests of the United States. This section was a direct slap at Congressman Trent Lott, one of whose former staffers had been appointed as ambassador to Barbados, with a collateral appointment to Antigua and Barbuda, which State wanted to close but Lott and his protégé did not. This provision was, however, repealed in the subsequent bill, in 1989,[121] and the post remained open until budget pressures finally brought about its closure in 1994. Finally, section 124 of the FY 1990–91 bill, showing some recognition of changing world circumstances but a continued interest in fine-tuned management of post openings and closings, was a "sense of the Congress" resolution that the president should "take all practicable steps to reopen the United States consulate in Bratislava, Czechoslovakia." This was shortly done, much to the pleasure of Senator Pell.

Ambiguities still remained, especially with respect to the status of the waived provision in the FY 1988–89 Authorization Act. Authorization staffers, some new to this tiresome dispute, and their State counterparts thought the time had come to regularize ways of dealing with the issue while preserving the positions of all concerned. Thus, the FY 1992–93 Authorization Act (in sec. 112) added a new section 48 to the Basic Authorities Act that apparently prohibited expenditures of funds for closing posts or for the Bureau of Administration if posts were closed (thus bowing in the direction of the recalcitrant Senate staffer responsible for the 1988–89 language). However, exceptions were provided if Congress was notified forty-five days before planned closing and if the reprogramming requirements of the Basic Authorities Act were followed, which State believed provided the needed flexibility. This compromise was eased by the recognition that funding for numerous new posts in the former Soviet Union and elsewhere needed to be found, and that closing lower-priority posts was an obvious, logical choice.

In late 1992, the outgoing Bush administration notified Congress of its intention to close some twenty posts in fiscal years 1993 and 1994, which was reaffirmed in January 1993. The new administration chose to let this decision stand and, after considerable consultation, notified the Congress on May 10, 1993, that it would proceed with the Bush plan with only very minor changes, leaving one small embassy open and delaying the closing of

---

121. Sec. 121 of the FY 1990–91 Authorization Act repealed the earlier provision.

two other posts.[122] Surprisingly, given the history of this volatile issue, the executive branch largely got its way this time. Eighteen of the twenty posts proposed for closure were not formally objected to by Congress. State gave way on only two: Apia, Western Samoa (because of the strong interest of a delegate from American Samoa, who was a member of the International Operations Subcommittee of HFAC); and Curaçao, Netherlands Antilles (in deference to Senator Pell and his staff director, who expressed serious concern about closing it and who intimated that cooperation in other matters would be easier for them to provide if the post were left open). Still later, in the spring of 1995, Secretary Christopher announced that as many as twenty-five additional posts, including some small embassies, would have to be closed, owing to budgetary constraints. As always, the acceptance of these closings by Congress, later reduced to nineteen, depended on which posts were finally picked.[123] Predictably, when the list was sent forward in June, Senator Pell raised reservations about closing down the Zurich post, on the grounds that it would be harmful to Liechtenstein (and his friend, the Grand Duke) to receive services from Embassy Bern, somewhat farther away![124]

Congress was cross-pressured. Section 2205 of the House version of the FY 1996–97 State Authorization Bill required that the secretary of state develop a worldwide plan for consolidation "wherever practicable, on a regional or areawide basis, of United States missions and consular posts abroad," and there was a similar Senate provision (section 1103). Yet both were dropped from the conference report: even in a financial crunch, apparently, endorsing post closings was too much.

Looking beyond these specific events, one must conclude that post closings will remain an issue. Although there are fewer than a hundred consul-

122. The relevant communications were letters to Congress from Under Secretary John F. W. Rogers on November 6, 1992, and January 14, 1993; and from Under Secretary J. Brian Atwood on May 10, 1993.

123. Memorandum from Christopher to Steering Committee Members and SMI Team Leaders, "Strategic Management Initiative Recommendations," May 5, 1995, attachment entitled "SMI—Secretary's Decisions," p. 6. For a speculative list of the posts likely to be selected, see "State Department Seeks to Shutter 21 Consulates," *Washington Times*, June 2, 1995. A refined listing appeared in "19 Posts to Close, but Workers Spared," *Foreign Service Journal* 72 (October 1995): 19. By May 1996, fourteen had been closed, with decisions "deferred" on the rest owing to congressional concerns (discussion with a knowledgeable State Department officer, May 13, 1996).

124. I was told this by a State Department officer who participated in the SFRC briefing on these closings, July 21, 1995. State had the foresight to instruct the ambassador to Switzerland to make a prior call on the Grand Duke in order to reassure him!

ates still open and the pool of possible closures is thus reduced, budget problems will continue to prompt reexaminations; as Christopher's 1995 announcement suggested, some minor embassies will have to be closed as well. As one perceptive commentator (a State Department officer who believes in very broad representation abroad and thinks that we should not close embassies if relations continue) has written: "Determining the relative importance of posts, both for resource allocation purposes and making judgments as to the disposition of posts, is necessarily subjective, hence imprecise."[125]

In contrast, it is interesting that the somewhat similar 1993 decision of USAID to close twenty-one missions (almost 20 percent of its *total* number) by the end of FY 1996 sparked much less heat, was approved by the secretary of state, and was accepted by Congress.[126] Arguably, Congress bought the executive argument that foreign assistance should be conducted in a businesslike way but would not, for symbolic reasons, accept a similar premise for diplomatic and consular posts.

In this chapter we have seen the creativity that Congress can muster to put its stamp on foreign policy, particularly with respect to "second-level" issues on which the president cannot afford to spend much political capital to win. The day-to-day interaction is sometimes as telling for outcomes as the grander issues that receive all the public attention. Such interaction, over time, can affect the overall balance between the two branches and certainly can make a difference in the operational efficiency of the executive. Despite the congressional assertiveness detailed here, to assess the mid-1990s as being the moment of the "Imperial Congress," as one prominent former executive-branch official does,[127] seems overstated. As seen, the executive can also mete out penalties and rewards.

---

125. Alphonse F. La Porta, "Overseas Posts: Locations, Functions, and Staffing," annex I to the *State 2000* report, p. 264; table 3, on pp. 266 and 267, contains a very useful summary of post openings and closings between 1970 and 1992. Information on subsequent closings was provided by the legislation affairs staff in the State Department's Office of the Under Secretary for Management.

126. This decision and the schedule for the specific missions to be closed was announced in a USAID general notice on November 19, 1993. In 1995, the number to be closed was revised upward to twenty-seven, again with little opposition from Congress. USAID's dire budgetary straits made it likely that many more would eventually have to be closed.

127. Joseph Califano, "Imperial Congress," *New York Times Magazine* (January 22, 1994): 40–41.

# CHAPTER SEVEN

# MYTHS IN EXECUTIVE–CONGRESSIONAL RELATIONS

Now that the current budgetmaking structure and some of the complexities of matching resources to policy execution and operations have been described, several myths in the conventional wisdom concerning foreign policy funding warrant attention. All of these generalizations hold some truth, but each requires qualification. Interestingly, there is little evidence that the 1994 Republican takeover of both houses of Congress changed the picture in any significant way, although the nuances differ. Institutional predilections remain very influential in determining how the Congress conducts itself in the foreign policy arena.

## Things Are Now Worse Than Ever

Some argue that relations between the foreign affairs agencies and the Congress have in recent times been at an all-time low. Besides the lack of a natural "foreign affairs constituency" to provide pressure and support, observers point to the disputes one can expect when Congress is controlled by one party and the presidency by another. Also, it is said, constitutional/ institutional disagreements are more intense than before the Vietnam War. Indeed, cooperation between the branches is frequently argued to be at its nadir.

Such generalizations are too easy. The assertion that having Congress and the executive controlled by the same party will fix whatever problems exist is dubious: interbranch relations have only intermittently been smooth, re-gardless of the partisan alignment. Institutional differences will always be with us, as the Founding Fathers undoubtedly thought necessary. Indeed, anyone who recalls the troubled sixties and early seventies, when Otto Pass-man and John Rooney, respectively, were in charge of the House Foreign Operations and Commerce-Justice-State appropriations subcommittees, is likely to need some persuasion that things are worse now.

Rooney, a New Yorker and a liberal Democrat (and therefore, one would think, an internationalist) was resolutely convinced that bureaucrats, espe-cially in the Foreign Service, were lazy and given to extravagance at public expense. One 1964 summary noted that Rooney had been called "one of the most powerful men in America, in a negative way," and that he was said to have cut more than a billion dollars from agency budgets over a ten-year period.[1] His intense questioning of virtually every item in State's budget submission became legendary, as did his use of informants within the de-partment and his influence in some personnel decisions. But once he took a State appropriations bill to the House floor, it was rare indeed that it was challenged, so some have argued that he actually served as a shield for the department.[2]

A look back at Figure 1 shows that during the Johnson administration buildup of the federal budget in the mid-1960s, funding for Function 150, especially for State, was flat, heavily owing to Rooney. He was given to endless sniping on small items, whether they were travel allowances, repre-sentation funds (he called this a "whiskey allowance"), or what he consid-ered to be excessive funding for the Foreign Service Institute. On the other hand, he also fought reductions for the International Information Service in 1953, only to criticize its successor, the United States Information Service,

1. James Reston, *New York Times*, cited in "Rooney, John J(oseph)," *Current Biography Yearbook, 1964* (New York: H.W. Wilson, 1965), p. 379.
2. For the flavor of Rooney's activities, see William L. Rivers, "The Foreign Policy of John J. Rooney," *Reporter* 24 (June 22, 1961): 36–38 (the point about serving as a shield for State is made on p. 37). See also Richard F. Fenno, Jr., *The Power of the Purse: Appropriations Politics in Congress* (Boston: Little, Brown, 1966), pp. 277, 279, and 459, for Rooney's im-pact. Fenno makes the same point as Rivers about Rooney's protecting the Department of State (p. 459). This sort of reputation is not all that rare. In 1995, for example, three of the four new Republican appropriations subcommittee chairmen—Senator Mitch McConnell (Foreign Operations), Representative Hal Rogers (CJS), Representative Sonny Callahan (For-eign Operations)—demonstrated similar protectiveness for "their" accounts, particularly im-portant in a time of intense budgetary pressure. Senator Phil Gramm (CJS) was quite a different personality, inflicting considerable pain on State and USIA, somewhat mitigated at the full SAC level by Senator Mark Hatfield, the chairman of that committee.

two years later, as being "futile" and "more interested in propagandizing the American public than in combatting Communism overseas."[3] On retirement in 1974, Rooney was succeeded by John Slack, who while less colorful was only marginally more sympathetic about the resources needed to carry out an effective policy abroad.

Meanwhile, there was a roughly similar story going on with respect to foreign aid. Here Otto Passman of Louisiana held sway for a similar period as Rooney, and with much the same results. Having been handpicked by Appropriations Chairman Clarence Cannon to chair the subcommittee, once the former "had become convinced that a maximum budget-cutting pattern would prevail,"[4] Passman single-handedly kept a very tight rein on foreign economic assistance. It was once claimed by Passman that the Kennedy administration offered to drop long-term project financing if Passman would step down as subcommittee chairman.[5] Only in 1964 was the Johnson administration able to achieve a significant funding increase, over Passman's opposition, but this was a rare loss. In 1965, the new chairman of the full committee, George Mahon, decided that the balance was too negative and replaced two anti-aid Democrats on the Passman subcommittee with two more favorably inclined members.[6]

By the early 1990s, in marked contrast, it can be argued that all four of the relevant appropriations subcommittees and their key members (Representatives David Obey and Neal Smith in the House, Senators Pat Leahy and Fritz Hollings in the Senate) had become sophisticated and knowledgeable about international programs and operations. That they did not always agree with the State Department, USIA, or USAID is not the same thing as being implacable opponents. Until the realities of GRH set in, for example, there was a major increase, assisted by Democrats in key congressional positions, in foreign assistance. Figures 2a and 2b show this trend.

The pattern was somewhat similar for State Department operations. There was at least as much impetus from Congress for the large buildup in overseas security programs carried out by State from 1986 to 1988 as there was from the department itself, and some on the Hill argued that State was too timid. The mid-1980s were not a bad time for overall departmental

---

3. The Rooney entry in *Current Biography* (see note 1 above), pp. 379–80, is the source for this section unless specified otherwise.

4. Fenno, *The Power of the Purse*, p. 145.

5. *New York Times*, August 5, 1961, cited in Burton M. Sapin, *The Making of United States Foreign Policy* (New York: Praeger, for Brookings Institution, 1966), pp. 42–43, n. 7.

6. Fenno, *The Power of the Purse*, p. 146.

operations; and once again, it was the pressures of GRH that reversed the trend toward what the executive regarded as adequate funding. The same picture was perhaps most clearly seen for information and cultural affairs programs run by USIA. Charles Wick, the Reagan administration's director of the agency, proved to be a genius at selling his programs to Congress, even in the face of skepticism from many foreign affairs professionals elsewhere in the executive branch.

The pattern was modified somewhat with the retirement and death of HAC Chairman William Natcher in early 1994. Obey was chosen as the new chairman, over Smith, while retaining his role as chairman of the International Operations Subcommittee. Smith moved to chair the Labor, Health and Human Services, and Education Subcommittee, with Representative Alan Mollohan of West Virginia replacing him at CJS. Mollohan showed a tendency to judge each program on its strengths and weaknesses, rather than, as Smith had frequently done, starting with the numbers that he believed had to be met and then looking for programs to adjust. This is a nuance, and possibly an artifact of a new chairman learning the ropes. In any event, Smith remained on the CJS subcommittee and there were no staff changes, so the approach to the FY 1995 bill varied only in subtle ways from the Smith years.[7] Of course, all this changed with the 1994 elections.

In 1995, with new Republican chairmen all around, there were some surprising pluses. Chapter 8 recounts many of the specifics for that year, but some initial observations are pertinent here. Starting with appropriations in the House, Hal Rogers, longtime ranking member of CJS, assumed control with Alan Mollohan now as ranking minority member. Although the CJS bill for FY 1996 was the source of major controversy, little of it came from the State part of the bill. While funding for peacekeeping and for USIA was severely reduced, the key accounts for State operations and administration survived at livable levels. Allowing for the overall pressure on discretionary funding, it was appropriations business as usual. Only the very close observer would have noticed much difference from 1994.

Foreign Operations was more interesting. Sonny Callahan of Alabama assumed the chairmanship, with the longtime member Charley Wilson of Texas as ranking minority member. The new appropriations chairman Bob Livingston of Louisiana (chosen by Speaker Newt Gingrich over several more senior Republicans because of his fealty to the budget-cutting mantra)

---

7. The analysis here is based in part on discussions, in June 1994 and subsequently, with a knowledgeable State Department legislative officer who worked closely with the appropriators.

and the peripatetic Obey, now ranking minority member of the full committee, both kept a close eye. A distinct asset was Livingston's choice as staff director, James W. Dyer, who in earlier years had been a congressional relations officer at State and who both understood and was sympathetic to the foreign affairs agencies. Callahan, known for never having voted for a foreign operations appropriation, proved to be much more of an appropriator than a budgetary/isolationist zealot; like Rooney a generation before, when the "Foreign Ops" bill came to the House floor it became his bill, and he defended it fiercely. The problem that year came from a tendency to add substantive items to almost all appropriations bills.

The House Foreign Affairs Committee, which became the House International Relations Committee (HIRC) in the general renaming of House committees in 1995, continued its quixotic quest for relevance, with Ben Gilman and Lee Hamilton merely switching positions, and its generally moderate approach was pushed in a more radical direction by larger House forces and close oversight by the leadership. Chris Smith of New Jersey became chairman of the HIRC Subcommittee on International Operations, but except for the abortion issue (about which more later) he was relatively moderate, perhaps tempered by the presence on the subcommittee of Ben Gilman and the former chairman Howard Berman. Even under the pressure to conform to new Republican priorities, older patterns of operation showed surprising strength—in particular the successful anti–Jesse Helms effort by the Republican HIRC member Doug Bereuter of Nebraska against some of the more extreme elements of Helms's reorganization plan (Chapter 8).

The Senate showed its own peculiarities, but was hardly a surprise. Helms and Pell switched positions on the SFRC, with the activist Olympia Snowe of Maine, newly elected to the Senate, chairing the SFRC Subcommittee on International Operations. This committee, given the predictably intense pressure for major changes and cutbacks from Helms, became more partisan than it had been for most of its recent history, with the moderate Republicans Richard Lugar and Nancy Kassebaum falling in line behind Helms on critical votes, which they had not always done when in the minority. But observers of the committee had no difficulty recognizing it; in style and efficiency, it clearly resembled the committee of earlier days, once the additional power of Helms was accounted for.

On appropriations, the Senate Foreign Operations Subcommittee operated much as before, with McConnell and Leahy exchanging roles and continuing to advocate well-known positions regarding foreign assistance.

There was relatively little trouble with respect to relations between them and USAID. Senate CJS, however, showed the confusion of this uncertain and perplexing year. Senator Phil Gramm of Texas became chairman, while Fritz Hollings once more became the ranking minority member, as he had been more than a decade before. Gramm's foibles were well known, and an element of hostility was added by his highly visible contempt for State and the Foreign Service.[8] But late in the year, with the departure of Senator Bob Packwood, Gramm eagerly gave up his chairmanship to move to the Budget Committee—always his goal—leaving CJS to be headed by Judd Gregg of New Hampshire, an unknown though clearly conservative quantity. This move took place after Senate action on the bill had been completed but before the conference between House and Senate occurred, and it made little initial difference.

Thus, while the full extent and import of the modifications occasioned by the Republican assumption of power in Congress could not be fully understood as of early 1997, initial signs are that less had changed than might have been expected. Indeed, the seemingly hard times for foreign affairs during 1995 must be viewed in the context of the larger, systemwide paradigm shift against Washington and toward devolution. At the macro level, the times may be at least temporarily worse for *any* discretionary account; but at the micro, foreign affairs level, there was a surprisingly strong sense of continuity. The foreign affairs tail will never wag the domestic politics dog, but it does have some strength, even if its support base remains narrow. Not the least elements in this conclusion were the ambitions of some Republican leaders—Dole and Gingrich come to mind—whose national aspirations required the demonstration of an internationalist sensitivity.

To pursue this point, throughout the 1980s until the mid-1990s, there were indications (even in 1995), that all but the hard right thought that more needed to be spent in support of international affairs. The same sentiments were occasionally expressed early in the Clinton administration, after the Cold War was over, and were reflected in the reasonably successful "Big Pie" exercise leading to the president's FY 1995 budget and a similar enhancement for the FY 1996 request discussed above. On balance, my cautious guess is that the 1995 frenzy to reduce international affairs spending

8. Explaining his tough approach toward State's budget as CJS appropriations chairman in 1995, Gramm said: "I thought the American people were more interested in law enforcement and fighting drugs than in building marble palaces and renting long coats and high hats." Quoted from the *Washington Post* by Carroll J. Doherty, "Gramm Tougher on State than Helms," *CQ Weekly Report* 53 (September 16, 1995): 2815.

will most likely dissipate as those who were a part of it become more conversant with the nation's international interests, when and if general budget pressures lessen. As has been seen, there were early signs of this in 1997. There will continue to be intense disagreements about how the money should be spent. But an intelligent executive strategy of sharing information and plans less grudgingly with the Congress is a necessary first step for producing better results.

There is a tendency in the State Department to regard whatever circumstances one finds oneself in as unique and to consider one's problems in isolation. In fact, the recent budgetary problems facing State and its sister agencies, notwithstanding those conservative Republicans whose credo seems to be "No Foreign Aid, Ever," are best explained primarily as extensions of the presidential–congressional "budget wars" impacting the entire federal government. Branches, not parties, may count most over time, although partisan differences may sometimes seem to overwhelm institutional ones.

## Foreign Affairs Funding Is Bipartisan

Parties do count. Foreign affairs professionals in the executive branch have traditionally underestimated the partisan basis of legislative activity *within* each house, even if in 1995 they may have overestimated it. Perhaps the normal perception occurs because so much emphasis has been given to the existence and importance of a bipartisan foreign policy.[9] Thus, career officials take for granted the importance of sustaining the capabilities of State and the other foreign affairs agencies, or foreign assistance, or contributions to international organizations. They presume that serious members and staff, of either party, will automatically share their assumptions. It follows naturally, to them, that it does not much matter who is president and whether he is of the same party that controls Congress. They also see foreign affairs as distinct and separate from domestic policy and domestic political concerns. When partisanship raises its head, it is an unexpected and unplanned for phenomenon.

9. For a representative example, see Henry Kissinger and Cyrus Vance, "Bipartisan Objectives for American Foreign Policy," *Foreign Affairs* 66 (Summer 1988): 899–921. There are many others.

What is sometimes forgotten is that agreement on abstract goals is not the same thing as agreement on means, and that there can be incentives for maintaining a posture of opposition. The process of legislation encourages horse-trading; but to trade, you must have something to deal. For foreign affairs funding, the currency is usually amendments, sometimes added to legislation solely so that the other side will have to give you something to have them removed. Such amendments often take the form of policy pre-scriptions ("policy mandates" in the 1995 lexicon), but they might equally well concern funding constraints, organization, changes to diplomatic privi-leges and immunities, diplomatic reciprocity, security, refugee affairs, or au-thorities for specific officials or agencies.

There is another way in which the generally partisan orientation of Con-gress affects the executive. When Congress and the presidency are in differ-ent hands, the inherent trust between State Department officials, for example, and key chairmen and members of Congress is simply not the same as when they are of the same party. Because those in State, including political appointees, almost always are thinking in terms of what they per-ceive to be the national interest, good management, or adequate resources—all politically neutral factors in their eyes—they tend to forget the necessarily more partisan orientation of those who must soon run for elec-tion again, against the other party.

As Stanley Heginbotham correctly noted in 1983, even when Congress and the executive are of the same party, the path is by no means smooth:

> Many executive-branch officials—including the staff of the Na-tional Security Council, State Department political appointees, and career Foreign Service officers—consider members of Congress and their staffs to be insensitive to the need for privacy and confidential-ity in foreign relations. They view the legislators as predisposed to grandstanding, prone to disrupting important incremental day-to-day shifts in relations with other countries, dilatory and unpredict-able in their legislative actions, ignorant of basic foreign-policy reali-ties, and parochial in their approach to global issues.
>
> Members of Congress and their staffs are often just as firmly con-vinced that foreign-policy officials are unquestioning in the advocacy of administration policies, obsessed with the minutiae of ritualized diplomatic exchanges, insensitive to broad patterns of American in-terests, more concerned with the interests and needs of their foreign counterparts than with the democratic processes of their own gov-

ernment, arrogant in their belief that their academic training and field experience give them a monopoly on foreign-policy wisdom, hypocritical in their claim exclusively to represent the national interest, and skilled primarily in stanching the flow of meaningful information to Capitol Hill.[10]

A recent example of the failure of some players, in this case in the executive branch, to understand such very different institutional cultures and imperatives occurred in 1993, when State's legislative affairs officers received strong guidance from department leaders to avoid controversies with members and staff responsible for the department's authorization and appropriations bills. The theme was, "We're all Democrats now, and we'll be able to work out mutually agreeable outcomes." Not surprisingly, this proved to be naive; congressional operatives followed their institutional inclinations, and the number of issues was as great as ever, even though the tone was more amicable than in earlier years. In fact, the authorization bill foundered in the Senate owing to one such disagreement, concerning international broadcasting (to be discussed below).

Executive actions or inactions that are inconsistent with what key members desire are easily interpreted as slights of either an institutional nature, showing a disregard of congressional prerogatives, or a partisan one, trying to do political harm to members of the other party. A classic case occurred in 1991, when State's congressional schedulers showed more concern, in the eyes of House CJS Chairman Neal Smith and his staff, for the needs of the Foreign Operations (Obey) Subcommittee than for CJS. The result, as described by Richard Munson:

> Representative Neal Smith, for instance, complained at length about the lack of cooperation from the State Department's Congressional Affairs Office. Even Representative Harold Rogers, who usually defended the Bush administration as the Commerce, Justice, State and the Judiciary Subcommittee's ranking Republican, declared, "I'm as frustrated as the chairman is with the State Department's congressional relations office. On the one hand, they can be unresponsive, rude, and arrogant. On the other hand, they can be unresponsive, rude, and arrogant." When the subcommittee endorsed Smith's pro-

10. Stanley J. Heginbotham, "Dateline Washington: The Rules of the Games," *Foreign Policy* 53 (Winter 1983–84): 158.

posal to slash the office's budget by 87 percent, two State Department staffers blanched and staggered out of the conference room.[11]

Only direct and repeated pleadings with Smith by Secretary Baker and his deputy, Lawrence Eagleburger, led to a restoration of funds for the congressional relations bureau. At one point, Baker interrupted a Mexico-to-Europe trip to land in Washington for a midnight meeting with Smith to make his case at the latter's Washington office. Predictably, in the meantime there was considerable acrimony within State over who was at fault.[12]

"Blame avoidance" also has something to do with congressional attitudes. Executive officials, in turn, are often flabbergasted by legislative branch reactions—and so the gulf between the two deepens. Not all members are equally disposed to find such plots, of course, nor are all executive officials equally insensitive to the possible turf battles within Congress, where good public policy can take a back seat to war between congressional contenders. The needless Pell-Hollings spat on the FY 1990–91 State Authorization Bill in November 1989, discussed in Chapter 5, is a classic example. One component of such problems is staff interests and concerns; it is my opinion that the "win–lose" mentality of staff on both sides makes solutions harder rather than easier.

In short, partisanship and institutional differences tend to reinforce each other. While coalitions have often been built across party lines, and while numerous Democratic committee and subcommittee chairmen have come to the aid of foreign affairs agencies headed by Republican appointees in recent years,[13] to view resource acquisition and management as essentially bipartisan is to misunderstand congressional–executive dynamics.

# No Payoff, No Help

The assertion that Congress will not help because there is no payoff is closely related to the "foreign affairs has no constituency" argument. The connection, obviously, is that doing what constituents want brings political success. Sometimes it seems that the reverse notion is more accurate—that

11. Munson, *The Cardinals of Capitol Hill*, pp. 48–49.
12. Personal experience.
13. As well as vice versa, to some extent, after 1994.

whatever payoff there is comes from opposing foreign assistance, in being known as a harsh critic or even an enemy of the Department of State. A variant sometimes heard combines the two: "You don't know who your friends are, and unless you accept our criticisms and proposals, you'll get even worse." This "We're from the Congress, and we're here to help you" approach is frequently viewed by the executive as a Trojan horse. Dan Mica and Olympia Snowe, the chairman and ranking member respectively of the International Operations (State Department) Subcommittee during the late 1980s, fairly or unfairly are most frequently cited as recent exemplars of this approach. Their activities with respect to the Moscow embassy is a good example. Similarly, during his unsuccessful 1988 Senate primary run in Florida, Mica focused heavily on the security of post operations in Cuba.

There are, however, examples of members who have attempted to protect and strengthen the department and related agencies, gaining little political advantage doing so. In recent years, Dante Fascell, chairman of the House Foreign Affairs Committee until the end of 1992, and Neal Smith, chairman of the Commerce-Justice-State Appropriations Subcommittee in the House from 1980 to 1994, stand out especially as "heroes" from State's perspective; but others, perhaps less consistently, have also made major contributions. This is not to say that either Fascell or Smith uniformly endorsed State's actions. As mentioned, Fascell was exasperated by the insufficient funding requests coming from State and, more recently, was frustrated by the Reagan and Bush administrations' unwillingness to find ways to increase revenues so that State could be funded higher.

Smith was inherently conservative in his handling of funding requests, scrutinizing in particular new programs, which although they begin modestly, may have major implications for the "outyears." He also became increasingly insistent that other agencies represented at posts abroad pay a fair share of the expenses they incur, rather than receiving services gratis or at low cost from State. To the extent such an effort was successful, of course, expenses were likely to be transferred from his bill to other appropriations accounts, thus freeing up more resources for the department and especially for other accounts funded by CJS. Hal Rogers exhibited many of Smith's characteristics after joining the subcommittee, especially after becoming chairman in 1995.

On the Foreign Operations side, Senators Leahy and McConnell and Representative Obey were generally supportive, regardless of which party held the presidency. Yet they never gave up their independence or their willingness to criticize USAID and other agencies, sometimes harshly.

As noted, the base of support for all international affairs programs is quite narrow. A few powerful friends can help, but the executive branch agencies soon become highly dependent on them. A broader coalition would greatly reduce the risk that the absence of a primary supporter at a critical time, or a contrary vote forced by political realities, might lead to a major defeat. Fascell's temporary absence from the conference on the FY 1988–89 Authorization Bill, for example, arguably led to the defeat of an HFAC effort to correct a modest but troublesome problem with respect to providing housing for members of the Foreign Service who were assigned to the U.S. mission to the United Nations. A crisis does not result from such accidents, but they do demonstrate how fragile is the executive's ability to manage congressional outcomes.

# Iron Triangles Do Not Count

If there are no natural constituencies, then one might assume there are no interest groups to interact with agencies and committees in search of satisfying mutual interests. The "iron triangle" explanation (interests, congressional supporters, bureaucrats with like concerns) is a traditional foundation of congressional studies (although some argue it is not as pertinent as earlier because of the proliferation of interest groups). Be that as it may, this literature is derived almost exclusively either from the domestic environment or from defense procurement.[14] Little attention has been given to whether or not the same phenomenon exists in the international affairs arena. In fair measure, it does. National interest and partisan politics, it turns out, are not the sole motivating forces.

---

14. The classic work, of course, is David B. Truman's *The Governmental Process: Public Interests and Public Opinion*, published originally in 1953 and recently republished by the Institute of Governmental Studies, University of California–Berkeley, in 1993. Earlier and of similar importance was V. O. Key, *Politics, Parties and Pressure Groups* (New York: Thomas Y. Crowell, 1948). See also Roger H. Davidson, "Breaking Up Those 'Cozy Triangles': An Impossible Dream?" in S. Welch and J. G. Peters, eds., *Legislative Reform and Public Policy* (New York: Praeger, 1977); Hugh Heclo, "Issue Networks and the Executive Establishment," in Anthony King, ed., *The New American Political System* (Washington, D.C.: American Enterprise Institute, 1978); and, perhaps the earliest of all, E. P. Herring, *Group Representation Before Congress* (Baltimore: Johns Hopkins University Press, 1929). For an exception to the lack of coverage of special interests in foreign affairs literature, see Lindsay, *Congress and the Politics of U.S. Foreign Policy*, pp. 157–58.

As one might expect, the difference is that the interests are different. First, the existence of lobbies keyed to the interests of specific foreign countries and orchestrated by them is a phenomenon not present in the domestic environment. The foremost examples are the Israeli and Greek-oriented groups, but the Canadians and the Taiwanese, among many others, are not to be ignored. To an extent not usually understood "outside the Beltway," earmarks in foreign assistance frequently are the result of interactions with U.S.-based private organizations whose financial interests are tied to grants and contracts for carrying out USAID projects, and who persuade key members to protect them. Although opinion is split, some close observers believe that the concerns of some of these groups, as conveyed to their allies in Congress, contributed heavily to the failure to enact new baseline foreign assistance legislation in 1993–94.[15] They certainly came into play in 1995 (see Chapter 8).

There are other examples. The close relationship between farm interests and P.L. 480 programs has often been remarked. Other connections are less obvious. Employee unions also make their opinions known,[16] and certain members pay close attention. Sometimes "interest politics" becomes almost silly, as with the efforts of the moving and storage industry to stop State from establishing its own storage facility for the household goods of members of the Foreign Service.[17] Architectural and construction contractors are not shy about making their views known to Congress when they lose out in competitive bidding for embassy construction projects. Even the California wine industry surfaces from time to time.[18]

15. See Chapter 3. My comments here are based on discussions with USAID legislative officials, 1993–95. For additional details on how these organizations currently operate, see Francine Modderno, "Focus: The Growing Clout of NGOs," *Foreign Service Journal* 72 (July 1995): 32–37.

16. The American Federation of Government Employees (AFGE) represented USIA employees from the early 1970s until late 1993, when the American Foreign Service Association (AFSA) mounted a successful challenge and won a representation election, restoring the status quo ante. AFSA also represents Foreign Service members in State, USAID, and the Departments of Agriculture and Commerce. Both these employee organizations have a history of activism with the Congress, pursuing not only employee but sometimes policy interests.

17. The conference report on the FY 1989 State Department Appropriation Act devoted extensive space to this quarrel, which was set off by the efforts of the moving and storage industry, working with one House committee member. The amounts of money involved were small, and State's proposal stemmed from dissatisfaction with commercial storage providers; but apparently the precedent was worrisome.

18. A California wine amendment first appeared in the Foreign Service Act of 1980, P.L. 96-465, sec. 905. The House version of what was to become P.L. 100-204, the FY 1988–89 Foreign Relations Authorization Act (sec. 125), contained another example, which was

Perhaps the most notable demonstrations of interest activity in foreign affairs resource politics are the somewhat parallel histories of foreign assistance to two sets of uneasy "partners": Israel and Egypt, Greece and Turkey.

## Israel and Egypt

Editorializing in 1986 about the FY 1987 allocations for foreign assistance, the *Washington Post*, while lamenting the maldistribution of foreign assistance (e.g., 40 percent of all economic support funds going just to Israel and Egypt), nevertheless noted the reality that "Egyptian aid has been tied to Israel aid since Camp David. The Israeli aid is kept high, in turn, not merely by that country's special history and needs but by its domestic political constituency; that is the motor that makes the whole aid program go."[19] Some have characterized assistance to Israel as having "taken on the aspects of an international entitlement program, seemingly as automatic as Social Security benefits. Year in and year out, usually with no debate, Congress earmarked about one-fifth of the $15 billion foreign aid budget for Israel. . . . When Egypt was included, the annual level of aid earmarked by Congress for the two countries rose to more than $5 billion by 1992, one-third of all U.S. foreign assistance spending."[20]

Table 6 presents a comparison of the Egyptian and Israeli cases since FY 1966. Until FY 1973, programs for both countries were relatively modest, with almost nothing for Egypt after the mid-1960s. In 1974, there was a major emergency-assistance effort for Israel in the aftermath of the Yom Kippur War in 1973, after which levels remained relatively stable, albeit with a significant beginning of increased economic assistance for Egypt, until 1979. In that year, of course, the Camp David summit meeting occurred. After the summit, President Carter requested $4.8 billion of loans and grants to be shared by Israel and Egypt, in addition to the regular aid program of about $2 billion and $1 billion, respectively.[21] As Table 6 shows,

---

dropped in conference in lieu of report language reaffirming the 1980 provision. A new generation of staffers did not realize what their California predecessors had already done! Section 905 and the later report language required that whenever possible, American products, especially wines, should be used at embassy functions and stocked at commissaries abroad. This is a sensible idea, and the natural inclination of ambassadors, but one wonders whether it really needs to be the subject of legislation.

19. "Foreign Aid: Maldistribution . . ." (editorial), *Washington Post*, December 21, 1986.

20. "The History of U.S. Aid to Israel," *Congressional Quarterly Almanac* 48 (1992): 540. This is a good short overview of the Israeli program.

21. Ibid.

Table 6. U.S. Foreign Assistance to Israel and Egypt, FY 1966–FY 1994

| Fiscal Year | Israel | | | | | Egypt | | | | |
|---|---|---|---|---|---|---|---|---|---|---|
| | Economic | Military | Total | Grants | Loans | Economic | Military | Total | Grants | Loans |
| 1994 | $1,200.0 | $1,800.0 | $3,000.0 | $3,000.0 | $— | $606.4 | $1,300.8 | $1,907.2 | $1,902.0 | $5.2 |
| 1993 | 1,200.0 | 1,800.0 | 3,000.0 | 3,000.0 | — | 753.3 | 1,301.8 | 2,055.1 | 2,055.1 | — |
| 1992 | 1,200.0 | 1,800.0 | 3,000.0 | 3,000.0 | — | 933.8 | 1,301.8 | 2,235.1 | 2,194.7 | 40.4 |
| 1991 | 1,850.0 | 1,800.0 | 3,650.0 | 3,650.0 | — | 997.9 | 1,301.9 | 2,999.8 | 2,139.7 | 160.1 |
| 1990 | 1,194.8 | 1,792.3 | 2,987.1 | 2,987.1 | — | 1,093.4 | 1,295.8 | 2,389.3 | 2,196.4 | 192.9 |
| 1989 | 1,200.0 | 1,800.0 | 3,000.0 | 3,300.0 | — | 968.2 | 1,301.5 | 2,269.7 | 2,119.2 | 150.4 |
| 1988 | 1,200.0 | 1,800.0 | 3,000.0 | 3,000.0 | — | 873.4 | 1,301.5 | 2,174.9 | 2,021.9 | 153.0 |
| 1987 | 1,200.0 | 1,800.0 | 3,000.0 | 3,000.0 | — | 1,015.2 | 1,301.8 | 2,317.0 | 2,125.3 | 191.7 |
| 1986 | 1,898.4 | 1,722.6 | 3,621.0 | 3,621.9 | — | 1,293.3 | 1,245.8 | 2,539.1 | 2,321.6 | 217.5 |
| 1985 | 1,950.1 | 1,400.0 | 3,350.1 | 3,350.1 | — | 1,292.0 | 1,176.7 | 2,468.7 | 2,254.9 | 213.8 |
| 1984 | 910.0 | 1,700.0 | 2,610.0 | 1,760.0 | 850.0 | 1,104.1 | 1,366.7 | 2,470.8 | 1,333.3 | 1,137.5 |
| 1983 | 785.0 | 1,700.0 | 2,485.0 | 1,535.0 | 950.0 | 1,005.1 | 1,326.9 | 2,332.0 | 1,193.7 | 1,138.3 |
| 1982 | 806.0 | 1,400.0 | 2,206.0 | 1,356.0 | 850.0 | 1,064.9 | 902.4 | 1,967.3 | 1,005.3 | 962.0 |
| 1981 | 764.0 | 1,400.0 | 2,164.0 | 1,264.0 | 900.0 | 1,130.4 | 550.8 | 1,681.2 | 788.7 | 892.5 |

| Year | | | | | | | | | | |
|---|---|---|---|---|---|---|---|---|---|---|
| 1980 | 786.0 | 1,000.0 | 1,786.0 | 1,025.0 | 761.0 | 1,166.4 | 0.8 | 1,167.3 | 602.0 | 565.3 |
| 1979 | 790.1 | 4,000.0 | 4,790.1 | 1,825.0 | 2,965.1 | 1,088.1 | 1,500.4 | 2,588.5 | 607.8 | 1,980.7 |
| 1978 | 791.8 | 1,000.0 | 1,791.8 | 1,025.0 | 766.8 | 943.0 | 0.2 | 943.2 | 146.1 | 797.1 |
| 1977 | 742.0 | 1,000.0 | 1,742.0 | 990.0 | 752.0 | 907.8 | — | 907.8 | 110.9 | 796.8 |
| TQ | 78.6 | 200.0 | 278.6 | 150.0 | 128.6 | 552.5 | — | 552.5 | 108.9 | 443.6 |
| 1976 | 714.4 | 1,500.0 | 2,214.4 | 1,225.0 | 989.4 | 464.3 | — | 464.3 | 112.6 | 351.7 |
| 1975 | 353.1 | 300.0 | 653.1 | 444.5 | 208.6 | 370.1 | — | 370.1 | 71.3 | 298.8 |
| 1974 | 51.5 | 2,482.7 | 2,534.2 | 1,551.5 | 982.7 | 21.3 | — | 21.3 | 11.8 | 9.5 |
| 1973 | 109.8 | 307.5 | 417.3 | 50.4 | 366.9 | 0.8 | — | 0.8 | 0.8 | — |
| 1972 | 104.2 | 300.0 | 404.2 | 50.4 | 353.8 | 1.5 | — | 1.5 | — | 1.5 |
| 1971 | 55.8 | 545.0 | 600.8 | 0.3 | 600.5 | — | — | — | — | — |
| 1970 | 41.1 | 30.0 | 71.1 | 0.4 | 70.7 | — | — | — | — | — |
| 1969 | 36.7 | 85.0 | 121.7 | 0.6 | 121.1 | — | — | — | — | — |
| 1968 | 51.8 | 25.0 | 76.8 | 0.5 | 76.3 | — | — | — | — | — |
| 1967 | 6.1 | 7.0 | 13.1 | 0.6 | 12.5 | 12.6 | — | 12.6 | 12.6 | — |
| 1966 | $36.8 | $90.0 | $126.8 | $0.9 | $125.9 | $27.6 | $— | $27.6 | $11.2 | $16.4 |

SOURCES: *U.S. Overseas Loans and Grants, Series of Yearly Data*, vol. 1: *Near East and South Asia*, "Obligations and Loan Authorizations, FY 1946–FY 1991." (Washington, D.C.: U.S. Agency for International Development [FA/B/RPA], 1992); *U.S. Overseas Loans and Grants and Assistance from International Organizations* (Washington, D.C.: U.S. Agency for International Development [FA/B/RA], 1995), individual country tables, pp. 10, 13 (for FY 1991–94 only).

NOTE: Slight discrepancies in totals because of rounding. TQ = transitional quarter.

the balance after 1979 shifted much more heavily to grants, rather than loans, especially for Israel, with a rough relationship of 3:2 between the two countries. An exception to this linkage occurred in the early 1990s, however, when in the context of the Gulf War, the United States, after a notable congressional debate, forgave $6.7 billion of Egyptian debt repayments (while at the same time increasing Israeli aid dramatically).[22]

Besides the large amounts of assistance routinely appropriated, the impact of the Israeli lobby was evident in the generous assistance conditions: "[B]eginning in fiscal 1985, lawmakers had included language in foreign operations bills stating that it was the 'policy and intention' of the United States that aid provided under the Economic Support Fund (ESF) be at least equal to Israel's debt repayments to the U.S. government. Israel used most of the $1.2 billion it receives annually under the ESF program to pay military debts."[23] Perhaps even more favorable than this "positive float," guaranteeing enough aid to pay debts, was a provision unique to Israeli aid that allowed large portions of U.S. aid to be deposited in Israeli accounts at the beginning of the fiscal year, rather than being spread out over twelve months. Thus, Israel was able to earn interest from U.S. banks that could be used for whatever purposes it chose, increasing the amount of funding available and bypassing the appropriations process.[24]

By the end of the 1980s, however, domestic and international circumstances had changed, leading to questions about whether this very favorable approach should continue. When Republican Senate leader Bob Dole dared in 1990 to raise the question of what level of aid to Israel was appropriate in light of new requirements with respect to the emerging democracies of the former Soviet Union, a major controversy was generated.[25] Secretary of State Baker, proposing a somewhat similar plan to provide new resources

22. Ibid. and Table 6.
23. Ibid. See also Table 6 for the specific data. By way of perspective, however, it should be remembered that at the same time the issue of housing guarantees of some $10 billion for Israel was on the table.
24. For an evaluation, see Clyde H. Farnsworth, "Israel Has a Unique Deal for U.S. Aid," *New York Times*, September 23, 1990.
25. See Bob Dole, "To Help New Democracies, Cut Aid to Israel, Four Others" (op-ed article), *New York Times*, January 16, 1990. For an analysis of the controversy that followed, see John Felton, "Dole Takes on Israeli Lobby, Proposes Cutting U.S. Aid: His Plan Would Provide Money to Help Panama and the New Democracies in Eastern Europe," *CQ Weekly Report* 48 (January 20, 1990): 196–98; and Helen Dewar, "Voices Rise as Foreign Aid Does Not: Fixed Priorities, Deficit Leave Little for Meeting New Demands," *Washington Post*, February 18, 1990.

for new needs, was also unsuccessful.[26] In the first year of the Clinton administration, the president was similarly "Challenged on Share of U.S. Aid Going to Israel and Egypt,"[27] Another, little-remarked factor was the realization that all this assistance, especially in the case of Egypt, made little difference in the development of these troubled economies.[28]

Yet, as of mid-1996, there had been little change. Israel's domestic supporters, even though its major lobbying group, AIPAC, had experienced internal difficulties,[29] continued to leave assistance to Israel sacrosanct, even in 1995. Willy-nilly, especially in light of Egypt's emerging role in the 1990s as a bulwark against terrorism and other Muslim fundamentalist threats, assistance for Egypt followed. In fact, at times that assistance was "de-linked" from the Israeli allocations, as with President Bush's successful campaign for Egyptian loan forgiveness as a consequence of Egypt's strong stand against Iraq in the 1990–91 Gulf War.[30] Meanwhile, Israel also played an important role, resulting in proposals and actions to increase aid to Israel as well, in effect creating a parallel situation, linked not to the Camp David accords but to the conflict with Iraq.[31]

26. John Felton, "With Little Maneuvering Room, Budget Holds Few Surprises," *CQ Weekly Report* 48 (February 3, 1990): 343.

27. *New York Times*, March 9, 1993.

28. See, for example, William E. Schmidt, "A Deluge of Foreign Assistance Fails to Revive Egypt's Striken Economy," *New York Times*, October 17, 1993; and John Lancaster, "U.S. Aid Has Yet to Lift Most Egyptians: After $19 Billion over 20 Years, Economy Remains Stagnant," *Washington Post*, April 5, 1995.

29. For details on AIPAC, see Lloyd Grove, "The Men with Muscle: The AIPAC Leaders, Battling for Israel and Among Themselves," *Washington Post*, June 14, 1991; and Michael Weiskopf, "Head of Pro-Israel Lobby Forced Out," *Washington Post*, June 30, 1993. Earlier discussions of note include Charles R. Babcock, "FEC Rules Pro-Israel Lobby, PACs Are Not 'Affiliated,' " *Washington Post*, December 22, 1990. Finally, two unpublished papers, while not easily available, present useful comments on the interaction of lobbying groups, the president, and Congress on foreign policy issues. See Mitchell Bard, "Presidential Dominance in Foreign Policy-making: The Case of U.S. Middle East Policy, 1945–1984," prepared for delivery at the annual meeting of the American Political Science Association, Chicago, September 3–6, 1987; and David A. Dickson, "Pressure Politics and the Congressional Foreign Policy Process: A Study of the Jewish-American, Arab-American and African-American Lobbies," prepared for delivery at the annual meeting of the American Political Science Association, San Francisco, August 30–September 2, 1990 (see pp. 5–7 for a succinct history of AIPAC).

30. See, for example, Carroll J. Doherty, "Bush's Plan to Waive Egypt Debt . . . Raises Questions About Israel," *CQ Weekly Report* 48 (September 15, 1990): 2932–33; as well as Doherty's later article, "Egypt Wins, El Salvador Loses in Foreign Aid Funding Bill," *CQ Weekly Report* 48 (October 27, 1990): 3627–29, which concludes that, in order to get this deal, the president had to accept restrictions on aid to El Salvador.

31. See, for example, Dan Balz and Molly Moore, "President Moves to Aid Economies of Gulf States," *Washington Post*, September 26, 1990; and Eric Schmitt, "U.S. Ready to Send Israelis New Arms as Signal to Iraq," *New York Times*, September 1, 1990.

But this situation may not be permanent. With the Republican assault on foreign assistance in 1995, the issue was reborn, even though some critics of foreign aid were careful to exempt the Middle East, at least for the moment.[32] Jesse Helms's comments that government-to-government assistance should be replaced by assistance to people, while provoking an impassioned response from one congressional Democrat, may yet prove to have been a portent of a radical shift in the public mood. Still, such a shift was not seen as of the FY 1996 appropriations (even though almost all other accounts were substantially reduced).[33]

## Greece and Turkey

Another, less potent, example of the impact of domestic considerations on foreign assistance, together with an unavoidable (however much development purists would like to deny it) link of assistance to clear-cut U.S. foreign policy interests, concerns those old antagonists Greece and Turkey. Turkey, a front-line country in the Cold War era, was and is nonetheless a subject of opprobrium because of its role in Cyprus and its treatment of its Kurdish population, the first of which has engaged the enmity of the large and vocal Greek American community. In addition, both countries have U.S. bases, which has led to "disguised rent" in order to retain base rights. Another important element has been the prominence of Greek Americans on key congressional foreign affairs committees, in particular Paul Sarbanes on the SFRC and Olympia Snowe on HFAC and then SFRC. Take 1987, for instance, as summarized by *Congressional Quarterly,* discussing the HFAC markup of the FY 1988 Foreign Assistance Authorization Bill:

> Another tumultuous debate occurred over military aid to Greece and Turkey, two rivals in the eastern Mediterranean with whom the United States has tried to maintain solid diplomatic ties. . . .
> Pro-Greek members of Congress virtually every year try to cut mil-

32. See Thomas W. Lippman, "Mideast Aid Survives Budget Ax: Israel-Egypt Funds Retain Broad Support," *Washington Post,* October 23, 1995. See also Chapter 8 below concerning pressure placed on the "AIPAC Democrats" in the House to vote for the State/Foreign Assistance authorization bill on the floor since it had full funding for Israel, even though it was deemed liable to veto by the White House on other grounds.

33. See Deborah Kalb, "Sen. Helms Comments Spark Concern over U.S. Aid to Israel: New York Rep. Jerry Nadler Circulates a Petition Urging Helms to Reconsider Proposal to End Foreign Aid to Israeli Government," *The Hill,* February 15, 1995. Nadler was acting in response to a February 6 interview with Helms, also carried in *The Hill.*

itary aid to Turkey or take other steps aimed at forcing that country to withdraw some or all of its troops—now around 30,000—that occupy part of the island nation of Cyprus.

The pending foreign aid bill . . . figures reflect a 7-to-10 ratio that Congress has informally followed when deciding on funds for these countries.

The report continues by describing a series of amendments offered by one member or another punishing Greece, rewarding Turkey, or vice versa.[34] Of course, as we have seen in a previous chapter, all this came to naught because there was no authorization bill passed in 1987, the appropriators having waived the requirement for one, as they routinely did. However, as Table 7 shows, the appropriators did preserve the 7:10 ratio (Greece/Turkey) for military assistance.

Although the administration never felt bound by the 7:10 ratio, the formula continued to survive until FY 1991, the status quo apparently being an easier outcome than the major changes proposed by proponents for either country. For FY 1992, however, Turkey, like Egypt, benefited from its prominent role in the Gulf War. In 1991, the administration proposed that funding for Greece remain fixed at about $350 million, about 56 percent of the $625 million proposed for Turkey.[35] In later years, unlike the Israel-Egypt case, Turkish support began to wane. For FY 1996, for example, the administration requested economic support funds in the amount of $100 million for Turkey, but the conference report imposed a limit of $33 million, both for budgetary and human rights reasons.[36]

The impact of the special cases of these four countries on the overall foreign assistance program can be seen graphically in Table 8. Ever since 1976, they have accounted, year in and year out, for approximately 40 percent of

34. Steven Pressman, "Disputes Dim the Future of Foreign Aid Bill: House Panel at Odds with Administration," *CQ Weekly Report* 45 (April 4, 1987): 618. Later that year, the House appropriators reaffirmed the 7:10 ratio, with an estimated military assistance level of $343 million for Greece and $490 million for Turkey. For subsequent discussions, see Pat Towell, "House Panel Makes Major Cuts in Foreign Aid Appropriations," *CQ Weekly Report* 45 (August 1, 1987): 1726; and Pat Towell, "Foreign Affairs Panel Approves a New Authorization Measure," *CQ Weekly Report* 45 (August 8, 1987): 1814–15.

35. See Carroll J. Doherty, "Mideast Countries Top List in '92 Budget Request," *CQ Weekly Report* 49 (March 8, 1991): 624.

36. See "U.S. Foreign Assistance Levels, Fiscal Year 1996," summary prepared by USAID's Bureau of Legislative and Public Affairs, November 1996. The actual amount, $33.5 million, is appropriated in sec. 568 of H.R. 1868 (P.L. 194-107). The House had originally provided only $21 million.

Table 7. U.S. Foreign Assistance to Greece and Turkey, FY 1966–FY 1994 (000s)

| Fiscal Year | Greece | | | | | Turkey | | | | |
|---|---|---|---|---|---|---|---|---|---|---|
| | Economic | Military | Total | Grants | Loans | Economic | Military | Total | Grants | Loans |
| 1994 | $— | $283.6 | $283.6 | $0.1 | $283.5 | $0.4 | $406.0 | $406.4 | $1.4 | $406.4 |
| 1993 | — | 315.3 | 315.3 | 0.3 | 315.0 | 200.4 | 453.1 | 653.5 | 203.5 | 450.0 |
| 1992 | — | 350.3 | 350.3 | 30.3 | 320.0 | 1.4 | 503.6 | 505.0 | 480.0 | 25.0 |
| 1991 | — | 350.6 | 350.6 | 30.6 | 320.0 | 250.4 | 553.7 | 804.1 | 754.1 | 50.1 |
| 1990 | — | 349.1 | 349.1 | 30.5 | 318.6 | 14.7 | 501.2 | 515.9 | 430.3 | 85.6 |
| 1989 | — | 350.7 | 350.7 | 30.7 | 320.0 | 60.4 | 503.5 | 563.9 | 473.9 | 90.0 |
| 1988 | — | 344.1 | 344.1 | 31.1 | 313.0 | 32.4 | 493.3 | 525.7 | 347.7 | 178.0 |
| 1987 | — | 344.3 | 344.3 | 1.3 | 343.0 | 103.1 | 493.5 | 596.6 | 416.3 | 180.3 |
| 1986 | — | 431.9 | 431.9 | 1.2 | 430.7 | 119.6 | 618.4 | 738.0 | 328.6 | 409.5 |
| 1985 | — | 501.4 | 501.4 | 1.4 | 500.0 | 175.9 | 703.6 | 879.5 | 309.5 | 570.0 |
| 1984 | — | 501.4 | 501.4 | 1.4 | 500.0 | 139.5 | 718.3 | 857.8 | 209.3 | 648.5 |
| 1983 | — | 281.3 | 281.3 | 1.3 | 280.0 | 286.0 | 402.8 | 688.8 | 313.8 | 375.0 |
| 1982 | — | 281.3 | 281.3 | 1.3 | 280.0 | 301.1 | 403.0 | 704.1 | 261.1 | 443.0 |
| 1981 | — | 178.0 | 178.0 | 1.5 | 176.5 | 201.0 | 252.8 | 453.8 | 137.8 | 316.0 |

| Year | | | | | | | | | | |
|---|---|---|---|---|---|---|---|---|---|---|
| 1980 | — | 147.5 | 147.5 | 2.4 | 145.1 | 198.1 | 208.2 | 406.3 | 80.4 | 325.9 |
| 1979 | — | 172.3 | 172.3 | 32.3 | 140.0 | 69.6 | 180.3 | 250.0 | 5.4 | 244.6 |
| 1978 | — | 175.0 | 175.0 | 35.0 | 140.0 | 1.1 | 175.4 | 176.6 | 1.2 | 175.4 |
| 1977 | — | 156.0 | 156.0 | 34.0 | 122.0 | 0.2 | 125.0 | 125.0 | 0.2 | 125.0 |
| TQ | 65.0 | 34.1 | 99.1 | 34.1 | 65.0 | — | 125.0 | 125.2 | 0.2 | 125.0 |
| 1976 | — | 190.6 | 190.6 | 34.6 | 156.0 | — | — | — | — | — |
| 1975 | — | 86.0 | 86.0 | — | 86.0 | 4.4 | 106.0 | 110.4 | 35.4 | 75.0 |
| 1974 | — | 67.5 | 67.5 | 15.0 | 52.5 | 5.5 | 192.6 | 198.1 | 123.1 | 75.0 |
| 1973 | — | 79.9 | 79.9 | 21.9 | 58.0 | 22.9 | 241.8 | 264.7 | 235.7 | 29.0 |
| 1972 | — | 110.7 | 110.7 | 50.7 | 60.0 | 66.9 | 222.3 | 289.2 | 234.2 | 55.0 |
| 1971 | — | 100.8 | 100.8 | 82.8 | 18.0 | 82.7 | 214.0 | 296.7 | 224.9 | 71.8 |
| 1970 | — | 68.9 | 68.9 | 68.9 | — | 90.2 | 182.2 | 272.4 | 198.7 | 73.7 |
| 1969 | — | 127.7 | 121.7 | 107.7 | 20.0 | 91.3 | 179.2 | 270.5 | 207.7 | 62.8 |
| 1968 | 0.7 | 67.1 | 67.8 | 67.8 | — | 85.8 | 172.3 | 258.1 | 190.1 | 68.0 |
| 1967 | 1.7 | 93.1 | 94.8 | 94.8 | — | 150.0 | 187.6 | 337.6 | 202.7 | 134.9 |
| 1966 | $17.7 | $102.4 | $120.1 | $105.9 | $14.2 | $160.2 | $149.3 | $309.5 | $164.5 | $145.0 |

SOURCES: U.S. Overseas Loans and Grants, Series of Yearly Data, vol. 1: Near East and South Asia, "Obligations and Loan Authorizations, FY 1946–FY 1991" (Washington, D.C.: U.S. Agency for International Development [FA/B/RPA], 1992); U.S. Overseas Loans and Grants and Assistance from International Organizations (Washington, D.C.: U.S. Agency for International Development [FA/B/RA], 1995), individual country tables, pp. 164, 183 (for FY 1991–94 only).

NOTE: Slight discrepancies in totals because of rounding. TQ = transitional quarter.

Table 8. Annual U.S. Foreign Assistance for Selected Countries, FY 1975–FY 1994 (000s) (Figures in parentheses are percentages of total amounts)

| Fiscal Year | Israel | Egypt | Turkey | Greece | Total | All Other | Grand Total |
|---|---|---|---|---|---|---|---|
| 1994 | $3,000.0 (18.9) | $1,907.2 (12.0) | $406.4 (2.6) | $283.6 (1.8) | $5,597.2 (35.3) | $10,273.8 (64.7) | $15,871.0 |
| 1993 | 3,000.0 (18.5) | 2,055.1 (12.7) | 653.5 (4.0) | 315.5 (1.9) | 6,024.1 (37.2) | 10,173.9 (62.8) | 16,198.0* |
| 1992 | 3,000.0 (19.6) | 2,235.1 (14.6) | 505.0 (3.3) | 350.3 (2.2) | 6,090.4 (39.1) | 9,498.6 (60.9) | 15,589.0 |
| 1991 | 3,650.0 (21.0) | 2,299.8 (13.8) | 804.0 (4.8) | 350.6 (2.1) | 7,104.4 (42.6) | 9,559.6 (57.4) | 16,664.0 |
| 1990 | 2,987.1 (19.0) | 2,389.3 (15.2) | 515.9 (3.3) | 349.1 (2.2) | 6,241.4 (39.7) | 9,485.6 (60.3) | 15,727.0 |
| 1989 | 3,000.0 (20.4) | 2,269.6 (15.5) | 563.8 (3.8) | 350.7 (2.4) | 6,184.1 (42.1) | 8,504.3 (57.9) | 14,688.4 |
| 1988 | 3,000.0 (21.6) | 2,174.9 (15.8) | 525.7 (3.8) | 433.1 (2.5) | 6,044.7 (43.8) | 7,746.4 (56.2) | 13,791.1 |
| 1987 | 3,000.0 (20.7) | 2,317.0 (16.0) | 596.6 (4.1) | 344.3 (2.4) | 6,257.9 (43.2) | 8,230.0 (56.8) | 14,487.9 |
| 1986 | 3,621.0 (21.8) | 2,539.1 (15.3) | 738.0 (4.4) | 431.9 (2.6) | 7,330.0 (44.1) | 9,296.0 (55.9) | 16,626.0 |
| 1985 | 3,350.1 (18.9) | 2,468.7 (13.6) | 879.5 (4.6) | 501.4 (2.8) | 7,199.7 (39.7) | 10,928.0 (60.3) | 18,127.7 |
| 1984 | 2,610.0 (16.8) | 2,470.8 (16.0) | 857.8 (5.5) | 501.4 (3.2) | 6,440.0 (41.5) | 9,083.7 (58.5) | 15,523.7 |

| 1983 | 2,485.0 (17.5) | 2,332.0 (16.4) | 688.8 (4.8) | 281.3 (2.0) | 5,787.1 (40.8) | 8,413.9 (59.2) | 14,201.0 |
|---|---|---|---|---|---|---|---|
| 1982 | 2,206.0 (17.9) | 1,967.3 (16.0) | 704.1 (5.7) | 281.3 (2.3) | 5,158.7 (41.9) | 7,164.5 (58.1) | 12,323.2 |
| 1981 | 2,164.0 (20.5) | 1,681.2 (15.9) | 453.8 (4.3) | 178.0 (1.7) | 4,477.0 (42.4) | 6,072.6 (57.6) | 10,549.6 |
| 1980 | 1,786.0 (18.4) | 1,167.3 (12.0) | 406.3 (4.2) | 147.5 (1.5) | 3,507.1 (36.2) | 6,187.3 (63.8) | 9,694.4 |
| 1979 | 4,790.1 (34.6) | 2,588.5 (18.7) | 250.0 (1.8) | 172.3 (1.2) | 7,800.9 (56.3) | 6,044.2 (43.7) | 13,845.1 |
| 1978 | 1,791.8 (19.9) | 943.2 (10.5) | 176.6 (2.0) | 175.0 (1.9) | 3,086.6 (34.2) | 5,927.3 (65.8) | 9,013.9 |
| 1977 | 1,742.0 (22.4) | 907.8 (11.7) | 125.2 (1.6) | 156.0 (2.0) | 2,931.0 (37.7) | 4,853.2 (62.3) | 7,784.2 |
| TQ | 278.6 (10.7) | 552.5 (21.2) | 125.0 (4.8) | 99.1 (3.8) | 1,055.2 (40.5) | 1,548.0 (59.5) | 2,603.2 |
| 1976 | 2,214.4 (34.5) | 464.3 (7.2) | — (0.0) | 190.6 (3.0) | 2,869.3 (44.7) | 3,543.1 (55.3) | 6,412.4 |
| 1975 | 653.1 (9.4) | 370.1 (5.3) | 100.4 (1.5) | 86.0 (1.2) | 1,209.6 (17.5) | 5,711.7 (82.5) | 6,921.3 |

Sources: *U.S. Overseas Loans and Grants, Series of Yearly Data*, vol. 1: *Near East and South Asia*, "Obligations and Loan Authorizations, FY 1946–FY 1991" (Washington, D.C.: U.S. Agency for International Development [FA/B/RPA], 1992); *U.S. Overseas Loans and Grants and Assistance from International Organizations* (Washington, D.C.: U.S. Agency for International Development [FA/B/RA], 1995), individual country tables, pp. 4, 10, 13, 164, 184 (for FY 1991–94 only).

Note: Data include security and economic assistance, both loans and grants. TQ = transitional quarter.

*For purposes of comparison, FY 1993 totals exclude a one-time $12 billion International Monetary Fund replenishment.

*all* bilateral U.S. foreign assistance. It is hard to sustain the argument that if economic development were the primary goal (the current term of fashion is "sustainable development"), taking into account the global situation and where the opportunities for progress are most favorable, that such a tilt to the Mediterranean and Middle East would have occurred. Rather, this special distribution shows that foreign assistance will perhaps always be subject to the twin pressures of domestic politics and U.S. foreign policy imperatives. Politics is always local.


# A Leap of Faith: Funding Follows Policy Changes

If the concept of matching policy priorities and resources has any currency, it must mean that when there are significant changes on the world scene, governments will realign their policies to take account of the changes and will in turn reallocate resources. We have already seen, however, several instances in which this rather obvious truism did not govern. But there is an even more obvious example of what has been called the "March of Dimes syndrome." When polio is cured, the March of Dimes has two choices: go out of business or find another childhood disease. It should not surprise that most organizations, including the March of Dimes, choose the latter course.

An almost classic case of this primordial instinct to adapt for survival (Darwin was right!) can be seen in the recent history of U.S. foreign broadcasting operations. The primary instruments[37] of these activities have been (1) the Voice of America (since 1942, the U.S. "official" radio, analogous to the BBC or Radio Moscow), a sometimes uneasy component of USIA, and (2) Radio Free Europe and Radio Liberty, dating from 1949 and 1951, respectively, which were intended to function as "surrogate broadcasters, providing to audiences behind the Iron Curtain the news and information to which they would have access if they had their own free press. . . . Both VOA and RFE/RL drew heavily for staffing on emigres from the countries served; they understood it to be part of their mission to encourage and sup-

---

37. There have also been special-purpose operations, such as Radio/TV Martí, intended to broadcast to Cuba and, more recently, plans for "Radio Free Asia." Both of the latter tend to sustain the same point, that special interests are a primary element in what the government does in overseas broadcasting.

port the pursuit of freedom by providing full information to the people of totalitarian lands."[38]

For many, the fall of the Berlin Wall and the subsequent collapse of the Soviet empire in 1989 called into question whether this Cold War approach to information (some would say propaganda) could justifiably be continued, at least in its current form. At issue was the cost of proposed new facilities as well as the self-interest of other parts of the foreign affairs community faced with budget shortfalls. Of particular interest was a new joint Voice of America and BIB (Board for International Broadcasting, the parent entity for RFE and RL) transmitter/relay station, proposed for construction in Israel (the location, of course, serving some unrelated purposes just considered) and intended originally to improve capabilities to reach into Eastern Europe and some of the Soviet republics.

In early 1990, even though Eastern Europe had already broken away from the Soviet bloc and although the Soviet Union itself was showing signs of imminent major change, the Congress authorized $207 million and appropriated $183.5 million for FY 1990 to begin the transmitter project.[39] State had attempted informally to squelch this appropriation in the hope that Function 150 shortfalls in other areas might thus be accommodated under the BEA cap, but to no avail. By late 1991, when the next authorization bill was under consideration, skepticism about the need for the transmitter was more pronounced. While not willing to make a formal request to cut it, OMB indicated it was not wedded to the transmitter (although of course the BIB and USIA, the parent organization of the VOA, continued to support it). Even the Israeli government, with a stake in the project because of fees to be paid and construction jobs to be created, gave informal indications that cancellation would not be a cause célèbre.[40]

Finally, in 1993, although there continued to be ambivalence about what should be done in the long term concerning the radios, the transmitter issue moved to resolution. The Clinton administration, after a review on assuming office, requested the deletion of funding for the transmitter, and that request was accommodated in the Authorization Bill for FY 1994 and 1995

---

38. *The Report of the President's Task Force on U.S. Government International Broadcasting*, Publication no. 9925 (Washington, D.C.: U.S. Department of State, December 1991), p. 5.

39. The authorization was contained in sec. 301(c) of the Foreign Relations Authorization Act, Fiscal Years 1990 and 1991, P.L. 101-246, February 16, 1990; the appropriation was in Title V of the Departments of Commerce, Justice, and State, the Judiciary and Related Agencies Appropriations Act, 1990 (P.L. 101-162).

40. I participated in some of these conversations.

and in the Supplemental Appropriations Bill for FY 1993.[41] The administration did, however, request $125 million for a transmitter in Kuwait. That request was deleted by the House authorizers with an explanation that the new broadcast entity being proposed in the bill (see below) should assess the need for it; they also questioned "the appearance of rewarding a country that has participated in the Arab League boycott of Israel," and the Senate committee expressly prohibited the use of funds for a transmitter in Kuwait. The final act did the same.[42] Clearly, the Israelis and their American supporters remained a force to be reckoned with, especially when supporting their position could conserve scarce funds!

The larger issues of government-sponsored international radio (and television) broadcasting will likely remain. On April 29, 1991, for example, the Bush White House press office announced the creation of an independent, bipartisan Presidential Task Force on U.S. Government International Broadcasting, the purpose of which was to review the best structure and organization for the future "in the overall context of U.S. foreign policy and public diplomacy."[43]

Apparently some in the Bush administration, in particular OMB Director Richard Darman and perhaps even USIA Director Henry Catto, hoped that the task force would conclude it was time to downsize broadcasting efforts and perhaps to phase out RFE and RL.[44] Instead, when the task force reported in December 1991, perhaps influenced by the intervening failed coup in the Soviet Union during August,[45] it concluded that "this is no time to abandon or degrade America's great international broadcasting endeavor," that the VOA should "go global" (with particular emphasis on China), and that RFE/RL should continue as surrogates until the new states could develop better broadcasting capabilities. As a consequence, there would be a

41. Sec. 217 of the House version, H.R. 2333, repealed sec. 301(c) of the 1990–91 authorization cited above (see note 39) and became sec. 315(b) of the final law. The appropriation provision was a rescission of $180 million in the Supplemental Appropriations Act of 1993, P.L. 103-50, July 2, 1993.

42. *Report of the House Foreign Affairs Committee to Accompany HR. 2333*, p. 47. The authorization bill as passed, P.L. 103-236, April 30, 1994, in sec. 226, expressly prohibited the use of any appropriated funds for a short-wave transmitter in Kuwait.

43. The White House announcement is reprinted as app. 1 in *The Report of the President's Task Force on U.S. Government International Broadcasting* (note 38 above), pp. 25–27.

44. This point was rather explicitly made to me by OMB officials serving in 1990–91. Interviews, spring and summer 1993.

45. For this possibility, see "Commerce Justice State Appropriations," *CQ Almanac* 47 (1991): 542; and *The Report of the President's Task Force*, p. 16.

"pronounced need" for their continuing services, at least until the end of the decade.[46]

The task force, while arguing for much closer technical cooperation among all the broadcasting operations, rejected the notion that there should be a radically new organizational structure that would combine RFE and RL into a single unit with the VOA. In fact, the task force supported moving Radio Martí and a possible Radio Free Asia under the BIB, since they acted more as surrogates for nonexistent independent radios in target countries than as official radios like the VOA. A single organization, it was argued, would likely come about through attrition if the surrogates were eventually phased out.[47]

The Bush administration was not especially pleased with this outcome, but thought it prudent not to argue the point in an election year, especially when the campaign was consciously de-emphasizing international matters and given the powerful lobby support for RFE and RL. The issue was left for later.

On June 15, 1993, the Clinton administration, after extensive internal discussions amid a good amount of acrimony, announced a different approach. While each of the radios (including the VOA) would remain independent, they would all be governed by an independent board appointed by the president with congressional approval. In effect, the existing BIB would be replaced by the new entity; and the VOA, by being under that structure, would likely have greater policy independence.[48]

Both the House and the Senate version of the Authorization Bill for FY 1994 and 1995 included provisions that (in somewhat different ways) provided for the new approach. After protracted discussion that was seen as increasingly arcane by all but the most engaged, a compromise that drew on both was finally accepted in April 1994.[49] Whether the BIB and the expa-

---

46. *The Report of the President's Task Force*, "Summary of Findings," p. 7.

47. Ibid., pp. 15–22.

48. White House announcement, June 15, 1993. See also R. Jeffrey Smith, "Conflict over U.S. Radio Stations Eases: Clinton Plan Would Achieve First Major Restructuring Since Cold War," *Washington Post*, June 16, 1993.

49. Title III of the bill reported by the full Senate Foreign Relations Committee and Part B of Title II of H.R. 2333 as passed by the House were entitled the "United States International Broadcasting Act of 1993" and the "International Broadcasting Act of 1993," respectively. The compromise, in the conference report, was Title III, "United States International Broadcasting Act," of the delayed State Authorization Act for FY 1994 and 1995, P.L. 103-236, April 30, 1994.

triate staff of the two surrogate radios, well organized, well supported, vocal, and happy in their Munich base (the Clinton plan called for downsizing and a full-scale relocation to Washington and Prague) would quietly accept the changes, however, was a big problem.[50] To take one example, RFE and RL as independent grantees could set their own salary schedules, subject to general guidelines and German law; VOA employees were paid according to normal U.S. government procedures. When Senator Russell Feingold, during consideration of the Senate provision just cited, noted the high salaries of the president of Radio Free Europe/Radio Liberty, Inc., and other senior officials ($316,000 for the former, including cost-of-living allowances for being based in Germany) and argued they should be paid at U.S. government scale ($120,000 would have been the maximum), he was strongly opposed by Senator Joseph Biden, long an active supporter of almost all forms of broadcasting, who argued for the independence of the surrogates and threatened a filibuster after Feingold prevailed, 15–4.[51] While the reason for Biden's strong feeling is unclear, his threat was taken seriously. Senate floor consideration of the entire FY 1994–95 Foreign Relations Authorization Bill was deferred until early 1994, pending a compromise. One was ultimately found, but the outcome was uncertain until the very end.[52] The delay dismayed many authorizers, who were forced once

50. The Munich staff strongly resisted this move, promoted by Czech President Václav Havel and the BIB, which would lower operating costs. In an obvious attempt to stop this maneuver, RFL's new president, longtime staffer William W. Marsh, resigned in January 1994, only three months after assuming his position. See John M. Goshko, "New President of Radio Free Europe Quits: Proposed Relocation to Prague Is Cited," *Washington Post*, January 11, 1994. Agreement was first reached to privatize and move the archives of the radios to Prague ("Radio Free Europe Near Accord with Financier George Soros to Privatize Its Research and Archives Operation and Move Them from Munich to Prague," *New York Times*, March 20, 1994). Congress, in the FY 1994–95 Foreign Relations Authorization Act (sec. 308[k]), wanted the new broadcasting board created by the act to make the decision whether or not to move, but allowed the president to prevail so long as he certified that "significant national interest" required it and notified Congress, providing a detailed plan. Later in 1994, President Clinton exercised this option, and the move took place. For the moment, Havel showed that he had more clout, at least with the Clinton administration, than the RFL/RL functionaries in Munich! These details are from a BIB official, June 24, 1994, February 17, 1955, and May 9, 1996. Information on the decision to move can be found in Craig R. Whitney, "U.S. Moves and Retools Radio Free Europe and Radio Liberty," *New York Times*, August 21, 1994.
51. Al Kamen, "In the Loop: Radio Free Europe Gets Static on Pay," *Washington Post*, July 21, 1993.
52. For a good short summary of these events, see David Binder, "Senators Battle over Foreign Broadcast Cuts," *Washington Post*, October 31, 1993.

again (in the CJS bill for FY 1994) to ask the appropriators to waive the requirement of authorization before obligation of appropriations.[53]

There are even larger issues, of course, such as whether the way of the future may not be private international broadcasting (at least for television), such as CNN or BBC World Service Television, which would be more independent than any government radio and less costly for the taxpayers of nations now operating government broadcasting services.[54] The almost viewerless (because of Cuban jamming) TV Martí continued to be funded at routine levels ($24.8 million for FY 1997) in no small measure because of its symbolic import for Cuban Americans in Florida (with its twenty-five electoral votes).[55] On the other hand, Radio Liberty and Radio Free Europe, already reduced to $75 million in the Clinton administration budget request for FY 1996 (from almost $230 million in FY 1995), sustained a further last-minute reduction of $46 million in the Senate CJS markup in order to provide funds for U.S. merchant shipping.[56] While this last cut was restored

53. The waiver extended until April 30, 1994, to allow time to attempt to pass an authorization bill. In the conference report, however, the appropriators could not resist twisting the knife, especially in light of recent history, most notably the "section 614" brouhaha of 1989–90 discussed at length in Chapter 5 above. They noted, first, that "the conferees have taken this action because the necessary authorizing legislation has not been enacted into law and the prospects for action are uncertain." Thus, they had "taken the only responsible action." They continued:

> Requiring annual or biennial authorization for spending levels is an important process, but prohibiting the obligation of appropriations in the absence of such authorization is unduly restrictive. *Therefore, the conferees strongly recommend that the authorizing committees give the most serious consideration to offering legislation to repeal section 701 of the United States Information and Educational Exchange Act of 1948 and section 15 of the State Department Basic Authorities Act of 1956.* (emphasis added)

The sections cited are those requiring authorization before the obligation of appropriations for the two agencies. The quoted language accompanies Amendment no. 170 and is found in *Congressional Record* 139 (October 14, 1993): H7999 and in the printed conference report, H. Rept. 103-293, 103d Cong., 1st sess. (Washington, D.C.: GPO, October 14, 1993), pp. 104–5.

54. For a thoughtful discussion of this issue, concluding that privatization is best and examining arguments on both sides, see "Cross-Frontier Broadcasting: And Nation Shall Speak Guff unto Nation," *Economist* 323 (May 2, 1992): 21–24.

55. Guy Gugliotta, "TV Martí Signal Clear on the Hill: Despite a Dearth of Viewers, Broadcasts to Cuba Still Will Be Funded," *Washington Post*, October 25, 1995. Interestingly, the final CR for FY 1996 also mandated a move of TV Martí's headquarters from Washington, D.C., to Miami.

56. Michael Dobbs, "Post–Cold War Message May Be Muted: Radio Free Europe, Sister Station Threatened by U.S. Budget Cuts and Political Maneuvering," *Washington Post*, October 17, 1995.

in conference, it was another example of the tendency to shift funds from Function 150 to domestic purposes in the CJS subcommittees; it also shows that Václav Havel, the Czech president who had just engineered the move of RFE/RL, had fewer votes than either the Miami Cubans or the U.S. merchant marine!

New circumstances, and in this instance changing technology, *ought* in my opinion to force a change in the ways in which overseas activities are carried out. This case also presents a classic example of why the transition is so difficult. Yet, faced with declining resources and a raft of new situations, there is little choice.

# CHAPTER EIGHT

# TRAIN WRECKS HAPPEN

## *Continuity and Change, 1995*

The Democrats' debacle in the 1994 midterm elections brought noticeable changes in the handling of issues of money and foreign affairs. Initially, it appeared that a revolution in relationships between the branches was in the offing, featuring intransigent opposition and greatly heightened hostility. But in retrospect, it is just as plausible to view most of the trends discussed above as continuing, albeit sometimes with greater force and emphasis. The developments of the eighteen months from the November 1994 elections through the spring of 1996 do place many of those trends in even sharper focus. They provide some stark examples of the uneasy and arguably growing tensions between Congress and the executive—institutional as well as heavily partisan in nature—when carrying out their joint foreign affairs responsibilities. There are worrisome indications of how uncertain the future may be, at a time when the United States must in large measure supply world leadership if there is to be any.

## Early Warnings

The results of the 1994 election were barely in when the first signs were seen that 1995 would be a turbulent year. For one thing, the longtime antagonist of the State Department and of many international programs and activities, Senator Jesse Helms of North Carolina, opted to become chairman

of the Senate Foreign Relations Committee.[1] Although he wrote a concilia-
tory letter to Secretary Christopher on the night of the election,[2] within a
few days Helms gave clear signals that a period of greater contentiousness
had arrived, not least in his explosive comments about the fitness of President Clinton to be commander in chief, followed shortly by the suggestion
that the president should not venture onto military bases in North Carolina
without protection.[3] Along with Senator Mitch McConnell, the new chair
of the Senate Foreign Operations Appropriations Subcommittee, Helms
quickly indicated that a major review of funding levels and foreign policies
of the Clinton administration would be in store, including "the so-called
foreign aid program," the separate status of what he considered to be the
liberal/elitist Foreign Service, relations with the United Nations, and the
Middle East peace process.[4] They were true to their word.

# The 1995 Agenda

Topically, the 1995 foreign affairs congressional agenda resembled that of
the immediately preceding years: namely, the requirement for State Depart-

---

1. In 1981, when the Republicans controlled the Senate, Helms had opted for the Agriculture Committee chairmanship for essentially North Carolina reasons, with Senator Richard
Lugar of Indiana chairing Foreign Relations. In 1987, when the Democrats reassumed control,
Helms won a close battle with Lugar to become ranking member of the SFRC, leaving Lugar
to be the senior Republican on the Agriculture Committee. In 1995, with no real challenge,
Helms again used his seniority to become chairman of the SFRC, with Lugar taking Agricul-
ture. For an overview of Helms's approach in 1995, see Barry Yeoman, "Statesmanship vs.
Helmsmanship," *The Nation* 262 (February 5, 1996): 11–15.

2. Robert F. Hopper, a State legislative officer, is the source for this information, May 1996.

3. See Bradley Graham and Dan Morgan, "Shalikashvili Rebuts Helms on Clinton's Ability
as Commander," *Washington Post*, November 20, 1994; Richard Cohen, "Chairman Jesse,"
*Washington Post*, November 23, 1994; Steven Greenhouse, "Helms Is at Center of Storm After
New Clinton Criticism," *New York Times*, November 23, 1994; and Helen Dewar, "Saying
Helms Vows to Hold His Tongue, Dole Won't Deny Him Chairmanship," *Washington Post*,
November 24, 1994.

4. John M. Goshko and Daniel Williams, "U.S. Policy Faces Review by Helms: State Dept.
Nemesis to Flex Muscle as Chairman of Foreign Relations," *Washington Post*, November 13,
1994. On foreign assistance, see John M. Goshko, "Foreign Aid May Be Early Test of New
Hill Order: Helms, Set to Head Key Senate Panel, Rattles Budget Saber as AID Braces for
Funding Battle," *Washington Post*, November 21, 1994; Steven Greenhouse, "Republicans
Plan to Guide Foreign Policy by Purse String: On the Hill, More Hostility About Spending
Overseas," *New York Times*, November 13, 1994; and Steven Greenhouse, "Foreign Aid and
G.O.P.: Deep Cuts, Selectively," *New York Times*, December 21, 1994.

ment and foreign assistance authorization acts as well as parallel CJS and "Foreign Ops" appropriations measures. On the policy side, questions concerning the role of the United States with respect to peacekeeping activities in Bosnia and Haiti, whether the START II treaty should be ratified and, in a spillover from domestic politics, the international ramifications of population control programs and abortion were equally present. Each of these familiar elements, however, proved extremely contentious, involving even the survival of some of the agencies—notably USAID, USIA, and ACDA—as well as major challenges to long-established programs. When the dust had settled, the changes were less dramatic than many had predicted, but there was little reason to hope for any basis of mutual understanding about how to deal with foreign relations. In this chapter, some major developments of 1995 are explored thematically in order to show their continuity with, and their departures from, the past.

# The Downward Funding Spiral Continues

First of all and coloring much of everything else, the decline in U.S. international affairs funding continued and accelerated. President Clinton's FY 1996 request for $21.2 billion for Function 150 was immediately pared down to $18.3 billion under the budget resolution and, after some small reallocations, to $18.49 billion at the end of the process. This was a $2.8 billion reduction, about a 13 percent overall cut from the request level, and some accounts were reduced substantially more.[5] Limitations on flexibility for the executive were more pronounced than these dollar cuts might suggest. As a USAID summary noted,

> The overall FY 1996 [Foreign Operations] appropriations bill provides $12.1 billion, 18% below the $14.8 billion requested by the President and 11% below the FY 1995 enacted levels. . . . Programs administered by USAID (other than ESF for Israel and Egypt, which were earmarked at request levels) were cut by an aggregate 22% from the request. . . . Assistance to the NIS [Newly Independent States of the former Soviet Union] and Eastern Europe programs

5. Data from OMB, the House Budget Committee, and State's S/RPP and M/FMP offices, at various times from spring 1995 to May 1996.

were reduced by 19% and 32%, respectively, from the levels requested.[6]

That the United States, according to OECD figures, ranked at the bottom of all developed nations in the percentage of GNP devoted to foreign assistance,[7] a fact noted with some frequency in Hill debate, carried almost no weight with Congress.

Domestic political realities were more compelling than the American international presence and obligations. Whether one used administration or Republican congressional numbers, the results were the same: a downsizing of government and a disaffection for Washington would sharply reduce federal funding. And for foreign affairs, which was either invisible or unpopular depending on the audience, the immediate future was bleak indeed.[8]

## Foreign Affairs: Still an Afterthought

This should not be surprising. The engine for these reductions was not primarily antipathy toward funding international activities, although the "new isolationists" were but the latest embodiment of the long-term skepticism of many in Congress, especially on the Republican side. Some believe that intended or not, the cuts would place America's leadership role at risk, almost by default. Even traditional Republican leaders, while having to accommodate those who had brought them majority status, found themselves confronting radically different and disconcerting approaches to international affairs.[9]

6. USAID summary, "Foreign Assistance Levels, Fiscal Year 1996" (undated, but prepared in late October or early November 1995).

7. Data from OECD studies, as provided by a bulletin from the White House Task Force on International Affairs Resources: "Advancing American Leadership: The Budget for International Affairs (Function 150)," *Bulletin* no. 15, June 26, 1995. See also "Development Aid Rises, but . . . ," *Christian Science Monitor*, May 14, 1996, for data on the twenty-one developed nations that were members of the OECD's Development Assistance Committee (DAC).

8. Among many discussions, see Jackie Calmes, "Clinton's Fiscal '97 Budget Reflects Major Shift Toward Ending Deficits and 'Big Government,' " *Wall Street Journal*, February 6, 1996; and Dick Kirschten, "Yep, Foreign Aid's Going South," *National Journal* 26 (December 12, 1994): 2931.

9. There have been endless commentaries on this point. Three of the more useful ones are Robert S. Greenberger, "As Congress Sharpens Knives to Cut Foreign Aid, Critics Warn of Damage to U.S. Policy-making," *Wall Street Journal*, May 18, 1995; Carroll J. Doherty, "New

For some, this international indifference was "an insidious form of isolationism" with almost no attention given to foreign affairs and to the role the United States should play in the world, in large measure owing to the attitudes and lack of experience of the new Republicans in the House. As elsewhere in the grinding budget debate, the hard and serious questions, from a public policy point of view, were not being asked: notably, "How big a cut is too much?"[10]

Be this as it may, the proximate cause for the budget reductions was the "Contract with America" espoused by most of the new Republican House majority, which placed elimination of the federal deficit by 2002 as its absolute highest priority. The impact on government expenditure was potentially even more draconian because of the parallel insistence on significant tax cuts. In consequence, virtually all discretionary federal programs, including many that had a more directly perceived positive impact on important segments of the public than international affairs, faced the same challenges. Only defense escaped to some degree, although it had taken major reductions in earlier years. At the macro level, international affairs was once again an afterthought, as it had been in the 1987 and 1990 budget summits. In the November 1995 agreement which brought to an end the first and shorter of two government partial shutdowns, international affairs was not even one of the areas that the administration insisted had to be protected during efforts to reach a balanced budget in seven years (by 2002), using CBO numbers.[11] In the negotiations, moreover, there was no longer any thought of "fencing" or protecting international affairs as a separate category, as had been done in 1990.[12]

---

Generation Challenges Established Orthodoxy," CQ Weekly Report 54 (February 3, 1996): 306–8; and Helen Dewar, "World of Difference: GOP Generations Vie on Global Affairs," Washington Post, April 9, 1996. Also typical are Bob Dole, "Who's an Isolationist?" (op-ed article), New York Times, June 6, 1995; and Arthur Schlesinger, Jr., "New Isolationists Weaken America" (op-ed article), New York Times, June 11, 1995. Mainstream internationalist views were expressed in two Washington Post editorials, "Cheap Shots at Foreign Affairs," September 15, 1995, and "The Irresponsibles," March 24, 1996, and in David Gergen's "Looking Beyond Our Borders," U.S. News and World Report 119 (April 15, 1996): 84.

10. This paragraph paraphrases David Gordon, a former HFAC staffer then working on foreign assistance who subsequently moved on to the Overseas Development Council, AFSA Friday Forum, Department of State, Washington, D.C., February 9, 1996.

11. These areas were Medicare, Medicaid, the environment, and education. Also cited were tax fairness, welfare reform, agriculture, defense funding, and veterans' benefits, but not international affairs. Letter from Leon E. Panetta to Bob Dole, November 24, 1995.

12. Robert D. Reischauer, "The U.S. Budget: A Valentine's Day Tale of Sweet Nothings," Economic Strategy Institute Noontime Lecture, Washington, D.C., February 14, 1996, in response to a question from the author.

It is, of course, true that even if there had been no overall drive to reduce the size and activism of government (admittedly hard to conceive given the forces that brought the Republicans to power in 1994), times likely would have been difficult for international affairs. To take one example, there was increasing skepticism, even among true believers, about the efficacy of foreign assistance.[13] The failure to enact final FY 1996 budgets until January 1996 for USAID and not until late April for the Department of State and USIA led to uncertainties that made a bad situation worse.[14] When the pressure to reduce government's cost and scope was combined with these factors—not to mention the hostility of Senator Helms and other conservative Republicans who had assumed central roles in Congress plus the ineptitude of some committees (especially House authorizers) in managing legislation—the impact was in certain areas devastating.

## Merger: A Surrogate for Program Elimination?

The determination of the newly empowered Republican members to force foreign affairs activities in radically new directions was perhaps most obvious in the yearlong efforts of Helms, HIRC Chairman Ben Gilman, and others to reorganize the agencies of the foreign affairs community and to abolish several of them. For many, these efforts went far beyond the usual rationales for reorganization—economy, efficiency, and the end of duplicative efforts—to the very future of the core activities through which U.S. interactions with the rest of the world are carried out. And they ignored the conventional wisdom that reorganizations could never work if they were forced by Congress on a reluctant executive branch.

Immediately after the election, the shocked Clinton White House began to assess where they stood, and among other things concluded that the administration's push for a smaller, less costly government—increasingly the theme of the National Performance Review, even before the election—was one positive element that should receive greater emphasis. As early as the Monday after the election (November 14, 1994) NPR Deputy Director John

---

13. One of the best of many commentaries to this effect in 1995 and 1996 was Howard W. French's "The World: Donors of Foreign Aid Have Second Thoughts," *New York Times*, April 7, 1996.

14. Ben Barber, "Funding Uncertainty Foils Foreign Affairs Agencies Abroad," *Washington Times*, January 22, 1996.

Kemensky announced to agency representatives that as the result of a Clinton-Gore meeting on November 10, there would be a new emphasis on reinventing government, although the form of this metamorphosis was not yet known.[15] On December 19, phase two of NPR was officially launched, with an emphasis on eliminating programs, devolving responsibilities where possible to state and local governments, and further reducing the size of the federal government.[16] The next day, Elaine Kamarck, a senior policy advisor to Gore and his link to NPR, was even more blunt in encouraging agencies and departments to submit radical ideas for change and streamlining. Showing the source of this initiative, she was also frank in stating that the new exercise would be controlled much more explicitly than its predecessor by political appointees.[17] On January 3, 1995, Gore sent a memorandum to the heads of all government agencies, asking for "various options for reorganizing themselves before the Republican-dominated Congress does it for them."[18]

Indeed, there was already a case in point in the international area. In mid-December 1994, Senator Mitch McConnell, the incoming chairman of the Foreign Operations Appropriations Subcommittee, indicated his intention to propose legislation that "would abolish AID and have the State Department carry out its functions."[19] Interestingly in light of events to follow, Jesse Helms, the incoming chairman of Foreign Relations, apparently told McConnell that he was impinging on the prerogatives of the SFRC and that

---

15. As USAID's NPR liaison, I attended this meeting.

16. See, for example, Ruth Marcus and Stephen Barr, "Sizing Up New Climate on Hill, Clinton Chose Downsizing," *Washington Post*, December 21, 1994.

17. At an NPR agency liaison meeting, which I attended.

18. Elaine Sciolino, "State Dept. May Absorb 3 Independent Agencies, Foreign Aid and Arms Control Involved: Sweeping Before the Republican Broom Hits the Floor," *New York Times*, January 11, 1995.

19. See Dick Kirschten, "Washington Update: Mitch, Dick Want to be Heard, Too," *National Journal* 27 (December 17, 1994): 2974–75; and Ben Barber, "State Aims to Grab Control of 3 Key Agencies: Future of AID, USIA, ACDA at Stake," *Washington Times*, January 11, 1995. See also "Flaws in a Foreign-Policy Design" (editorial), *Atlanta Constitution*, December 16, 1994, for a critique of McConnell's merger plan. The *Washington Post* made a similar argument in a January 6, 1995, editorial, "Open Season on AID?" which noted that the agency faced a "two-front war" both within the administration and against McConnell and other key Hill Republicans, and which made a central AID argument that foreign assistance under control of the State Department "would likely be treated exclusively as a tactical weapon of America diplomacy with not much regard for the needs of international development or U.S. economic interests." See also "Foreign Aid Ruse" (editorial), *Christian Science Monitor*, January 6, 1995, which criticized McConnell's plan as making many of the same mistakes as the Clinton administration, tying foreign policy too closely to domestic policy.

his bill would never receive a hearing. This declaration may have been in part because the Helms staff was working on a plan to abolish USAID, a plan that may have been preempted by McConnell's staff in a display of appropriator one-upmanship![20]

In response to McConnell and other likely threats, shortly after the election USAID's very effective public affairs staff stirred up a torrent of articles and editorials favorable to foreign assistance and to the agency. This campaign was to be easily diverted to additional tasks shortly thereafter.

All this provided an opportunity which was quickly exploited by some at State, who believed that budgetary stringency in the new Republican-controlled Congress was inevitable, and that one way to preserve core functions was to consider merging the smaller foreign affairs agencies into the Department of State. This would, they thought, reduce overhead and costs, with the added incentive of bringing more policy coherence to the administration's foreign affairs efforts. Even before the election, building in part on the unhappiness of State Department regional assistant secretaries over coordination failures in developing an overall, coherent foreign policy owing to the "extreme turf consciousness" of other foreign affairs agencies, some senior officials at State had begun talking about developing a more integrated structure. The day after the election, they were reenergized by the additional argument that the very limited budgets which seemed inevitable made consolidation all the more important, a viewpoint that was reinforced through quiet conversations with Republican congressional staff.[21] When McConnell's proposal begain to circulate, an additional argument was that an administration plan was needed to preempt him and provide the president and the secretary of state with an opportunity to shape reorganization.[22] Once the State Department plan came to light, however, skeptics outside the department quickly noted it would virtually ensure that State's perspectives dominated, and they began to protect their turf.[23]

State prepared a draft plan, which reflected "absolute acceptance" of the

20. Congressional relations sources in USAID and State.

21. Interview with Craig Johnstone, a key State Department participant in these early deliberations, May 1, 1996.

22. Barber, "State Aims to Grab Control . . ."

23. To some, the plan seemed to follow the "Willie Sutton theory of reorganization." Perhaps apocryphally, Sutton, the well-known bank robber, was asked, "Why do you rob banks, Willie?" To which he responded, "Because that's where the money is!" These critics believed that some in the Department of State, in the area headed by the under secretary for global affairs, facing great difficulty in funding their programs, saw a merger as a way to gain access to some of USAID's program resources and to reallocate them.

desirability of "genuine amalgamation" by all seventh-floor principals. Secretary Christopher, in part because of the NPR search for bold proposals, raised the issue with the vice-president, who was initially very enthusiastic. Christopher himself, while certainly not opposed, may have done this more to be responsive to Gore's appeal than as a committed advocate in the same way his staff was. In any event, the plan was sent to NPR just before the holidays. Christopher apparently saw this as a high-stakes issue he did not want to lose.[24]

After the Christmas break, an interagency principals' meeting chaired by Gore was convened on short notice on Friday, January 6, 1995, to consider the State Department proposal. Beginning a pattern to be repeated throughout the year, the session, while courteous and businesslike was also very contentious, with USAID and other agency representatives strongly opposed to the plan. Later, Secretary Christopher was reported to have been " 'caught flat-footed' by the vehement opposition to the changes."[25] State was arguing that world changes and those in Congress made reorganization necessary in order to retain some initiative in the face of hostile congressional leadership; AID and other opponents countered that a major change under these circumstances "would look more like capitulation than determination."[26]

At a second meeting, on January 10, agency heads came equipped with papers making their cases. Some reflected afterward that it was at this point that the contest began to turn against State because of intense resistance. Not surprisingly, each side criticized the other for the poor quality of its staff work.[27] By the next day, reflecting the common Washington practice

24. See note 21 above.

25. Quoted in an unsigned article (Globe Staff), "Christopher Is Said to Tell Aides He Wants to Resign His Position," *Boston Globe*, January 10, 1995. Elaine Sciolino, "Clinton Said to Reject Offer by Christopher to Quit," *New York Times*, January 12, 1995, suggests the same. Obviously, whatever the secretary's intention at the time, he did not depart. On January 11, Reuters quoted Christopher as stating that he had an important agenda for the year. On January 13, Daniel Williams reported in the *Washington Post* that "Secretary of State Christopher Gets Vote of Confidence from President Clinton." The White House apparently had canvassed inside and outside the administration concerning whether Christopher should be retained. A proud man, it is plausible that the secretary might have contemplated leaving after being undercut in this fashion. Interview with a senior foreign affairs official, May 16, 1996.

26. Globe Staff, "Christopher Is Said to Tell Aides . . ."

27. Various participants. While this reaction no doubt reflected in part a natural tendency to find staff work that supports one's own position to be of higher quality than staff work that does not, USAID did have some serious problems with State's presentation, which they found to be full of inaccuracies regarding AID's willingness to participate fully in integrated country

that such bureaucratic frays are fought out as much in the press as in private, press outlets carried detailed stories clearly based on leaks from participants.[28]

Over the next two weeks, the battle became increasingly intense, both in private and in public. Atwood was especially vocal, particularly at a development assistance conference on January 15.[29] His public affairs campaign, already in place, was easily retargeted to the antimerger battle. State leaders interpreted this move as AID taking the offensive against them. In fact, Atwood prided himself as a team player, and would likely have been willing to live, however reluctantly, with the unfavorable outcome.[30]

As opponents hoped, the White House proponents of smaller government soon decided that the costs were not worth paying in this instance. By January 24, the *Boston Globe* was reporting that the plan had been set aside,[31] news that was confirmed two days later by others.[32] On January 27, the vice-president's office issued a press release which mandated reviews of consolidation and of possibilities for greater efficiency in many foreign affairs sectors (e.g., arms control, public affairs, policy coordination, missions abroad, refugee and disaster relief, trade, and sustainable development). Tellingly, its major element was that "the review concluded that the Arms Control and Disarmament Agency, the Agency for International Development, and the United States Information Agency are essential vehicles for the accomplishment of their missions under the overall foreign policy guid-

---

planning. At Atwood's direction, USAID asked Leon Fuerth, Gore's foreign policy advisor, to withdraw the State paper (interview with senior foreign affairs official, May 16, 1996).

28. See, for example, Sciolino, "State Dept. May Absorb 3 Independent Agencies"; John M. Goshko, " 'Super State Department' May Absorb Other Agencies: Clinton Considers Consolidating AID, ACDA, and USIA," *Washington Post*, January 11, 1995; Dick Kirschten, "USS Foggy Bottom's No Happy Ship," *National Journal* 27 (January 21, 1995): 197; and even a *Washington Times* editorial, "At State, a Super Non-Starter," January 12, 1995.

29. "Atwood Defends AID and aid," *Washington Post*, January 16, 1995.

30. Interview with Atwood, May 16, 1996. See also Thomas W. Lippman, "Entrenched Constituencies Help Kill Merger: Proposed Absorption of 3 Foreign Policy Agencies by State Dept. Fails Quickly and Bitterly," *Washington Post*, February 3, 1995, which is the best short press article on the episode to this point, though inaccurate in stating that "Atwood told Christopher he would resign if the plan went through."

31. Paul Quinn-Judge, "Plan for a New 'Super' State Dept. Is Shelved," *Boston Globe*, January 24, 1995. The *Globe* appeared to have especially good White House sources during this episode.

32. Thomas W. Lippman, "Gore Is Said to Reject Merger of Foreign Policy Agencies," *Washington Post*, January 26, 1995; Steven Greenhouse, "Gore Rules Against Merger of A.I.D. and Others into State Dept.," *New York Times*, January 26, 1995.

ance of the Secretary of State."[33] It also promised a reduction of $5 billion in Function 150 expenditures over a five-year period.

Atwood and his allies appeared to have won. But as has been seen throughout his book, some things are never truly over.

Senator Helms, although originally lukewarm to the merger plan (he would have preferred outright abolition of USAID and termination of its programs), in part because it might increase the power of some in State whom he was not fond of,[34] could not resist the temptation to use this issue in his efforts to realign U.S. foreign policy, and by the by cause some discomfort for the administration. Helms's first shot was not long in coming, in the form of an article entitled "Christopher Is Right,"[35] in which he argued that the idea was "bold and innovative" but had been subverted by the "bureaucratic hierarchy." He also wrote that when the SFRC took up the State authorization bill, he would introduce his own consolidation plan. Helms provided no specifics, though.

February 1995 saw ongoing administration attempts to ferret out the details of the Helms plan, which apparently did not yet exist except in sketchiest form. The counterattack by the threatened agencies against the merger was revved up again. Meanwhile, the executive branch agonized over whether to attempt preemption or to meet Helms partway by including some merger ideas in their version of a draft State Department authorization bill or, alternatively, to hold fast in defense of Gore's decision. This issue was never effectively resolved, and in a departure from years past, no formal draft legislation was sent to Congress, lest it look pale by comparison.[36] At the same time, Helms's opposition to foreign assistance continued to be clear, leading to the conclusion that his plan was not designed to deliver

33. Office of the Vice-President, White House, press release, January 27, 1995.

34. E.g., Deputy Secretary of State Strobe Talbott and Under Secretary of State Tim Wirth. "As I understand it, Strobe Talbott is pushing this," Helms said on January 11. "He wants to be secretary of state. We'll see about that." Quoted in "State Department Offers Own Cuts to Pre-empt Republicans," *CQ Weekly Report* 53 (January 14, 1995): 170.

35. Jesse Helms, "Christopher Is Right" (op-ed article), *Washington Post*, February 14, 1995, appearing the morning that Secretary Christopher testified before the SFRC to defend the FY 1996 foreign affairs budget request. Carroll J. Doherty, "Helms Puts His Own Stamp on Cuts Gore Rejected," *CQ Weekly Report*, 53 (February 18, 1995): 540, puts the Helms initiative in context, and summarizes some provisions of the plan.

36. Discussions with several participants in State, USAID, and OMB. Some desired provisions, however, were passed informally to the House and Senate committees and made their way into the draft legislation. This fairly widespread practice is known colloquially as "tossing it over the transom."

"more effective overseas assistance." Rather, it was "a weapon to be used in the Republican assault on major elements of President Clinton's foreign policy."[37] It was probably also seen as a way to embarrass the vice-president, according to some participants.

The first direct encounter occurred when Christopher appeared before the SFRC and Helms on February 14 to defend the coming year's international affairs budget request. Helms's support for the "Helms-Christopher plan" left the secretary somewhat uncomfortable, as an exchange at the hearing showed:

> In a joking reference to the article,
> Christopher said, "Mr. Chairman, let me first say that I'm always grateful for your support whenever I receive it, in whatever newspaper." But he added that he accepted Gore's conclusion that the cost of the merger "would be greater than the benefits that would ensue" and would jeopardize the agencies' internal reform efforts.
> "Of course," said Christopher . . . "we'll look at whatever you come up with, whatever you recommend."
> "Mr. Secretary, I recognize the position you're in," Helms responded. "Let me assure you that from this committee, with a number of senators as cosponsors, will come something that you and the vice president will indeed be obliged to look at. And I thoroughly disagree with the conclusion of the vice president . . . that it would cost more than the benefits."

Atwood, on C-SPAN, had stopped just short of calling Helms an isolationist, characterizing the plan as "mischievous" and as demonstrating views reflective of an isolationist sentiment. Helms's response to Atwood was typical of his cordial style masking a firm resolve:

> "I like Brian and I think he's doing a good job. But I understand he went on [televison] and gave me down in the country about my reorganization plan. It's not my reorganization plan, it's going to be the committee's reorganization plan."
> To Christopher, Helms said. "Give Brian my best regards."[38]

37. "The Real Foreign Aid Debate" (editorial), *Washington Post*, February 18, 1995.
38. The quotations from the February 14 hearing come from Thomas W. Lippman, "Helms's Praise Has Christopher Explaining: Merger Plan Sounds a Lot Like the One Gore Rejected," *Washington Post*, February 15, 1995. Lippman also quoted Atwood as calling Helms an isolationist. Atwood says that is not what he said, although he did characterize the *plan* as isolationist. Interview with Atwood, May 16, 1996.

On March 15, Helms, accompanied by Gilman of HIRC and by Senator Olympia Snowe (newly arrived from the House and now the chair of the SFRC Subcommittee on International Operations which would have initial jurisidiction over the merger issue) sketched out their plan at a press conference. As promised, it abolished AID, ACDA, and USIA and used nongovernmental voluntary agencies to channel assistance overseas. Press coverage was extensive, viewing the plan as an initial maneuver in a major battle to come.[39] At subsequent hearings, Helms scheduled former Secretaries of State Eagleburger and Baker and several others in support of merging the agencies (March 23, 1995), and he solicited letters from other former secretaries to the same end. On March 30, the administration (Atwood, USIA Director Joseph Duffey, Moose of State, and ACDA head John Holum) had its day, getting a somewhat frosty reception amid signs that some Democrats were not altogether unsympathetic to a merger of some sort.[40]

The interagency atmosphere meanwhile was becoming more tense, with the smaller agencies assuming that some in State were working closely with Helms and his House counterpart Ben Gilman, who soon was preparing his own merger plan for inclusion in the House version of the foreign relations authorization bill.[41] Although Gilman indicated that he wanted to find a way out of the situation short of a merger, he would be told by the House leadership that he had to go along. Even so, he told a senior USAID staffer

39. See, for example, Thomas W. Lippman, "Helms Outlines Foreign Policy Reorganization: Prolonged Hill Battle Expected over Agency Merger Proposal," *Washington Post*; Steven Greenhouse, "Helms Seeks to Merger Foreign Policy Agencies: A Senator Sees Savings; the State Dept. Sees Chaos," *New York Times*; Ben Barber, "Reinventing Foreign Affairs: Helms Plan Would Ax 3 Agencies, Save Billions of Dollars," *Washington Times*; and Michael Ross, "Tackling Foreign Policy, GOP Aims to Privatize Functions, Merge Agencies," *Los Angeles Times* (Washington edition). All appeared on March 16, 1995.

40. Ben Barber, "Feinstein, Kerry Tilt to Helms: Express Support for Giving 3 Agencies' Duties to State," *Washington Times*, March 31, 1995. Kerry was to cause concern for the antimerger forces in USAID and elsewhere throughout the episode, since he favored considerable consolidation and, moreover, wanted to strike an agreement with Helms. As will be seen, a deal was the last thing those who were against the merger plan wanted.

41. Among the by-products of this interagency sniping was a rather scurrilous list of "Top Ten Reasons Not to Merge USAID and State," which emerged from the bowels of the AID bureaucracy. Among the printable items included were these: "It would be exorbitantly expensive to send all of USAID's employees to expensive finishing schools and change their names so they had a 'III' after them"; "Poor, hungry people hardly ever hold cocktail receptions"; "USAID logo would have to be changed to pinstripe"; and "Brie and chablis are much more expensive to ship to refugee camps than bulgur wheat and water purification units." The AID leadership moved quickly to suppress this item—but not soon enough. Indeed, I was given a copy by an amused State Department senior manager!

later on that "we're not going to let you die."[42] By early April, the anti-merger forces, with the vice-president's decision supporting them, had been able to force a White House diktat that there was to be no discussion or cooperation with Congress on the merger idea and no contingency planning within the executive branch in anticipation of a possible forced consolidation.[43] House (HIRC) hearings in April were again confrontational, although elements of the Helms plan (such as a private foundation to carry out residual foreign aid activities) were stripped out, and there was more infrastructure within the "new" State department to manage them.[44]

Throughout the spring, the campaign was fought in the press as well as in Congress, with the antimerger forces having the upper hand (if one may measure) the result by the number and strength of relevant articles).[45] In Congress, however, the Republican proponents had the votes, despite warnings that a veto was likely. At times, the byplay was almost comic. Beginning a pattern that was to be repeated, an internal USAID E-mail described the agency's tactic as being to "delay, postpone, obfuscate, derail." The memo

42. Gilman's views were cited by a USAID legislative affairs officer who participated in these meetings (interview, June 13, 1996). As with some other new Republican chairmen, Gilman was suspect as a moderate, and the threat existed that his chairmanship might be in jeopardy if he did not go along with "Contract" plans to abolish some agencies. See, for example, Carroll J. Doherty, "Gilman Under Party Pressure," CQ Weekly Report 53 (May 13, 1995): 1335. For a more general treatment of Gilman, see Thomas W. Lippman, "Foreign Policy Chief Known for His Personal Diplomacy: Gilman's Bipartisanship May Be Both Flaw and Strength," Washington Post, January 26, 1995.

43. USAID and State Department legislative affairs officers are my source for the White House position.

44. Republican Congressman Doug Bereuter of Nebraska sponsored the amendment to remove the development foundation from the bill. On April 4 and May 9, Atwood, Duffey, Moose, and ACDA (Holum in April, his deputy Ralph Earle II in May) appeared before HIRC, making the same arguments as in the Senate.

45. Former Deputy Secretary of State Clifford Wharton argued, "Consolidate? Yes, but Not as Jesse Helms Would," Washington Post, February 21, 1995; and Stephen S. Rosenfeld provided a piece, also in the Washington Post (May 19, 1995), entitled, "Jesse Helms's Power Play: A Radical Assault on the Balance of Power in Making Foreign Policy." Atwood gave an extensive interview to the Washington Post, conducted by Thomas W. Lippman and entitled "Inside: AID—Battling for Independence and Against a Perception," appearing on March 2, 1995; and editorials favorable to foreign assistance were printed by papers ranging from the Hartford Courant (January 21, 1995) to the Orlando Sentinel (January 24, 1995), the Miami Herald (May 1, 1995), and some sixty others between the November 1994 elections and April 1995, according to a USAID release prepared in mid-April. AID also tried to drive home the impact on specific areas as Atwood visited them: see, for example, Rachel Zimmerman, "Local USAID Contractors Nervously Await Budget Knife," Business Journal (Portland, Ore.), March 3, 1995.

found its way to Helms's staff, which promptly issued it as a press release under the title "Captured Enemy Documents."[46]

After Democratic attempts to sidetrack the merger failed, and with the usual policy issues and "pet rocks" being included, the HIRC marked up the bill (which became H.R. 1561) in May.[47] On May 15, Helms for the first time issued a full version of his plan, only two days before the SFRC markup. Administration witnesses earlier had largely been guessing about what was included! In an almost unprecedented outcome, all the votes taken were decided on a straight party-line basis. Included was a Kerry-sponsored alternative merger plan, which would have required the administration to propose a reorganization plan eliminating at least one agency.[48] Unlike the House, the Senate bill (S. 908) did not include a foreign assistance authorization.[49]

As H.R. 1561 went to the House floor on May 23, it was met by a SAP (Statement of Administration Policy) stating that in its committee form, the president's advisors would recommend a veto, and then by a presidential statement explicitly threatening one.[50] The House leadership had hoped to pass the bill quickly, but the Democrats managed to stall it on procedural and policy grounds, so that in the end it had to be carried over until after Memorial Day.[51] The merger, unwarranted "policy mandates," and low

46. May 5, 1995. Later on, several additional memos with the same title were issued by Helms's press spokesman, Marc Thiessen.

47. Robert F. Hopper, a State Department legislative affairs officer, coined the term "pet rocks" to characterize idiosyncratic amendments offered by individual members.

48. Throughout the year, Kerry attempted to find viable compromises, believing that the administration, in light of reduced funding, had to come to grips with a consolidation of functions and perhaps a merger. However, he was also attempting to protect the president's prerogative to set the organizational structure and to decide *what* should be cut or merged. This left him at odds with many in the administration, unwilling to accept what more neutral observers felt was almost inevitable.

49. For dates, witnesses, and votes on amendments, see the two committee reports: Committee on International Relations, House of Representatives, *American Overseas Interests Act of 1995, H.R. 1561*, H. Rept. 104-128, pt. 1, May 19, 1995; and Committee on Foreign Relations, *Foreign Relations Revitalization Act of 1995, S. 908*, S. Rept. 104-95, June 9, 1995.

50. The SAP was dated May 22, 1995, and Secretary Christopher sent letters providing more detail to Gingrich and Gilman that same day. The president's comment, made during a Rose Garden appearance, was the next day. Atwood and others had lobbied internally for months for such a presidential statement, about which many in State and some others were at best lukewarm.

51. See Carroll J. Doherty, "Democratic Unity Stalls GOP Juggernaut: House Republicans Put Off Final Action on Bill to Chop International Aid Apparatus," *CQ Weekly Report* 53 (May 27, 1995): 1513–16.

funding levels were all bitterly contested, but perhaps the most notable event was Representative Henry Hyde's unsuccessful if thoughtful attempt to repeal the War Powers Resolution.[52] On June 8, the contentious bill passed by a vote of 222–192, well short of the margin needed to sustain a veto, as the president noted with pleasure in another Rose Garden statement.[53]

Also in early June, the SFRC completed a highly partisan markup of its parallel legislation (two bills, separating foreign assistance authorization from the rest). On July 26, the Senate took up S. 908, its version of the State authorization bill with consolidation provisions attached.[54] Once again, Secretary Christopher threatened a veto of the bill in its current form.[55] Almost immediately, the Democrats began to signal that they would seek extended debate on the bill. After two separate attempts by the leadership failed to gain cloture (on July 31 and August 1, by identical votes of 55–45), with only Pell (philosophically opposed to cloture) joining the Republicans, Dole pulled the bill.[56] Normally this would have been the end, but Helms persisted, saying that the game was not over. He also said that the SFRC would conduct no business meetings to act on confirmations, treaties, or other matters until the administration began to talk about consolidation. On August 1, Helms's staff began to issue daily "Helms Held Hostage" press releases attacking the administration, in particular Atwood.[57]

A few days later, around August 7, word began to circulate that Wendy Sherman, State's assistant secretary for legislative affairs, had approached Bud Nance, Helms's chief of staff, about beginning discussions. The other agencies, not consulted, felt this was premature, especially since there was

52. See Chapter 6 above for Hyde's efforts.
53. See Carroll J. Doherty, "House Approves Overhaul of Agencies, Policies," *CQ Weekly Report* 53 (June 10, 1995): 1655–57. President Clinton said that "this bill would take us in an isolationist direction at a time when America is ready to lead in the world. I am gratified that argument was persuasive to enough Members of the House to sustain a possible veto." White House press release, June 8, 1995.
54. The parallel foreign assistance authorization, S. 961, never reached the floor.
55. Letter from Christopher to Helms, July 25, 1996.
56. Cloture, the procedure under Senate rules for limiting debate, requires sixty votes in favor to be invoked.
57. On shutting down the SFRC, see Ben Barber, "Helms Set to Halt All Action by Panel: Democrats Stall Foreign-Aid Cuts," *Washington Times*, August 2, 1995. For a more dispassionate account, see Eric Pianin and Helen Dewar, "Senate Democrats Stymie Helms's Bid to Kill Three Foreign Policy Agencies," *Washington Post*, August 2, 1995. On the "hostage" issue, see Guy Gugliotta, "Capital Notebook: Helms Finds No Art in AID's Performance," *Washington Post*, August 1, 1995.

no agreement on a possible counterproposal. The same day, Helms issued a press release stating that because of this demarche, he had scheduled an SFRC business meeting on August 10 to consider pending nominations. It did result in the committee's voting out all pending nominations, but only a few were confirmed by the full Senate before August recess; the rest would wait until December.

On August 11 two important meetings occurred, together demonstrating the difficulties within the administration. The first was a contentious executive-branch "Function 150" meeting, during which the smaller agencies, led by Atwood, complained that an approach should not have been made to the Helms staff without prior agreement. AID insisted that either Sarbanes, a strong defender of the agency's continuing independence, or his representatives be at the table in any talks (a reflection of skepticism about how strongly Kerry would defend their position); and that, on the executive side, others at Sherman's level, for example USAID's assistant administrator for legislative and public affairs Jill Buckley or her deputy, Bob Boyer, must also be present. It was at about this time that a USIA congressional relations officer offended Sherman by suggesting that State was condoning a version of "Sophie's Choice," by being willing to discuss with Helms which of State's "children" would be sacrificed to save the others.[58]

The second meeting was between President Clinton and Senator Helms. Earlier, the White House had asked Helms's aid in confirming White House staffer Mark Gearen as Peace Corps director, notwithstanding the impasse over SFRC business. Helms told the administration's emissary, Erskine Bowles, from North Carolina and an old Helms family friend as well, that he might be able to help, if Bowles could help him see the president personally about his merger plans. Bowles could. Since no prior mention was made of this meeting to Atwood or the others, on the later excuse that the White House had insisted on secrecy, the other agencies viewed this turn of events as further evidence that State had broken ranks. At the meeting, the Helms staffer Steve Berry made the argument for the merger proposal, finding the president cordial but noncommittal. The vice-president presented the case against a merger, taking the same line as in his January 27 announcement

58. The reference, of course, was to William Styron's classic 1979 novel by that name, in which Sophie Zawistowski, a Polish Catholic woman taken by the Nazis, is forced by a sadistic SS doctor to choose which of her two children to send to a concentration camp in order to save the other. While eliminating an agency was hardly equivalent to the Holocaust, the department's staff working on the issue badly underestimated the depth of feeling in the smaller agencies, contributing to the interagency tension.

not to pursue the approach. Chief of Staff Leon Panetta, Deputy National Security Advisor Sandy Berger, Christopher, and Sherman were there, but as noted no one was present from the other agencies, and there was no resolution.[59] A subsequent Hill meeting between administration and Senate staffers led nowhere, although Sherman agreed that the administration would detail specific problems with the Helms bill in early September.

Little occurred in September, although HIRC, after a couple of failures, finally succeeded on September 27 in reporting its recommendations for items to be included in the initial CR, which was necessary as the end of the fiscal year approached without appropriations legislation having been passed. Those recommendations included the consolidation plan originally passed in H.R. 1561.

On September 28, Helms tried again to obtain a Senate floor vote on his merger plan, this time threatening to hold up action on the executive notification required to allow payment of assistance to the Palestinians, a key element of the peace agreement signed that same day. Some in the White House, and some Senate Democrats, tiring of the impasse, began cautiously to advocate allowing Helms a vote on a freestanding resolution, arguing that, if necessary, it could be prevented from becoming law. Reflective of this mood, what appeared to be a breakthrough occurred on September 29, when the acting Senate majority leader, Senator Dan Coats, was successful in winning unanimous consent for using S. 908 as a vehicle for a merger vote. The agreement provided that a single managers' amendment would be in order, to be presented by both sides with four hours of debate; the amended version of S. 908 was then to be substituted for the House bill, H.R. 1561. The advantage of this procedure was that it used the existing place in the queue of the Senate calendar held by S. 908 and also bypassed what would likely be almost endless numbers of amendments and an inability to control debate.[60] If it worked, it would provide for relatively painless Senate passage of a State authorization bill and then conference with the House. As it turned out, there were enough ambiguities about what had been agreed to that resolution was still months away. The key issues were

59. Al Kamen, "In the Loop: Hunter Meets Hunted," *Washington Post*, September 8, 1995. The title refers to the irony of the presentation being made by Berry, who as a State Department official in the Bush administration had been accused of improperly assisting efforts to research Clinton's passport files for politically useful information about the now-famous trip to the Soviet Union while at Oxford. Berry had been demoted over the episode; he was eventually cleared.

60. The unanimous consent agreement concerning S. 908 is printed in *Congressional Record* 141 (September 29, 1995): S14777.

still whether the agreed language would mandate abolition of one or more agencies, how much in savings would be required, and how many positions would have to be cut.

On the executive side, October brought several White House meetings attempting to develop an administration position on the desired contents of the managers' amendment to S. 908. OMB urged the use of a dollar figure for cuts based on the president's budget proposal, with no set number of agencies to be abolished, while Secretary Christopher opposed endorsing any dollar cut, since he wished to revisit (and increase) the OMB numbers for Function 150 (as he would continue to do, with some success, until he left office in January 1997). Others, including Atwood, were more willing to include specific cuts, so long as they did not exceed what was likely to be proposed by the president in any event.

Things were no better in the Senate. On October 18, a Kerry-Helms negotiating session disintegrated, after Kerry offered a cut of $1.2 billion over four years (Helms's position at the time was for a $2.5 billion cut over five years) and also proposed changes in other provisions of S. 908. Helms thought that the managers' amendment was to be limited to the consolidation issue, leaving the rest of his bill intact and protected from filibuster, and he accused the administration and its Senate allies of bad faith. Predictably, he canceled an SFRC business meeting that had been called to deal with nominees and treaties. (The meeting had been scheduled as a part of the unanimous consent agreement.) The SFRC was back in its "hostage-taking" mode.[61]

On October 31, Majority Leader Dole, at Helms's urging, attempted to bring pressure in yet another way: he declined to bring the extension of the Middle East Peace Facilitation Act (MEPFA) to the Senate floor. (An extension was necessary owing to the failure to pass the "Foreign Ops" appropriation bill, which contained regular funding for the peace process in Palestine and Israel.)[62] His grounds were that the administration had failed to negotiate with the Senate on Helms's merger proposals. Two days later, on November 2, further reflection led the Senate leadership to decouple MEPFA and the authorization bill, largely because of a Dole decision that it was better politically not to give the Palestinians an excuse to disrupt the peace process. A thirty-day extension passed by voice vote. The House had al-

---

61. A good overview of the situation as of late October can be found in Dick Kirschten, "The Helmsmen of the GOP," *National Journal* 27 (October 28, 1995): 2684.

62. See Thomas W. Lippman, "Aid to Palestinians Held Up In Senate: Helms Feud with State Dept., Abortion Fight May Lead to Cutoff," *Washington Post*, November 1, 1996.

ready adjourned, so the extension technically was not in place, necessitating a temporary closing of the New York PLO office. Kerry apparently helped this decision by agreeing to further negotiations on the merger. With respect to the latter, the focus was now on the size of the funding cut to be required, in the range of $1.6 to $2.1 billion, depending on the source.[63]

By November 17, press reports had it that Helms and Kerry had reached agreement on reductions in Function 150 funding over five years in the amount of $1.7 billion from FY 1995 enacted figures, of which only 30 percent could come from programs and not more than 15 percent from State operating accounts. This approach would leave more than $900 million to be absorbed by USAID and USIA operations. The result, those agencies argued, would be the death of one or the crippling of both. Other controversial provisions remained, including a 50 percent cut in USAID staffing; also, all other-agency personnel assigned abroad would be detailed to State, rather than remaining on the books of their home agencies. Some interagency hostilities resulted, since other agencies believed State had proposed the 15 percent limit on the amount from State operations,[64] an initiative not approved by OMB. In due course, the administration (pushed hard by Atwood) told Kerry it would not back the arrangement; other SFRC Democrats, especially Senators Sarbanes and Feingold, took the same position. Helms, having initially promised to move SFRC business, including nominations and treaties, once again declined to do so after the agreement fell apart. On the same day, November 17, *all* Republican members of the committee, including Kassebaum and Lugar, privately not sympathetic to Helms, signed a letter to Kerry supporting Helms's position and noting that most experts considered a serious assessment of "the existing antiquated management of U.S. foreign affairs" to be necessary.[65] Helms at the same time accused Kerry of adding new provisions to the deal after being roughed up by his Democratic colleagues, an accusation that Kerry denied. Thus, at the congressional Thanksgiving recess, little had been accomplished except

63. Details in this paragraph come from USAID congressional liaison staff, November 1996.

64. Under Secretary for Management Richard Moose and the State Department legislative staff made the argument for this protection of core diplomatic functions quietly to Hill staffers. The other agencies took this as a sign of State's weakness and of its fear that it could not hold to such a level of cuts in executive branch negotiations for subsequent years, and they were quick to make this point to their State colleagues. Naturally, such goings-on did little for executive branch harmony. Conversations with participants, November and December 1995.

65. Thomas W. Lippman, "GOP Allies Sign Letter for Helms: Chairman Supported in Foreign Policy Tiff," *Washington Post*, November 20, 1995.

an increase in the level of acrimony. This was all small potatoes, of course, since it occurred simultaneously with the larger budget contretemps and with the November shutdown of most of the federal government after the failure to agree on a continuing resolution.

After the recess, on-again, off-again talks resumed, and continued for almost two weeks, with agreement held to be close more than once only to fall apart.[66] An agreement to count severance pay for employees of the European radios (a one-time item in the USIA 1995 appropriation) as a part of the 1995 enacted base was one feature of the emerging negotiations. This feature meant that spending for the outyears would be compared with 1995, and the differences *each year* would be counted as savings against the agreed cut. Since the severance pay (on the order of $100 million in 1995) did not appear in any of the five following years, spending for each was reduced by the same amount and was thus to be counted as a savings each year! This ploy became a key to agreement on the agreed $1.7 billion cut, since it would provide some $500 million in apparent savings over the five-year period and would reduce the cuts from USIA and USAID operations to around $450 million, which seemed inevitable, even under the president's proposed budget.[67]

Perhaps symbolically, on Pearl Harbor Day, December 7, Helms and Kerry finally announced agreement on their managers' amendment, which in addition to the authorization bill included timing for consideration of two important arms control treaties (START II and the Chemical Weapons Convention) and confirmation of several ambassadors and of Foreign Service promotees.[68] On December 14, the Senate adopted the agreement, in

66. See Al Kamen, "In the Loop: Puncturing the Point Man," *Washington Post*, November 17, 1995 (about Kerry's problems within his own party); Ben Barber, "Helms Shunned in Offer to End Foreign Aid Battle," *Washington Times*, November 17, 1995; Chris Black, "Helms, Kerry Return to Impasse: Deal on International Development Aid, Ambassador Appointments Collapses," *Boston Globe*, November 24, 1995; and Leslie Phillips: " 'Senator No' Puts U.S. Foreign Policy on Hold: Helms' Reorganization Push Halts Treaties, Appointments," *USA Today*, December 5, 1995.

67. Of all the scorekeeping creativity discussed in this book, counting a one-time expenditure as providing reductions for each of five more years may be the most bizarre example; but without it, there could have been no agreement. The figures are arrived at as follows. Total cut: $1.7 billion. Maximum amount from programs (30%): $510 million. Maximum amount from State operations (15%): $245 million. Balance (from USIA and USAID operations): $955 million. Of which from severance pay: $500 million. Thus, $455 million was left, to be taken from operations of the two agencies.

68. The needed procedural steps, in the form of a series of unanimous consent agreements on the Senate floor, are found in *Congressional Record* 141 (December 7, 1995): S18288–31. See also Neil A. Lewis, "Helms, After Winning Leaner Foreign Policy, Clears Way to Approve

the form of a substitute for the bill, by voice vote, and then routinely passed the amended authorization bill (S. 908) 82–16. There was, however, considerable rancor between Helms, on the one hand, and Senators Biden and Sarbanes, on the other, who were urging a vote against the bill. In keeping with the earlier unanimous-consent decrees, a large number of pending ambassadorial nominations were confirmed immediately thereafter, and Dole promised that the START II treaty would receive early consideration.[69] Although Helms had been unable to achieve outright abolishment of any agencies, he had forced his way into the game, changing the terms of the debate and demonstrating an ability to make life miserable for the foreign affairs establishment.[70] What remained was a conference on the authorization legislation.

The rest of December and January were taken up with the longest government shutdown in history, the Washington blizzard of 1996, and frantic efforts to reach an overall seven-year budget agreement, each of more import to most than the State authorization bill. By February, House and Senate staffers were attempting to craft a conference report while Congress was in recess. These efforts were largely boycotted by the Democrats, although they did sit in as observers and note takers. Before they would agree to work toward a bill that could be supported, the Democrats insisted there must be several fixes agreed to by the Republicans in both houses: viz., the Chris Smith population/"Mexico City" language (see following section), livable authorization levels, and nothing more radical than the Kerry-Helms compromise on the merger. The Republicans continued to assert that they desired a bipartisan bill and were attempting to resolve remaining issues.

On February 28 and 29, the formal conference finally met. Although improvements had been made during staff discussions, the administration continued to find the bill unacceptable.[71] The Republicans hoped to attach the bill to the next CR, required by March 15, but Senate Appropriations Chairman Mark Hatfield, the key player vis-à-vis the CR and a firm supporter of population programs, continued to oppose doing so if the bill

Ambassadors," *New York Times*, December 9, 1995; and Helen Dewar, "Senate Deal on Foreign Policy Agencies Ends Impasse on Envoys, Treaties," *Washington Post*, December 8, 1995.

69. The Senate debate on the bill is found in *Congressional Record* 141 (December 14, 1995): S18616–39.

70. For one assessment, see Dick Kirschten, "Foreign Policy: Helms Has Had Quite a Ride," *National Journal* 27 (December 23, 1995): 3177. A negative view appeared in a *Washington Post* editorial, "Held for Ransom," on December 17, 1995.

71. As is typical, the administration had provided detailed comments on both versions of the bill and on what it would accept (letters from Sherman to Helms and Gilman, February 28, 1996).

contained either the House authorization version of the population language or, alternatively, the appropriations one-year language as permanent legislation. The Republicans much preferred the CR approach, rightly fearing that a freestanding bill would be much easier to veto than the entire CR, since the latter would shut down much of the government for a third time. When the conference resumed on March 5, the Democrats tabled an alternative version based on Kerry-Helms, developed in consultation with the administration. Republicans stated they would take it under advisement, during a short recess in the conference. In fact, they were making frantic attempts to attach some portions of their plan to the CR, which would (1) mandate abolition of one agency, thus allowing the House freshmen to claim that they had succeeded in abolishing *something,* and (2) limit the waiver of authorization for State, ACDA, and USIA to April 1, thus keeping the conference alive, since an authorization bill would be needed after that date.[72] The antimerger forces, for their part, were uneasy about what the administration would do if this ploy were successful and if faced with shutting down the government. It seemed possible that the White House might accept this language and deal with the problem in another way, perhaps through a signing statement, as it had in January concerning the appropriations population compromise. Authorizers were in one of their periodic frenetic efforts to remain relevant. But the attempt to use the CR failed.

Authorization conferees fell back to their only remaining recourse and agreed on a conference report for a freestanding authorization bill. Among other things, the report required that the three small foreign affairs agencies all be abolished, although there was provision allowing the president to waive this requirement for two of them (still ensuring that the freshmen could claim at least one scalp). Also kept in place was the "Foreign Ops" appropriations language on population program restrictions.[73] With the conference report scheduled to be taken up in the House on March 12, on March 11 it elicited an explicit veto threat: "If the conference report on H.R. 1561 is presented to the President in its current form, the President will veto the bill. While steps have been taken to improve the bill, it still

72. Details come from USAID legislative affairs officers, March 1996.

73. Technically, on the population issue, the conference report was silent, thus leaving standing the appropriations language. The text of the conference report is printed in *Congressional Record* 142 (March 8, 1996): H1987–H2032. Press discussions include "Congress Sends White House a Compromise Foreign Spending Bill," *New York Times,* March 8, 1996; Helen Dewar, "Foreign Agency Plan Puts Onus on Clinton," *Washington Post,* March 8, 1996; and Carroll J. Doherty, "State Department: Conferees Agree on Bill to Abolish an Agency," *CQ Weekly Report* 54 (March 9, 1996): 634.

contains numerous provisions which do not serve U.S. foreign policy or U.S. national interests."[74] The SAP cited the forced consolidation of agencies, low authorization levels, changes in the Taiwan Relations Act and in relations with Vietnam, provisions restricting U.S. participation in international organizations, and failure to remove family-planning restrictions in the Foreign Operations Appropriations Act as making the bill unacceptable.

Nonetheless, on March 12 the House passed the conference report by a partisan vote of 226–174, close to the margin by which H.R. 1561 had been passed in June 1995, again insufficient to override a veto. For two weeks, tactical considerations and other pressing business precluded Senate action. Finally, it was passed by a party-line vote of 52–44 on March 28, again not enough to override.[75] Predictably, on April 12, President Clinton vetoed the bill. Clinton's veto message was unusually explicit and lengthy in explaining this decision.[76] Although not having nearly the votes needed, Republican House leaders scheduled an override vote for April 23, only to postpone it as it became clear that the long-sought final CR would be passed later that week (as it was on April 25) and that it would not contain language requiring an authorization bill. And so the last weapon to force a State authorization bill was removed, and with it any chance in the 104th Congress for enacting a consolidation or abolishment of any of the agencies.[77] But there was one final, almost chimerical act. Having no chance, the House still attempted on April 30 to override the president's veto. The vote

74. Office of Management and Budget, Executive Office of the President, *Statement of Administration Policy: H.R. 1561—Foreign Relations Revitalization Act of 1995*, March 11, 1996.

75. For House action, see Carroll J. Doherty, "State Department: House Sends Foreign Affairs Bill to Uncertain Fate in Senate," *CQ Weekly Report* 54 (March 16, 1996): 712; for the Senate, see "Foreign Relations Bill Faces Veto," *Washington Post*, March 29, 1996; "Foreign Affairs Bill Faces Veto," *International Herald Tribune*, March 30, 1996; and Carroll J. Doherty, "State Department: Clinton with Veto Pen Poised, Gets Agency-Cutback Bill," *CQ Weekly Report* 54 (March 30, 1996): 893.

76. White House press release, April 12, 1996, reprinted in *CQ Weekly Report* 54 (April 20, 1996): 1974. See also Jerry Gray, "State Dept. Budget Is Vetoed; Clinton Protests Planned Cuts," *New York Times*, April 13, 1996; and "President Vetoes Foreign Policy Bill," *Washington Post*, April 13, 1996.

77. See Carroll J. Doherty, "Foreign Policy: GOP Not Giving Up On Agency Cuts," *CQ Weekly Report* 54 (April 20, 1996): 1059. On the eventual passage of the CR, see Michael Wines, "House and Senate Vote to Approve '96 Spending Bill: A Truce in Budget Wars," *New York Times*, April 26, 1996; and Jackie Calmes, "Historic Budget Battle Ends with a Whimper, as Congress Approves Funding Deal for 1996," *Wall Street Journal*, April 26, 1996. The CR was H.R. 3019, which became P.L. 104-134, April 26, 1996.

was 234–188 in favor of the override, well short of the two-thirds majority needed.[78]

While it could be argued that the failure to enact foreign affairs reform legislation demonstrated the weakness of the legislative branch, such an interpretation fails to capture just how much this eighteen-month-long episode impeded the conduct of other foreign affairs business between the branches and how it was a likely precursor of future difficulties. It is hard to imagine that reorganization and consolidation of the foreign affairs agencies will disappear from the agenda, especially in times of sharply reduced financing. As has been seen, important foreign affairs matters are long-lived, and failure the first time around hardly precludes later action.

Predictably, at the beginning of the 105th Congress, the consolidation issue returned with force. In confirmation hearings for Secretary of State–designate Madeleine Albright, Helms reviewed the history of conflicts in 1995, and was emphatic in his determination to pursue the question. In response, Albright took a milder line than in the president's veto message on the 1995 Foreign Relations Authorization Act just described: "Let me say that on the issue of reorganization and consolidation. . . . I think it's very important for us to have an effective and efficient foreign policy mechanism. And I look forward very much to discussing the issue with you. . . . I have an open mind and I wish to have some discussions with you on the subject." Within the administration, another intensive review began in March, bringing with it renewed inter-agency tensions. This time, however, the result was different. On April 17, the White House announced that the president had decided to propose a reorganization plan bearing notable similarities to that vetoed two years earlier. USIA and ACDA were to be merged into the State Department. USAID was to report directly to the secretary of state and have "certain shared administrative functions," with State, while remaining "a distinct agency." The department itself was to undergo "a new round of internal reinvention to incorporate new organizations and to manage new responsibilities." Initial congressional reaction was cautiously positive (Senator Helms's spokesman said the plan appeared to be "a big victory") while final judgment was reserved pending development of the details. It was widely assumed that the reorganization plan was a sop to

---

78. House Fails to Override Foreign Policy Bill Veto," *Washington Post*, May 1, 1996. A last-gasp effort by Gilman to sell the merger case, in a column in the *Washington Times* of April 30, 1996, had little impact.

Helms, the price of his allowing a Senate vote on the important chemical weapons (CBW) treaty, a notion given currency by the fact that the reorganization plan was made public within hours of the Senate scheduling a vote on the treaty! Once again, following a now familiar pattern, the North Carolinian had creatively used the leverage he had to obtain results he wanted on other issues.[79]

For the sake of simplicity, this section has focused on the authorizing committees and their interaction with the executive. The appropriators were players, too, as will be seen below.

## Policy Mandates and Micromanagement

Intertwined with the highly visible merger dispute were many others. They demonstrate two features resembling those of previous years: (1) attempts by Congress to place its stamp on the nation's foreign policy, and (2) efforts to achieve a fine-grained control over agency operations. In both instances the power of the purse remained a potent tool.

Several examples help make this point. First, the perennial issue of attempting to recognize Jerusalem as the capital of Israel made one of its frequent reappearances, though less creatively than in the 1987 Helms version (Chapter 6 above). Politicians in both parties have found the idea of forcing a move of the U.S. embassy to Jerusalem attractive, for it has great appeal to American Jewish voters, if not always to the Israeli government. President Clinton had supported the idea during the 1992 campaign, for example, although on May 9, 1995, when Senate Majority Leader Dole and House Speaker Gingrich introduced legislation (S. 770 and H.R. 1595) that would have required groundbreaking in Jerusalem by 1996 and occupancy of an

---

79. Albright quotation from Senate Foreign Relations Committee, "Hearing to Consider the Nomination of Madeleine Albright for Secretary of State," p. 81. For details on the hearing, see Carroll J. Doherty, "Albright Wields Persuasive Powers at Confirmation Hearing," *CQ Weekly Report* 55 (January 11, 1997): 133–34. Plan details quotations from Office of the White House Press Secretary, press fact sheet, April 18, 1995, issued after press briefings the previous day. For linkage with the chemical weapons treaty vote, see John F. Harris and Thomas W. Lippman, "Clinton Agrees to Shift Foreign Policy Agencies: Move Comes as Senate Sets Chemical Arms Vote," *Washington Post*, April 18, 1997. Helms's spokesman, Mark Thiessen, was quoted in Steven Lee Myers, "State Dept. Set for Reshaping, Pleasing Helms," *New York Times*, April 18, 1997.

embassy there by 1999, the president quickly came out in opposition.[80] Later in the year, the issue surfaced again, amid commentary linking it to presidential politics and the quest for support from the American Jewish community. This time Dole picked up on a revised version of the bill, S. 1322, originally offered by Senator Jon Kyl. After a veto threat, a compromise was reached: the required groundbreaking in FY 1996 was eliminated, but State's Foreign Buildings Office was allowed to spend only 50 percent of its FY 1999 appropriation if the move had not occurred. In an addition that allowed the president to accept the legislation, he could waive these provisions for an indefinite number of six-month periods if U.S. national security interests in his judgment so required. On October 24, the Senate and the House both passed the legislation overwhelmingly, by votes of 93–5 and 374–37, respectively, and the White House, realizing that a veto would be overridden, decided to let the bill become law without being signed by the president.[81] This bill was a good example of conditional funding. Unless the embassy in Jerusalem opened on the specified schedule (if the president did not waive the requirement), other construction funding would be withheld. This episode again illustrates the potential power of focused interests, especially AIPAC, and is a clear (if nonlethal) example of how domestic politics can cause foreign policy difficulties.

A variation on the theme of withholding funding as a weapon occurred in April 1996 when Senator Mitch McConnell (R–Ky.), chairman of the

80. Carroll J. Doherty, "Foreign Relations: Clinton Opposing Embassy Move," *CQ Weekly Report* 55 (May 13, 1995): 1338; Thomas W. Lippman, "Dole Seeks to Make Jerusalem Home of U.S. Embassy in Israel," *Washington Post*, May 10, 1995; and Clyde Haberman, "With Calls for U.S. Embassy in Jerusalem, Israel Isn't Pleased," *New York Times*, May 8, 1995. For pros and cons, see Douglas J. Feith, "To Promote Peace, Move the Embassy" (op-ed article), *New York Times*, May 29, 1995; Joseph C. Harsch, "An Unpeaceful Move" (opinion), *Christian Science Monitor*, May 23, 1995; Richard Cohen, "Jerusalem Remembered: Never Mind the Peace Process When There's a Sound Bite to Be Had" (opinion), *Washington Post*, May 11, 1995; and Claiborne Pell and Lee H. Hamilton, "Embassy in Jerusalem? Not Yet" (opinion), *Christian Science Monitor*, June 1, 1995. A scathing and cynical Israeli view is Akiva Eldar, "Dole Toys with Jerusalem" (op-ed article), *New York Times*, May 12, 1995.

81. The bill became the Jerusalem Embassy Act of 1995, P.L. 104-45, November 8, 1995. See the following, all appearing on October 25, 1995: Martin Sieff, "Jerusalem Embassy Bill Passes; Clinton Won't Veto," *Washington Times*; Helen Dewar, "Congress Approves Move of U.S. Embassy to Jerusalem by Mid-1999," *Washington Post*; and Stephen Labaton, "Congress Backs Israel Embassy Switch, but Gives Clinton an Out," *New York Times*. The Senate debate on S. 1322, which makes the electoral connection of this bill rather clear, is printed in *Congressional Record* 141 (October 23, 1995): S15465–88 and S15491–95, and in 141 (October 24, 1995): S15520–35. The House debate appears in *Congressional Record* 141 (October 24, 1995): H10680–89 and H10691–92.

SAC Foreign Operations Subcommittee, threatened to withhold future peacekeeping appropriations until the Clinton administration explained why it had failed to seek congressional approval before sending U.S. troops to Macedonia as part of a U.N. force in 1993. The issue turned on the requirements of the U.N. Charter and the implementing U.S. statute, the United Nations Participation Act (UNPA). UNPA required the president merely to notify Congress if the forces were "observers," and he had done so. McConnell argued that in fact the troops were "combat ready" (a second designation under the act, requiring congressional approval) and that the president therefore had been in violation.[82] Perhaps because this was not a serious challenge, but more a "shot across the bow," McConnell chose not to pursue the matter after State provided a detailed letter explaining why the "observer" provision had been correctly invoked.[83]

In a related vein, Congress and the president once again had great difficulties over whether and under what limitations to commit U.S. troops as peacekeepers, this time to Bosnia. There were significant divisions within both branches, and clearly the inclination was to try to gain political advantage.[84] Finally, with the conclusion of the Dayton accords in December 1995, both houses after contentious debate declined to pass legislation that would have barred funding for support of the troops, but they went out of their way either to actively oppose or at least not to support President Clinton's policy. The Senate, led by Dole, eventually passed a resolution stating that the president could commit U.S. troops, but that he should also take steps to strengthen Bosnia government forces. The House, still in the grasp of its antagonistically anti-Clinton freshmen, opposed the deployment while at the same time stating support for the troops and arguing for neutrality among the several factions.[85] Use of U.S. forces abroad continued to be the

82. See Rowan Scarborough, "Senator May Halt Funds for Macedonia Mission," *Washington Times*, April 9, 1996. The issue received renewed prominence at this time because of Army Specialist Michael New's court-martial for refusing to become a U.N. peacekeeper. Part of New's argument was that the mission was not a legitimate one because Congress had not been notified, the same argument that McConnell subsequently picked up. Domestic politics played an obvious part, in that New was a Kentucky constituent of McConnell!

83. Letter from Barbara Larkin, acting assistant secretary of state for legislative affairs, to Senator McConnell, May 10, 1996.

84. Donna Cassata, "Foreign Relations: Congress Bucks White House, Devises Its Own Bosnia Plan," *CQ Weekly Report* 53 (June 10, 1995): 1653–54.

85. The Dole legislation was S.J. Res. 44; the House version was H. Res. 302. See Pat Towell and Donna Cassata, "Bosnia: Congress Takes Symbolic Stand on Troop Deployment—Both Chambers Voice Support for U.S. Soldiers, Refuse to Endorse Clinton's Policy," *CQ Weekly Report* 53 (December 10, 1996): 3817–18.

most contentious of any foreign policy issue between the branches, and it was the source of an agonizing consideration of the proper roles of each.

Another example of a complicated issue involving both houses, authorizers and appropriators, interest groups, and domestic politics, as well as being an issue that spilled over into other issues, was the previously mentioned dispute over foreign assistance for population control and family planning. On assuming office, one of President Clinton's initial actions was to scrap the "Mexico City" policy (named for an international meeting at which it was developed), which dated from the early Reagan administration.

With their party gaining control of Congress, right-to-life Republicans were determined to make a full attack here and elsewhere on legalized abortion in whatever form, and the first session of the 104th Congress was filled with skirmishes in this war. Here, right-to-lifers were adamant in their resolve to restore the old Reagan policy, including prohibitions on funding for any organization that supported abortions or abortion counseling, whether or not it used federal funds for these activities. In particular, such private organizations as the London-based International Planned Parenthood Federation or international ones like the United Nations Population Fund were targets. Of special importance was the lead role of Representative Christopher H. Smith (R–N.J.), a sincere and intractable foe of abortion, who not incidentally was the new chairman of the HIRC subcommittee, International Operations and Human Rights, which was jurisdictionally responsible for State Department authorizing legislation. This single issue stalled passage of the "Foreign Ops" appropriations bill for several months, forcing USAID to be included in that part of the government which was furloughed in late 1995 and again in early 1996, and delaying all foreign assistance including that for Israel and Egypt, none of which was in disagreement, from October until late January.

Of great interest here is the endgame. By October 24, the "Foreign Ops" appropriations conference had adjourned, having reached agreement on every provision except the "Chris Smith language," which was modified somewhat but still remained unacceptable to Senate conferees.[86] The next week, the conference report was adopted by the House on October 31, and by the Senate on November 1, with large bipartisan majorities. But the House insisted on the Smith restrictions, and the Senate voted again to re-

86. Carroll J. Doherty, "Appropriations: Foreign Aid Bill Snags on Family Planning," *CQ Weekly Report* 53 (October 28, 1995): 3315–17.

move them.[87] On November 15, the House tried again, once again insisting on its provision, 237–183.

The Senate conferees then attempted a creative, if dubious, ploy. First adopting a substitute amendment which endorsed the Clinton administration's family-planning policy, they then tabled both that amendment and the contending Smith provision from the House on a single 54–44 vote. The Senate argued that by tabling both provisions, in effect leaving population funding without restrictions, the conference report was cleared for presidential action. The House, not surprisingly, took a contrary view, arguing (correctly) that the Senate could not bind the House unilaterally and that the issue of disagreement could not be severed from the rest of the conference report.[88] Eventually, the Senate decided not to send the conference report to the White House. Meanwhile, the threat of a second government shutdown loomed, and the appropriators became increasingly determined to pass as many of the remaining appropriations bills as possible. For Foreign Operations, there was pressure from assistance recipients caught up in the population fight, highlighted by Israel. The situation was not eased by the appearance of Israeli Prime Minister Shimon Peres in Washington in mid-December, shortly after the tragic death of his predecessor Yitzhak Rabin and with Israel's $3 billion more than two months overdue.

In this tight situation, HAC Foreign Operations Chairman Sonny Callahan tried to find a way out. First he proposed that funding to population groups be cut by 50 percent from 1995 amounts unless those groups pledged not to lobby for or perform abortions, even using their own funding. This idea was rejected outright by Chris Smith, with the Republican leadership disinclined to push him too far. On December 13, Callahan introduced and the House passed a new version. It struck the Smith language but also stated that the waiver of the authorization requirement for foreign operations included in the conference report would not apply to bilateral population assistance or to the UN family-planning program. This would have meant that FY 1996 population funds could be obligated only after the unlikely enactment of a foreign assistance authorization bill. Thus it was "lose–lose"; no restrictions, no funding. The White House stated that it

---

87. Carroll J. Doherty, "Appropriations: House, Senate Remain at Odds over Family Planning Aid," *CQ Weekly Report* 53 (November 4, 1995): 3387–88. The House vote on the conference report was 351–71, the Senate's 90–6, and the Senate insisted on its position 53–44.

88. For details, see Carroll J. Doherty, "Appropriations: House Resists Senate Gambit on Foreign Operations Bill," *CQ Weekly Report* 53 (November 18, 1995): 3351.

would veto the appropriation (having already shown in other cases, for example CJS, that it would do so), while the Senate, because of its tabling ploy the previous month which procedurally ended consideration of the population funding issue, could not bring up the new Callahan provision unless it were possible to obtain unanimous consent, almost as unlikely as passing a foreign assistance authorization.[89] There matters stood, and when the government once again shut down on December 15 because of the lack of a CR, USAID was among the missing.

In January 1996, a way out was found which satisfied no one. There would be no funding for population programs (unless an authorization were passed in the interim) prior to July 1. After that date, assuming no authorization, these programs would be funded at 65 percent of the FY 1995 level (a cut of $192 million from that year, and $88 million below the conference report level); a further restriction required that these funds be obligated on a strictly proportional basis over fifteen months until September 1997, thus creating a management nightmare as well as a funding shortfall. This last feature soon became known as "metering." At the same time, the Smith restrictive language was dropped, to his displeasure.[90] The appropriators in this instance passed the issue back to the authorizers, where it continued to be a problem for the ill-fated authorization conference. The president signed the "Foreign Ops" conference report on February 12, and it became P.L. 104-107.

This was not the end. Supporters of the population programs—in particular, Senate Appropriations Chairman Mark Hatfield—began efforts to find a way to restore funding to the conference level, and to remove restrictions on the use of funds. His tactic was to include, during negotiations for the "permanent" CR (which would fund those parts of government that did not have regular appropriations bills for the rest of FY 1996), language allowing the president to spend funds without the restrictions if he could show that those restrictions decreased demand for family-planning services and as a consequence would actually increase abortions.[91] After several

89. Details of this back-and-forth struggle come from an internal USAID legislative report, December 13, 1995, and from Carroll J. Doherty, "Appropriations: Abortion Imbroglio Stalls Foreign Aid Bill," *CQ Weekly Report* 53 (December 16, 1995): 3820.

90. Carroll J. Doherty, "Appropriations: Family-Planning Compromise Helps Foreign Aid Pass," *CQ Weekly Report* 54 (January 27, 1996): 227.

91. See Barbara Crossette, "U.S. Aid Cutbacks Endangering Population Programs, U.N. Agencies Say," *New York Times*, February 16, 1996; and "Family Planning Fiasco" (editorial), *Washington Post*, March 12, 1996. There was a considerable press battle over this international version of the volatile abortion issue. Examples include Julia Duin, "Pro-Lifers Divided

failed attempts, a flurry of negotiations in late April forged a final CR agreement on April 24, overwhelmingly passed by both houses and signed by the president. In the last-minute compromises, Hatfield was unable to sustain his position. The low funding level and obligation restrictions remained in place.[92] Meanwhile, attempts to reach agreement during the State authorization bill conference, which the appropriators had invited, were of no avail. Nothing was included in that bill, leaving the appropriations restriction intact. In the end this made no difference, since the conference report was vetoed and not repassed. None of the participants was satisfied with the outcome, as is so often the case.

There were many other controversies, arising from the seemingly irresistible practice of encrusting foreign affairs authorization bills with every member's foreign policy prescriptions. In late May 1995, as the House took up the combined authorization bill, these predictable but controversial provisions surfaced as always, giving "directions to President Clinton on a long list of matters . . . from tiny questions of detail to major policy issues."[93]

It could be debated endlessly whether this bill was worse than its predecessors—any administration official who has worked this legislation at one time or another no doubt feels that the bill he or she had to deal with was the worst—but this one was notable in some respects. Even Larry Eagleburger, the Republican secretary of state at the end of the Bush administration, felt that the Republican Congress had gone beyond too far: " 'The House has gone crazy,' he told National Public Radio. 'The restrictions and

---

on Family Planning: Hatfield Sponsors Third World Funds," *Washington Times*, March 18, 1996; Judy Mann, "Extracting Their Pound of Flesh" (opinion), *Washington Post*, February 2, 1996; and Christopher H. Smith, "Big Bucks for International Abortion" (op-ed article), *Washington Times*, March 27, 1996. Smith, of course, sponsored the restrictions. His article drew extensive comments thereafter in letters to the *Washington Times*. A very thoughtful "after action" article, relating the domestic and international contexts, as well as the role of interest groups and activists on both sides, is Eliza Newlin Carney, "Poor Planning," *National Journal* 29 (May 4, 1996): 1017.

92. USAID Assistant Administrator for Legislation and Public Affairs Jill Buckley, "Legislative Report," April 26, 1995: "The conferees also agreed not to include Senate language to ease the current funding restrictions on USAID's and other international population planning programs." See also Al Kamen, "In the Loop: Your Witness," *Washington Post*, May 1, 1996, for discussion of a technical glitch whereby the Hatfield fix was initially included in the CR by mistake, not unlike what happened with the foreign-military-financing episode and the FY 1991 Foreign Operations Appropriation Act, discussed in Chapter 4 above.

93. Anthony Lewis, "Abroad at Home: Capitol Power Grab," *New York Times*, May 26, 1995.

demands on the President are an absolute attack on the separation of powers.' "[94]

Some of the most notable policy provisions in the bill, H.R. 1561 as passed by the House, included the following:

- establishing a special envoy with the rank of ambassador for Tibet (sec. 2302)
- substituting the pro-Taiwan provisions of the 1979 Taiwan Relations Act for the subsequent 1982 agreement which normalized diplomatic relations with China (sec. 2601)
- terminating the arms embargo on Bosnia (sec. 2607)
- providing detailed interpretations of the U.S.–North Korea "Agreed Framework" of 1994 (secs. 2641–45)
- prohibiting funds to be used to return involuntarily individuals who had fled their home countries to avoid possible torture (secs. 2661–62)

Added to these provisions, which would have had the force of law had the bill been enacted, were some sixteen "congressional statements" on policy issues expressing opinions or a sense of the Congress about how foreign policy should be carried out. There were also several detailed restrictions, instructions, or prohibitions of funding for particular purposes (e.g., U.N. assessments).[95] In the foreign assistance titles of the bill, there were many more provisions, including of course the strong Chris Smith limitations on population programs.

On the micromanagement side, in addition to the abolition of the smaller agencies, the House would have

- created a coordinator for counterterrorism, although State already had a nonstatutory one (sec. 2301);
- similarly created a coordinator for human rights and refugees, replacing two assistant secretaries approved in the last authorization bill, in 1994 (sec. 2303);
- established an assistant secretary for human resources, largely duplicating the functions of the director general of the Foreign Service (sec. 2305);

94. Ibid.
95. See Chapter 6 for more on peacekeeping and U.N. funding.

- required the U.S. permanent representative to the United Nations to be subordinate to the secretary of state (sec. 2306); and
- specified the number of members in each agency's foreign service cadre (sec. 2351).

Some of the most offending provisions were expunged in conference, along with similar ones added by the Senate, but what was left was still much too much for the administration to accept. President Clinton's veto message of April 12, 1996, took particular exception to Asian policy provisions, especially those reviving the Taiwan Relations Act and restricting funds to normalize relations with Vietnam, hampering "the President's ability to pursue our national interests there and potentially jeopardizing further progress on POW/MIA issues." He also cited the merger provisions, limits on participation in international organizations, and low levels of authorization which would "adversely affect the operation of overseas posts of the foreign affairs agencies and weaken critical U.S. efforts to promote arms control and nonproliferation, reform international organizations and peacekeeping, streamline public diplomacy, and implement sustainable development activities." A final main objection was the failure to "remedy the severe limitations placed on U.S. population assistance programs" in the foreign operations bill.[96]

A final example demonstrates the degree of contentiousness and unwillingness to trust the administration on the part of HIRC. During early 1995 hearings, USAID's assistant administrator for management Larry E. Byrne had testified that the $465 million included in the committee's mark for USAID operating expenses would force the agency into violation of the Antideficiency Act (31 U.S.C. 1341) well before the end of FY 1996. Committee leaders asked the GAO to prepare a report on the validity of this assertion; when completed, the report largely substantiated the USAID contention. Nevertheless, Chairman Gilman sent a letter transmitting the report to Administrator Brian Atwood on September 11. That letter focused on some GAO criticisms rather than on the major point, and it concluded with the statement "Please let me know when you are ready to brief us on your plans to operate AID at the budget levels no greater than those recently approved by the House or Senate." On September 19, Atwood replied that the Gilman letter was "disheartening" and that "it failed to recognize the many difficult decisions we have taken to reduce and reform USAID and I

96. The quotations and summary are from the veto message of April 12, 1996.

believe it did not accurately represent the GAO's position." He continued by reminding Gilman that the GAO report endorsed the main point: namely, the real risk of mandatory obligations exceeding appropriated funds at the $465 million level. Atwood also provided five pages of specific improvements that had been made, many of which (such as cutting missions and people) reduced operating costs. He concluded that "it does not strike me as responsible to force an agency into anti-deficiency when GAO has affirmed that we cannot operate through the fiscal year at the OE level that the House voted to authorize."[97]

## Iron Triangles Again: The Dangers of Single-Issue Politics

Another continuing trend in the events of 1995 was the almost pervasive activity of a wide range of interests in attempting to influence congressional foreign affairs outcomes. Congress and the executive did not fight their battles alone.

Perhaps most obvious was the impact at several key points of AIPAC, and (to some extent) the Israeli government, in addition to the law requiring movement of the U.S. embassy to Jerusalem. On the authorization bill, a major effort was needed to convince the so-called AIPAC Democrats, strong supporters of Israel, to hold the line and vote against the Republican version (both in committee and subsequently on the floor) in that it provided full funding for Israel and the Middle East peace process. While there was no real Democratic expectation of defeating the bill outright, it was important from their perspective to demonstrate that there were enough votes to prevent override of a possible veto. Led by Representatives Howard Berman and Gary Ackerman, the latter arguing that GOP motives were clear because "with the exception of aid to Israel, they made the bill unacceptable to everyone on the Democratic side,"[98] the Democrats were successful in overcoming AIPAC. It had been asked by the administration not to support the bill, but had done so because of the favorable Middle East provisions.

In other cases, AIPAC got its way, and of course Israel was fully funded

97. Quoted from the Gilman–Atwood and Atwood–Gilman letters.
98. Kenneth J. Cooper, "African American–Jewish Alliance Stalls House Vote on Foreign Aid Bill," *Washington Post*, May 26, 1995.

in the Foreign Operations Appropriation Act. Most telling were (1) the unblocking of MEPFA funding at the end of October, at the height of the battle over population assistance and general budget issues, and (2) the facilitating of an agreement on the "Foreign Ops" appropriation, given the felt need by all American politicians involved to free up assistance to Israel.

Israel was by no means the only nation actively trying to promote its interests legislatively. At the end of the long conference struggle over the State authorization bill, in April 1966, the Chinese Foreign Ministry issued a diplomatic protest over the anti-Chinese elements in the bill. The latter would "pose gross encroachments upon China's sovereignty and wanton interference in China's internal affairs," according to a Chinese spokesman.[99]

And as seen already, pro-choice and pro-life groups were heavily engaged during the population assistance program battle. Even as the bill's sponsor (Chris Smith) attacked the work of the International Planned Parenthood Federation,[100] opposing groups mounted a strong attack in favor of restoring full funding for these programs, with Smith supporters weighing in as well.[101] In seeking a compromise on the issue which would free up all the rest of foreign assistance funding, USAID faced a delicate problem with the pro-choice groups, which had a major interest in continuing these programs as little changed as possible. They used the sympathies of the White House very effectively, conveying the strong possibility of a veto if the "Mexico City" provisions remained in either the authorization or the appropriations bill. It was a bitter blow when they were unable either to restore funding or remove restrictions on its use.

Even the internal executive lobbies had their day. In the January 1996 temporary-funding legislation which allowed the government to reopen, a device called "targeted appropriations" was employed to deflect political heat by providing full-year funding for programs that appeared to be popular with the public, even as the rest of the government operated under short-

---

99. Quoted in James Morrison, "Embassy Row," *Washington Times*, April 3, 1996.

100. Julia Duin, "Smith Draws Bead on 'Abortion Lobby,'" *Washington Times*, April 19, 1996.

101. See, for example, letters to the *Washington Times* (April 2, 1996) from the president of Population Action International and from officials of Negative Population Growth Inc. and the American Life League. These were joined on April 8 by a letter from the president of the Alan Guttmacher Institute, co-author of a study attacked by Smith because of its conclusion that by reducing unintended pregnancies, population assistance programs would actually reduce the number of abortions.

term CRs and faced another shutdown. In international affairs, two such activities were included: consular affairs (reflecting press stories and complaints to members about the difficulties encountered when passports and visas could not be obtained) and diplomatic security for posts abroad. The latter, while obviously important at a time of renewed terrorism threats, was a less obvious choice over all the other programs, international and domestic, not so favored. However, State's management, supported by the department's diplomatic security bureau, readily acquiesced in including it when it was proposed by some on the Hill, apparently concerned that they would be blamed should there be a terrorist incident at a diplomatic mission abroad.[102]

Another internal example occurred during the administration's early deliberations over State's proposal to merge the foreign affairs agencies into the department. Many groups, having a vested interest in as much independence and visibility as possible for arms control, public diplomacy, or foreign assistance activities, weighed in against the possible merger. The result: "In the end the three agencies escaped the ax because Gore's team decided the amount of money a merger could save was not worth what one senior official called the 'grief' it would provide."[103]

Part of the clout of external lobbies, of course, came from "the mother's milk of politics": campaign contributions. Dole, for example, had been particularly helpful to a rabbi from Brooklyn, an important campaign fundraiser, who enlisted his help in obtaining USAID funding for a project in Russia that had been rejected. While a link between fund-raising and Dole's intervention was difficult to prove, it does not take a great stretch here to assign credibility to the connection (nor in other cases, involving members of both parties).[104]

Perhaps most telling of all, however, was the obvious impact of lobbies on the "Foreign Ops" appropriations bill. After all, that was where the money was. Dan Morgan in the *Washington Post* captured the realities of the situation beautifully, contrasting the "stormy foreign aid debate" in the full House as the authorization bill was being debated in June 1995 with the simultaneous "proceedings taking place in a crowded meeting room,

---

102. Senior diplomatic security official, April 29, 1996; State Department legislative affairs officers, April 30, 1996.

103. Thomas W. Lippmann, "Entrenched Constituencies Help Kill Merger," *Washington Post*, February 3, 1995. The same forces came into play when the action shifted to Congress.

104. See Serge F. Kovaleski, "Dole Fund-raiser Got Helping Hand: Project Proposal Won Grant After Initial AID Rejection," *Washington Post*, April 8, 1996.

where a House Appropriations subcommittee was drafting next year's foreign aid spending package one line at a time."[105] Among those working the appropriations markup were Turkey, a former congressman representing Azerbaijan, an Alabama condom-maker, Archer Daniels Midland, the ever-present family planners, refugee support groups, and a variety of U.S. business interests.[106]

In short, high politics, foreign policy directions, and constitutional issues were certainly not the only factors influencing legislative outcomes. The interests of specific groups and organizations were at least as important as the "sausage" of foreign affairs legislation was being prepared.[107]

## Budget Summits and Scorekeeping Again Prove Dangerous

The 1995 budget debates recalled the similar crises in 1987 and 1990, though somewhat less the difficulties of 1993. Summits displace the normal processes and the usual players. If anything, the key negotiations were held at even higher levels and with a smaller number of participants than earlier. Ultimately, they were between the president and the Republican leaders of the two houses, and even budget committee chairmen were excluded from some important sessions. The appropriators were on the outside looking in, until the very end when they were heavily involved in the March and April deliberations on the final CR.[108] Inevitably, at the level of abstraction in-

---

105. Dan Morgan, "Where Foreign Aid Gets Down to Business: While House Debates Policy, Appropriations Panel Deals with Real Dollars," *Washington Post*, June 12, 1995.

106. Ibid.

107. Bismarck is reputed to have said that there are two things one would do well not to watch being made: sausages and tax legislation. Few who have been through the process would exclude appropriations markups from this warning.

108. While past budget summits had also been limited to the leadership and the budget chairmen, Clinton's personal involvement was unprecedented, and clearly affected the dynamics of the long, arduous process. See Ann Devroy, "For Congress, Negotiators, More Talk Than Action: Top Leaders' Budget Meetings Just a Prelude to Bargaining," *Washington Post*, January 2, 1996; Eric Pianin and Ann Devroy, "Both Sides Cite Progress Despite Budget Rhetoric," *Washington Post*, January 4, 1996; and Eric Pianin and John F. Harris, "Negotiators Near Pact on '96 Funds," *Washington Post*, April 24, 1996. A fascinating account of the negotiations, obviously based on insider conversations, is Michael Weisskopf and David Maranis, "Inside the Revolution: Endgame," a four-part series appearing in the *Washington Post*, January 18–21, 1996.

volved, small accounts such as the entire Function 150—unless they were one side or the other's social-political agenda—were all but ignored. Such a process cannot produce sensible prioritization, nor protect national interests in areas where some subtlety is required.

A second area is also of concern. The reader has perhaps grown tired of my railing against the vagaries of scorekeeping as it has affected international affairs. Yet, in the 1995 budget discussions, a macro version of these effects was introduced, in the long and arcane dispute over whether CBO numbers should be used in scoring the various budget proposals. Admittedly, earlier discussion of scorekeeping has focused on the expenditure side, the rate at which appropriations should be counted as contributing to the deficit. This time, scorekeeping came into play vis-à-vis the economic assumptions. The twenty-day government shutdown in December and January came about because of disagreement over small differences in projections about economic growth over a seven-year period. Really this was an argument over the unknowable, over what one respected expert called the "huge unreality for everybody's numbers."[109] Obviously, 1995 had done nothing to place either federal budgeting as a whole or its international affairs component on a more logical basis.

# Authorizers and Appropriators Redux: Waivers and More Fragmentation

One vignette illustrates that the ongoing differences between authorizing and appropriating committees were alive and well, even after the sea change in congressional organization in 1995. H.R. 1561, the American Overseas Interests Act of 1995, containing both the State/USIA and foreign assistance authorizations for fiscal years 1996 and 1997, passed the House on June 8, 1995. It included an authorization of approximately $645 million for the Development Assistance Fund (DAF), a primary component of the bilateral economic assistance administered by USAID. On June 22 the "Foreign Ops" appropriation bill was brought to the House floor, including $669 million for the DAF account.[110]

109. Reischauer, "A Valentine's Day Tale" (note 12 above).
110. Because of a realignment of child survival and tropical-disease-control funding in the authorization bill, the figures used are different in that bill; but all agreed that the amount at issue was between $645 million and $669 million for the core functions. See *Congressional Record* 141 (June 27, 1995): H6326–30.

On June 27, during continuing debate on the measure, the HIRC authorizations chairman Ben Gilman, with a freshman member of the committee (Sam Brownback, R–Kans.), introduced an amendment to reduce the appropriated amount by $24 million—explicitly to match the authorized amount. At the same time, they agreed that the overall amount proposed by the appropriators for their bill was within both the authorized amount and budget resolution ceilings. The appropriators explained that increasing the DAF was an integral part of a bipartisan compromise, without which the Democratic members would not support the appropriations bill, and further that what was at stake was not only a question of jurisdiction and of authorizers protecting their turf, but also an attempt to lower even more the account funding for the controversial population programs.[111]

Gilman's attempt to reduce the funding was rejected by a vote of 202–218.[112] How the votes divided was very revealing. Within the House as a whole, 79 percent (180 of 227) of the Republicans supported Gilman, while only 11.5 percent (22 of 192) of the Democrats did so. Among HIRC members, there was essentially a straight party-line vote. Only the moderate Jim Leach (R-Iowa) voted against Gilman among the twenty-three Republicans, and all sixteen of the voting HIRC Democrats opposed the chairman and supported their party's position. The appropriators, on the other hand, generally placed defense of their bill above any partisan position. Twenty-two of the thirty-two Republican appropriators voted against Gilman, including Chairman Livingston and all members of both the Foreign Operations and the CJS subcommittee. Not unexpectedly, appropriations Democrats voted overwhelmingly against Gilman as well (2–22).[113] The old pattern of appropriators deciding what was acceptable, then defending their bills on the floor against all comers—as in the days of Passman and Rooney—had survived the Republican revolution![114]

111. On this point, see comments during the debate by Representatives Charles Wilson, ranking member of the "Foreign Ops" Subcommittee, and David Obey, ranking member of the full committee. *Congressional Record* 141 (June 27, 1995): H6327.
112. Roll call no. 420, *Congressional Record* 141 (June 27, 1995): H6330. For the votes of individual members, see *CQ Weekly Report* 53 (July 1, 1995): 1952–53.
113. This analysis of party votes draws from the explanation accompanying Roll call no. 420, "House Votes," *CQ Weekly Report* 53 (July 1, 1995): 1952. The analysis of committee votes is my own.
114. This in spite of the highly partisan atmosphere in the House at the time. The next day, in order to show their displeasure at not gaining an additional seat on the Ways and Means Committee to balance a new Republican, angry Democrats employed a variety of dilatory tactics to force the House to stay in session all night considering the bill. That the new Republican, Greg Laughlin of Texas, had defected from the Democrats earlier in the week, probably

Obviously, one strand of all this was the requirement for authorization before obligation of appropriations; for if both bills had survived as passed, the extra $24 million for DAF would have not been authorized. The requirement for authorization would then have had to have been waived, and the appropriators were clearly willing to do so. This early indication of indifference to what the authorizers thought, coupled with the Senate impasse over its version of the authorization later in the summer, caused Gilman to be concerned that the authorization process and his committee's raison d'être would be bypassed. On August 3, 1995, he sought the speaker's help in fighting off any attempt by the appropriators (likely aided by the administration) to waive the requirement for authorization, since he was

> concerned that granting these waivers will effectively kill our efforts to bring about change in the area of foreign policy. . . . I would appreciate whatever assurances you can provide that you will work with my Committee to ensure that the Administration is not able to defeat our efforts by obtaining a waiver of the statutory authorization requirements through the appropriations process.[115]

The next day, Gingrich replied to Gilman that

> I continue to strongly support your legislation that would bring our foreign affairs agencies into the post–Cold War era. Further, I share your concern over any Administration effort to circumvent the authorization process. . . . I do not foresee circumstances under which I would support any effort, over your objections, to waive the authorization requirements that would be satisfied by enactment of H.R. 1561.[116]

Such circumstances, of course, did arise later on during this complicated and contentious year. In 1995, unlike the 1989–90 and 1993–94 episodes when it was finally possible to enact a State authorization act, there were just too many obstacles.

It soon became clear that, as in every year since 1985, there would be no

---

after having been promised the Ways and Means seat, only made matters worse. Michael Wines, "Democrats Rock Around the Clock til Daylight: A Frustrated Minority Ties Up Legislation," *New York Times*, June 30, 1995.

115. Letter from Gilman to Gingrich, August 3, 1995.
116. Letter from Gingrich to Gilman, August 4, 1995.

foreign assistance authorization. While the House had passed a combined State–foreign aid bill (H.R. 1561), the SFRC quickly divided the two parts and marked up its State bill (to become S. 908) on May 17; its companion (S. 961), though reported from committee on June 21, never came close to floor action.[117] At the very beginning, the authorizers had failed to carry out half of their major legislative responsibilities.

By September 28, when the first of many CRs was passed, it was almost a foregone conclusion that there would be a full waiver of authorization for the "Foreign Ops" bill; this was far less certain for CJS. Each short-term CR (this time there were a dozen altogether) contained its own time-limited waivers; the issue for CJS was whether a waiver would be included in a final appropriations act or in a final CR for the rest of FY 1996.

From October through early January, congressional consideration of the "Foreign Ops" appropriation bill, as we have seen, resembled Ping-Pong. The late January compromise allowed an agreement for the foreign operations bill to be attached to the January 26 CR. This move would avoid potential floor problems and the time constraints on passing it as a free-standing bill.[118] Meanwhile, there was no progress on the CJS bill, so the issue of authorization remained moot. In yet another wrinkle, though, during the consideration in early March of what was to become a CR for the rest of the fiscal year, Gilman with the support of Majority Leader Dick Armey attempted to persuade HAC Chairman Bob Livingston to attach some key parts of the State authorization bill, including merger provisions, thus lessening the possibility of a veto which faced a freestanding bill. Livingston, with the strong support of his chief of staff, Jim Dyer, was adamantly opposed, but he (reluctantly) agreed to give the authorizers a few more weeks by including a waiver of the authorization requirement until only March 31, rather than for the whole year. Those close to the negotiations attributed Livingston's position to his lack of respect for the authorizers, in particular HIRC.[119] After the unexpectedly long delay for the CR

117. Some executive branch officials believe that Helms never intended to bring a foreign assistance authorization to the Senate floor. As chairman of the committee reporting it, he would almost have had to support its passage—something he did not wish to do.

118. Ironically, as noted above, a flaw in drafting meant that the foreign operations bill was not in fact attached to the CR. Since all parties were in agreement about the intent of Congress, lawyers decided it should be signed as freestanding legislation. It was enrolled separately by the clerk of the House and signed by President Clinton on February 12, 1996, as P.L. 104-107.

119. Conversations with administration congressional relations officers, March 1996. This was not the first attempt to place authorizing language in the "Foreign Ops" appropriations

lasting until late April, during which the authorization conference report had been passed and vetoed, the final result was no language regarding the authorization issue in the CR. Thus, the prior authorizations stood and no new authorizing legislation was required.[120]

One conclusion to be drawn from these events is that while it is all well and good for there to be a requirement for authorization before appropriations can be expended, in extremis ways will be found to fund the government, even if the authorization must be sacrificed. The power of the purse is used within Congress as well as between the branches!

# Reform Is Among the Victims

One final aspect of the events of 1995 warrants mention here, although fuller discussion fits most naturally in the next chapter. With the great confusion and the overwhelming focus on the reduction of the deficit, reform efforts designed to match resources and policy, especially interagency ones, were left battered. Some internal efforts (both in USAID and in State, for example) fared better. On the Hill, the reforms initiated in the 104th Congress, never conspicuously directed toward this goal in any event, predictably produced few results.[121] Whether either reform effort could be revived would await the 1996 elections and the views of those then in charge of the two branches.

One small benefit for the executive was that, even with all the interagency sniping over the merger, the pressure then collectively faced made it imperative "to work more closely together than they ever had before. For months on end there were weekly (and more) conference calls and meetings at which strategy and basic approaches were discussed. Once this happened, even though no one liked the meetings, it was harder for the hill to play divide and conquer and the charges of each agency cutting its own deals diminished a bit."[122]

---

legislation. In October 1995, Sam Brownback, a freshman HIRC Republican, had attempted to persuade Livingston to attach the merger legislation to the Foreign Operations conference report. He was rebuffed then as well. See Dan Morgan, "Steep Learning Curve for Appropriators: House GOP Newcomers Test Power Held by 'College of Cardinals,'" *Washington Post*, November 2, 1995.

120. Continuing resolutions, by their nature, "continue" past requirements, including prior authorizations, unless language to the contrary is specifically included in them.

121. See Chapter 9 for additional comments on reform in the 104th Congress.

122. Note to me from Robert F. Hopper, May 17, 1996.

# Everything Is Related to Everything Else

The short conclusion is that 1995 was a terrible year for building a partnership to manage international affairs. The executive felt it had insufficient flexibility to operate and carry out foreign policy, while the congressional comfort level was so low that members were heavily disinclined to grant such freedom of action. Yet the foreign affairs events of 1995 clearly fit easily, if at times noisily, into the broader context of executive–legislative interactions presented in other parts of this book. Even with the dramatic surface changes that Republican majorities brought to the 104th Congress and to relationships with the Democratic presidency, most of what has been described here has direct antecedents in earlier periods.

It must be concluded that while there are close interrelationships between funding, organizational considerations, policy goals, politics, and the personalities of the key players, the context in which foreign affairs issues are played out through executive–legislative interaction is heavily institutional. Whoever is in control of each branch, there will be disputes between them that can be traced back to earlier battles and, ultimately, to the constitutional arrangements that strongly define the nature of the branches. Thus, struggles for control of the foreign policy apparatus and how it is employed will surely continue. At best, they will reflect the fact that, especially in an uncertain world, foreign-policymaking is a serious and difficult business. At worst, they will demonstrate the triumph of mindless politics over what is good for the nation.

# CHAPTER NINE

# WHERE DO WE GO FROM HERE?

*Fixes*

The troubled nature of congressional–executive foreign policy/power-of-the-purse interactions leads us to an obvious question: Are improvements in the process possible? It is important to be clear at the outset about what is meant by "improvement." For some, improvements would be whatever enhances the power of one branch relative to the other.[1] A second category might be those changes intended to take the politics out of the process, making it more technical and more "logical." Reforms intended explicitly to serve either of these purposes seem unlikely to be made or, even if formally instituted, to achieve their intended purposes. Yet it can be argued strongly that existing executive–legislative budget interactions, at least as they relate to foreign affairs, do not allow significant policy/resource issues to be addressed frontally. Without abrogating the constitutional responsibilities of either branch or developing a sterile, depoliticized process, ways need to be found to link policy priorities more closely with the application of resources in a time of new challenges coupled with severe budget constraints. Ideally, too, broader national purposes need to replace the narrow parochial ones so frequently observed.

---

1. Former Senate Majority Leader and White House Chief of Staff Howard Baker, for example, explicitly advocates returning more budget power to the president. In remarks at a Brookings conference in 1993, he blames the 1974 Congressional Budget Act for taking away "the president's control of the national agenda in tax and economic and fiscal policy. Too often, the president's budget was simply declared dead on arrival. The Congress went on its merry way in passing its own budget, or in one case passing no budget at all. But to get rid of divided government and bring some degree of balance between the White House and the Con-

To begin with, all of the institutions involved are "in trouble"[2] whether one is speaking about the executive branch (see NPR report of the vice-president), the Congress (see the work of the Joint Committee on the Organization of Congress), the Department of State ("State 2000"), USIA (1991 task force on international broadcasting, Clinton administration proposals, NPR), USAID (Hamilton-Gilman, Ferris, SWAT team, Carnegie, Helms, Gilman),[3] or the government as a whole. There was, by the early 1990s, a broad consensus that our institutions of governance did not work as they must (and not only with respect to the marriage of policy and budgets). It was this pervasive sentiment, in part, that produced a climate in 1995 which was favorable to the radical reorganization efforts in foreign affairs as well as the parallel initiatives affecting many other parts of the government.

Global governmental renewal ("reinvention" is a term overused and not very accurate, in my view) is much too broad a subject for this book, but we may isolate some possible changes relating to money and foreign affairs that show promise for improving the situation, assuming always that there is a general will and a perceived incentive to discard the status quo. Some would argue that everything has been tried before, that there is nothing new.[4] But my argument is that with respect to the effective conduct of foreign affairs as it involves money, the attempt should be made. Reforms applicable to the executive branch are a sensible starting point, since budget preparation begins there and since the executive constitutionally has primary foreign affairs responsibility.

# Executive Reforms

## The Climate for Change

There are numerous impediments to the development of a logical foreign affairs budgeting process. Several are especially vexing and largely responsi-

---

gress, the president, whether he is a Democrat or Republican, has to be given more effective authority over fiscal matters." Quoted in Sundquist, ed., *Beyond Gridlock?* p. 65.

2. The first line of the first Brookings/AEI report on renewing Congress begins, "Make no mistake about it. Congress is in trouble" (p. 2). The second report was cited above; the first is Thomas E. Mann and Norman J. Ornstein, *A First Report of the Renewing Congress Project* (Washington, D.C.: American Enterprise Institute and Brookings Institution, 1992).

3. Full citations to these studies may be found above.

4. See, for example, Philip G. Joyce, "The Reiterative Nature of Budget Reform: Is There Anything New in Federal Budgeting?" *Public Budgeting & Finance* 12 (Fall 1993): 36–48. Joyce gives a useful short summary of major attempts at budget reform since the Budget and Accounting Act of 1921.

ble for the tangled history of earlier reform initiatives. Obviously, they must be coped with if future efforts are to have a better chance of success.

First of all, there has been a general lack of concern about resource issues, resulting in a tendency to equate them with what has been called mere "housekeeping." A related problem is the ambivalent perspective exhibited by many at State with respect to operating such programs as foreign assistance or cultural exchange. Like resource issues, they are not pure diplomatic activities; thus they are seen as secondary in importance. This in turn helps explain a third problem which has received special attention: the organizational fragmentation of the executive-branch foreign affairs community. If these "secondary" activities are segregated in separate agencies, they are more easily put out of mind at State. The result has been a lack of coordination and a proliferation of special interests surrounding each agency and program, making overall priority-setting extremely difficult. In a time of increasingly tight resources, this state of affairs is no longer acceptable.

## Some Useful Starting Points

Formulation of an integrated, executive-branch international affairs budget tied to policy priorities would not require starting from scratch. Some building blocks already exist.

First, State has made a good (if tentative) start, since 1989, in developing a program planning system, which has become more workable each year. As often happens in State, image has not overtaken reality; the process is better than its reputation. But it is necessary that it not be allowed to die, and similar initiatives in other agencies must also be incorporated in a coordinated cross-agency effort.

There is also progress vis-à-vis elements of other agencies, such as the long-standing efforts in USAID's Latin America Bureau and in parts of USIA. Moreover, in 1994 and 1995 all of USAID undertook a major reengineering of its planning and operating processes, and the new system was operational by 1996. These initiatives, however, are not yet fully exploited.

The State process, by its fourth annual cycle in 1993–94, was gradually becoming more integrated into the resource management process. Mission Program Plans (MPPs)—prepared by embassies and other missions—should have obviated the need for separate mission budget submissions, and Bureau Program Plans (BPPs) were used as basic documentation to formulate and justify bureau resource requests. Unfortunately, planning and resource-management (particularly budgeting) exercises were still viewed by some bureaus and posts as disconnected. Annual preparation of five-year plans was seen as a burden. Another problem is that the program planning process focused on resource implications for State programs and accounts only, even though at the MPP level all agencies participated at most posts and staffing for all agencies was projected. Timing was also a problem. If bureau plans are completed only after the shape of the budget has already been determined, they are of little use in meshing plans and budget requests. Post and bureau deadlines as early as the third planning cycle were set with the budget preparation calendar in mind, but it was difficult to meet those deadlines, a necessary condition if there is to be useful input, and as of mid-1996 the problem remained. While the planning and budget processes were, by then, more closely harmonized than earlier, they were a long way from being completely synchronized.

By 1995, there were both continuing improvements and indications of future difficulties. Instructions remained identical with those of the previous year, so new software was not required and only an annual plan update was required, rather than a completely new submission. These were significant simplifications. Another positive change was the growing inclusion of Function 150 elements beyond the State Department, in resource planning as well as in staffing. At the same time, the MPPs appeared to be of greater utility in the field than they were in Washington, and the importance of the BPPs was distinctly limited. Another potential problem was that the two State staffers who had been the driving force in developing the planning process since its inception moved on to other duties, and management of the process was then placed in the hands of a team. MPPs continued, but the bureau plans, the key element for consolidation across the department, were initially suspended in 1995 pending the outcome of the department's Strategic Management Initiative, which it was initially thought might produce significant operational changes necessitating new guidance for preparing the plans. SMI did not produce such results, and the BPPs were eventually prepared in simplified form.[5] More generally, Under Secretary for Management Richard Moose was reported initially to be skeptical of the

5. The second phase of the SMI was announced by Secretary Christopher in a "town meeting" with State Department employees on March 20, 1995. Eventually, for 1995, bureaus other than those in the management area were asked to submit reports based on the MPPs, though not full plans. M-area bureaus were required to submit standard MPPs. By early 1996, the department's leadership had declared victory, but little of concrete use had emerged from the SMI exercise. Details on MPPs and BPPs from State Department officers closely involved with the process, May 1996.

true value of the planning process, and at least one well-placed senior official speculated that while it was being improved each year, the process had perhaps "peaked" and started to decline.[6] By the end of 1995, however, Moose had become a strong supporter of the process, especially when it was an absolute necessity to prioritize because of declining resources. An additional factor cited for his change of opinion was that these plans contained much of the information required to be reported by the Government Performance and Results Act (GPRA).[7]

With this spotty history, it is uncertain whether the planning process will be continued and become a major tool in matching resources and priorities.[8] But there is a chance.

Second, State's internal budget-formulation process is gradually becoming more refined, informed by (slowly) improving databases and by the use of bureau program plans earlier in the cycle. These steps have been encouraging improvements and some integration of budget formulation with foreign policy objectives. While State's internal budget staff in the late 1980s was relatively inexperienced, it was talented and became hardened by the difficult times under BEA imperatives and during the authorization/appropriation imbroglios of that period.

Third, much has been learned about how to run integrative processes, in part through the efforts of the D/P&R staff since it was created in 1986 and, since 1993, by its successor, the Resources, Plans, and Policy Office (S/RPP). The natural centrifugal forces toward independence, however, both within State and especially within other agencies, must nonetheless be confronted. Fortunately, there is now enough useful experience to provide something to build on with respect to a more comprehensive effort, assuming that the political and bureaucratic will exists.

6. Details in this paragraph come from interviews with several closely involved officials, March–May 1995 and April–May 1996.

7. Interviews with an M policy analyst, November 29, 1995, and a senior Function 150 budget manager, May 1, 1996. Among other things, GPRA requires each agency and department to produce a strategic plan linking resources and expected results.

8. One observer, a career officer serving as ambassador at an African post (and one who is more knowledgeable than most about planning issues, owing to his experience at State), summarized the situation toward the end of 1995, *after* the developments just discussed: "The existing mission program plan exercise is flawed. A minimum level of joint planning in an organized sense takes place in the preparation of MPP; it is viewed largely as a State Department driven exercise. MPP is strong on program and policy objectives and weak on consolidation, resource allocation, staffing, and funding." Unclassified cable to the secretary of state and others, November 29, 1995.

## A Unified International Affairs Budget: Prospects

It is hard to deny that the use of scarce resources would be much improved if the executive could develop a true Function 150 budget that systematically weighed currently divorced segments against one another and presented firm priorities to Congress. However, such a budget, whatever its form, would be a classic example of "top–down" budgeting, as opposed to the often advocated "bottom–up" approach. It is simply not possible to prioritize effectively without a central decisionmaker. This would have to be either the secretary of state or the OMB director, ideally operating on the basis of guidelines from the president. Such a system would not necessarily be in the interests of either the disparate parts of Congress which now consider the various parts of Function 150 or, for that matter, the many engaged elements of the executive branch, since in each case independence of action would be circumscribed by the overall plan. Some, including myself, briefly entertained the hope that the BEA of 1990, because of its "fences" or "fire walls" isolating Function 150 from outside competition, might facilitate the development of such an approach. As of 1996, however, only modest progress has been made, although interest remained in parts of the executive branch, notably in the S/RPP office in State.[9]

In its late 1992 report, the State 2000 Task Force had recommended that the policy planning staff (S/P) and the D/P&R office be merged, in an effort to force resource use to be related more closely to explicit policy priorities.[10] While it was not implemented with the other early Christopher-period State Department organizational changes, this idea retained currency. In fact, 1993 was a time of confusion as Deputy Secretary Wharton delayed selection of a new D/P&R director, and his eventual choice promptly took another assignment on Wharton's departure that November. Meanwhile, the previously discussed "Big Pie" exercise, preeminently the kind of cross-150 effort this staff was created to manage, was directed by a retired Foreign Service officer, Craig Johnstone, brought back for the purpose, and not by D/P&R.

However, it was soon decided to upgrade the D/P&R office and to institu-

9. For example, guidance issued on September 24, 1993, concerning preparation of FY 1995 budget submissions by State, AID, and USIA, moved beyond initial attempts the preceding year to formulate the 150 budget in broad policy categories. See the next section for new and old categories. The idea was to make the budget presentation more consistent with foreign policy goals.

10. At pp. 25–27 in the report, with more detail in Bacchus, "Resource Allocation," annex B to State 2000, pp. 145–58.

tionalize this function, now recognized to be important. On January 20, 1994, an internal State Department memorandum announced creation of S/RPP, formed by adding some policy analysts from the policy planning staff to D/P&R and elevating its reporting point to the office of the secretary. It was to be headed by Johnstone. This change was clearly intended to achieve much the same purpose as the *State 2000* recommendation to create an Office of Strategic Planning and Resources.[11] The terms of reference for the new office included acting as a resource to senior management in all the foreign affairs agencies "to assist in developing policies, plans and programs to achieve foreign policy goals"; to advise them "on management of the International Affairs (Function 150) Budget, coordinating the resource requirements of the foreign affairs agencies to enable the Secretary to present integrated international affairs resource requests"; to recommend "resource allocations to fulfill policy priorities and maximize efficient use of scarce resources"; to conduct "policy reviews to ensure clear definition of goals and continuity between programs, resources, policies and goals"; and to work closely with others in the department and throughout the administration to coordinate budgetary and legislative strategy.[12]

While it was hardly an immediate success, creation of this office at least demonstrated increasing recognition of the need for closer matching of policy and resources and for greater integration. Further impetus was given on March 31, 1994, in an unusual departmentwide meeting of assistant secretaries and key budget managers, at which Deputy Secretary Talbott and Under Secretary for Management Moose laid down the law about the necessity to embrace the department's program planning mechanism, as a means of marrying policy priorities and scarce resources. At the same meeting, S/RPP Director Craig Johnstone made it clear that his office was intended to be the primary locus for close cross-agency coordination of the entire Function 150.[13]

Johnstone soon revealed an ambitious plan for doing all this (which was in some measure implemented) and confirmed the suspicions of other agencies, including OMB, that with the backing of Christopher and Talbot, he wanted State (i.e., his office) to play the brokering role. Some at OMB believed he should have confined himself in this regard to State and USAID, while working in a more collaborative way with OMB with respect to the

11. Discussions with advocates of the S/RPP approach, late 1993–April 1994.

12. Details come from an internal State Department memorandum, January 20, 1994, and from senior officials who participated in formulating the proposal.

13. I was present at this meeting.

rest of the function. There was also the feeling that S/RPP did not attempt enough program reviews, although others do note that the attempt was made to build in more performance goals. In other agencies, some thought he attempted too dominant a role, which "at worst was offensive to the head of the independent agency." Yet there were some successes, notably in achieving higher submission numbers for the FY 1996 budget. On the Hill, results in 1994 (for FY 1995) were reasonable given the tight budget situation, although the attempt to redefine the budget in functional categories continued to be met with indifference.[14]

The second full cycle for S/RPP began in the spring of 1995, during preparation of the FY 1997 budget. This budget was assembled in the context of the dramatic events of that year, described in Chapter 8 above. Johnstone had hoped that the process would change in several ways from what had gone before. First, on the State side, he wanted to involve the regional assistant secretaries more deeply, now that the 1994 experiment using the under secretaries as focal points had shown its weaknesses. Second, he wanted the internal State budget development and the cross-agency Function 150 processes to be more integrated throughout. A third important objective was to show that the independent foreign affairs agencies could work together.[15] To these ends, Secretary Christopher sent a memo, prepared by S/RPP, to the heads of USAID, USIA, and ACDA. After noting that "given the certainty of impending budget cuts for FY 1996, I believe it is imperative that we begin our FY 1997 planning by developing a strategy for dealing with dramatically reduced funding levels," Christopher proposed a process based largely on six interagency teams, each chaired by a regional assistant secretary of state. The memo also stated the secretary's objectives for the review, as good a set of goals for an integrated process as is likely to be found:

> I am hopeful that this process will serve a number of objectives. First, it will help us to set realistic priorities for our programs and make rational decisions on the use of our scarce resources. Second,

14. This paragraph is based on interviews with senior budget officials in OMB, State, USIA, and USAID, February–May 1995.

15. Interview with Johnstone, May 2, 1995. As seen in the discussion of the proposed merger of foreign affairs agencies, presented in Chapter 8, a lack of close coordination among the agencies was one reason that some in State, including Johnstone, advocated consolidation around the time of the 1994 congressional elections. By 1996, he had come to believe, like Allen Schick twenty years earlier, that a truly integrated Function 150 budget would require organizational consolidation and unified leadership. Interview, May 1, 1996.

it will help break down the barriers between policy formulation and program implementation, ensuring that policy makers have a voice in and an understanding of program development, and program managers contribute to and have knowledge of policy formulation. Finally, we will clearly demonstrate the ability of the International Affairs Agencies to work together on policy and program and development, proving that consolidation of the foreign affairs agencies is not a necessary prerequisite to effective foreign policy management.[16]

Predictably, this memo was not well received by the smaller agencies, leading to tense consultations between their leaders and State. They believed that the proposed approach placed entirely too much power with the assistant secretaries of state, and they demanded higher-level leadership and intervention. In due course, an uneasy compromise was reached, with Johnstone and Talbot presiding, but it was demonstrated once again that the degree of coordination required to integrate the Function 150 budget will not be easy to come by.[17] One thoughtful observer with experience at OMB, State, and USAID believes that S/RPP could serve its most useful role not in the budget formulation stage, but *later on,* once resources are available, when as an agent of the secretary it would be listened to with greater credibility and less controversy.[18] That may be so, but it would hardly unify the foreign affairs function.

Still more difficult than integrating Function 150, but even more desirable, is the notion of a consolidated process that prioritizes *all* budgeted federal activities that have a major impact on international relationships. There are obvious definitional problems, but ways to begin are suggested below. One expert has proposed what might be called a "National Security Budget," including primarily intelligence and defense activities;[19] a more expansive version would create a "Function 150 Plus" budget, cutting across all agencies.[20]

16. State Department memorandum, Warren Christopher to the heads of USAID, USIA, and ACDA, May 19, 1995.

17. Details in this paragraph come from discussions with participants in the process, May 1995. To take one example, I was present at an internal USAID meeting on June 1, 1995, at which Administrator Brian Atwood, discussing the planned leadership role for State Department regional assistant secretaries, said: "This is not acceptable to us."

18. Richard Nygard, USAID budget director, April 19, 1995.

19. Suggested in 1990 by Robert F. Hopper, a member of the legislative staff of the Department of State's under secretary for management.

20. This idea was given prominence by the "State 2000" task force, in particular Lannon Walker.

## Program/Performance Budgets: Panacea or Placebo?

U.S. federal budgets traditionally have been structured on the basis of object classes or general purposes, such as "salaries and expenses" or "foreign buildings." In effect, they are directed toward the input side of spending, rather than on what is accomplished with the funds, and they place a strong emphasis on control of expenditures. But at least since the 1920s and 1930s, there have been voices arguing for greater emphasis on the management of expenditures to carry out specific functions, and thus greater attention to outputs rather than inputs. A milestone in this movement was the report of the Hoover commission, which apparently coined the term "performance budgeting" to describe what had previously been known as "functional" or "activity" budgeting. At about the same time, another reform movement emerged which, while sharing the conviction that it was desirable to concentrate on outputs, went one step further: to emphasize the objectives or purposes to be achieved. If the key for the performance budgeting school was management, then that for program budgeting was and is planning. The McNamara period in Defense was perhaps the high point of this program budgeting movement. The classic article on these distinctions, still often cited, suggested that "as a general rule performance budgeting is concerned with the *process of work* (what methods should be used) while program budgeting is concerned with the *purpose of work* (what activities should be authorized)."[21]

There are many other formulations of the differences between input, or object class, budgeting and budgeting that shifts the focus to the output side, or to performance, to what actually is accomplished. In effect, the earlier assumption was that if money was appropriated for a specific purpose, then that was all that was required. Under output formulations, this assumption would no longer hold. Either the work actually done (performance budgeting) or the purposes served/goals achieved (program budgeting) would be the organizing concept.

The latest proponents of performance budgeting (who also advocate strategic planning) have been the authors of Vice-President Gore's National Performance Review (NPR) report, released in September 1993. About the

21. Allen Schick, "The Road to PPB: The Stages of Budget Reform," *Public Administration Review* 26 (December 1966): 251. Much of the commentary in the previous paragraph derives from this article. A current formulation which updates Schick's argument can be found in Don A. Cozzetto, Mary Grisez Kweit, and Robert W. Kweit, *Public Budgeting: Politics, Institutions, and Processes* (White Plains, N.Y.: Longman, 1995), chap. 7, "The Search for a Budget 'Theory,' " pp. 185–222.

existing situation, they concluded: "[T]he budget process is characterized by fictional requests and promises, an obsession with inputs rather than outcomes, and a shortage of debate about critical national needs. We must start to plan strategically—linking our spending with priorities and performance."[22] Despite half a century of advocacy, shifting to "outputs" still seemed too hard.

One difficulty, of course, is that the budget process moves inexorably forward, with as many as four different annual processes in progress at once. Thus, there is little time to explore what happened in prior years in order to judge performance or outputs.[23] This is especially true for projects and activities having a long lead time: e.g., major development efforts where the true impact may always be hard to measure (many variables can affect the result, and not only foreign assistance activities). Definitive results may be measurable only after decades. Benchmarks along the way may help, but assessing results will always be difficult.

While performance budgets and program budgets are related and share an output orientation, one recent work argues that the former tend to focus on "what each administrative unit is trying to accomplish, how much it is planning to do, with what resources." In contrast, a program budget "divides expenditures by activities" and is sometimes related to a planning process

> where goals are stated and expenditures allocated in an effort to reach those goals. The emphasis in this format is on the appropriateness of current spending priorities and the possible need for tradeoffs between programs. *Program budgets have the most potential for allowing legislators to review the policy implications of spending decisions.*[24]

22. NPR (see Chapter 3, note 21, above), p. 16. A more detailed explanation of the Gore exercise as it related to budgeting issues was an accompanying report: *Mission-Driven, Results-Oriented Budgeting*, also issued by the GPO, dated September 1993 but made public in late 1994.

23. By 1993, although AID's Center for Development Information and Evaluation (CDIE) was attempting a rather sophisticated evaluation of AID programs, the results had not been routinely injected into budget preparation. In February 1995, however, a consultant, Howard H. Raiken, produced the latest in a series of reports on this issue, *Performance Results Measurement Data and Reporting System: Conceptual Framework* (Washington, D.C.: USAID, February 17, 1995).

24. Irene S. Rubin, *The Politics of Public Budgeting*, p. 76, emphasis added.

A similar linkage between planning and budgeting is inherent in the proposal presented in the following sections.

In an experiment whose acceptance by Congress was at best lukewarm, as noted, the FY 1995 and FY 1996 foreign affairs budget presentations by the Clinton Administration were reconfigured into new categories conforming to the central elements of its announced foreign policy. Instead of the traditional categories such as humanitarian assistance, security assistance, conduct of foreign affairs, information and exchange activities, and international financial programs (see Table 1, for example), these new budget requests were arrayed by groupings such as "Promoting U.S. Prosperity through Trade, Investment, and Employment," "Building Democracy," "Promoting Sustainable Development," "Promoting Peace," "Providing Humanitarian Assistance," and "Advancing Diplomacy."[25] This change was clearly an attempt to tie resources to broad priority areas (i.e., more to outputs than to inputs) as well as, of course, to make foreign assistance and agency operations more palatable to Congress. While this was a step in the desired direction, regrouping accounts is only the beginning of effectively prioritizing among them. Unfortunately, even though this modest advance survived OMB scrutiny, the reaction of Congress, especially the appropriators, was not encouraging; and, with the failure to enact a basic new Foreign Assistance Act (see Chapter 3 above), Congress insisted on the old categories. The administration prepared its FY 1996 and FY 1997 budget submissions using both the old and the new categories.

## The Critical Change: Linking Resources to Policy

A fundamental tenet of the approach proposed here is the necessity to link explicit priorities with resource allocation throughout the entire process

25. For FY 1995, see U.S. Department of State, Bureau of Public Affairs, *FY 1995 International Affairs Budget Request* (February 7, 1994) as well as the *FY 1995 Budget of the United States Government* (Washington, D.C.: GPO, 1994). For FY 1996, see the analogous documents, the former being dated February 6, 1995. Because other proposed USAID changes, such as a new Foreign Assistance Act and reformed organization and procedures, were not yet in place for FY 1995, one OMB official characterized this change, in the spring of 1994, as "old wine in old bottles." Budget professionals at OMB, in Congress, in the CBO, and even in the foreign affairs agencies continued to track the process by the traditional subfunctions. Nevertheless, the S/RPP office continued to use both the new and the existing categories in its FY 1997 submission. See its summary, "Highlights of the FY 1997 International Affairs (Function 150) Budget Request," March 18, 1996.

from budget formulation to enactment. In the following sections I suggest one way this might be done in the preparation stage, prior to submission of the president's budget to Congress.

In its late-1992 report, State's management task force—State 2000—began the annex on resource allocation by stating that

> one primary finding of this Task Force is that the U.S. government must have a strategic foreign affairs planning process, and that it, in addition to serving other purposes, must be closely linked to formulation of the Federal budget and other resource management decisions.

The annex continued by explaining why:

> We assume tight foreign affairs budgets. Without a means of forcing hard choices among contending priorities in an increasingly complicated and busy world, we believe it will not be possible to conduct a coherent foreign policy that clearly serves national interests. Without such a process tying resources to foreign policy priorities . . . we will not be able to use our limited resources in the most effective ways. . . . [O]nce priorities are established, our programs and operations must be structured and supported in ways which make them real. *Resource allocation must follow strategic planning which produces policy priorities.*[26]

If one grants the plausibility of this argument, bringing such a process into being is still a major undertaking. Still, the history of failed attempts does provide lessons on how some of the pitfalls can be avoided.

*First, high and low policy must be linked.* Foreign policy goals and objectives must be clearly and explicitly examined for longer-term resource and management implications, and the trade-offs must be determined. The resulting decisions must then be crosswalked into specific budget requests, financial plans, and personnel actions. Priorities cannot be solely within the purview of resource managers; if they are, especially when funding is tight, every incentive will be for the cheap to drive out the important. All too many of our policy gurus would not recognize a true budget; they simply

---

26. Bacchus, "Resource Allocation," p. 145, emphasis in original. The immediately following paragraphs, on previous lessons, are drawn closely from the same source (p. 151).

have no experience in the realities of program operations, financial requirements, or infrastructure costs. The obvious implication is that these two disparate kinds of professionals must work it out together.

*Second, such a strategic planning and resource allocation process,* integrated across functional and major programmatic categories, *cannot be run successfully if the key decisionmaker is below the secretary/deputy secretary of state level.* Under secretaries may be able to make the trade-offs, subject to the occasional appeal upward, within sectors directly under their control (T in the past for security assistance, M for accounts such as S&E, foreign buildings, and the like), but they will not be viewed as sufficiently impartial to trade off their own functions equitably against others, even within State.

*A third reality is that any such process, to be effective, must be parsimonious.* If those who must do the work are actively to support the process, the process must be simple. This reality is particularly true for senior officials who must play a significant role in a successful process, such as ambassadors, assistant and under secretaries, the deputy secretary, and the secretary (and their counterparts in other agencies, especially USIA and USAID). It seems clear that separate, comprehensive planning and budgeting processes would impose too much of a burden. The two must be closely linked and merged to the maximum extent possible. Especially for the foreign affairs community with its far-flung installations, time will be at a premium. It must not be wasted.

With these warnings in mind, we may now consider what kind of a process might reasonably meet these requirements and avoid the clear pitfalls.

## Strategic Planning and Resource Allocation: How Might It Work?

The president must be able to present to Congress an integrated foreign affairs strategy and budget that clearly reflects policy choices and, when necessary, must be able to convey changes in priorities even after the budget is submitted for congressional action. To accomplish this, the process of program planning and budget formulation would need to have certain key features.[27]

It is fundamental that the process begin with a statement of broad foreign

27. The following description closely follows Bacchus, "Resource Allocation," pp. 152–54.

policy priorities and goals endorsed by the NSC and the president. The initial draft of this annual directive might be prepared for NSC consideration by an appropriate State Department office charged with strategic planning and resource allocation (under the current structure, the new S/RPP office), but it must have a government-wide imprimatur. This directive would also facilitate consideration and inclusion of international activities funded outside Function 150, such as drug enforcement. It would specifically address priorities for the next fiscal year, but would also lay out broad guidelines for a five-year period—a rolling strategic plan. These goals and objectives would be much more useful if they were drawn up with specific attention to later resource allocation applications.

Concurrently, OMB would issue its closely related planning guidance (preliminary budget marks) for budget submissions due later in the year. Budget guidance, too, should provide broad guidelines for future-year financing.

The secretary of state would follow up on this initial presidential guidance. This phase is a mixture of policy goal-setting and resource allocation, but with the emphasis shifting to the budget. State's strategic planning and resource office (called SPR in the *State 2000* report, S/RPP in the 1994 version) would elaborate on the presidential guidelines, setting goals and more detailed marks for each region. This step would require close coordination with other agencies and with State's under secretaries. Planning marks would be provided for all Function 150–funded regional activities, major worldwide programs, and domestic operations, both for State and for other affected agencies. Under secretaries would coordinate the process within their areas (e.g., Management for support programs, personnel, buildings, etc.; Global Affairs for drugs, terrorism, refugees, environment, and democracy programs; Political Affairs for field submissions from geographic bureaus).

At the next level of specificity, assistant secretaries would further elaborate guidance and resource marks for overseas missions and for elements of major global programs, requiring submissions from ambassadors and program managers that show all participating agencies' resource requests in a single, integrated budget document. That is to say, Mission Program Plans (MPPs) would, as now, include the activities of all agencies at a given post, but they would also result in a direct budget input for all affected accounts, not just for the State Department accounts as currently. Collated and prioritized regional plans, which would aggregate the mission submissions, would become the primary building blocks of budget preparation. A parallel process would exist for major worldwide programs. The timing and format of the programming/budget cycles/documents would need to be reconciled.

Ideally, most interagency disputes would be resolved at the ambassadorial/program manager level, since these officials already have the authority and responsibility to fashion integrated country and program plans. Ambassadors, of course, cannot move money from one agency's account to another. But they can recommend projected budgets that would call for shifts among agency budgets or for a different resource profile. They can also recommend, through the department and the congressional process, formal transfers and reprogrammings, both of which would be called for if new priorities emerged that had not been included originally.

Assistant secretaries would then aggregate field submissions and thrash out any remaining interagency disputes. Under secretaries would intervene as necessary at this stage, with the goal of leaving only the most important trade-offs for the secretary's decision.

The budget formulation "endgame" would resemble, albeit in a more orderly way, that described for recent years. The State Department resource staff would take the various submissions and integrate them into an overall presentation to the secretary, flagging the key decisions to be made before sending the proposed budget to OMB and the president. In making these decisions, the secretary would consult as necessary with agency heads. Secretarial recommendations for Function 150 would be definitive; for non-150 international programs, they would reflect agreements made during the planning/budgeting process. Agency heads could appeal, but the process would work best if there were a presumption that the secretary had done what the president asked.

Finally, OMB would recommend to the president what the aggregated funding level should be, but would not second-guess priorities. This step would be facilitated if relevant OMB staff had been involved throughout the process. OMB would also assess the "fit" of non–Function 150 international programs with the overall budget plan. These recommendations, naturally, would be adjusted to conform to final presidential decisions.

At the next stage, agency budget preparations would be carried out in ways similar to those in the current process, under the direction of CFOs/comptrollers. However, because of the decisions made earlier in consolidating country and regional budgets and their worldwide program counterparts into larger units, the latter task should be somewhat easier than it is now. In particular, trade-offs among contenders for resources would already have been decided (within available funding). Congressional presentation documents would be prepared according to agency/account requirements, as at present, but would also reflect the new approach.

Figure 5 illustrates this proposed process and the approximate timing requirements. It emphasizes among other things the complexities that arise from no fewer than four budget cycles being under way simultaneously.

Once the president's budget is submitted to Congress, the emphasis should be on the relevance and priorities of the foreign policy goals and objectives sought and the appropriateness of the programs and overseas partners selected to attain them. Ideally, functional/sectoral allocations and earmarks would disappear (although it must be recognized that they generally exist because of fundamental political differences between an administration and Congress and not just because of flaws in the budget and appropriations processes).[28] Once appropriations were made, the executive, in consultation with Congress, would be able to transfer or reprogram monies among major foreign policy priorities among and within regions. This procedure would follow established rules (e.g., percentages of receiving accounts and limits), as now, but with greater flexibility. Changes to authorizing and appropriations legislation would be needed.

There is an additional integrative instrument that might profitably be used under certain circumstances: apportionment. This post-appropriations action is the means (once the secretary of the treasury has issued warrants establishing the amount of money, by account, authorized to be withdrawn from the Treasury) by which OMB makes funds available for the accounts and agencies to which they have been appropriated. Apportionments are distributions that limit the amounts available for obligation; they are usually divided by time periods (to avoid Anti-Deficiency Act violations) or by specific activities.[29]

The key here is that OMB has the ability, subject to the reporting requirements of the Impoundment Control Act of 1974, to withhold apportionments if it is not satisfied that funds will be obligated in accordance with overall agreed priorities. Such withholding already occurs in some cases, but it could be given more emphasis. Thus the OMB director and the secretary of state, in concert, could insist that sectoral assistance funds (e.g., in the narcotics-control area) be used for the highest-priority projects. Cur-

---

28. For a discussion of the pervasive appeal of earmarking, though not in the area of foreign affairs, see Mary Jordan, "Funds from Friends in High Places," *Washington Post*, October 10, 1993.

29. See Schick, Keith, and Davis, *Manual on the Federal Budget Process*, p. 207; or Schick, *The Federal Budget*, p. 206.

Fig. 5 An Integrated Foreign Affairs Strategic Planning and Resource Allocation Process

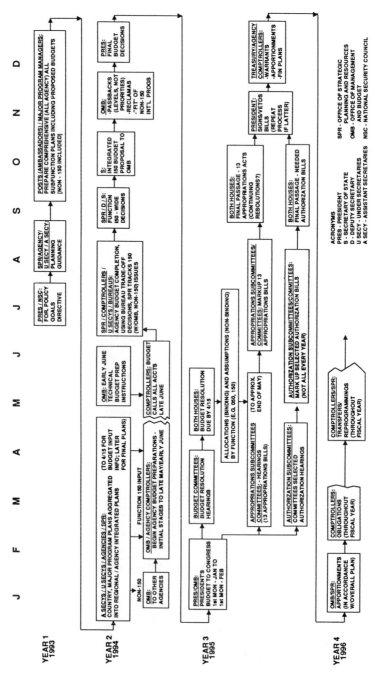

SOURCE: Office of the Under Secretary of State for Management, *State 2000: A New Model for Managing Foreign Affairs*, Publication no. 10029 (Washington, D.C.: U.S. Department of State, December 1992), p. 157.

rently, for example, there is no guarantee that the bulk of the narcotics funds which are appropriated to USAID accounts will be obligated in accordance with the plan established by State's assistant secretary for international narcotics matters, the person who technically has the job of providing overall policy guidance and coordination across agency lines. Apportionment control could in theory largely remedy this problem. Congress, however, might find fault with this device unless there was full, prior consultation and unless the integrated plan used to determine whether or not to apportion had been presented to them. Even so, this approach warrants consideration as one means of giving teeth to support agreed priorities.

## Caveats

With the proposed process in mind, several things need to be accomplished in order to avoid some major potential difficulties. Otherwise, the process will fail, as previous attempts demonstrate.

First, any attempt at overall international affairs budget prioritizing must be closely incorporated into OMB's total budget review process. If not, agencies both in Washington and in the field will resist inclusion in a State-led process, and will likely be supported by their congressional authorizing and appropriating committees. Similarly, the appeal rights of independent agency heads—i.e., their ability to make a case to the president—must be honored; these rights are likely to be used only infrequently, but the possibility adds legitimacy to the process.

State, if given such a task, must also take care that budget integration does not denigrate or undercut the roles played by the various foreign affairs agencies and by other departments in making the case to the Congress and the public for those areas where they have special responsibility and expertise (e.g., DOD for peacekeeping and military aid, USAID for economic aid, Treasury for international financial institutions). In a time of increasing conflict between domestic and international accounts for shares of the budget pie, the expertise of all the foreign affairs agencies must be engaged.

Finally, if integrating Function 150 will be difficult, then going beyond these clearly identified international activities to programs having an international impact but carried in other budget functions will be even more daunting. As Allen Schick correctly noted in 1975, there is a direct relationship between domestic and international programs in many areas, and it is not feasible to segregate one from the other. His argument remains pertinent, if not controlling, to this day. Instead of trying to place programs having both domestic and international ramifications in one category or the other, says Schick, it would be more desirable "to merge international and domestic activities in the same function whenever pursuit of the international objective is critically dependent upon domestic actions."[30] His larger point is that the goal should be "to foster a budget environment in which policymakers tackling [domestic] issues are sensitized to the impact of their decision on the foreign policy of the United States."[31] Schick does not believe that such an environment would necessarily make international programs more vulnerable to domestic pressures but that, to the contrary, "the budgetary isolation of international affairs makes it an easy pick for budget cutters."[32]

Schick's solution would be to reorganize the entire federal budget across functional lines. Currently, this idea does not seem politically feasible; nor, as he would agree, does redefining Function 150 to include such programs seem realistic. What does seem doable is to force all overseas expenditures, from whatever function or source, to fit an overall conceptual scheme. This effort will require attention and enforcement from the center. State could follow up on presidential decisions, but ultimately the White House would have to ensure compliance.

## Implementation in the Clinton Administration

The basic premises of an approach like the one just described, as recommended in the *State 2000* report, were accepted by the Christopher team when it assumed control of the department and were reflected in an implementation directive (issued on February 5, 1993) that made a large number of organizational and process changes largely derived from that report.[33]

30. Schick, "Congressional Use of Its Money Power," p. 458.
31. Ibid.
32. Ibid.
33. Warren Christopher, "Message to State Department Employees," February 5, 1993, printed in Bureau of Public Affairs, U.S. Department of State, *Dispatch* 4, no. 8 (February 8, 1993). With respect to resource allocation, the directive stated: "In a time of tight budgets and increasing demands on international affairs resources, clearer priorities must be established for the International Affairs Budget Function 150 Account if Administration initiatives are to be realized. Under the direction of the Deputy Secretary, who will coordinate management of international affairs resources, the Policy Planning Staff shall provide policy guidance so that general spending priorities may be established. A deputy in S/P shall work closely with the Office of Policy and Resources (D/P&R) to link the policy planning and resource allocation processes."

However, it is instructive to look briefly at what was done and what was not done. The State 2000 task force, as mentioned, had recommended that the existing D/P&R staff and the policy planning staff (S/P) be merged in order to force policy considerations and resource allocation to be considered together. This recommendation was opposed by both units: the head of D/P&R was concerned that he would lose immediate proximity to the deputy secretary; the incoming head of the policy planning staff did not want to see S/P become a budget shop, fearing that this would undermine its credibility as a major player in foreign policy development. Hence the compromise quoted in note 33. Little of consequence occurred in 1993; but 1994, as described above, brought one more attempt.[34]

In USAID as well, something just as tentative occurred. The new leadership of the agency, in particular Administrator J. Brian Atwood and Chief of Staff Richard McCall, assumed their positions committed to the necessity for a policy–resource linkage. Early discussions concerning reorganization of the agency assumed that the budget office would be moved from the purview of the assistant administrator for management to become part of a reconstituted policy bureau, in essence going back to a pattern that was in existence before 1992, when USAID's *last* reorganization had separated policy and budget functions. However, when the final plan was announced in October 1993, the two offices stayed separate, and a complicated scheme was established to take care of the necessary coordination.[35] Again, both parties seemed to feel they would lose something in a merger, yet both stated their commitment to working closely together. Personalities also played a part, as did uncertainties about how USAID's policy bureau should be fitted into overall agency operations. The result was the USAID efforts to mesh policy and resources were more ad hoc than originally hoped. Later in the administration, the budget shop, strongly supported by Assistant Secretary

---

34. Conversations with all the individuals involved, January 1993–March 1994.

35. The final version of the reorganization plan, issued on October 1, 1993, touched on this issue several times, most completely on p. 7: "The Bureau for Management works closely with PPC in developing the Agency program budget. PPC [the Bureau for Policy and Program Coordination] establishes overall policy guidance and determines program priorities. In the annual budget process, operating bureaus and offices propose their resource needs and how they can best achieve the Agency's policy objectives. The Management Bureau is responsible for assembling and executing the Agency budget as part of a collaborative process, working with PPC on program-related matters. The Director of the Budget Office reports to the Assistant Administrator for Management and also serves as a key advisor to the Director of PPC." USAID General Notices, *Agency Reorganization*, USAID: Washington, D.C., October 1, 1993.

for Administration Larry E. Byrne, a powerful force in USAID's leadership, came to dominate a weak policy bureau.[36]

So long as such separatist attitudes prevail between planners and budgeters, it is unlikely that the executive branch can make the necessary changes. Next, it is essential to consider the equally important congressional part of the equation and to explore whether the prospects for improvement are better there.

# Congressional Reforms

The U.S. Congress, through the work of the Joint Committee on the Organization of Congress, recently engaged in its most thorough internal review in a generation. Chaired jointly by David Boren and Lee Hamilton, with Pete Domenici and David Dreier as vice-chairmen, this committee conducted comprehensive hearings and in late 1993 published its recommendations in separate House and Senate reports[37] (since the two houses could not agree on all particulars). The review generated several additional commentaries, some of which have already been cited.[38] This is not the place for a full-dress analysis of the committee's findings. Instead, the focus here will be on the implications for foreign affairs programs and funding. The present section begins with an issue that, although it is below the threshold for a broad-gauged study of congressional operations, is perhaps among the most important for a focus on the role of Congress in funding foreign affairs.

## Consolidate Function 150

Even without a unified executive-branch foreign affairs budget, and certainly to accompany such a change, a realignment of congressional responsi-

---

36. Details come from several senior USAID officials involved in this process, May–July and December 1995.

37. The two reports, both bearing the title *Organization of the Congress*, were issued as H. Rept. 103-413 and S. Rept. 103-215 (Washington, D.C.: GPO, 1993). Each was in two volumes. Volume 2, containing very useful background papers and summaries of testimony, was identical for each report.

38. In particular, see the two AEI/Brookings studies from the "Renewing Congress" project (cited above at note 2; and Chapter 6, note 90).

bilities to place maximum jurisdiction for Function 150 in one set of appropriations subcommittees would add much needed coherence.[39] It might even force the executive to move in the right direction. The simplest way of doing this would be to move responsibility for funding State Department and USIA operations away from the CJS subcommittees and add it to the "Foreign Ops" subcommittees. As a result, the lion's share of Function 150 would be in one place, thus allowing (it can be argued) more-considered congressional judgments to be made about trade-offs within the function.[40] To take one small example, should agricultural development activities be funded via the U.N. Food and Agricultural Organization, now under CJS jurisdiction, or via direct U.S. programs through USAID (now under Foreign Operations) and USDA (funded by the Agriculture subcommittees)? Among other things, the current approach leads to incremental budgeting, not to fundamental reassessments.

A second argument for consolidation is that it would prohibit "poaching" of foreign affairs funding to support other programs, as has happened in the past at times when the International Affairs function was not "fenced."[41] The assumption, of course, is that under the current system, if there is an open competition for resources within the CJS subcommittees, foreign affairs programs and activities will lose out; that is, State and USIA will suffer reductions in order to increase programs in Justice and Commerce. And there is such a risk. But it is misleading to assume that foreign affairs concerns would *always* lose out: the context and the specific programs in contention might well alter the outcome in favor of certain kinds of foreign affairs activities, as has happened in the past. On balance, however, the possible diversion of Function 150 resources to other purposes remains a cause for worry.

Another potential advantage would be the opportunity to reflect executive branch priorities more directly. In 1990, for example, it is widely believed that, owing to State's disinclination to weigh in on how the FY 1991 Budget Act allocations should be divided among the four sets of subcommit-

39. See Chapter 2 for the history of the current distribution of Function 150 among four sets of appropriations subcommittees.

40. Some Function 150 funding would still be handled elsewhere: about a billion dollars a year for the "Food for Peace" program would remain with the Agriculture subcommittees (a telling sign of its true purpose), and a very small amount with the Labor subcommittees. The latter could easily be added to "Foreign Ops" as well; however, these are distinct activities, and combining the rest alone would still provide significant consolidation.

41. See the discussion in Chapter 5 and Tables 3a–c, 4a–c, and (in particular) 5, showing what happens when international activities are not protected.

tees having responsibility for Function 150, too much emphasis was placed on economic support funds and on contributions to international organizations, and not enough on State operations.[42] Consolidation would in effect remove such decisions from the full Appropriations Committee and place them with the new Foreign Affairs Subcommittee, where it might be assumed that there is more real knowledge about programmatic requirements. As it is now, the division of Function 150 among multiple sets of subcommittees makes across-the-board trade-offs within the function impossible. Thus, the real allocation fight takes place within subfunctions (e.g., how to split up economic assistance) rather than between them (e.g., whether more should go to international organizations for peacekeeping or for economic assistance).

The working levels in OMB (associate directors and division chiefs for international affairs) have long advocated such a consolidation, arguing that nuts-and-bolts State Department operations, hardly the sort of programs that elicit much support, would benefit if there were one set of subcommittees. With a few exceptions, however, it has been found that State itself was not interested in a consolidated 150 presentation, either for executive branch presentations or congressional consideration.[43]

But what about the other side of the coin? If such a reform were to occur in Congress, the executive would likely be quite wary of placing almost total control of international affairs funding in the hands of only four members (the chairmen and ranking majority members of the two subcommittees). Even less inviting to some, the importance of a handful of staffers to the foreign affairs agencies would be enormous. Under the current decentralization, there are more possibilities for appeals if one or another set of subcommittees proves recalcitrant.

A somewhat related idea has been suggested from time to time by knowledgeable State and OMB staffers. Starting from the assumption that the goal

---

42. This opinion was expressed at the time in State Department budget circles. These personnel blamed the Bureau of Legislative Affairs and the D/P&R staff for not arguing the point strongly, asserting that they did not want to exacerbate relationships with the appropriators, especially on the foreign assistance side. The previous year, State had attempted to influence 302(b) allocations, only to be met by cries of outrage from the Foreign Operations subcommittees, who argued (especially Senator Robert Kasten, the ranking minority member in the Senate) that this was properly the business of Congress, not the executive. Kasten's feeling was that the administration's position disadvantaged "Foreign Ops" to the benefit of the CJS subcommittees with respect to possible funding levels.

43. James Barie, former OMB international affairs division chief, July 29, 1993. Other OMB staffers, past and present, generally confirm this view.

is to maximize funds for current Function 150 activities, the argument has been that military assistance funding should be shifted from the International Affairs function to the Defense function, where it would be a much smaller part of the whole and would therefore attract less attention. However, given the close scrutiny the military assistance account receives—recall the competition for funding to Egypt vs. Israel and to Turkey vs. Greece—it seems problematic that such a shift would necessarily increase overall resources, especially in light of recent pressures to reduce the Defense Department budget. This idea might have made more sense in the early 1980s, during the Reagan defense buildup, when the notion was most seriously discussed.

## Better Prioritizing

Consolidation of appropriations jurisdiction is not the only possible way to prioritize. On the authorizations side, the current situation is somewhat more favorable to across-the-board consideration, if only because SRFC and HIRC already have principal jurisdiction over Function 150. Although, like the appropriators, the authorizers consider various parts of the needed legislation in different subcommittees, at some stages the practice already exists whereby the larger package is drawn together at the full committee level. Foreign assistance authorization in HIRC (earlier HFAC), for example, has traditionally been considered initially by the various regional subcommittees, but the final bill has been consolidated by the full committee. Moreover, on both sides of the Capitol, the authorizing committees already provide priority listings to the two budget committees in an effort to influence the assumptions accompanying the annual budget resolutions. It should be recalled, however, that the more explicit such priorities become, the less room there is for maneuver by the currently freewheeling appropriations subcommittees. The change suggested here, therefore, would fly in the face of the incremental, "amendment by amendment" congressional style, and thus undoubtedly would be resisted. Moreover, some caution is needed when ascribing inevitably better outcomes to a process that would be structured more like that in the authorizing committees, given their painful track record described throughout this book.

## Disciplined Use of Control Devices

Except for those directly involved, the cumulative weight of the application of congressional control mechanisms (discussed in Chapter 6) generally goes unnoticed. Despite the resulting complications for administrators of foreign affairs programs and activities, there is little sympathy for bureaucrats. Amendments, reports, certifications, and other requirements imposed for essentially political reasons—to make a point, to send a message, to respond to constituency pressures, or to pay back earlier alleged transgressions—can seriously frustrate effective operations. This is not to say that many such actions, seen as obstacles by the executive branch, are unwarranted with respect to the larger public interest—only that they can impede the successful completion of actions mandated by Congress.

Nonetheless, it would be useful for Congress to exercise greater discipline in the application of such devices. The goal should be to keep those which assist legitimate oversight and constrain executive excesses or mistakes, and to eliminate those which unnecessarily hamper flexibility. It is especially necessary that the executive possess the ability to respond rapidly to changing circumstances and unanticipated crises, when time generally does not permit seeking and gaining legislative endorsement in the normal ways. One classic example has already been seen, relating to an unplanned-for and unpredictable need for funds to evacuate Americans from the Middle East in 1990, at a moment when State's small emergency account was depleted. A more flexible transfer authority would have made the solution easier. Such problems are almost inevitable with respect to disasters, humanitarian assistance, or essential, time-sensitive international peacekeeping operations.

Obviously, constraints on operational flexibility can be traced to a simple lack of trust between the branches, but some are the result of gamesmanship and a desire to teach a lesson. More explicit explanations of priorities by the executive may help to focus the issues and alleviate suspicions, but they could equally well highlight areas where Congress, once it knows the facts, may disagree. Given recent history and the general trend toward congressional assertiveness, a better climate allowing greater freedom of action will not be easy to come by. Still, the right approach to the Hill by the foreign affairs agencies could almost certainly improve the situation, and should be tried. One useful suggestion, which came from the Congressional Joint Committee's House members, was to eliminate unnecessary reporting requirements and to "sunset" all required reports unless reauthorized.[44]

In these times of intense partisanship, the kind of institutional discipline suggested here may not be in the cards. If one party controls the Congress

44. H. Rept. 103-413, recommendation 35, p. 24. No action was taken on this proposal.

and the other the presidency, it may just be too much to ask one side to ignore an opportunity to make life difficult for the other. The problem is arduous enough when the issue is *only* constitutional—the separation of powers. When partisanship, especially if mean-spirited and ideological, is added, prospects are not good. But if sound governance is the objective, rather than just winning, such discipline becomes imperative.

## Trade-offs: Flexibility vs. Protection

Another aspect of flexibility (or the lack thereof) that has come into play in recent years has to do with the GRH and especially the BEA ceilings, or "caps," on spending. The former, with its risks of sequestration, strongly discouraged add-ons, however meritorious or crucial the purpose. Even transfers were made difficult because of scorekeeping conventions which meant that different kinds of accounts were held to outlay at different rates. The practical effect was that those accounts which might be the most likely sources of emergency funding—since they funded longer-term programs and since deferred spending would not be fatal to them—produced lower spendable amounts (potential outlays) for a given transfer amount, precisely because the spending was stretched out over a longer period.

All this leads to an argument for the easier movement of funds from one account to another in order to give agencies the ability to respond more effectively to new circumstances. State, for example, has consistently sought more flexible transfer and reprogramming authority in recent years, only to be met with great skepticism, especially by the CJS appropriations subcommittees; similarly, in USAID's proposed 1993 substitute for the Foreign Assistance Act of 1961, it was hoped that limits on amounts transferable from one account to another, as well as requirements to report minuscule program changes, would be eliminated. The larger point, of course, is that changes are inevitable in a complex undertaking. A looser rein will result in better management, if the necessary trust exists.[45]

---

45. AID also hoped to develop a revised approach to notifications, freeing it from the requirement to inform Congress each time it proposed to change spending beyond minimal amounts for specific projects within an account, which for Development Assistance alone forced from 750 to 1,000 annual notifications, mostly noncontroversial (AID legislative counsel, December 1, 1993). The new approach would require notifications only for changes in Strategic Objectives, a much broader grouping than individual projects. As of mid-1996, though, only modest progress had been made in convincing appropriators to accept the new, less restrictive approach (AID senior legislative affairs officer, February 8, 1995, and May 1996).

Flexibility, however, is not always desirable. It depends on who has it. For example, the possibility of moving funds from International Affairs to Domestic Programs, as the CJS subcommittees did in the pre-BEA period of the late 1980s, is obviously easier when there are *no* caps to contend with. The FY 1994 CJS Act, the first to be passed after the demise of the separate category caps of the BEA which were in effect the three previous fiscal years,[46] showed a return to the same pattern (with an estimated $320 million proposed by the administration for International Affairs being moved to domestic accounts in the Commerce and Justice departments, primarily by the CJS subcommittees).[47]

Thus, the greater appropriations flexibility before 1990 and after 1993 was not necessarily a blessing for the foreign affairs agencies. As I have argued above, one way of addressing this problem would be to lodge as much of Function 150 as possible in one pair of appropriations subcommittees. It would then be harder to move funding from 150 to other functions. Greater transfer/reprogramming authority, already mentioned, is usually seen by the executive branch as a particular boon, since the executive and not Congress must formally initiate such actions. Even here, however, flexibility is not always desirable—as, for instance, when, without it, all programs must be sequestered while, with it, politically strong accounts (e.g., inspectors general) might escape with few if any cuts and others might be forced to take a disproportionate "hit." In any event, the level of skepticism about greater executive branch capability to move funds without legislation will inevitably continue; such authority will continue to be seen by many in Congress as infringing on their legislative prerogatives. Unless and until there is greater mutual trust—not likely anytime soon—this situation will not change.

## Conserving Member Time to Encourage Focus

Reference has already been made to the efforts of the Joint Committee on the Organization of Congress. What is striking about the proposals made

46. It will be recalled that the three categories were Domestic Discretionary Spending, Defense, and International Affairs.

47. The $320 million figure is derived from Table 4c, by comparing appropriated amounts with the administration request and then comparing the result with what would have been appropriated had each department or account been subjected to the same 6.1 percent reduction by which the *total* amount appropriated in the bill was less than the total request. Thus, State received almost $308 million less, USIA slightly more than $11 million less, and related agencies about $1 million less than would have been the case with a proportional cut. Although

to and by it, especially those pertaining to the authorization, appropriations, and budget processes, is how many are keyed to the problem of overload and the felt need to reduce pressures on members' time. Inevitably, of course, many of the changes nominally directed to this laudable purpose would result in redistributions of power, both within the two houses and between Congress and the executive. Many of the reactions to these ideas are most easily understood in the context of likely winners and losers. Two broad areas of reform intended to address the overload issue have to do with (1) the frequency of congressional budgeting activities and (2) the structure and organization of the legislative branch.

## Biennial, Not Annual, Budgets

Perhaps no reform proposal has received so much recent attention as that of moving from annual to biennial budgets, with corresponding changes in the budget, authorization, and appropriations processes. This has been advocated by the vice-president's NPR, outside experts, and some witnesses before the congressional joint committee as a partial solution to the overload problem. Proponents see annual budgeting as resulting in the inability by Congress to spend adequate time on important issues of public policy and prioritizing or to carry out effective oversight of executive branch activities.[48] The theory is that biennial budgets would make both executive branch budget preparation and congressional consideration less frenetic and would allow time for more effective review and assessment.[49]

Advocates of biennial budgeting usually argue along the lines of Senator Wendell Ford, a longtime supporter:

> A 2-year budget cycle not only provides for more long-term planning on all levels of government and eliminates redundancies in the budget process, it also provides much needed time for program oversight—oversight that can help prevent another savings and loan cri-

---

this figure is a construct, it is given some validity by a conversation I had with a senior OMB official who estimated, on October 7, 1993 (even before the bill was enacted into law), that the switch from international to domestic accounts in the absence of internal caps for FY 1994 would be on the order of $300 million.

48. See NPR, p. 17, as well as Stephen Barr and Eric Pianin, "Two-Year U.S. Budget Is Pushed: Gore Group's Draft Back Funding Limits, Civil Service Changes," *Washington Post*, August 31, 1993. The latter source accurately predicts the reactions, pro and con, that this proposal generated.

49. NPR, p. 17. See also the joint committee testimony below.

sis, oversight that can target instances of waste or abuse, oversight that can save the taxpayers dollars.[50]

Representative of thoughtful opposition to biennial budgeting was Congressman Anthony Beilenson, a member of the House rules and budget committees and the chairman of a task force on the budget process between 1982 and 1984, to which he refers:

> [W]e decided not to pursue a 2-year plan of any sort because budget circumstances changed so quickly that we believed that a 2-year budget plan and/or appropriations bills would be outdated by the second year as, in fact, in reality they always seem to be. We felt that the likely outcome of having a 2-year process would be doing an updated budget resolution and very detailed supplemental appropriations bills in the second year, in which case there is no great point in having a biennial process.
>
> My own feeling is that the same argument against biennial budgeting holds true today. However, I do want to note that the task force report encouraged authorization committees to authorize programs for multiyear periods, which I still think is a very good way of reducing the amount of legislation and workload . . . and giving committees more time for oversight, which I think is something we need to do a great deal more of and a great deal better than we currently do.[51]

It is highly doubtful, though, whether many in Congress, in particular the powers on the appropriations committees, would be willing to give up the opportunity to exert their influence on an annual basis.[52] Many authoriza-

50. Wendell H. Ford, *Testimony Before the Joint Committee on the Organization of Congress, April 1, 1993*, Committee Print, p. 3. The joint committee deliberations were published as separate committee prints, unnumbered, for each date. This and subsequent citations are from these individual prints, unless specifically noted otherwise. The hearings, however, are summarized in vol. 2 of the two joint committee reports, cited above (note 37).

51. Beilinson testimony, March 23, 1993, pp. 4–5.

52. Consider the testimony of Senator Robert Byrd and Representative William Natcher, the two appropriations chairmen, before the joint committee. Both strongly opposed biennial appropriations. Byrd said, among other things: "I think that if we have a two-year appropriations, the bureaucrats downtown . . . would be very much less likely to follow and carry out the intent of Congress if they knew that they weren't going to have to come back for two years." Natcher argued that there would be more work than proponents realized and that oversight activities would be undercut. See Eric Pianin, "Gore Panel Enters Political Minefield on Budget: Proposed Biennial Approach Is Seen as Encroaching on Domain of Powerful Legislators," *Washington Post*, September 5, 1993.

tions are already multiyear (the Foreign Relations Bill, a subject of discussion throughout this book, for example, authorizes annual amounts, but does so two years at a time), and the 1990, 1993, and 1995–96 budget negotiations moved in the direction of multiyear budget targets. What is clear is that the annual appropriations cycle invites an imperfect match between evaluation of the success of programs and activities and the subsequent amounts appropriated for them. On the other hand, biennial appropriations would clearly run the risk of being out of date during the second year. Even so, there is some appeal in the idea of treating the needed outyear revisions by exception, rather than starting over even when there are no changes.

What is striking is that the divisions on this issue were institutional rather than partisan. The leadership and key individuals on the authorization and budget committees tended to favor biennial budgeting, while the appropriators clearly did not.[53]

One intermediate proposal, by the AEI/Brookings "Renewing Congress" project, might improve matters without stumbling on the difficulties of an across-the-board biennial budget. While arguing that appropriations need to be annual, the authors also conclude that

> the budget process should be performed on a two-year cycle, with basic fiscal policy guidelines set only once per Congress, in its first year.
>
> Biennial budget resolutions and biennial reconciliation would reduce the time devoted to budgeting and free time for other legislative and oversight activities. We are less persuaded that biennial appropriations make sense.[54]

What to make of all this? Most probably, the impact for foreign affairs would cut both ways. For longer-term programs, such as foreign buildings

53. For example, Senators Domenici, Boren, Kassebaum, Nunn, and William V. Roth, as well as former Senator (and a Budget Committee ranking member) Henry Bellmon, were advocates. So too were House Majority Leader Gephardt and the Democratic and Republican Freshman Caucuses. In opposition besides Byrd, Natcher, and Beilenson were virtually all members of the appropriations committees of both parties in both houses. For a more complete list, see the full hearings, the Pianin article cited in note 52 above, and Eric Pianin, "OMB Opens Campaign for a Biennial Budget: Proposal Is Part of 'Reinventing Government,' " *Washington Post*, October 8, 1993. OMB Director Panetta had been a longtime proponent of biennial budgeting, going back to his experience on the House Budget Committee.

54. Mann and Ornstein, *First Report of the Renewing Congress Project*, p. 46.

and major foreign assistance programs, the greater certainty of a longer budget cycle would be an operational plus. And assuming the absence of "artificial" fences, which as we have seen tend to protect Function 150, biennial budgeting might provide fewer chances for appropriations subcommittees to divert funds to domestic or other purposes.[55]

On the other hand, given their lack of relevance to the constituency concerns of most members, unexpected but important Function 150 funding requirements might be especially difficult to accommodate in the off years through supplementals or BEA emergency provisions, except in the case of true emergencies where there is a broad consensus for immediate action.[56] Finally, it is hard to know what the impact on oversight would be. Authorization bills for State and USIA are already on a two-year cycle, so here presumably there would be little change: oversight would continue to be idiosyncratic rather than systematic, assuming no other changes. While it is possible that the appropriators would carry out more oversight if more time were available, for them the issue of whether to provide funding or to increase or decrease it generally drives oversight; it is even possible that a biennial cycle could result in *less* appropriations oversight!

In sum, it seems rather clear that while there might be some advantages in reducing the work load associated with annual appropriations legislation, biennial budgeting is not a cure-all for the problems of meshing the foreign policy needs of the country with the funding to carry out associated

55. The term "artificial" was the characterization of Chairman Neal Smith of the House CJS Appropriations Subcommittee, discussing the FY 1994 CJS bill with State Department officials. He felt that the BEA fences for fiscal years 1991–93 forced him to fund his part of Function 150 at higher than warranted levels. However, since they were arrived at by exactly the same processes that limits on specific functions have been arrived at under budget legislation in effect since 1974, they merely placed additional, aggregated caps at a higher level of generality. This information about Smith's views comes from a conversation I had on October 14, 1993, with a State Department congressional affairs staffer present at the discussion.

56. A case in point was the inability of the department and the administration, in February 1994, to convince Congress that $670 million in unanticipated peacekeeping costs warranted "emergency" treatment under the BEA (which would have meant no offsetting cuts were needed) at the same time that an extra $1.2 billion to pay for drawdown of the U.S. troops in the Somali peacekeeping force was granted this treatment. Bringing U.S. troops home was seen, apparently, as an imperative; vaguer peacekeeping requirements were not. This business became part of the Emergency Supplemental Appropriations Bill (to fund earthquake recovery in California), to which, inevitably, various other items desired by members were added. See Helen Dewar, "Congress Approves Quake Relief Bill in Time for Recess," *Washington Post*, February 12, 1994; and "Congress Passes Measure Providing $8.6 Billion for Quake Relief," *New York Times*, February 12, 1994. Later in the year, as noted above, cuts in foreign assistance provided sufficient headroom in Function 150 for the offsets needed, and so the $670 million for peacekeeping was appropriated.

programs. And while both the House and the Senate members endorsed biennial budgeting (including biennial budget resolutions, biennial appropriations, and at least two-year authorizations) in their joint committee reports,[57] strong opposition by key appropriators doomed the idea, at least for the moment.[58]

## Radical Changes in Jurisdictions

Another series of proposals to the joint committee concerned process and organization rather than timing. The future for these ideas is even more problematic than for biennial budgeting, because they would affect power relationships even more directly. Once again, the nominal starting point was the perceived need by proponents to reduce overload and allow more time to do what is most important.

One example of the overload problem was referred to throughout the series of joint committee hearings, most often by Senator Boren. After noting the complications for oversight when "you have a government agency reporting to 20 different subcommittees or 30 different subcommittees," because there are more than 30 committees and subcommittees between the two houses, Boren moved on to what many consider the crux of the problem:

> Part of it is because we're members of far too many committees. The average Member of the Senate is a Member of 12 committees and subcommittees. We go up to a high of 23 with various Members having waivers. . . . [S]ome witnesses . . . suggested that if we could really reduce—start with the processes of reducing the number of committees that Members can serve on and stopping the waiver process—and then go on from that, we would find probably, that a lot of committees—subcommittees especially—would become under-populated once you really had to choose between the things that really matter to you—and then trim back significantly.[59]

57. H. Rept. 103-413, pp. 4–5, 18–19; S. Rept. 103-215, pp. 13–14.

58. See, for example, "Inside Congress: Congressional Reform," CQ *Weekly Report* 52 (January 8, 1994): 6; and Richard E. Cohen, "Congressional Chronicle: Talk—and more Talk—About Reform," *National Journal* 26 (January 1, 1994): 33.

59. Senator David L. Boren, joint committee hearing, April 1, 1993, p. 5. This statement was made during an exchange with Senator Wendell Ford, in the course of the latter's testimony.

Thus, limiting the number of committees on which an individual could serve—and there were endless suggestions about how this might be done—was the most frequently heard proposal and, at least in the abstract, the most appealing to members.

More radical suggestions would move directly to the idea of reducing the number of committees themselves, which of course would result in fewer places to assign members. Most prominent among such proposals was Senate Resolution 13, whose primary sponsor was Senator Nancy Kassebaum (and similar legislation applying to the House was promoted by Representative Robert Walker). Kassebaum's explanation of her plan (which by late 1993 was cosponsored by thirteen of her colleagues, including Senators Nunn, Lott, and Kerry) is illuminating and worth quoting at length:

> The legislation would consolidate the existing three-step spending process that we now have into two steps. Today, the spending cycle begins . . . with the Budget Committee exercising de facto control over policy priorities . . . by drafting and enforcing the budget resolution. The cycle ends with the Appropriations Committee resetting priorities within budget parameters. Sandwiched in the middle are the authorizing committees, whose influence on spending priorities has become increasingly limited.
>
> We are proposing to merge the authorizing and appropriations process into one step for allocating funds within the overall budget limits. . . .
>
> I think the current system is redundant. How often do we waste time repeating the same debate—once during the authorization and again during appropriation. This does nothing to improve the deliberation of this body. . . .
>
> The Budget Committee would be replaced by a Leadership Committee . . . comprised of the Chairmen and Ranking Members of all other committees. So this is a body that would set priorities . . . and be responsible. . . . The individual Chairman and Ranking Members then would enforce the budget limits through their individual committees, allocating resources within limits that have been set by the Leadership Committee. They would judge both the merit and the priority of individual programs—functions now divided between the authorizing and the appropriating committee.[60]

60. Kassebaum testimony, March 16, 1993, p. 2. Some in Congress were not so squeamish

Although this plan was seen by some as an attack on the appropriators by beleaguered authorizers, in fact it is better seen as a merger of the two processes and of the committees that now carry them out. There are critics, however, who think that without separate appropriations committees, there would be insufficient checks on spending. The usual justification for this argument, so frequently cited on the floor by appropriators, is that since 1945 appropriators have provided some $200 billion less than has been requested by various presidents.[61] Kassebaum's response was that while it is not the appropriators' fault that the deficit has skyrocketed, the current process is not efficient: "It is wrong to characterize our proposal as an attack on the Appropriations Committee. Rather, it is an attack on an unworkable division of labor that purports to have one group set policy while another spends money and, in fact, leaves nobody accountable."[62]

Kassebaum is probably right. Wags have argued that, of the three processes—budget, authorization, and appropriations—there is room only for two: take your pick!

At the same time, it is likely that the leadership of both houses will continue to see the appropriations process as the last, best hope for action in cases of gridlock, because of the government's primal need for funding. However sloppy the process, *there will be appropriations*—if not through the usual thirteen bills, then through CRs or omnibus bills. As one centrally positioned appropriations staffer told me, "For better or for worse, the leadership needs the appropriators. It's hard to get things done otherwise."[63]

Even if merging the authorization and appropriations committees has little chance of success—current interests of chairmen and ranking members on both sides would come into play as well as more philosophical considerations—simplification is very seductive. Another alternative might be to merge the appropriations and budget processes, although this possibility has received almost no public attention. There is the risk that this tack would be

---

about admitting that they were in favor of abolishing the appropriations committees. See, for example, the discussion of Representative Dana Rohrabacher's plan in *National Journal* 25 (March 20, 1993): 703; as well as Kenneth J. Cooper, "GOP Freshmen Seek to Abolish Key Panel as Part of House Overhaul," *Washington Post*, March 31, 1993. The latter piece was a summary of the proposal that would be made to the joint committee by the Republican House Freshmen on April 1, 1993.

61. See Richard Munson, "Deforming Congress: Why Those Capitol Hill Budget Reforms Could Cost You Plenty," *Washington Post*, September 5, 1993.

62. Senator Nancy Kassebaum, "Taking Exception: Cardinal Rule for Congress," *Washington Post*, September 13, 1993, responding to Munson, "Deforming Congress."

63. HAC subcommittee clerk, July 28, 1993.

more parochial in the priorities it would set, compared to the choices made by a Kassebaum-style leadership committee; but, given the current role of the full appropriations committees in translating the budget resolution levels into allocations for the appropriations subcommittees, it might be less of a change and thus more acceptable.

It is undeniable that the interaction between appropriators and authorizers may be more difficult than that between either of these and the budget committees. Many of the episodes already presented in this book turn on the former relationship, and many witnesses before the joint committee dealt explicitly with this problem. Among the most eloquent was Representative George Brown, then chairman of the House Science, Space, and Technology Committee and a long-term critic of appropriators for exceeding their briefs:

> There is little doubt that the historical tension between the Authorization and Appropriations Committees has worsened in the past decade. Witnesses before this committee have argued that much of the tension is due to unresolvable policy differences, or will disappear with unified Government in which the Congress and executive branch are controlled by the same party, or that the situation is correctable with more aggressive legislative action on the part of the authorizer[s].
>
> [But] . . . the problem is severe and not as easily solved as some have suggested. . . . Let me suggest these simple proposals. . . .
>
> First and most importantly, Members in both Houses should serve either on authorization committees or Appropriations Committees, but not both. . . . [F]undamental imbalances are created when Members in the Senate are permitted to serve on both committees. Inevitably, members will prefer to legislate an appropriations bill or the accompanying report which by their nature under the rules of both Houses are [more] protected from debate, amendment and perfection than the corresponding authorization bills.
>
> And, secondly, although the House has rules to prevent unauthorized appropriations and legislation in appropriations bills, the rules are routinely waived. . . . Waivers to these rules should be allowed only in extraordinary circumstances and only with the concurrence of the authorizing committee. . . .
>
> And, third and last, I believe that all reasonable changes should be

considered which would require enactment of multi-year authorization legislation prior to enactment of appropriations legislation.

[A]lthough there are times when policy differences preclude action on authorization legislation, in many cases authorization bills languish simply because it is more convenient for Members to deal with policy in appropriations bills and in report language. *But if the Houses cannot find the time and will to deal with authorization bills, then the authorization and appropriations processes should be compressed into a single step, and I will strongly support such action.*[64]

Senator Richard Lugar, a member of the joint committee and chairman of the SFRC in the early 1980s, provided a foreign affairs example of the authorization–appropriation difficulties during the same session of the joint committee:

My experience as Chairman of the Foreign Relations Committee came this way: We finally got a foreign aid bill, the first time that it had occurred in a decade. . . . It was so surprising to the Appropriations Committee people who dealt with foreign aid that they had gone about . . . rewriting the bill as they usually do. I went over to see my good friend, Mark Hatfield, who . . . was Chairman of the Appropriations Committee. I said Mark, this has changed; you know, we have authorized money. You ought to read what we said. And that is what we want done. And there is going to be a fight if it is not done. Mark was really helpful.

But that was the last time the Foreign Relations Committee passed foreign aid bills. The foreign aid people on appropriations had gone back to their old tricks; and, essentially, they write the bill. And many administrations like it. . . . That way, [they] don't have to deal with two committees. You can simply go to the bottom line, the conference of last resort, the final night and write in what you want.[65]

---

64. Brown testimony, March 16, 1993, pp. 24–25, emphasis added. Editing as in original.

65. Comments by Lugar during Kassebaum testimony, March 16, 1993, p. 11. Lugar apparently forgot that one additional Foreign Assistance Authorization Bill passed, in 1985 for FY 1986 and 1987 (P.L. 99-83, August 8, 1985), but his general point about the tendency to operate solely on the basis of appropriations with respect to foreign assistance is correct. Lugar went on to express his distaste for this "final night" approach to legislation and to "mumbo jumbo" reconciliation (p. 12).

Lugar is probably right about the attractiveness to the executive branch of dealing just with the appropriators. Given the proclivity for the authorizing committees to play "secretary of state for a day," this alternative must seem less complicated. However, as also noted, when the executive becomes embroiled in authorizer/appropriator disputes, as happened over the Foreign Relations Authorization Act for FY 1990–91 during late 1989, the tactic becomes less attractive.

There may be another way to deal with this problem of overlap and turf battles between authorizers and appropriators, short of merging the two processes. Senator Barbara Mikulski, an Appropriations Subcommittee chair, testifying two days after Lugar and Brown, made it clear she did not favor the Kassebaum proposal for a merger, but did agree that clarification was needed: "I believe we can accomplish her same objectives, which I support, through selectively streamlining the authorizing process. . . . [T]here should be one authorization committee and one appropriations committee, one authorization for each major agency and one appropriations subcommittee linked to this. . . . [C]ongressional oversight has become scattered and the potential for real problems develop very quickly."[66] Presumably, Mikulski would find attractive the idea of putting responsibility for all of Function 150 in one set of appropriations committees, with the parallel authorizing function in HIRC and the SFRC.

Proposals for reducing the number of committees extend beyond merging authorization and appropriations, for example, to consolidating authorization committees in a way somewhat parallel to the Mikulski notion just cited. Senator John Glenn, then chairing the Government Affairs Committee, found the committee and subcommittee structure of the Senate to have so much overlap between the budget, authorizing, and appropriations processes that "it literally becomes legislative WPA. We're just making work for ourselves, and unnecessarily."[67] Glenn believes that to avoid redundancy and reconsideration of the same issues over and over, restructuring and simplification are called for: "[T]his would be a general upheaval, and I understand that, but I think five or possibly six major committees could take in most of the functions of Government. For instance, what if we had a Department of Human Resources, that took in all of those functions; a Department of Natural Resources; a Department of National Defense; another one

66. Mikulski testimony, March 18, 1993, p. 12.
67. Glenn testimony, June 24, 1993. Reprinted in *Interbranch Relations*, S. Hrg. 103-122, p. 62. Glenn thoughtfully explores many of the options discussed here.

of Economic Affairs; of International Relations; and perhaps a sixth of Rules and Administration?"[68]

Glenn thinks this kind of functional structure ideally would be applicable to the executive as well as to Congress, but would at least start with the latter. He recognizes the problem that fewer committees and subcommittees mean fewer chairmanships: "[O]ver in the Senate, it's become almost a custom that you try to have a subcommittee for each new Senator coming in. We don't quite meet that, but we don't miss it very far."[69]

There can be less radical fixes than either merging authorizing and appropriating committees or massively reducing the number of committees. Some have argued that simplification of congressional processes, even without any modification of committee structures—for example, by recasting and simplifying the rules of each chamber and then adhering to them—could go a long way toward providing what is needed. In this vein, if it were possible to move authorizing committees out of the money process, and the appropriators out of the legislative business, the roles of each set of committees would be clarified and there would be less duplication and fewer turf battles of the kinds described throughout this book. Under such an approach, the authorizers might provide permanent authorization for agencies and programs, but would not set program levels, the area where the authorizers are alleged to conflict with appropriators. The latter, by the same token, would not change the parameters of programs or create new ones. Whether the authorizers, especially in today's climate, would be willing to go this far is questionable, however.

In the end, the joint committee reports bowed to the intractability of the committee issue. They did not propose major jurisdictional changes, the merger of authorizing and appropriations committees, or a reduction in the number of committees (although they did each propose a modest reduction in the number of subcommittees). Instead, they attempted to limit the number of assignments individual members might have and, in the Senate, to limit chairmanships, though not in a way that would preclude the problem of the same senator serving as chairman of both an authorizing committee and the parallel appropriations subcommittee. Despite the constant theme of overload, in the end both houses were reluctant to give up multiple committee memberships and greater chances to have a chairmanship.[70] Again

68. Ibid., p. 60. Presumably, Glenn meant committees, not departments.
69. Ibid., p. 61.
70. For recommendations about subcommittee reduction and the membership provisions, see H. Rept. 103-413, pp. 5–6 and 9–10, and S. Rept. 103-215, pp. 4, 7–9, 11–12.

fragmentation was shown to serve the interests of individual members, if not of Congress as an institution. As will be discussed below, in the Republican 104th Congress there were some limited reductions in committees and subcommittees, following joint committee recommendations to some extent.

## Scorekeeping Again

Two additional changes in the way Congress addresses foreign affairs funding, both in the area of scorekeeping, warrant consideration. Although of less import than those discussed earlier, each of these changes has some appeal, at least in most parts of the executive branch.

First, assuming that there continue to be both authorization and appropriations committees, the tendency of the former to want to demonstrate fiscal responsibility (and, as will be shown, to constrain the freedom of action of appropriators) by scoring authorization bills as if they were appropriations should be reexamined. To repeat, statutory scorekeeping requirements apply only to appropriations measures; scoring authorization as well can mean that some funds allocated to foreign affairs cannot be used. To take a simple example, suppose that the 602(a) and (b) process allocates $5 billion to the CJS subcommittees for Function 150. Assuming these subcommittees decide to follow this budget resolution guidance (no longer mandatory for FY 1994 and later years), they retain the flexibility to appropriate the total as they see fit (so long as authorization exists or the requirement for it has been waived), dividing it among all their 150 accounts to fund the full range of State Department and USIA activities. However, there must be sufficient authorization for each account or line item, as well as for the total appropriated. And that is where a problem can arise. If the authorizers provide $400 million for account (a) and $600 million for account (b), then the appropriators cannot increase the appropriation for (a) to $500 million, even if they decide that (b) should be limited to $500 million; the best they could do would be to use $400 million for (a). If they resolve that (b) should not be higher than $500 million then $100 million of the allocation would not be used.

This outcome could mean a major resource loss for foreign affairs. The traditional way of avoiding this problem would be for the authorizers to provide sufficient authorizing "headroom" to cover any amount likely to be appropriated or even to authorize "such amounts as may be necessary" for an account, a formula often used in the past. If the first approach were followed, however, the total authorized would be well above the budget resolution allocation, assuming that all accounts were treated this way, leaving the appropriators to make final choices; and if the second applied, the authorization bill could not be scored at all, and the appropriators would be entirely in charge. There is no easy answer, but the problem can be mitigated if the authorizers and appropriators are in close touch and arrive at common figures early enough in the process to ensure that the two pieces of legislation match up in the amounts provided for each account.

The other scorekeeping problem, that of a mismatch between budget authority levels and outlay amounts, may be virtually impossible to solve, so long as *annual* measurements of efforts to reduce the federal deficit are a political imperative. The source of this problem, of course, is the need, on the one hand, to know the total dollar cost of a project or of operating an agency and, on the other, to know how much is projected to be spent each year. Because outlays "lag" from one year to the next, it not infrequently happens that outlays, owing to prior-year spending decisions, will be so high as to force new current-year budget authority to be reduced because otherwise outlays would exceed the limits. Under current rules, the appropriators have no choice but to do so, thus distorting spending patterns over time. What is clear, moreover, is that scorekeeping needs to be more transparent, better understood, and less arcane and that the process must be codified so that the rules are more widely understood. Arguably, the best course of action would be to pay less attention to this year's BA figures and to scrutinize both current-year and outyear outlays more closely. Foreign affairs, like all categories, would benefit from such an approach.

# Nontraditional Approaches: Capital Budgeting, Asset Management, and Innovation Funds

A final set of innovations, which would have to be accepted by both branches, would recognize that there are many kinds of federal spending, with very different short- and long-term implications. Generically, these proposals attempt to take advantage of the differences between spending for current operations and spending for infrastructure or investment purposes, to add flexibility, and to stretch scarce resources. They would also require greater trust between the branches.

Some would take certain kinds of activities "off budget," funding them in ways that do not require appropriations. Generally, executive agencies and occasionally their congressional supporters have found these approaches more appealing than have OMB or the budget committees.

Under *capital budgeting* proposals, operating expense accounts and investment accounts would be handled separately. As one proponent of this approach explained to the joint committee,

> [W]e really have no idea how much we are borrowing to run the day-to-day operations of the Government . . . as compared to those things in which we are investing—highways, bridges, airports, water and sewer systems. We make no differentiation. . . . Other subsets of Government and almost every business recognizes that you have got to make some differentiation between what it costs to operate your business or your government and what you are investing in the future. Capital budgeting makes that recognition.[71]

Some advocates of capital budgeting would make further distinctions. For example, one possibility is that the federal budget would have to be balanced for operating accounts, but the government could borrow for investment purposes (i.e., for the capital projects accounts).[72] And under some plans, only the amount to be expended in a given year would be scored. Under current procedures relating to credit reform in the 1990 BEA, for example, the entire cost has to be counted in the initial year, making attractive techniques such as lease-purchase virtually impossible: "The deficit in some sense . . . is distorted now because capital expenditures are in effect expenses all in the year in which they are authorized and appropriated."[73] As a consequence, "[W]hat our current budget system is doing is forcing us, because we're in an annualized outlay budget, not to consider the benefits of purchase versus lease versus other forms of ownership and use. And so a capital budget gives us the tool to make those financial decisions."[74]

71. Representative William F. Clinger, Jr., testimony, March 18, 1993, p. 25.
72. Representative Robert E. Wise, Jr., testimony, March 18, 1993, p. 26. Senator Paul Sarbanes, in his February 1995 comments to a group of foreign exchange students (noted in the Introduction), made the same point. He also argued that a significant yet unrecognized part of the federal deficit problem, the root cause of so much pressure to adopt a balanced budget amendment at that time, was the inclusion of major capital items. He argued that they should not be considered as part of the deficit, but rather as investments.
73. Clinger testimony, p. 33. See also the testimony and written statements of Representatives William Orton and Christopher Cox at the same hearing (pp. 35–51, 78–97).
74. Orton testimony, p. 41.

In foreign affairs, an obvious application would be the acquisition of new facilities overseas where, as noted, problems of either full or piecemeal funding have been exacerbated by credit reform. Lease-purchase, especially during conditions of uncertainty (e.g., installations in the former Soviet republics), is preferable either to renting over an extended period without purchase possibilities or to launching major construction or full purchase when long-term needs are unclear.

Capital budgeting as described so far would still be on budget, although under the plans proposed funding for capital projects would be considered differently for purposes of scoring (and for controlling their impact on the deficit). There is a more radical approach that has had some recent currency in State: *asset management.* It would go another step, taking certain programs, basically in the foreign real-estate and buildings area, off budget for practical purposes and making them self-contained. This approach, if exploited, would have taken advantage of the fact that the department owns properties in some capitals—Tokyo and Berlin in particular—that have appreciated geometrically in value because of their prime locations in superinflated real-estate markets. If some of these properties were to be sold intelligently, some believe, it would be possible to obtain replacements for a small fraction of the amounts received. The rest could be invested, and the proceeds used to finance the foreign buildings account, rather than relying on annual appropriations. For example, if it were possible to generate $250 million a year (which a $5 billion account with a 5 percent return would do, not a farfetched premise), that alone would exceed the average annual funding for construction over the past two decades. Timing is important: the Tokyo real-estate market collapse in the 1990s made this idea much less attractive there than earlier, but new opportunities will no doubt present themselves.

A possible alternative to outright sale, actually proposed by a commercial consortium, would have had the United States allow two high-rise buildings to be constructed on a portion of the land occupied by U.S. family housing in Tokyo, with one replacing lost housing and the other being used for commercial leasing. The United States would also have received some $200 million annually in rental fees and would have gained title to the office high-rise after twenty-five years. The attractiveness of this alternative to selling the property outright was obvious. Necessary funding for the FBO account would still be forthcoming, while retaining the entire property and avoiding having such a large sum made available all at once would prevent its becoming a target for diversion for deficit reduction or for other spending purposes.[75] While nothing that grandiose proved possible, FBO's upgraded real-estate division continues to explore opportunities to sell unneeded property assets in order to generate funds for needed construction.[76] Recent examples include sale of the DCM residence in Kuala Lumpur for $6 million, with a replacement possible at $500,000 and the profit being available for other needs; the sale of surplus properties in Germany to pay for a new embassy in Berlin; and the disposition of little-used property in Bangkok to generate needed funds for housing upgrades in Tokyo.[77]

There are still other creative approaches. One, somewhat similar to capital budgeting but in theory available for broader purposes, is the *innovation capital fund,* sometimes called a "revolving capital investment fund." The NPR, for example, recommended that USAID should work with OMB to establish such a fund to provide the resources quickly needed to improve its information and financial-management system capabilities.[78] Deficiencies in these areas were widely acknowledged by both the executive branch and Congress, but most thought that the needed resources simply could not be found. NPR suggested a variety of means to skirt this issue: (1) retain cost savings from efficiency measures in an innovation fund account and use them for specific projects; (2) make across-the-board cuts to initiate such a fund, then replenish those accounts initially cut with the savings that result from the improved systems; (3) obtain authority to borrow innovation funds from program accounts, paying back the loan with interest from the savings of the new systems; (4) request a separate appropriation or emergency supplemental appropriation to provide seed money for a capital fund, with the principal ultimately being repaid to the Treasury through payments from the end users of the innovations. Each of these approaches entails some difficulties, but following general business practices of borrowing for capital investment with an obligation to repay would increase financial

75. I was a participant in some of the State Department meetings at which these various options were discussed (1988–91). Neither deal was actually made, in part because of the decline of the Tokyo real-estate market and in part because of fears that the political risks of trying to retain use of the capital generated were too great.

76. Some of the problems with asset management came from within the U.S. government. State and Treasury at one point differed about whether or when to sell Tokyo property, and the GAO, after the fact, questioned why sales had not been made while the market was high. See James Morrison, "Embassy Row: State's Real Estate," *Washington Times,* May 2, 1995.

77. Details here come from a senior FBO official, January 24, 1995.

78. Recommendation AID05, "Agency for International Development," in *Accompanying Report of the National Performance Review* (Washington, D.C.: Office of the Vice-President, September 1993), pp. 31–35. Because of clearance delays in the White House, this report was not made public until July 1994.

management flexibility. In the USAID example, OMB vetoed submitting any of these options for congressional consideration, although some additional funds for the same purpose were requested in the FY 1996 budget submission.[79]

One final possibility has received considerable attention not only for foreign affairs activities but for a diverse range of government undertakings: viz., *retention of user fees* and charges to help fund that part of the government providing the services used. At several times during the 1980s, for example, State sought the capability to retain a specific portion of the substantial fees it earns from issuing passports and visas each year to fund modernization and automation of the systems used to produce and verify those documents. In each case, OMB declined to approve such innovations; historically it likes taking items off budget no more than the appropriators.[80] Yet the notion that users of specialized services provided by the government should pay for them and that the fees collected should go in the first instance to paying the costs for those services, is appealing. This idea was advocated by the NPR for a number of government services, though not explicitly for any provided by the foreign affairs agencies.[81] With OMB casting a blind eye to the proceedings, State managed, in 1993–94, to obtain authorizations for several activities of this kind, including the retention of fees for commercial services under controlled conditions, for certain categories of nonimmigrant visas, and for provision of foreign language services such as translation and interpretation to other federal agencies.[82] There is likely to be greater movement in this direction in the future, if ways can be found to satisfy Congress (particularly appropriators) that they will have sufficient oversight over the funds earned and expended by the government.

79. The NPR recommendation was AID05.01, which may be found on p. 34 of "Agency for International Development" (ibid.).

80. Some experts think that if such an arrangement were in place and the funds were used for system improvements, fewer people would slip unnoticed through the checking system. In light of the fact that the alleged leader of the group responsible for the World Trade Center bombing should have been excluded from the United States, and managed to enter partly because of antiquated verification systems (see Chapter 6), the idea has become more attractive.

81. See the NPR report, *Creating a Government that Works Better & Costs Less*, for a listing of recommendations for all agencies, pp. 134–53 and 160–68.

82. These provisions are found in secs. 136, 140, and 193, respectively, of P.L. 103-236, April 30, 1994. In the FY 1996 CJS appropriation, building on this authorization history, fee retention for these purposes was in fact granted, with OMB acquiescence, and was retained in the FY 1997 appropriation. The FY 1998 presidential budget submission sought authority for $595 million in fee retentions. Because appropriated funding would be reduced by the same amount, some in State thought this was risky, given the possibility of shortfalls in fees collected, with no way of making up the difference.

The devices and approaches discussed in this section, all of which share some potential for adding flexibility to the funding of foreign affairs programs and activities, may seem mundane, sometimes technical, and essentially unrelated to great constitutional issues. Yet they are all a part of the total picture. That such innovative approaches are not used more widely draws us back to the central point: Congress does not trust the executive to spend properly funds over which Congress cannot, if it chooses, exercise substantial oversight and control. Significant changes here seem likely to occur only if a compact between the branches can be orchestrated.

# Congressional Reforms in the 104th Congress: So What?

In the end, the voluminous work of the Joint Committee on the Organization of Congress, which provided much of the substance for the present chapter, had almost no direct impact. Following publication of the separate House and Senate reports at the end of 1993, the intention was for each house to conduct hearings and present formal legislative proposals. To assist in this process, Ornstein and Mann issued a third "Renewing Congress" report in March 1994, attempting to synthesize what had been proposed with an eye to what was politically possible.[83] Their advice was essentially ignored. The Democratic leadership in both houses proved to be uninterested in the proposals—despite clear signs that the public was becoming disgusted with congressional operations and mores (e.g., exemptions from laws applying everywhere else). Even from the beginning, Mann noted, "it was clear that the leadership had absolutely zero interest in forming a new joint committee."[84]

To be sure, there were some modest changes in the House during the 103rd Congress, but none addressing the proposals noted above in this chapter. Four select committees were eliminated, and minor restrictions were imposed on the number of subcommittees to which a member could

---

83. Thomas E. Mann and Norman J. Ornstein, *Renewing Congress: A Progress Report* (Washington, D.C.: American Enterprise Institute and Brookings Institution, 1994).

84. Quoted in Eliza Newlin Carney, "Capitol Hill Watch: Why Reform Moves Failed," *National Journal* 27 (October 15, 1994): 2412.

belong. There were also technical changes in floor rules, intended to protect authorizers and the minority.[85] But little of note was accomplished.[86]

But reform was not quite dead. The "Contract with America," endorsed by the preponderance of Republicans running for the House in 1994, gave considerable attention to proposals that were advocated by Republicans to the joint committee, but not adopted. Roger Davidson summarized them as including the following:

> reducing the number of committees and cutting committee staffs by one-third, limiting terms for committee chairs, requiring committees to meet in public and banning proxy voting. To restrict budget-making they would require "zero-baseline" budget estimates (that is, unadjusted for inflation) and three-fifths majorities to pass tax increases. Congressional accountability would be enhanced by auditing congressional operations and by applying to Congress all federal workplace laws (this latter already adopted by the House in 1994).[87]

After intensive internal consultations—with Representative David Dreier, who had been the House vice-chairman of the joint committee, playing an active role and providing a link to the earlier effort—the House Republicans incorporated almost all these elements in the House rules adopted on January 4, 1995.

85. For a useful chart summarizing changes in the 103d Congress and comparing them to those which I discuss next, after the Republicans took charge of both houses, see Roger H. Davidson, "Congressional Committees in the New Reform Era: From Combat to the Contract," chap. 3 in James A. Thurber and Roger H. Davidson, eds., *Remaking Congress: Change and Stability in the 1990s* (Washington, D.C.: CQ Press, 1995), p. 33.

86. Among the useful commentaries on why Congress failed to enact any major changes in 1994, see Eliza Newlin Carney, "Dead Ended: A Joint Committee Set Up to Study Congress's Many Inefficiencies Labored for Six Months and Produced Few Major Challenges to the Status Quo. Now the Panel's Modest Proposals Are Going Nowhere, in Part Because House and Senate Leaders Aren't Interested," *National Journal* 27 (July 23, 1994): 1733–37; as well as a series of weekly reports, primarily by Richard Sammon, under the heading "Organization," in *CQ Weekly Report* 52 (1994). They are: July 9, pp. 1855–56; August 6, p. 2219 (by Stephen Gettinger); September 17, p. 2559; September 24, pp. 2659–60; October 1, p. 2755; and October 8, p. 2855. For an insider's "after action" report on the work of the joint committee, see Thomas E. Mann, "Renewing Congress: A Report from the Front Lines," chap. 11 in Thurber and Davidson, eds., *Remaking Congress*, pp. 174–85.

87. Roger H. Davidson, "Governing After 1994: Political Tides and Institutional Change," *Extension of Remarks*, Newsletter of the Legislative Studies Section, American Political Science Association (December 1994): 16. One summary of the Contract with America, along with an assessment of the prospects for its adoption, is "Republicans' Initial Promise: 100-Day Debate on 'Contract,' " *CQ Weekly Report* 52 (November 12, 1994): 3216–19.

Three standing committees (District of Columbia, Merchant Marine and Fisheries, and Post Office and Civil Service) as well as twenty-five subcommittees were abolished, their responsibilities being transferred to other committees. With few exceptions, primarily Appropriations and Government Reform and Oversight, committees were limited to five subcommittees. Included was the renamed International Relations Committee (formerly Foreign Affairs), reduced from nine to five subcommittees. Members were limited to two full committee and four subcommittee assignments, and were allowed only one chair. Staff was reduced by 30 percent and, perhaps at least as important, all committee and subcommittee staff appointments were controlled by the full committee leadership, one of several steps reducing the power of the subcommittees. Provisions with respect to baseline budgeting, ending proxy voting, term limits for the speaker and committee chairmen, and open committee meetings were also included.[88]

Not part of the formal rules, but important to the way the House operated in the 104th Congress, were several steps that centralized power in the hands of the leadership (particularly Speaker Gingrich). These steps included Gingrich's appointments of committee chairs according to their commitment to the party agenda (Representative Bob Livingston became chairman of Appropriations, even though he was only fourth in seniority); the use of ad hoc task forces composed of members appointed personally by the speaker to handle certain issues, bypassing the committees; and tight control over scheduling. To a great extent, Gingrich was building on the enhanced powers of the speaker in force since the 1970s, but he showed a special facility (initially) for maximizing the possibilities. Whether his own members would continue to applaud this style remained to be seen; for the moment, though, it was extremely effective.[89] Later on, of course, Gingrich

88. For summaries of the changes, see "For the Record: New House Rules," *New York Times*, January 6, 1995; and David S. Cloud, "GOP, to Its Own Great Delight, Enacts House Rules Changes," *CQ Weekly Report* 53 (January 7, 1995): 13–15. For a later, more extensive discussion, see C. Lawrence Evans and Walter J. Oleszek, "Congressional Tsunami? Institutional Change in the 104th Congress," a paper prepared for delivery at the annual meeting of the American Political Science Association, Chicago, August 31–September 3, 1995. Table 1 (pp. 33–34) of the latter paper is especially useful.

89. Among many commentaries on the Gingrich style, see especially Jackie Koszczuk, "Gingrich Put More Power into Speaker's Hands: Chairmen Put Aside Objections over Shift in Hopes of Keeping Control of Congress," *CQ Weekly Report* 53 (October 7, 1995): 3049–53. Gabriel Khan, "Gingrich Plan: End to Panels?" *Roll Call*, October 9, 1995, provides additional information on the use of task forces, held to operate with one simple mandate: "accountability to the Speaker." Another discussion of the declining power of House committee chairmen in 1995 can be found in Richard E. Cohen, "Capitol Hill Watch: Who's in Charge on Committees," *National Journal* 28 (May 13, 1995): 1180–81.

became unpopular with the public, and consciously assumed a lower profile, leaving much of the day-to-day management of the House to Majority Leader Richard Armey. After Gingrich's reprimand for ethics violations in January 1997, this pattern was certain to continue.

Predictably, the Senate was less inclined to accept major changes in operating style and mores. Initially, the one visible change was a reduction in committee staff which was considerably less than that in the House (on the order of 13 percent, compared with 30 percent).[90] No committees were abolished, and only three reduced the number of their subcommittees. Shortly after the election, incoming majority leader Bob Dole appointed a working group to consider possible reforms. Headed by Senators Domenici (who had been Senate vice-chairman of the Joint Committee on the Organization of Congress) and Mack, the group's report contained rather modest changes when it was presented on January 23, 1995. It was never brought to the floor, although several components (including those noted above) were considered separately.

Later in the year, the Republican conference did adopt a reform plan having considerable potential impact on the distribution of power in the Senate and paralleling some of the House changes. This plan was the work of a Republican Conference task force appointed by Dole and headed by Mack. Its genesis was sparked by the concern of some conservatives as to the loyalty of chairmen to the party agenda, a concern set off by the vote of Appropriations Chairman Mark Hatfield against the balanced budget amendment. After numerous modifications to the initial version the plan was adopted on July 19 (with an addition made on August 3). It featured six-year term limitations for committee chairs, ranking minority members, and all GOP party leaders except the majority leader and the president pro tempore; establishment of a Republican legislative agenda at the start of each Congress; modifications in the calculation of seniority; selection of chairmen by secret ballot, and a limit on chairmanships (except for Appropriations) to one full committee or one subcommittee for each member.[91] More radical changes, such as limiting filibusters or adopting a two-year budget cycle, received scant attention.[92] This outcome is not surprising,

90. See Chapter 6 for details on the size of congressional staff and the reductions made in 1995.

91. Details in this and the preceding paragraph, unless otherwise noted, come from Evans and Oleszek, "Congressional Tsunami?" pp. 24–27 and table 3.

92. On the former, see Helen Dewar, "Harkin Targets a Senate Tradition: Iowan Is Set to Launch Drive to Repeal the Filibuster Rule," *Washington Post*, November 20, 1994.

given the style of the Senate. In 1994, before the election, one analyst opined that free-lancing was so common that whoever became majority leader might find himself leader in name only.[93]

These changes in the 104th Congress did little to address the foreign affairs problems described earlier in this chapter. Function 150 remained divided, exactly as before, among four sets of appropriations subcommittees. Nothing was done either to protect Function 150 or to provide greater flexibility. While there were minor changes in committee and subcommittee jurisdictions, they were hardly radical.[94]

Nor were there any significant changes in the budget process that might promote logic and prioritizing for foreign affairs. While a seven-year budget resolution was adopted—the centerpiece of the year's conflicts between the president and Congress—appropriations remained annual. Explicit congressional efforts at prioritizing were swamped by a process turned on its ear. With the new Republican majority determined to have a balanced budget by the year 2002 while simultaneously enacting a significant tax cut, the importance or needs of any specific program, except defense, took a distinctly secondary place. Rather than assessing what was important to get accomplished and then deciding how to fund such high-priority activities, set dollar figures drove the process. Moreover, many arguments about the importance of a given activity and of maintaining funding for it were deflected on grounds that the pain must be shared across the board in order to cut expenditures sufficiently to balance the budget and allow for the tax cut.[95]

93. Graeme Browning, "Freelancers: Party Discipline in the Senate Has Eroded So Much that Whoever Becomes Majority Leader—Republican or Democrat—Is Likely to Become a Leader in Name Only," *National Journal* 27 (September 24, 1994): 2202–6.

94. The House did experiment with the rules process with respect to the GOP leadership's announced intention to promote more open rules and freer debate. See Guy Gugliotta, "House Republicans Promise More Freewheeling Debate on Legislation," *Washington Post*, December 1, 1994. As 1995 progressed, however, they were tied in procedural knots and unable to maintain any approximation of a schedule, at times resembling the Senate! The initial attempt to consider the State authorization bill is a case in point. See Chapter 8 and Evans and Oleszek, "Congressional Tsunami?" pp. 20–21.

95. For a good example of the dominant mentality, see the House floor debate on the FY 1996 Foreign Operations Appropriations Bill, where this point is made repeatedly. In introducing the debate, Subcommittee Chairman Sonny Callahan presented the objective most succinctly: "[R]ecognize the message the American people sent to us in November. They said to cut spending. They did not say to cut spending in every area that we deal with except foreign aid. They said cut everything." *Congressional Record* 141 (June 22, 1995): H6243. The complete debate can be found in the *Record* for June 22, pp. H6243–56; June 28, pp. H6446–80, H6483–558; and July 11, pp. H6756–69. Eventually, of course, the tax cut was thwarted.

Similarly, little changed with respect to exerting greater discipline in the use of congressional control devices. There were modest signs that, given low funding levels, there would be less frequent resort to earmarks in the foreign affairs bills, although favored items (e.g., foreign aid for Israel and Egypt) and disliked items (e.g., appropriations for the United Nations and, in particular, payment of arrearages) received the usual amount of attention and support or opposition. Reports continued to be ordered, contingency funding continued to be used and, given the heightened partisanship, there was little inclination to provide additional wiggle room for the executive. Scorekeeping, if anything, became a more prominent factor than before, since it is the device by which efforts at deficit reduction are measured. Authorizers, especially Senator Jesse Helms as head of the SFRC, used procedures to attempt very tight control of the amounts to be made available for foreign affairs. Helms failed only by reaching too far.

The reform agenda would have to wait for another day.

Even had there been greater change, none of the executive or legislative branch reforms discussed and sometimes endorsed in the present chapter offers a panacea. In a process as complicated and important as spending the people's money for international affairs, there is no "silver bullet."[96] The full impact of even those changes which might be agreed to is not always knowable, and this should add a cautionary note. One extremely knowledgeable observer of the congressional and budget scene, then CBO Director Robert D. Reischauer, was almost certainly correct when he advised the joint committee as follows:

> I think you can make a case for restructuring the operations and working of the Congress, which is what you are all about. But that shouldn't be driven by budget policy. It should be driven by an effort to streamline this institution, to make it more effective, to make the outcomes of your deliberation more to the liking of the membership.
>
> If you do that, I think we will have a more effectively working budget process. It will be a byproduct of that. You shouldn't go about the reforms because the budget is consuming your activity and if you could do something about the way the budget operated within

96. For a perceptive discussion of the most recent (failed) major Congressional reform effort before 1994, see Roger H. Davidson and Walter J. Oleszek, *Congress Against Itself* (Bloomington: Indiana University Press, 1977), which is a detailed study of the 1974 Bolling committee's attempt to restructure House committees.

the Congress it would make the rest of congressional life more efficient. I think that would be a mistake.[97]

Much the same advice ought to apply to the executive branch as well. *Outcomes* (defined in terms of the overall performance of the government and, in this instance, how well the nation's foreign policies are carried out and how well its interests are protected), not *inputs* (such as the technical aspects of budgeting or the amount expended on a particular activity or function), should be the focus of attention and should drive process changes. Changes will never be easy. The culture of government—the "rules of the game," to borrow from the notable work of Nathan Leites—are excruciatingly difficult to alter.[98] This fact was evidenced, notably, in the tentative approach to congressional reform and in the reaction to the work of the joint committee in 1993.[99] Yet, contrary to the tenor of this book at times, the budget is not everything. In the oft-quoted words of former CBO Director Rudolph Penner, "The process is not the problem. The problem is the problem."[100] Quick fixes cannot alter political dilemmas, but sensible changes can sometimes make them more manageable.

97. Reischauer testimony, March 4, 1993, p. 26.

98. See Nathan Leites, *Rules of the Game in Paris* (Chicago: University of Chicago Press, 1969). The notion that political cultures and institutions have rather specific rules by which they operate is essential to understanding them, not least in the context of the executive–legislative interaction over constitutional and budget matters. Leites further developed this idea in his subsequent work on "operational codes" for institutions.

99. See, for example, Kevin Merida, "Reform of Congress May Be a Case of 'Not in My Back Yard,' " *Washington Post*, October 21, 1993, written even before the recommendations of the chairmen and vice-chairmen of the joint committee were issued, let alone its final report. For comments about an important side issue—the desire of House members to put an end to Senate filibusters—see Merida's article just cited as well as Adam Clymer, "House Members Seek Senate Change," *New York Times*, October 21, 1993. Other easily accessible discussions include Kevin Merida, "Lawmakers See Promise, Peril in Effort to Reform Committee System," *Washington Post*, April 26, 1993; Kevin Merida, "2 Senate Reformers Urge 12% Staff Cut, Citizen Ethics Probes, Curb on Filibuster," *Washington Post*, November 5, 1993; Michael Wines, "Under Senate Streamlining Plan, the Powerful Would Be Less So," *New York Times*, November 5, 1993; and Kevin Merida, "House Reform Is in the Eye of the Beholder," *Washington Post*, November 26, 1993.

100. Quoted in "Roundtable on Budget Process Reform," Joint Committee on the Organization of Congress and Center for Congressional and Presidential Studies (American University), April 15, 1993, in vol. 2 of the joint committee report, p. 205.

CHAPTER TEN

# THE UNEASY PARTNERSHIP/
# RIVALRY CONTINUES

Under the U.S. Constitution, executive–congressional relationships in foreign affairs will never be smooth; the Founders intended it that way. How much partnership versus how much separation of powers will be an eternally shifting mix. Cooperation and confrontation will alternately come to the fore.

As was argued in the *State 2000* report, "For roughly the past quarter century, we have experienced a period of Executive–Congressional strife as each branch endeavored to fulfill its respective perception of its constitutional role in conducting the nation's foreign policy. By their nature, these roles generate tension. *Effective pursuit of the national interest is not promoted if these differences deteriorate into persistent, implacable confrontation.*"[1] The Tonkin Gulf Resolution was perhaps the beginning, followed and fed by Watergate, Nicaragua, Iran-Contra, Iraq and the Persian Gulf, Somalia, Haiti, and Bosnia.

A prototypical pattern has emerged. First, when faced with a situation where the president believes U.S. troops should be deployed, a Congress often controlled by the opposition and motivated in part by partisan considerations will adamantly oppose any involvement of American forces. If forced into acquiescing in or if unable to prevent the use of troops, Congress next attempts to impose limits on numbers and activities and, above all, to require that they be extricated by a date certain. Because the use of troops requires money, Congress has leverage here. At the same time, an attempt

1. *State 2000* report, p. 21, emphasis added.

is made to ensure that if the operation encounters difficulties, it is the president who is blamed. That such dissonance may increase the likelihood of failure (it can be of considerable advantage to an opponent to know that U.S. troops will depart by a set date, for example) is almost never acknowledged. There will be more such episodes in today's world of regional conflicts, civil wars, and readjustment.[2] Scowcroft and Kanter, two Bush administration critics of the Clinton foreign policy, seem correct when they say that "maneuvering in the complex environment of a Somalia—or Haiti or Bosnia—requires the agility of a ballet dancer, not the Mack truck of legislation."[3]

Norman Ornstein and Thomas Mann provide historical context:

> During the period from the Civil War through the Vietnam conflict, the general thrust of change in interbranch relations involved an expanded role for the federal government, accompanied by broad congressional delegations of discretionary authority to the executive branch. Since the early 1970's, however, the opposite has been occurring. Steadily increasing reassertions of congressional authority have led to executive branch charges of "micromanagement."[4]

Congress clearly has the authority to declare war, to raise and support armies, and the ultimate power of the purse. The president is the commander in chief, has the sole power to negotiate with foreign countries (subject in certain cases to Senate advice and consent), and also recognizes foreign governments, appoints U.S. representatives, and receives their foreign counterparts. These roles, presented in stark, general form in the Constitution, are straightforward only on the surface. Much is implied in these seemingly uncomplicated mandates. The reality, then, is great complexity and frequent ambiguity, particularly when resource issues are involved.

Some clear dangers exist, as *State 2000* warned:

> In the future international operating environment . . . continuation of interbranch conflict reminiscent of the past could be disastrous. As

2. See Chapter 8 for Clinton–congressional exchanges on Bosnia, in the context of the events of 1995. On the dangers of fixing a date certain for withdrawal of U.S. forces once engaged, see Thomas L. Friedman, "Foreign Affairs: Expiration Date: 12/20/96," *New York Times*, May 6, 1996.

3. Brent Scowcroft and Arnold Kanter, "Foreign Policy Straitjacket," *Washington Post*, October 20, 1993.

4. Mann and Ornstein, *Second Report of the Renewing Congress Project*, p. 78.

the domestic and international issue agendas merge, acknowledged Congressional responsibilities for the former cannot easily be separated from impact on the latter. The close interplay and symbiosis between . . . global issues . . . and the [domestic and world] economies is one obvious case in point. The great danger is that domestic interests will become poised against international ones in a potentially destructive zero-sum game. This is virtually guaranteed if perceptions of institutional prerogative reinforce a domestic–international dichotomy and rend the fabric of what we argue must be a seamless, integrated policy process.[5]

The great strengths of Congress lie in its collective insights into fundamental patterns of American interests, its ability to provide broad-gauged oversight of executive branch activities, its capabilities to inform and to win support from the public, and its political role as critic and sounding board. Nonetheless, the Congress is also fragmented, riven by jurisdictional rivalries between its houses, committees, and personalities, as has been seen in the very different perspectives of budgeteers, authorizers, and appropriators. Congress can suffer from a short attention span and become excessively attuned to the passions of the moment.

The president and his agents have the great instrument of the bully pulpit to forge a national and global consensus on fundamental policy initiatives, and also the means—organization, resources, and operatives—to carry out the activities needed to give life to policy goals. They also run the risk of doing great harm if they are, or if they appear to be, directionless in the conduct of the nation's international affairs. At the operational level, the executive must accept the doctrine of accountability: what the executive does is the people's business and, therefore, the Congress's business. However, if it is to have an enhanced capability to respond to a rapidly changing international environment, the executive must have greater flexibility than current circumstances now permit. It must be able to organize and reorganize itself, to prioritize resource use, and to realign activities as new circumstances and experience dictate, all the while keeping Congress engaged. Unless the legacy of distrust (manifested by overly detailed legislation) is overcome, the executive cannot perform as it must.

Collaboration between the Congress and the executive must be the norm if we are effectively to address the complex challenges of the new interna-

5. *State 2000* report, p. 21 (I was the primary drafter of the report's sections on this topic).

tional scene. This partnership must recognize not only constitutional imperatives but the differing strengths, characteristics, and capacities of each branch. The advantages of each must be understood, respected, and even deferred to. If they can be, the application of money to foreign affairs can be more responsive to the national interest. Warren Christopher's 1982 call for "Ceasefire Between the Branches: A Compact in Foreign Affairs,"[6] written between his two stints at the Department of State, still rings true.

More partnership is essential if we are to address the problems of matching policy goals and resources in foreign affairs. The conclusion must be that as a government we are not anywhere near being able to meet this challenge.

Neither the executive branch nor Congress is now structured to allow rational resource choices for the support of foreign policy, even in "normal" budgetary times. *The executive* has no effective process for developing an overall Function 150 budget, much less for comparing priorities between 150 and defense or domestic discretionary spending. *The Congress,* while in theory able to solve this prioritizing problem at the macro level via the budget resolution, cannot make comparisons within 150 once the budget allocations are "crosswalked" to appropriations, since the function is split among several appropriations subcommittees. Moreover, since subparts of Function 150 are considered with parts of other functions, at the micro level arbitrary trade-offs must be made between unrelated programs. Unless International Affairs is protected by its own ceiling as under the 1990 budget summit agreement, an approach that brings its own problems, foreign affairs often loses out to domestic programs.

All this might be more acceptable if there were a tradition of ample funding for our government's international activities. But as has been seen, except for the Marshall Plan era and during the first Reagan administration, foreign affairs appropriations have basically been flat. The importance of such funding has often been ignored or misunderstood by both Congress and the executive, and thus foreign affairs funding has been "caught" between the two much larger categories of defense and domestic discretionary spending. Unpopular programs and the lack of a natural constituency are prime causes.

Somewhat paradoxically, given the small financial stakes involved, Congress is now more assertive than earlier about foreign policy money issues,

---

6. *Foreign Affairs* 60 (Summer 1982): 989–1005. This article also shows that it is easier to analyze from the outside how things should work than to do so as an active player.

as well as for those involving high policy or the commitment of American troops. It is learning to use a wider range of "power of the purse" weapons to confront the president's constitutional prerogatives in foreign affairs.

The 1974 Congressional Budget Act and later modifications to it have made the process more complex and difficult, constitutional issues aside. Foreign affairs funding can no longer be considered in isolation. These factors, combined with strained relations brought about in part by congressional frustration over the inability to play a larger foreign policy role, can lead to disaster for coherent policy and operations, as I have sought to demonstrate throughout this book.

Today's "rules of the game" may be similar to those of the past, but they are not always what the conventional wisdom suggests. Issues concerning foreign policy funding are not isolated from partisanship, "turf," and interest politics, but some members do take a national interest approach even when there is no political advantage in doing so. One lesson is that "nuts and bolts" do count; they determine outcomes. Nuts and bolts are what the "money types" (budget and appropriations) do. If the political will exists, a better match of policy and resources is possible, although neither the National Performance Review in the executive nor the work of the Joint Committee on the Organization of Congress provides much reassurance that the necessary changes will occur in the near term. A true Function 150 budget for the executive branch could be a reality, although it would require giving more control to a central decisionmaker, who I argue would have to be the secretary of state. Congressional jurisdictional changes placing most of Function 150 in one set of appropriations subcommittees would be a logical counterpart, especially if the executive should move toward greater integration. More conscious prioritizing and overview by everyone involved would also be highly desirable. (I recognize that this flies in the face of incremental, "amendment by amendment" styles of setting policy.) While hardly earthshaking, the other changes proposed in Chapter 9 would each contribute to better integration of policy and resources.

America's preeminence in the post–Cold War world leaves us little choice except to lead. To do so, we must be much better equipped to carry out our responsibilities, which are in many ways expanding, with resources that will always fall short of what is needed. The conclusion seems inescapable: there is a pressing need to change the ways in which the public business of international affairs is done, whether in the realm of high constitutional politics or in the less exalted and less exciting work of constructing and enacting budgets that more directly serve our national purposes.

# APPENDIX A

## General Abbreviations and Acronymns

| | |
|---|---|
| 050 | Budget Function 050 (Defense) |
| 150 | Budget Function 150 (International Affairs) |
| ACDA | U.S. Arms Control and Disarmament Agency |
| AFSA | American Foreign Service Association |
| AID | Traditional acronymn for the U.S. Agency for International Development. USAID has been the preferred form in the Clinton administration. |
| AIPAC | American Israel Public Affairs Committee |
| BA | Budget authority (moneys appropriated to be expended) |
| BEA | Budget Enforcement Act of 1990 |
| CBO | Congressional Budget Office |
| CFO | Chief financial officer (one for each department/agency) |
| CJS | Commerce, Justice, State, the Judiciary and Related Agencies appropriations subcommittees in the House and Senate. Also used as shorthand for appropriations bills in the jurisdiction of these subcommittees. |
| CR | Continuing resolution (temporary appropriations act) |
| CRS | Congressional Research Service |
| DAS | Deputy assistant secretary (of state or another department) |
| DCM | Deputy Chief of Mission |
| DOD | Department of Defense |
| Foreign Ops | Foreign Operations and Export Financing appropriations subcommittees in the House and Senate. Also shorthand for appropriations bills in the jurisdiction of these subcommittees. |
| FSO | Foreign Service Officer |
| GA | *See* UNGA. |
| GAO | General Accounting Office |

GRH            Gramm-Rudman-Hollings (Balanced Budget and Emergency Deficit Control Act of 1985)

GRH II         Gramm-Rudman-Hollings II (Balanced Budget and Emergency Deficit Control Reaffirmation Act of 1987)

HAC            House Appropriations Committee

HFAC           House Foreign Affairs Committee (replaced in 1995 by HIRC)

HIRC           House International Relations Committee (replaced HFAC in 1995)

INS            Immigration and Naturalization Service

NGO            Nongovernmental organization (usually a foreign assistance conduit)

NPR            National Performance Review (White House, Clinton administration)

NOAA           National Oceanographic and Atmospheric Administration

NSC            National Security Council (White House)

OE             "Operating Expenses" account (USAID; like the Department of State and USIA's S&E)

OECD           Organization for Economic Cooperation and Development

OMB            Office of Management and Budget (White House)

OT             Outlays (moneys actually expended)

PC             Peace Corps

PLO            Palestine Liberation Organization

PPA            Program, Project, or Activity (element of a budget account)

PPDA           Peace, Prosperity, and Democracy Act of 1994 (the failed foreign assistance reform bill)

PVO            Private voluntary organization (usually a foreign assistance conduit)

RFE            Radio Free Europe

RL             Radio Liberty

SAC            Senate Appropriations Committee

S&E            Salaries and expenses account (Department of State and USIA; like USAID's OE)

SAP            Statement of administration policy (position on pending legislation)

SFRC           Senate Foreign Relations Committee

| SMI | Strategic Management Initiative (Department of State reform program, 1995–96) |
| UNGA | United Nations General Assembly |
| USAID | U.S. Agency for International Development (Clinton administration preferred acronymn; *see* AID) |
| USDA | Department of Agriculture |
| USIA | U.S. Information Agency |
| VOA | Voice of America |

## Department of State Organizational Acronymns

(May refer either to the incumbent of the position or to the office or organizational area headed by the incumbent)

| D | Deputy Secretary |
| E | Under Secretary for Economic and Business Affairs |
| G | Under Secretary for Global Affairs |
| M | Under Secretary for Management |
| P | Under Secretary for Political Affairs |
| T | Under Secretary for Security Assistance, Science, and Technology. Also called informally International Security Affairs. Changed in 1993 to Arms Control and International Security Affairs. |
| D/P&R | Advisor to the Deputy Secretary–Policy and Resources (replaced in 1993 by S/RPP) |
| DS | Bureau of Diplomatic Security |
| FBO | Foreign Buildings Office (Bureau of Administration) |
| INR | Bureau of Intelligence and Research |
| IO | Bureau of International Organization Affairs |
| M/COMP | Comptroller (replaced in 1989 by M/FMP) |
| M/FMP | Bureau of Finance and Management Policy (headed by Department of State's CFO) |
| OES | Bureau of Oceans, International Environmental, and Scientific Affairs |
| S/P | Policy Planning Staff |
| S/RPP | Office of Resources, Plans, and Policy (replaced D/P&R in 1993) |

# APPENDIX B

## Appendix Tables

Appendix Table 1    Outlays for International Affairs (Function 150) 1940–1997
(Data Source for Figure 1)

| Year | President's Budget Actual $ Millions (a) | Constant $ Millions (1987) (b) | % of Budget (c) | % of GDP (d) | Total Budget Outlays ($ Millions) (e) | GDP ($ Billions) (f) | GDP Deflator (1987 = 1.0000) (g) |
|---|---|---|---|---|---|---|---|
| 1940 | 51 | 521 | 0.54 | 0.053 | 9,468 | 95.4 | 0.0978 |
| 1941 | 145 | 1,437 | 1.06 | 0.128 | 13,653 | 112.5 | 0.1009 |
| 1942 | 968 | 8,682 | 2.75 | 0.683 | 35,137 | 141.8 | 0.1115 |
| 1943 | 1,286 | 10,726 | 1.64 | 0.733 | 78,555 | 175.4 | 0.1199 |
| 1944 | 1,449 | 12,491 | 1.59 | 0.718 | 91,304 | 201.7 | 0.1160 |
| 1945 | 1,913 | 16,766 | 2.06 | 0.902 | 92,712 | 212.0 | 0.1141 |
| 1946 | 1,935 | 16,220 | 3.50 | 0.911 | 55,232 | 212.5 | 0.1193 |
| 1947 | 5,791 | 38,710 | 16.79 | 2.598 | 34,496 | 222.9 | 0.1496 |
| 1948 | 4,566 | 29,592 | 15.34 | 1.851 | 29,764 | 246.7 | 0.1543 |
| 1949 | 6,052 | 38,255 | 15.58 | 2.304 | 38,835 | 262.7 | 0.1582 |
| 1950 | 4,673 | 28,599 | 10.98 | 1.758 | 42,562 | 265.8 | 0.1634 |
| 1951 | 3,647 | 20,908 | 8.01 | 1.163 | 45,514 | 313.5 | 0.1592 |
| 1952 | 2,691 | 16,540 | 3.98 | 0.790 | 67,686 | 340.5 | 0.1627 |
| 1953 | 2,119 | 12,377 | 2.78 | 0.582 | 76,101 | 363.8 | 0.1712 |
| 1954 | 1,596 | 9,042 | 2.25 | 0.434 | 70,855 | 368.0 | 0.1765 |
| 1955 | 2,223 | 12,343 | 3.25 | 0.578 | 68,444 | 384.7 | 0.1801 |
| 1956 | 2,414 | 12,659 | 3.42 | 0.580 | 70,640 | 416.3 | 0.1907 |
| 1957 | 3,147 | 15,602 | 4.11 | 0.718 | 76,578 | 438.3 | 0.2017 |
| 1958 | 3,364 | 15,838 | 4.08 | 0.751 | 82,405 | 448.1 | 0.2124 |
| 1959 | 3,144 | 13,980 | 3.38 | 0.648 | 92,098 | 480.2 | 0.2249 |
| 1960 | 2,988 | 12,709 | 3.24 | 0.592 | 92,191 | 504.6 | 0.2351 |
| 1961 | 3,184 | 13,228 | 3.26 | 0.616 | 97,723 | 517.0 | 0.2407 |
| 1962 | 5,639 | 23,016 | 5.28 | 1.016 | 106,821 | 555.2 | 0.2450 |
| 1963 | 5,308 | 20,865 | 4.77 | 0.908 | 111,316 | 584.5 | 0.2544 |
| 1964 | 4,945 | 19,049 | 4.17 | 0.791 | 118,528 | 625.3 | 0.2596 |

| Year | Actual $ Millions (a) | Constant $ Millions (1987) (b) | % of Budget (c) | % of GDP (d) | Total Budget Outlays ($ Millions) (e) | GDP ($ Billions) (f) | GDP Deflator (1987 = 1.0000) (g) |
|---|---|---|---|---|---|---|---|
| 1965 | 5,273 | 19,898 | 4.46 | 0.855 | 118,228 | 671.0 | 0.2650 |
| 1966 | 5,580 | 20,425 | 4.15 | 0.759 | 134,532 | 735.4 | 0.2732 |
| 1967 | 5,566 | 19,787 | 3.53 | 0.702 | 157,464 | 793.3 | 0.2813 |
| 1968 | 5,301 | 18,111 | 2.98 | 0.626 | 178,134 | 847.2 | 0.2927 |
| 1969 | 4,600 | 14,877 | 2.50 | 0.497 | 183,640 | 925.7 | 0.3092 |
| 1970 | 4,330 | 13,193 | 2.21 | 0.439 | 195,649 | 985.4 | 0.3282 |
| 1971 | 4,159 | 11,856 | 1.98 | 0.396 | 210,172 | 1,050.9 | 0.3508 |
| 1972 | 4,781 | 12,797 | 2.07 | 0.417 | 230,681 | 1,147.8 | 0.3736 |
| 1973 | 4,149 | 10,475 | 1.69 | 0.326 | 245,707 | 1,274.0 | 0.3961 |
| 1974 | 5,710 | 13,257 | 2.12 | 0.407 | 269,359 | 1,403.6 | 0.4307 |
| 1975 | 7,097 | 14,916 | 2.14 | 0.470 | 332,332 | 1,509.8 | 0.4758 |
| 1976 | 6,433 | 12,619 | 1.73 | 0.382 | 371,792 | 1,684.2 | 0.5098 |
| TQ | 2,458 | 4,649 | 2.56 | 0.552 | 95,975 | 445.0 | 0.5287 |
| 1977 | 6,353 | 11,503 | 1.55 | 0.331 | 409,218 | 1,917.2 | 0.5523 |
| 1978 | 7,482 | 12,621 | 1.63 | 0.347 | 458,746 | 2,155.0 | 0.5928 |
| 1979 | 7,459 | 11,579 | 1.48 | 0.307 | 504,032 | 2,429.5 | 0.6442 |
| 1980 | 12,714 | 17,902 | 2.15 | 0.481 | 590,947 | 2,644.1 | 0.7102 |
| 1981 | 13,104 | 16,763 | 1.93 | 0.492 | 678,249 | 2,964.4 | 0.7817 |
| 1982 | 12,300 | 14,697 | 1.65 | 0.394 | 745,755 | 3,122.2 | 0.8369 |
| 1983 | 11,848 | 13,497 | 1.47 | 0.357 | 808,380 | 3,316.5 | 0.8778 |
| 1984 | 15,876 | 17,398 | 1.86 | 0.430 | 851,846 | 3,695.0 | 0.9125 |
| 1985 | 16,176 | 17,114 | 1.71 | 0.408 | 946,391 | 3,967.7 | 0.9452 |
| 1986 | 14,152 | 14,537 | 1.43 | 0.335 | 990,336 | 4,219.0 | 0.9735 |
| 1987 | 11,649 | 11,649 | 1.16 | 0.262 | 1,003,911 | 4,452.4 | 1.0000 |
| 1988 | 10,471 | 10,106 | 0.98 | 0.218 | 1,064,140 | 4,808.4 | 1.0361 |
| 1989 | 9,573 | 8,853 | 0.84 | 0.185 | 1,143,172 | 5,173.3 | 1.0813 |
| 1990 | 13,764 | 12,200 | 1.10 | 0.251 | 1,252,515 | 5,481.5 | 1.1282 |
| 1991 | 15,851 | 13,452 | 1.20 | 0.279 | 1,323,441 | 5,676.4 | 1.1783 |
| 1992 | 16,107 | 13,221 | 1.17 | 0.272 | 1,380,856 | 5,921.5 | 1.2183 |
| 1993 | 17,248 | 13,784 | 1.22 | 0.276 | 1,408,675 | 6,258.6 | 1.2513 |
| 1994 | 17,083 | 13,333 | 1.17 | 0.257 | 1,460,841 | 6,633.6 | 1.2813 |
| 1995 | 16,434 | 12,541 | 1.08 | 0.234 | 1,519,133 | 7,004.5 | 1.3104 |
| 1996 est | 14,830 | 11,039 | 0.94 | 0.202 | 1,572,411 | 7,336.0 | 1.3434 |
| 1997 req | 15,035 | 10,885 | 0.91 | 0.195 | 1,635,329 | 7,707.6 | 1.3813 |

SOURCE: Office of Management and Budget, *Budget of the United States Government Historical Tables, Fiscal Year 1997* (Washington, D.C.: GPO, 1996), table 3.1, pp. 42–49, for columns (a)–(e); table 1.2, pp. 12–22, for column (f); table 1.3, pp. 23–24, for column (g).

NOTE: "Actual" = current year. Column (b) = (a) as adjusted by (g). Column (c) = (a) divided by (e). Column (d) = (a) divided by (f). Column (e) is on same basis as (a); i.e., current year, not adjusted. TQ = transitional quarter; est = estimate; req = request.

Appendix Table 2   Function 150 Budget Authority, Mandatory and Discretionary, FY 1976–FY 1997
(Data Source for Figure 2)

| Fiscal Year | 151 | 152 | 153 | 154 | Subtotal* | 155 | Total |
|---|---|---|---|---|---|---|---|
| | ← | | | $Millions | | | → |
| 1976 | 3,076 | 3,712 | 782 | 423 | 7,994 | 6,063 | 14,057 |
| TQ | 319 | 589 | 362 | 103 | 1,374 | −1,043 | 331 |
| 1977 | 3,550 | 3,954 | 1,054 | 400 | 8,958 | −744 | 8,214 |
| 1978 | 4,183 | 4,577 | 1,241 | 451 | 10,451 | 1,124 | 11,575 |
| 1979 | 5,084 | 5,772 | 1,318 | 506 | 12,680 | −2,298 | 10,382 |
| 1980 | 5,264 | 5,066 | 1,343 | 518 | 12,191 | 5,761 | 17,952 |
| 1981 | 4,420 | 5,068 | 1,465 | 555 | 11,508 | 15,844 | 27,352 |
| 1982 | 4,474 | 6,863 | 1,688 | 587 | 13,612 | 4,612 | 18,224 |
| 1983 | 4,711 | 8,142 | 1,830 | 688 | 15,371 | −4,632 | 10,739 |
| 1984 | 5,069 | 8,943 | 2,015 | 808 | 16,835 | 7,718 | 24,553 |
| 1985 | 6,496 | 13,730 | 2,501 | 950 | 23,677 | 2,776 | 26,453 |
| 1986 | 4,760 | 9,543 | 2,992 | 970 | 18,266 | −1,607 | 16,659 |
| 1987 | 4,902 | 8,213 | 2,582 | 1,031 | 16,727 | 1,997 | 18,724 |
| 1988 | 5,022 | 8,598 | 2,631 | 1,056 | 17,307 | −123 | 17,184 |
| 1989 | 5,296 | 7,666 | 2,775 | 1,126 | 16,862 | 390 | 17,252 |
| 1990 | 5,696 | 8,393 | 2,933 | 1,317 | 18,338 | 473 | 18,811 |
| 1991 | 6,778 | 9,061 | 3,238 | 1,243 | 20,320 | 2,369 | 22,689 |
| 1992 | 6,655 | 6,682 | 4,063 | 1,303 | 18,704 | 2,523 | 21,227 |
| 1993 | 6,992 | 5,491 | 4,327 | 1,248 | 18,058 | 14,275 | 32,333 |
| 1994 | 7,699 | 4,531 | 4,630 | 1,496 | 18,386 | −647 | 17,709 |
| 1995 | 7,661 | 4,626 | 4,063 | 1,421 | 17,771 | 8,100 | 25,871 |
| 1996 | 6,479 | 5,037 | 3,954 | 1,115 | 16,585 | −252 | 16,333 |
| 1997 | 6,978 | 5,023 | 4,167 | 1,162 | 17,330 | −715 | 16,615 |

SOURCE: Office of Management and Budget: *Budget of the United States Government Historical Tables, Fiscal Year 1997* (Washington, D.C.: GPO, 1996), table 5.1, pp. 75–78.

NOTE: TQ = transitional quarter.

*Subfunctions 151–154.

# INDEX

Page numbers in italics refer to tables and charts.